POSTCOLONIAL LACK

SUNY SERIES, INSINUATIONS:
PHILOSOPHY, PSYCHOANALYSIS, LITERATURE
Charles Shepherdson, editor

Postcolonial Lack

IDENTITY, CULTURE, SURPLUS

GAUTAM BASU THAKUR

Cover art: from "Across the Line" exhibition, Pavlov Institute, Kolkata. With permission from Ratnaboli Ray, Director of Anjali: Mental Health Rights Organization, and Smita Khator, photographer.

Published by State University of New York Press, Albany

©2020 State University of New York

All rights reserved

No part of this book may be used or reproduced in any manner whatsoever without written permission. No part of this book may be stored in a retrieval system or transmitted in any form or by any means including electronic, electrostatic, magnetic tape, mechanical, photocopying, recording, or otherwise without the prior permission in writing of the publisher.

For information, contact State University of New York Press, Albany, NY
www.sunypress.edu

Library of Congress Cataloging-in-Publication Data

Names: Basu Thakur, Gautam, author.
Title: Postcolonial lack : identity, culture, surplus / Gautam
    Basu Thakur.
Description: Albany : State University of New York Press, 2020.
    | Series: Suny series, insinuations: philosophy, psychoanalysis,
    literature | Includes bibliographical references and index. |
Identifiers: LCCN 2019036267 | ISBN 9781438477695 (hardback)
| ISBN 9781438477718 (ebook) | ISBN 9781438477701 (pbk)
Subjects: LCSH: Postcolonialism in literature. | Psychoanalysis
    and literature. | Postcolonialism in motion pictures. |
    Postcolonialism. | Psychoanalysis. | Identity (Psychology)
    | Other (Philosophy)
Classification: LCC PN56.P555 B38 2020 | DDC 809/.9335—
dc23 LC record available at https://lccn.loc.gov/2019036267

10 9 8 7 6 5 4 3 2 1

FOR BINU

"the captain whose ship has not [yet] been built"

CONTENTS

Acknowledgments — ix

Introduction — xiii
postscript — xxxiii

CHAPTER ONE The Subaltern Act of Freedom — 1

CHAPTER TWO Postcolonial. Animal. Limit. — 33

CHAPTER THREE Hysterization of Postcolonial Studies; *or,* Beyond Cross-Cultural Communication — 67

CHAPTER FOUR Fictions of Katherine Boo's Creative Non-Fiction, *or,* The Unbearable Alterity of the Other — 105

CHAPTER FIVE Political Correctness *Is* Phallic: Idaho Politics, *Black Panther*, and *Gran Torino* — 143

Conclusion: Particular Universal — 179
Notes — 197
Works Cited — 217
Index — 233

ACKNOWLEDGMENTS

This book was conceived between *two* lacks—the first and second LACK conferences held at Colorado College in 2016 and 2017 respectively. On my way back from the 2017 conference, I prepared the draft proposal for the book while waiting for my (delayed) connecting flight at Denver Airport (DEN). I thank the organizers of LACK, my fellow panelists from both years and those who attended the sessions and asked hard questions. For once in my life I am thankful for a delayed flight: it gave me the opportunity to draft the proposal. I am profoundly indebted to Molly Rothenberg for reading and commenting on my initial proposal. Her honest criticism helped me fine-tune the draft into the final project.

The manuscript was written during my sabbatical semester of Spring 2018 and revised over that summer. I am grateful to Boise State University, my department chair, and the dean of the college for granting me sabbatical.

I thank Charles Shepherdson for showing faith in me. Without him this project could not have taken wings. And I thank Andrew Kenyon at SUNY Press for his support and patience. I am also immensely grateful to Cynthia Col for preparing the index.

A number of friends provided feedback on early drafts, helped think through the project, and track down resources. In no particular order these beautiful souls are: Meghant Sudan, Ed Pluth, Anustup Basu, Arijit Sen, Rashna Singh Batliwala, Indranil Mitra, Michael Palencia Roth, Ritoban Basu Thakur, Manisha Basu, and Soma Mukhopadhyay. I thank Andrew Laird for inviting me to Brown University in Spring 2017 and Rachel Harris and George Gasyna for inviting me to the University of Illinois at Urbana-Champaign in Fall 2017. On both occasions I got the opportunity to share parts of this project with and learn from my colleagues at these institutions.

A separate round of thank you is reserved for Boise State's Albertson's Library. Without the support of our fantastic library staff this book could not have been completed. In particular, I thank Mary Aagard, Ash Whitwell, Audrey Williams, and Ana Kurland, and everyone at the Interlibrary Services for their prompt handling of my Interlibrary loan requests. Thank you to Will Cole, my undergraduate research intern for spring 2018. His support in the project is deeply appreciated.

I am lucky to have colleagues such as Ralph Clare (my "colonial cousin"), Edward "Mac" Test, Brian Wampler, and Whitney Douglas. They supported me in ways that I simply cannot contain in words. Thank you all. But I owe more than my heartfelt gratitude to the wonderful Whitney Douglas. She suffered these last twelve months from my pestering questions about verbs, adverbs, idioms, and clauses without expressing fatigue or annoyance. Thank you Whitney for your resolute friendship and endless supply of unique gifts (from "Shakespeare Insult Bandages" to Sigmund Freud coasters). Everyone needs a "Whit" in their lives and I am thankful to call her "my friend."

Speaking of friends, I must mention Sayandeb Chowdhury and Debshikha Bose. Without Sayan I could not have dared engage with Nabarun. Sayan is a Jeeves to my Wooster, while Debshikha has proved to be a true Ronnie. Her endearing cackle kept my spirits up throughout the writing process.

A very special note of gratitude is reserved for Ratnaboli Ray, the founder-director of *Anjali*, a mental health rights organization in Calcutta, and Smita Khator, an old friend from Calcutta. Ratnaboli and *Anjali* has been working for years to "establish Mental Illness within the mainstream health paradigm of India and to 'speak for' a large population of marginalized people with mental illness vis-à-vis their right to a professional and inclusive system of care and treatment" (http://www.anjalimentalhealth.org/). The cover of the book is a painting showcased at an exhibition organized by *Anjali*. I saw a photograph of the painting first on Smita's Facebook page and she put me in contact with Ratnaboli for getting required permissions. I thank them both for allowing me to use the painting and photograph on the cover of this book.

Dr. Marilyn Schuler played a special role in this project. Under her insistence I first read and presented a short talk on Katherine Boo's book at Boise's Black History Museum. This talk is the basis of my chapter 4. Chapter 4 is dedicated to my Grand-aunt, Purnima Roy Chaudhuri, or *Poo* as I called her. *Poo* witnessed the Bengal Famine as well as the globalization of the country. I lost her in 2018. She wanted to see me as a cricketer playing for India. "And when they ask you how you became a cricketer, let them know about me," she would say. I wonder what she thought when I decided to leave cricket in order to focus on my English major. Chapter 4 in this book is a humble homage to her and her generation.

Versions of chapters 1 and 4 were presented at the 2016 and 2017 LACK conferences; a conference version of chapter 2 was presented at the 2017 Modern Languages Association Annual Convention at Philadelphia. This has been recently accepted by Amit Rahul Baishya and Suvadip Sinha for their forthcoming collection of essays titled *Postcolonial Animalities*. I thank them both for this.

Lastly, I want to thank my family. My mother and brother in India for their support. To Reshmi, Rohitashwya (Binu), and EnZo (aka Ackbar), I can only say thank you for tolerating my writing schedules. But without them these pages would not exist.

INTRODUCTION

I. TO BEGIN (A DIFFICULT CONVERSATION)

Postcolonial Lack is an attempt to reconvene dialogue between two seemingly antagonistic disciplines—postcolonial studies and psychoanalytic theory. Though once collaborative, the relationship between the disciplines today is marked by mutual suspicion and is even borderline hostile. Postcolonial critics, for instance, charge psychoanalytic theory with overwriting the particularities of the non-West in favor of its uniform metaphysics of being, while psychoanalytic critics disapprove of postcolonial's advocacy for the marginalized as puerile identity politics. I believe, however, that there is a critical need for mending this relationship in the context of our neoliberal present. At a time when standard arguments against postcolonial studies either typically emphasize its redundancy in the changed climate of multiculturalism and/or accuse it for being complicit in promoting neoliberal ideologies, I contest that reconnecting the disciplines can make postcolonial studies relevant for the global present alongside making psychoanalytic theory more global.

The primary focus of this book is on arguing how postcolonial studies can collaborate with psychoanalytic theory and become more theoretically rigorous in its analyses of contemporary narratives of Othering, exclusion, and cultural appropriation. Indeed, a lot remains to be done for making psychoanalysis truly global, that is, "to historicize the psychoanalytic object and objective, invade its heredity premises and insulations, and open its insights...to cultural and social forms that are disjunctive to its originary imperatives" (Spillers 1996, 76). But that would require a separate monograph. In this book, my concern, limited as it might be, is with postcolonial studies and its lack(s).

The argument I make in this book is simple: in order to remain relevant in the global present, postcolonial studies must move from interrogating the politics of symbolic difference to exploring the excess, surplus, or lack that linger in the wake of exercises of self-representation. Put differently, I wish to see postcolonial studies accomplish the critical task of turning focus away from the symbolic and toward the real. This book demonstrates how the psychoanalytic concepts of the other (*objet petit a*), subjectivity qua desire or/ as lack ($), and nonbeing as surplus (jouissance) infuse greater analytic rigor into postcolonial interrogations of hegemony, othering, and subject making and how this enables us to consider the function of the real in colonial and postcolonial texts.

Postcolonial studies today has become a tool for either recovering, restoring, and recognizing muted voices or underlining the highly implicated condition of global subjectivity in matters of social inequality and injustice. These related exercises of rescue and rehabilitation of victims from global oppression and the exposition or acknowledgment of personal culpability in sustaining global inequality aim to satisfy two seminal conditions of neoliberalism. First, these appear to take action against or raise consciousness about injustice without taking any real action. Secondly, these keep people feeling good about the self-conscious and self-critical character of contemporary society without, again, requiring people to directly confront the structural or systemic conditions responsible for social inequity. In effect, on the one hand, postcolonial studies today is dominated by a competition for tragedy (i.e., discover who is the most victimized among all victims), anointing in process the victim of history as *the* only authentic subject (of speech). On the other hand, the need for continuous self-scrutiny in order to disavow even the remotest chance of being complicit in or identified with unequal exercises of power (for example, the #NotinMyName campaigns) has led postcolonial studies to focus on retaining particular identities against universalist demands of identity: "As British Muslims we utterly condemn ISIS who are abusing the name of Islam with their acts of terrorism. We call on fellow British Muslims to unite and denounce this evil group and their acts—which are done #NotInMyName" (#NotInMyName: n.p.). These trends have reduced the discipline into a redoubt for identity politics. In this book I ask: What can the discipline contribute beyond recovering, reconstituting, and reintegrating marginal identities. I must clarify, though, that the state of the discipline I am describing here is limited to my experiences of it in the U.S. academy and, at the same time, it is deliberately generalizing in order to be provocative. Routine practices of unearthing silenced voices and giving them representation in the mainstream have lulled the inherent strengths of the discipline and slight provocation is in order for waking it up from this stupor.[1]

The need to focus on *reconquest of silenced identities* has reached such a feverish pitch in the present that searches for marginal human voices are proving not enough (Abdel-Malek [1981] cited in Lazarus 2011, 255). Inspired by what Badiou terms twenty-first-century messianic environmentalism and the recent turn toward nonhumans and the environment, postcolonialists today are training focus on "rescuing" muted animals and abiotic things (Badiou 2018, n.p.; Grusin 2015). This cozying together of "old" and "new" academic cliques merely adds a layer to postcolonial's demands for rehabilitating excluded subjects—their insertion into and respectful accommodation within global culture—and for calling out implicated subjects. Caught up in these agendas, postcolonial studies makes the mistake of forgetting what theorists such as Gayatri Spivak and Edward Said often repeated. Namely, reversing symbolic positions—the self versus the Other, the center versus the margin, and the nonhuman instead of the human—only reproduces the existing hierarchy by another name (Spivak 1999, 9). And that domination and our association in domination, direct or indirect, is not simply a matter of ignorance that can be revoked by telling the ugly truths about complicity or by appealing to our morals. We should, rather, recognize these disciplinary orientations as symptomatic of the hegemonic control neoliberalism enjoys over the academy. As long as capitalism models conformity as well as scripts its opposition, postcolonial cultures and its literary, academic, and civil societies are destined to remain interpellated by the West (Nandy 1983, xii).

How can we *rescue* postcolonial studies from its current state? I submit the following: *hystericization of the discipline*; or, what Spivak advocates for upending the master's discourse, namely, *render it uncanny*. In *Critique of Postcolonial Reason*, Spivak writes:

> I have not tried to diagnose Kant's hidden "beliefs" here. I have constructed a version of a script *within* which his text may be seen as held. To read a few pages of the master's discourse allowing for the parabasis operated by the native informant's *impossible eye* makes appear a shadowy counterscene. (1999, 37; emphasis mine)

Spivak's methodology in this passage provides me both the cue to connect psychoanalytic theory to postcolonial studies and the framework with or from within which to interrogate postcolonial's habitual emphasis on binary opposition, exclusion, and othering. Put another way, by making the discipline uncanny, I demand it give up its "truth": that the radical kernel of this discipline is not identity critique or exposition of dominant ideology but, rather, as envisioned in Fanon, it is about examining ontology in relation to historicity. The "problem of history," that is, of colonialism and imperialism as historical material events, must be examined from the "psychoanalytic and ontological angels," Fanon had written in his thesis (2018, 257).

I find the division between early and late Fanon, that is, the "psychoanalyst Fanon" and the "political Fanon" or the Fanon of *Black Skins, White Mask* versus the Fanon of *Wretched of the Earth*, rather futile. Even if I do not always agree with Homi Bhabha's *reading* of Fanon or Fanon's reading of Lacan, I find attempts to dislocate the "later Fanon"—the Fanon who is more Marxist revolutionary than a witness to colonialism's effects on individual and collective psyche—overly disappointing. In my opinion, "Marxist" extrapolations tend to essentialize Fanon through a developmental argument. That is to say, early Fanon was naive, too invested in Western science and only through his experiences does he eventually realize true universality of Marx, hence the shift from psychoanalysis to revolutionary Marxism. While some consider this an appropriate historical overview of Fanon's thinking, I remain skeptical due to the psychologism invoked in this reading of Fanon's intellectual development not to mention being upset at the unnecessary infantilization of early Fanon. I prefer instead to think of Fanon as a complicated thinker exploring and examining conditions of colonialism from different perspectives. Simply put, I do not seek to privilege one set of his thinking over another and absolutely refuse to frame an argument for the development of this thought in terms of a naive beginning and a mature end. In fact, I consider Fanon's highlighting of ontology in relation to colonialism as his primary contribution. Put differently, Fanon shows how colonialism unravels the ontological uncertainty of both the colonizer and the colonized by exposing their beings as marked by the space of nonbeing or what exists between the colonial constructions of "white" and "black" identities. The subject emerges as split between these imaginary identities or, more pertinently, inhabits the gulf between these identities. The subject in the colony is not-All, never whole and never supported in history by some essential substance or master signifier. It exists only as a flicker between two signifiers but never in itself.

Peter Hudson offers a useful summary of this particular aspect in Fanon's writing. Hudson writes,

> Torn between two impossibles—to be white and to be black—the first barred and second an impossibility in its own terms as there is no black "being"—blackness produces no "ontological resistance"—"turn white or disappear" sums up the ontological void of the black colonised subject. Made to want to be white, but incapable of this—he is black; and his blackness seen through his own "white" eyes reduces him to "nothing." The colonial symbolic is so constructed as to give the black subject nothing to hold onto—no orthopaedic support for an identity—just a whiteness forever eluding him and a blackness that doesn't "exist" in any case. Within the colonial matrix, this is the ontological vortex that is the elementary colonial identity and lived experience of the colonised black subject; and all his compulsive (self-destructive) pathologies, his specific repertoire of "reactional" conduct, have their source in this primary ontological differential. So, fundamentally, colonialism is an ontological differential between white and black subjects; and this orders each and every sphere or sector of colonial society (including the economy). (2013, 264–65)

This understanding of the subject as lack—nonbeing as the signature of radical antagonism that results from colonialism and consequently determines social relations within colonial society—is not just a psychoanalytic perspective on the subject but the subject here represents the cause for the political. In other words, a realization of subjectivity (I or being) as the condition of and as contingent to the state of radical negation or nonbeing can galvanize newer imaginaries of emancipatory action. I say "newer" because the realization of nonbeing as the constitutive condition for all being, colonizer and colonized, helps free anticolonial struggle from the fantasy of reversing power structures. Fanon is quite clear on this point: decolonization does not end with the end of colonial rule or the replacement of the colonizer by the formerly colonized. The assertion of the colonized's black identity against the colonizer's white identity is only the first stage of liberation and must be followed by the dissolution of *all* identities in *the night of the absolute*: a new (universal) humanism founded on the suspension of all certainties of being is the true goal of decolonization (Fanon 2008, 112; see also, Ciccariello-Maher 2010). In other words, revolution cannot be limited to reversing symbolic binaries but, rather, must dismantle the system responsible for maintaining these binaries. Colonial experience is isomorphic with the experience of living in capitalism:

both introduce division in society forcing the majority to inhabit the space of in-betweenness or the state of limbo between the unavailable "white" and the impossible "black"—the space between "us" and "them." By asking, we reintroduce the affective agency of this in-between, unbearable space, or nonbeing, into considerations of postcolonial analyses, I am rooting for reorienting the focus of postcolonial studies toward the instance of the surplus in the mechanisms of othering, difference, and subject making.

II. THE POSTCOLONIAL SAMIZDAT

According to Terry Eagleton, there exists somewhere a secret handbook for postcolonial critics. This samizdat rulebook instructs both neophytes and vested scholars of the discipline in two fundamental rules. The first rule of postcolonialism is to deny postcolonialism. To call postcolonial "bogus" (as Spivak does in *Critique of Postcolonial Reason*) or to excuse one's self from the label "postcolonial critic" has become the *de rigueur* gesture, according to Eagleton. With every postcolonial book beginning by rejecting the notion of the postcolonial and asserting the impossibility of ever grounding what postcolonialism means, "[t]he idea of the post-colonial has taken such a battering from post-colonial theorists that to use the word unreservedly of oneself would be rather like calling oneself Fatso, or confessing to a furtive interest in coprophilia," avers Eagleton (1999, n.p.).

The second rule of postcolonialism: "Be as obscurantist as you can decently get away with" (ibid.). To Eagleton, postcolonialists are guilty of writing in styles inaccessible to the general reading public; their avowed sentiments for underlining the communicative gap between the center and the margins, the elite and the subaltern, nothing more than a sham. These ivory-tower academics are in reality capitalism's trusted vanguard. The secret handbook exists for training postcolonial theorists to substitute cultural frameworks in place of political analyses, thus leaving capitalism unchallenged and students unprepared to question the economic causes for (their) social inequality. As Eagleton sees it, postcolonialism is "a way of being politically radical without necessarily being anti-capitalist, and so is a peculiarly hospitable form of leftism for a 'post-political' world" (ibid.).

Eagleton's concern over the postcolonial underground sounds cannily similar to the neoconservative Stanley Kurtz's views about Edward Said's plot to destroy America. In his testimony to the "Subcommittee on Select Education,

Committee on Education and the Workforce U.S. House of Representatives," dated June 19, 2003, Kurtz charged Said and "postcolonial theory" with weakening American democracy and jeopardizing national security. Kurtz claimed, "Title VI–funded professors take Edward Said's condemnation of scholars who cooperate with the American government very seriously. For years, the beneficiaries of Title VI have leveled a boycott against the National Security Education Program, which supports foreign language study for students who agree to work for national security–related agencies after graduation." The boycott has "change[d] the purpose and nature of the program itself, which is to stock our defense and intelligence agencies with accomplished speakers of foreign languages." This resulted in the September 11 attacks because "transmissions from the September 11 highjackers went untranslated for want of Arabic speakers in our intelligence agencies" (Kurtz 2003, 9–11, 69–78).

Kurtz's view of postcolonial theory as an organized left-wing infiltration of the U.S. academy which has as its ultimate goal the destruction of U.S. political (democracy), cultural (Western civilization), and moral (Christian) values is analogous to the basic ideological motif of the new conservatives in Europe who believe that failing to overpower the West through the communist revolution, a secretive communist center plotted to gain control of the universities in order to destroy the "Christian ethical foundation" and secure the communist takeover of society. According to these European new conservatives, this underground operation began with the Frankfurt school, and current-day disciplines such as feminism, LGBTQ studies, or cultural Marxism, most commonly, are the natural outcomes of this plan (see Žižek 2018a, n.p.).

I mention these three critiques (Eagleton, Kurtz, European conservatives) because, one, they are symptomatic of the general criticism of the discipline, and, two, because irrespective of the critic's ideological situation, whether Left or Right, postcolonial studies always finds itself in the crosshairs of some of the most vitriolic censures. The most stinging criticisms of the discipline, however, came from postcolonial academics such as Benita Parry, Arif Dirlik, and Aijaz Ahmad, who through the 1980s and 1990s routinely censured the discipline's grounding in mid-twentieth-century French theory, especially berating the influence of Michel Foucault, Jacques Derrida, and Jacques Lacan on Edward Said, Gayatri Spivak, and Homi Bhabha. According to this critique, postcolonial's *linguistic turn* compromised its ability to convincingly analyze the material conditions of social oppression suffered by real individuals and real communities in the colony and the postcolony. In the last two decades, critics such as Slavoj Žižek and Vivek Chibber have reiterated similar arguments condemning the discipline as fashionable nonsense. Žižek and Chibber have both criticized the discipline for *culturalizing politics,* sidelining Marxist thought, and complementing neoliberal identity politics. According to them, the discipline's lack of focus on class and continued fascination with discursive practices of becoming and belonging have rendered it completely incapable of interrogating the current dispensations of global capitalism. Postcolonialism today fails to realize the modalities of ideological oppression inherent in oft-stated ideals of multiculturalism, tolerance, human rights, and democratic pluralism.

This double whammy—materiality and reality—ensured the divorce between postcolonial studies and French theory, including psychoanalytic theory. But this has since proven unfortunate for two reasons. One, separation from French theory never did manage to put postcolonial studies back on a path to Marx, and two, the separation shifted the discipline toward reparative work and pushed it farther away from radical theoretical imaginations of power, resistance, and otherness. What Žižek notes now as the condition of the discipline is the direct result of forgoing theory. As I have written elsewhere, the diminution of postcolonial studies resulted not from its investment in theory, but, rather due to its separation from theory (Basu Thakur 2015). Specifically stated, having forfeited the initial advantage of its connection to French theory, postcolonial studies suffers from a lack of theoretical rigor and this lack makes it incapable of pursuing qualified arraignments of contemporary maneuvers of self-representation and Othering. With exclusive focus being given to unearthing buried voices—contrastive communities, marginalized cultures, and exsanguinated identities—the discipline has become enmeshed in identity politics.

With the discipline leaning toward vacuous searches for competing victim voices, an unwanted competition has taken over postcolonial research. It is invested in unearthing, weighing, and measuring who has historically suffered more; which communities are the most marginalized; and which victim has the right to stake the strongest claim to historical persecution, trauma, and exploitation. But questions remain about methods used to quantify the different cases of oppression. What makes one community more exploited than the next and what new kinds of Othering are at work within these assessments? Or, to put it bluntly, how is it okay to protest exploitation of women and children in the United States but remain indifferent to, even complicit in, the oppression of Palestinian, Afghan, and Nicaraguan women and children by the U.S. military-industrial complex? Postcolonial studies in America today is that face of U.S./global liberalism which remains content with claiming rightful angst over historical suffering while being absolutely noncommittal regarding U.S. foreign policy. Seeking rehabilitation, recognition, and reparation for victims—the latter voices included in the syllabus and their plights recorded in new research tomes—postcolonial academic work in the global world does little more than coopt and sanitize potential radical activisms within the facile folds of an imagined neoliberal harmony. On the one hand, celebrating victim identity reduces political speech to testimonials of suffering that are to be empathized with and sincerely understood but never allowed translation into direct action against the system. On the other, substitution of political action with appeals and pleas seeking redress from the system responsible for producing the conditions of suffering destroys any scope of true political emancipation for the victims (Dean 2009). Yet a large section of the U.S. academy, including a substantial part of the postcolonial community, appears unmoved by the university's neoliberal turn. To them: *postcolonial is dead!*

III. POSTCOLONIAL IS DEAD; REIMAGINING POSTCOLONIAL STUDIES

In his passionate defense of postcolonial studies' continued relevance in the twenty-first century, Robert Young argues that as long as othering, exploitation, and hegemonic dominance exist, the discipline remains a crucial "*political project*—to reconstruct Western knowledge formations, reorient ethical norms, turn the power structures of the world upside down, refashion the world from below." In the "postracial" multicultural world, the discipline is needed for interrogating "the hidden rhizomes of colonialism's historical reach" and the muted or not immediately identifiable forms via which processes of self-representation at the expense of the Other continues to unfold in plain sight (Young 2012, 20–21). Young does not dismiss the argument that transformations in global cultures warrant changes in postcolonial studies' analytic praxis, most importantly the need to expand and revise existing understandings of the self-other relation. Unlike the nineteenth century, when alterity was symbolically constructed and selectively appropriated in order to constitute the image of Europe's sovereign self, we now need to add to this reading a theoretical understanding of the other as "not something produced [only] as a form of exclusion but [also as] fundamental to being itself" (ibid., 39). This is especially critical in the twenty-first century when popular opinion is toward celebrating, embracing, and protecting the Other to the extent of homogenizing them. For instance, our neoliberal societies prohibit and disavow any criticism of the Other, claiming the latter's suffering or victimhood should be their only identity. But is this really different from nineteenth-century practices of Othering? Is this not another way for sustaining the subject of the West in the era of globalization? What is the difference between the liberal, tolerant view of the Other and the conservative dehumanizations of people of color, LGBTQ communities, the immigrant, and the refugee? I discuss these questions in the chapters. For the moment, let me say that I consider Young's essay a clarion call to postcolonialists for moving beyond symbolic politics and into the politics of the Real. Or, past Otherness as symbolic to otherness as irreducible, uncanny, and traumatic. The latter manifests the fundamental impasse at the heart of the social and is both constitutive of social relations and disruptive of social communication. Correspondingly, this otherness eviscerates the fiction of the subject as master or the subject-supposed-to-know.

My book takes Young's call seriously. It seeks to theoretically ground his argument about reframing critical dialogue over radical alterity or otherness via what I deem necessary, namely, a *return* to Freudian-Lacanian psychoanalytic theory. I see this move as putting postcolonial studies beyond the cramping politics of symbolic difference and closer toward delivering the *political project* of examining the function and consequences of the antagonism constitutive of the social. For when we accept the emergence of being qua nonbeing or underline the irreparable antagonism structuring intersubjective relations, we return to discussing that which makes politics and discourse possible. Alenka Zupančič teaches us that politics covers up the impossibility of social relation by making the fundamental antagonism appear temporary, a passing impediment in the path of accomplishing perfect social harmony (Zupančič 2016). Commonly, political discourse gives an imaginary position and symbolic meaning to this temporary condition/impediment—it is the Other whose exclusion from the social promises the liberation from all antagonisms. In Nazi Germany this position was occupied by the figure of the Jew; in twenty-first century globalized India it is the Muslims, Dalits, and the seculars. Indeed, the logic of imperial-fascist ideology and the contemporary neoliberal ideology map together on this point—a perfect social state is impossible without the fantasy about the Other's excessive enjoyment. The Other as victim or the Other as the enemy within is excessive for the suffering they have experienced and/or for the threat they contain. Therefore, only by accommodating and/or excising them can a social utopia come into existence.

The "excess" I discuss in relation to the other, however, ruptures this very politics of Othering. I examine the other's surplus enjoyment that erupts suddenly to throw hegemonic behemoths of institutional classifications and symbolic categorizations into total disarray. Most commonly experienced in terms of the other's unfathomable desires (what does it want) and the other's confusing agency (why did it do that), this other is uncontainable, unknowable, and (hence) unsymbolizable. In the face of this other, prescience of selfhood folds into an absence and the subject-supposed-by-philosophy (*one who can know* or *loves to know*) dissolves or barely sustains subjectivity qua anxiety.

The other inhibiting Othering—the other which impedes or escapes symbolization—fills a lacuna in habitual postcolonial interrogations of the Other as the excluded self-referent (Young 2012, 36). Insofar as the other's surplus nonbeing unravels social identities as fiction and authority as indeterminate and fragile, discussing this irascible surplus helps reconceptualize the universal in terms of our shared ontological lack. Only when we understand the universal as not founded in a common positive element but a shared excluded one, that is, a universal of negated subjects, are we freed from thinking in terms of symbolic difference—master and the slave—and move closer toward a radical *politics of affiliation* among *all* ontologically divided subjects.

Shifting focus from difference to surplus does not mean ending examinations of the politics of Othering; rather, this shift adds to existent postcolonial interpretations of Othering by highlighting a new set of ethical and political considerations emerging in direct consequence of the other's irreducible alterity. In wanting postcolonial studies to recognize and mediate its oversight of the other-as-surplus, I wish to see the discipline know its lack. As the book's title conveys, what postcolonial studies lacks in the twenty-first century and what must be done in order to effectively interrogate past and continuing politics of exploitation, domination, and Othering can be routed through questions of the other's radical alterity without compromising on interrogating capital and the various discursive mechanisms of Othering.

Rounding off his attack on postcolonialism as "a brand of culturalism, which inflates the significance of cultural factors in human affairs," Eagleton counsels in "Postcolonialism and 'postcolonialism' " (1998) that the discipline should actively embrace "openness, dialogism, *a refusal of simplistic binary oppositions,* and *a due recognition of the mixed, unstable, undecidable, indeterminate nature of things*" (26). His advice for most parts has gone unheeded, as postcolonial analyses narrowed over time into historicist ventures. Responding to Young's call for reimagining the discipline and taking cue from Eagleton's advice, and in no less measure guided by rereadings of Fanon and Spivak via Lacan, this book underlines the need for routing postcolonial analyses of power relations and social dynamics through the question of ontology. But before this can be done, a difficult conversation must be enacted: How to get old enemies speaking to one another again? Bringing postcolonial studies to dialogue with psychoanalytic theory is easier said than done. Misunderstandings stemming from almost three decades of misreadings and misappropriations from both sides have constructed an insurmountable barrier between the disciplines.[2]

IV. SPIVAK'S *LOVE* LETTER

Spivak captures the postcolonial unease with psychoanalysis in her 1993 essay "Echo." She writes:

> I have always felt uneasy about the use of psychoanalysis in cultural critique since it is so culture-specific in its provenance. Like many others, I too have felt that Marxism, focusing on something on a much higher level of abstraction than the machinery, production, and performance of the mental theater, and as obviously global as capitalism, is not open to this particular charge. (*To say capitalism is all over the place is not as universalist as to say everyone has the same-pattern psyche.*)...
>
> For the use of feminist psychoanalysis in understanding sexual difference and gendering I feel some sympathy because it is so actively contestatory. But general cultural critique has always seemed to me to be quite another matter. *Without the risks or responsibilities of transference at least implicitly diagnostic and taxonomic, ignoring geopolitical and historical detail in the interest of making group behavior intelligible, and not accountable to any method of verification, the brilliance of psychoanalytic cultural criticism has always left me a bit suspicious.*
>
> *Yet Freud has remained one of my flawed heroes, an intimate enemy.* To his race, class, and gender-specificity I would apply the words I wrote about Charlotte Bronte more than a decade ago: "If even minimally successful, my reading should incite a degree of rage against the gendered/imperialist narrativization of history, that it should produce so abject a script for him." (2012, 219–20; emphasis mine)

INTRODUCTION

For a postcolonial critic to claim interest in Freud is to invite charges of Eurocentrism, of "race, class, and gender-specificity," Spivak announces in her *love letter* to Freud (ibid., 220). Interestingly enough, a few pages later in that same essay she revises her stand on Freud with help from Bimal Krishna Matilal: "Matilal," she says, "allowed me to make room for Freud in my intellectual world" (ibid.). But this Freud or Spivak's Freud is an ethical philosopher (like Derrida) whose primary contribution is recognizing "the aporia between terminable and interminable analyses" or the impossibility of knowledge-production/meaning making (ibid., 220–21). This anecdote of personal conversion notwithstanding, the habitual stance in postcolonial studies has always remained closer to Spivak's initial rejection of Freud. This has not only led to a foreclosure of Freud or psychoanalysis from postcolonial discussions but also, more disastrously, a disavowal of Spivak as one of the finest readers of Freud.[3]

The story is not too different on the other side. For a Freudian-Lacanian to show interest in postcolonial studies almost always earns the reproach: How can you claim to be a Lacanian if you acknowledge arguments about particularities? "Being Lacanian" implies proving detachment from the particular and siding with the universal. But, in my opinion, the psychoanalytic critique of postcolonial particularity is as banal as the postcolonial critique of the psychoanalytic universal insofar as both misunderstand one another. Neither seems to understand that the universal condition of lack can find diverse, particular expressions or that our particular expressions of alienation extending from feelings of not belonging to our families to not being of this planet are only isomorphic human characterizations of the unutterable experience of being severed from (imagined) wholeness.

Mrinalini Greedharry does an excellent job of summarizing this decades-old conflict between the disciplines. I will not repeat that narrative here, directing interested readers instead to Greedharry's book *Postcolonial Theory and Psychoanalysis: From Uneasy Engagements to Effective Critique* (2008). By avoiding retelling a known story, the gist of which is already captured in Spivak's passage above, I am choosing to go directly to my point about the disciplines being what, after Ashis Nandy, I will call "intimate enemies." But prior to that I wish to awaken readers to the basic differences between existing works that study the intersections between the disciplines and my focus in this book.

To begin with Greedharry, while it is one of the few recent works to attempt a disciplinary conversation between the old enemies—"what psychoanalysis has done for postcolonial studies and what postcolonial studies might do for psychoanalysis"—her book is more focused on postcolonial theorists who work with psychoanalytic theory (Fanon, Bhabha, Nandy, Kakkar, etc.) and is also not Lacanian in orientation. By contrast, *Postcolonial Lack* is "strictly" Lacanian in its understanding of, as well as examinations of, postcoloniality. Recent works that *are* Lacanian in orientation and focus on coloniality, decoloniality, racial identity, globalization, etc. include Derek Hook's *A Critical Psychology of the Postcolonial: The Mind of Apartheid* (2012), "Postcolonial Psychoanalysis" (2008), and "Fanonian Ambivalence: On Psychoanalysis and Postcolonial Critique" (2013; co-authored with Ross Truscott); Sheldon George's *Trauma and Race: A Lacanian Study of African American Racial Identity* (2016); some essays in George and Hook's coedited Special Issue of *Psychoanalysis, Culture, and Society*, titled "Lacanian Psychoanalysis: Interventions into Culture and Politics" (2018); Jamil Khader's *Cartographies of Transnationalism in Postcolonial Feminisms: Geography, Culture, Identity, Politics* (2014) and his essay "Žižek's Infidelity: Lenin, the National Question, and the Postcolonial Legacy of Revolutionary Internationalism" (2013) in Khader and Rothenberg's co-edited *Žižek Now: Current Perspectives in Žižek Studies*; Ilan Kapoor's *Celebrity Humanitarianism: The Ideology of Global Charity* (2012) and *Psychoanalysis and the GlObal* (2018); and, Azeen Khan's "Lacan and Race" (2018). However, while all these books and essays are mostly Lacanian in orientation, and though obvious intersections exist between Hook's readings on apartheid and race in South Africa and George's exploration of African American identity and my book, the latter remains exclusive in its singular focus on the discipline of postcolonial studies. Secondly, except for Greedharry, none of these works attempt to reestablish conversation between psychoanalysis and postcolonial studies as disciplines, remaining partial to using psychoanalytic theory for interrogating race relations in the contemporary world and/or for explaining the postcolonial global condition. I discuss the structure of the book and its textual/disciplinary focus in more detail in section VI of this introduction.

V. INTIMATE ENEMIES, POSTCOLONIAL STUDIES, AND PSYCHOANALYSIS

Postcolonial studies and psychoanalysis share a similar objective: interrogate the (im)possibility of university discourse and constructions of identity and social relations based on this discourse. What poses as knowledge or discourse is supported by fantastic master signifiers guaranteeing knowledge as absolute and objective. At one level, these master signifiers symbolize or symbolically assure us of power and completeness. On another level, the desire for the master signifier paradoxically attests to our inability to exist without fantastic objects, ideas, or things covering up the fact of our irreparable ontology. Simply put: we can neither endure knowing nor exist without compulsively overwriting our lack of knowledge. This condition is not descriptive of not having or not being but is, rather, illustrative of being as a condition of lack/non-being. The subject of lack is therefore indeed better rephrased and understood as *subjectivized lack* (Chiesa 2007, 6).

The colonized other (*objet a*) inhabits or constitutes the heart of the colonial sociosymbolic. It underscores the impossibility or absence of any master-signifier, or a prevailing symbolic big Other, guaranteeing the stability of this order. The other's nonbeing is the nonrelation(ship) deadlocking social relations between the master and the slave, the self and the other, the center and the margin(s), while its appearance in the order composes the moment of symbolic collapse. It is not that the symbolic irreparably collapses into an unredeemable heap but this is the moment when the symbolic's indeterminacy stands exposed. The appearance of the other or encountering this other opens up the void constitutive of as well as integral to the social. For what we think ails our being and how we think we know what ails us offer neither the truth about our being nor an identification of the real of our being. Being in this doldrum *is* what makes us human.

It is possible to explain the relation between postcolonial studies and psychoanalysis in another way: both expose the image as *construction*. Beget by fiction—an image of boisterous autonomy—this image, which precedes the social determination of the self in experiences of a violently mutable outside world, remains forever irreducible to the self (Freud 1991; Spivak 2003, 22; Lacan 2006, 75–81). This early image is distant from and incommensurable with the self. In the symbolic or the domain of the ego overseen by the presence of the Other, this primordial image appears as stain—a rupture in the complacent confident symbolic mesh that acts to absorb the subject's falls—and speaks of the universe as flaw and nonbeing as the only condition of existence (Lacan 2006, 694). What transforms this disemboweling primordial image of the real to present it *as lack* or desire is another fiction—the fiction of a big Other authorizing this desire and guaranteeing its potential fulfillment in a deferred space, time, and object.

"Real" reality is conditionally overwritten to appear absorbed in the image of the self. What we claim as the real image (identity) is beset by the logic of our present-day instagram(mar). We appear on Instagram as real—capturing us in real moments as real selves—when what we are really doing in these moments is that we are posing for the desire of the Other. Put differently, we (always) wish to see ourselves in the eyes of the Other. Sadly, postcolonial studies has ignored psychoanalysis's emphasis on the Other as empty, and accordingly their desire to investigate authentic identities has been hijacked by the desire of the Other. To be a postcolonial we have to remain committed to the Other's desire: we cannot question the dominant neoliberal laws of empathy, tolerance, and pluralism. Anyone questioning whether the other should be characterized homogenously with suffering and homologously with victim identities is promptly chastised for being intolerant, fascist, and Eurocentric. "Eurocentric" as if intolerance, homophobia, systemic oppressions of minority do not exist outside the West or within societies and communities from the non-West. We witness a nuanced ideology here. While such diasporic communities as Indians and Pakistanis in the UK can be charged with acts of bias as "honor killings," refugee populations insofar as they have experienced some form of heightened trauma are always excused from all charges of bigotry or prejudice. This liberal dispensation is yet again another point where contemporary conservative articulation intersects with (neo)liberal discourse. This book attempts to avoid this pitfall by seeking to *return* postcolonial studies to one of its original exegeses, namely, considerations of the radical nonbeing of the colonized other as the unimaginable truth of colonial and postcolonial social relations.

Postcolonial Lack claims that in order to remain relevant in the global present, postcolonial studies must move from interrogating the politics of symbolic difference to exploring the other's surplus. That is to say, we (re)turn to critically considering the other's irreducible nonbeing in postcolonial texts about fraught social relations. From others who retract themselves away from violent power struggles, libidinal economies, and capitalist commodity cultures to others that displace the human from its imaginary stewardship over this planet, this book highlights a new set of ethical and political considerations that emerge for studying postcolonial social relations in the context of the other's unbearable alterity. The chapters of this book expound upon how eruptions of the other's nonbeing—the other's surplus enjoyment as well as the other's lack (of desire)—disrupt the sociosymbolic. These are the moments when social relations are unraveled as constitutively marked by deadlocks and antagonisms which lead us toward (un)learning the routine politics and ethics of self-representation.

VI. STRUCTURE OF THE BOOK

The book is divided into two broad sections, with three chapters composing the first section and two chapters plus a conclusion the second. The first section focuses on rereading postcolonial literature and film by taking into account the function of the other as real. The second section focuses more on how liberal multiculturalism repeats, rephrases, and revisions colonial-era subject-making without appearing to undertake any form of Othering. If anything, these contemporary representations appear conscious, self-reflexive, and not unwilling to dig out their own implicated subject positions. Taken together, the two sections of this book seek "new" ways for ethically engaging with otherness as radical alterity.

The first three chapters explore and interrogate the other's sudden eruption in postcolonial literature and film. Focusing on the impossible figure of the subaltern (in Mahasweta Devi and Gillo Pontecorvo), postcolonial animals (a relic pterodactyl in Devi, again, and swarms of crabs in Amitav Ghosh), and the failure of cross-cultural communication (in Leila Aboulela and Tony Gatlif), I underline through these chapters the other as impediment; or, the emergence and/or realization of the other's radical alterity as recognition for the fundamental antagonism structuring all social relations.

Serially put, chapter 1 describes how the other's (subaltern's) surplus enjoyment tears a hole in the symbolic logic of dominant hegemony, thus opening up a space for reconceptualizing subaltern freedom. Chapter 2 discusses how animals displace established subject positions by bringing the radical extimacy of a 4.5-billion-years-old planet into intimate focus with our alienated relation to this planet. The third chapter, the most humanly oriented of these three, focuses on love, understanding, and dialogue in order to disclose how human endeavor to memorialize the other through archives only illustrates the impossibility of this task.

The second section illustrates how contemporary celebrations of identity politics, political correctness, and multiculturalist activism ideologically replace discussions of radical alterity with discussions of empathy, charity, and individuality. My comparative discussion of Katherine Boo's representation of urban precariats in chapter 4 shows contemporary critiques of globalization's effects on the poor in the global South are nothing but recycled presentations of the imperial fantasy of the third world as endemically corrupt, incorrigibly unchangeable, and politically inflexible. In then comparing Boo with Narayan

Gangopadhyay, a Bengali writer from the 1940s, in whose short story the urban poor appear differently, my end goal is not to erase Boo out of the scene but, rather, to underline my repeated emphases on seriously taking Spivak's critique that reversing binary oppositions is futile. Therefore, instead of criticizing Boo's representations as recycled clichés about the third world, I argue for understanding her unfortunate entrapment in the desire of the Other. I contend that Boo epitomizes the liberal postcolonial Western subject whose desire for politically correct representation of the other marks her out as another victim of identity politics. Due to her racial makeup Boo cannot ethically embrace the other and must always assume the morally sanctified position even when representing the most disturbing or disgusting others.

I carry this argument forward into the fifth chapter where I take up some recent discussions about identity politics. Beginning in my neck of the woods, the unremarkable and stereotyped state of Idaho, I claim first that the Democrat buildup in and competition for the state's 2018 gubernatorial race was underwritten by the *allure of images* or a politics over which candidate has a better (politically correct) image rather than being dominated by important policy questions. I use this instance to segue into discussing how, today, identity politics has ended up producing very different readings of films such as *Black Panther* (2018) and *Gran Torino* (2009). Conceived as a Spivakian exercise in unlearning, this chapter claims *Gran Torino* is a more racially as well as politically sensitive film than *Black Panther*. In the conclusion of this chapter, I return again to Idaho politics. Occasioning a trite exchange between the then Republican congressman Raul Labrador and the now retired Boise State University president Robert Kustra, I underline the emptiness of identity politics and how conversations directed by identity politics, and images associated with this politics, commonly obviate the real issues.

The book concludes with a chapter marked "Conclusion: Particular Universal," which, structurally speaking, should be received as a conclusion though it also works as a chapter specific to the discussions in the second half of the book. More specifically, it focuses on current debates over universalism and particularism and through this attempts to respond to the habitual charge against psychoanalysis, namely, that psychoanalysis passes off its Eurocentric imagination and bourgeois values as universal (Gibson 2003, 130). This charge in recent years have taken shape of the debate between the particular's right to exist against the universal's aggression and has been a pestering, to wit, lingering, issue for cultural and philosophical debates of the last quarter as well as for the more intimate conflict between psychoanalysis and postcolonial studies. I intervene in this debate, however, not from the psychoanalytic side but through Spivak. Interestingly, Spivak's usual response to the issue is similar to the response from the psychoanalytic side: She bifurcates the notion of universalism dependent on positive master signifiers—male, able-bodied, white-billionaire—to emphasize what "falls out" of signification every time we claim the universal on basis of master signifiers. In other words, as I read them, both Spivak and Lacan, expose the universal as empty. There is nothing that makes the universal *universal*, yet we strive after words and images that would make the universal the all-out success we want it to be when we only encounter the lack(s) of the universal. By showing the master signifier as empty—incapable of reproducing reason—I re-situate in the conclusion of this book what I claim throughout: equality is alterity.[4]

INTRODUCTION, *POSTSCRIPT*

Instead of prefixing an "author notes" to the "Introduction," I will use this *postscript* to address two points for which I did not have space in the Introduction. The *postscript* becomes crucial as well due to the interdisciplinary and comparative character of the book. The first note in this postscript is brief: it explains my use of author names. The second, a longer note, clarifies my use of the terms *other* and *Other*.

I. AUTHOR NAMES

When naming European/U.S. authors, I follow the established protocol of using last names. Therefore, Gatlif for Tony Gatlif or Boo for Katherine Boo. When naming non-Western/non-European authors writing in the vernacular, especially authors from South Asia, I use the protocol of using their first names, therefore, Mahasweta for Mahasweta Devi and Rabindranath for Rabindranath Tagore. However, when naming non-European authors writing in English, I revert back to the standard protocol followed in the United States of using last names. So, Ghosh for Amitav Ghosh and Aboulela for Leila Aboulela.

II. THE OTHER AND THE OTHER

The terms *other* and *Other* are used extensively in this book. The concept of the other is central to postcolonial theory while "other," written in lower case, and different from the "Other," written in upper case, are significant to Lacan's teachings. In order to avoid confusion over my use of the terms in this book, I offer the following annotation.

The "other" is a key concept in postcolonial studies. It is a sum of the diverse voiceless, exploited, and dehumanized colonized—"a primary means of defining" the identity of the colonizer (Ashcroft, Griffiths, and Tiffin 2007, 42). The other exists, therefore, as negated or lacking (civilization, speech, education, law, etc.) and helps consolidate the Self of Europe as master (positive) signifier.[1] Edward Said (*Orientalism* 1978) and Alain Grosrichard (*Sultan's Court* 1998 [1979]) elucidate how material practices (biopolitics) and fantasmatic beliefs (ideologies) interwork to reduce heterogeneous populations into monoliths—the other is primitive, despotic, Sotadic etc. Cleansed of all differences and irksome singularities, the other functions to consolidate the white aristocratic, able-bodied, and heteronormative European male as the ideal universal form of moral and political subjectivity. In itself the other is empty, filled out with Europe's repressed fantasies. This process of creating the "other" is termed "othering."

Postcolonial critics interchangeably use lower and upper cases for writing the other. Though Spivak stays cautious using upper-case Other to designate the locus of power in the colonial dialectic, that is, the colonizing Other, and the lower-case other for "colonized others...as subjects," her logic deriving from Lacan's differential writing of the terms, the extent to which this distinction (*à la* Lacan) can benefit postcolonial studies hasn't been fully explored (Ashcroft, Griffiths, and Tiffin 2007, 155–56). Following Spivak, and with the intention of making good on the above critique, I distinguish my use of the "other" from the "Other" thus: I use the lower-case other for designating the colonized as individual, particular, and singular and therefore distinguish it from the colonized as the Other or the colonized as symbolically determined in terms of difference from the self of the colonizer. Mind you: I am not strictly following the Lacanian determination of the big Other as the locus of Law preferring to orient my use of the terms *other* and *Other* on Lacan's concept of the other as radical alterity. My use of "other" specifically references the irreducible in the colonized Other. That is what *remains outside of, resistant to,* and in *excess of* imperial symbolizations of the colonized as *binary* Other. The other is radical alterity; the other's alterity marks it as a traumatic impossibility within the colonial sociosymbolic.

Put another way, the other is Fanon's zone of *nonbeing*. Occupying the space between the imaginary positive Self and the negated impossible Other, the other that remains in-between is an expression of radical negativity arranging the manifest relation between the Self and the Other. The other in the symbolic is this radical negativity positivized; its nonbeing being represents the essential antagonism at the heart of the colonial sociosymbolic and it is as this *being of nonbeing* that it constitutes the respective identities and hierarchical relationship between the colonizer and the colonized.[2] Put differently, the other is a rupture—the hole in the real—the aporia responsible for dislocating colonial social relations as well as supporting these relations.

As noted above, my conceptualization of the other in terms of impossible alterity and not symbolic difference draws from Lacan's *objet a*. By Lacan's own admission the *objet a* is "his most significant contribution to psychoanalysis," and one of his most elaborated, revised, and reimagined concepts (Fink 1995, 83). Fink notes that, "few concepts have so many avatars in Lacan's work: the other, *agalma*, the golden number, the Freudian Thing, the real, the anomaly, the cause of desire, surplus jouissance, the materiality of language, the analyst's desire, logical consistency, the Other's desire, semblance/sham, the lost object, and so on and so forth" (ibid.). My use of the other, however, specifically draws on the notion of the Real, or the other as a piece of the real. That is to say, I conceive the other as unsymbolizable alterity responsible for eviscerating the fiction of the subject. As surplus or excess, the other, to misquote the words of Collette Soler, "cannot be translated in terms of unconscious knowledge[,] cannot be measured[, is] beyond the subject," hence unbearable to the Self (Soler 2014, 107). In encountering this other, the subject confronts its own radical alienation—the gap within its desire, the fracture within its imagined omnipotence, the point at which it stands witness to the disappearance of its Self (Lacan Sem XI 1998). The other is hameographically linked to our fundamental condition as lacking subjects. Encounters with the other only substantiate this condition, thereby putting an end to imaginaries of power, authority, and identity. In its role as the site of unbearable enjoyment (*jouissance*), the psychoanalytic concept of the other is logically same as the other I designate as being in excess of or as surplus to the postcolony. Both perspectives articulate each other as a "negativity at work" (Zupančič 2016, 87). Psychoanalysis sees it inhabiting the core of the subject; I claim that it is inherent to colonial/postcolonial social relations. In focusing on the colonized as the symbolic Other and nothing more, postcolonial studies has given short shrift to this valuable concept. Re-linking with psychoanalysis, allows us, as I demonstrate in this book, to radically reimagine postcolonial theory for the global present.

Before concluding, a few sentences on the big Other. The upper-case Other or big Other in psychoanalysis is the Law—the symbolic Other—inaugurated by the paternal function or the *Name-of-the-Father*. The "Name-of-the-Father" cancels out the "desire of the Mother," thereby enabling the subject to move from being an object in the Mother's ravenous desire to becoming a subject of desire (Lacan 2006, 465, 688). The subject gains domicile in the symbolic order by acknowledging castration. Castration being the "payment" required for escaping the Mother's crocodilian desire. Castration "means that jouissance has to be refused in order to be attained on the inverse scale of the Law of desire" (ibid., 700).[3] Presented differently, it is the law apropos which the otherwise empty subject gains identity.[4] By contrast, I present the postcolonial Other as the reduced or distilled representation of the colonized as negative. As I use it in this book, the postcolonial Other functions as the prop or prosthetic which gives the subject of the West and the West as subject favorable terms for coming into existence. As far as possible, to contrast the psychoanalytic Other from the postcolonial Other, I have written the former as "big Other" and the latter as simply "Other."

ONE

The Subaltern Act of Freedom

I. SUBALTERNITY AND FREEDOM

It is difficult, if not downright impossible, to draw a straight line between subalternity and freedom. If we follow Spivak's definition of subalternity as position without identity—the subaltern occupies a position in society (it figures in censuses, voter's lists, etc.) but is bereft of political or voice-consciousness—then freedom can only exist as a negated concept in relation to subalternity. In other words, the question of subaltern freedom is directly contingent on reversing or eradicating the specific conditions of subalternity. The subaltern must transcend her peripheral position and enter the dominant center. However, insofar as the subaltern is strictly determined by a lack—its inability to self-represent—the possibility of subaltern (class) mobility is doubtful. This makes the proposition of subaltern freedom moot.

The paradox has led some critics to talk about an inherent "theoretical deadlock" in Spivak's theory: "The deadlock emerges from the fact that Spivak's concept of the subaltern displays a peculiar troubling quality, as it can only be defined *via negativa,* namely through its inherent status as a non-subject or non-agent" (Jong and Mascat 2016, 718). "The narrative of subalternity is always already subsumed by the discursive power of patriarchy, imperialism, and nationalism, which purport to both represent (in terms of politics) and re-present (in terms of artistic renditions) the subaltern subject," therefore, irrespective of whether the subaltern remains on the margins or enters the center, the subaltern always occupies a subservient position, is always subject to domination, and her actions are always inscribed with the logic of dominant hegemony (Shandilya 2014, n.p.).

Correspondingly, it has been also argued that in the rare case a subaltern manages to enter the hegemonic center, she no longer remains a subaltern and loses or forfeits all right to represent those she left at the margins. For once at the center, she becomes part of the center—she speaks as the center—and can no longer authentically represent those at the margins. This debate, readers will remember, erupted in the wake of the publication of Rigoberta Menchu's memoir, *I, Rigoberta Menchu* (1983). A K'iche' woman, Menchu was part of the indigenous resistance against the Guatemalan government and army during the Guatemalan Civil War (1960–1996). Her *Testimonio* brought to the world's attention the plight of the indigenous and their rights. While some critics applauded her work as the ultimate validation of subaltern speech, others questioned the authencity of the document on basis of some historical and personal details contained in the testimony. Summarized, the problem is, indeed, can the subaltern (ever) speak? For when at the margins its speech remains unheard; and when, having broken through into the center the subaltern attempts to speak about the condition of life on the margins, its speech is scrutinized and ultimately dismissed for containing minute irregularities (see, Beverley 1999, ch. 3). The subaltern is caught between two deaths: on the margins, it does not exist; but once at the center it can no longer stake claim on the margins. It seems there cannot be a (subaltern) act that actually ever frees the subaltern.

But these are not the only issues emerging from Spivak's theorization of the subaltern. Critics commonly accuse Spivak of *culturalizing* politics. That is, of substituting Marx with Derrida in her analyses of subalternity and class; of imposing a unitary subjectivity on the subaltern by framing subalternity via a poststructuralist fantasy of cultural identity; and of resigning the subaltern to its (im)possible condition of lack. The subaltern cannot speak, act, or be free and it appears that Spivak believes the only way the subaltern can exact some modicum of communication in a sociosymbolic heavily stacked against her is by dying.[1]

What if the subaltern's immobility, its definition via negativity, is not a "theoretical deadlock" but, rather, Spivak's *most* fundamental point about subalternity? I read or misread Spivak differently. Instead of thinking in terms of the subaltern's movement from margin to center, I find it useful to think of the subaltern as expository of the real condition of the social. Accordingly, I read the aphorism—*the subaltern cannot speak*—as Spivak's brutal and unambiguous identification of subalternity as social impasse. The subaltern names the insurmountable impossibility existing not just as a differential between the enlightened center and the brackish margin but as substantive of the impossible antagonism constitutive of this social relation. Pushing farther this line of thinking, I wager in this chapter a reading of subalternity as asynchrony, nonreciprocity, and nonrelation(ship).

We should exercise extreme caution with the hypothesis noted above. I am not suggesting we reduce the idea of subaltern nonrelationality into a coda for understanding oppositional identity politics or explaining the social as irreparably schismatic. Consider how a literal reading of the hypothesis risks silencing the subaltern by turning her into a formula for understanding the social: the absence of subaltern speech means society is irreversibly divided by class; consequently, responses to social inequality must take either one of two (hyperbolic) forms. First, if the nonrelational other is restricting the social from achieving its full harmonious potential, then we must erase this impediment (through the use of concentration camps or by building walls). We identify this as the conservative reaction. The second or the neoliberal response states that we remain deeply empathic toward the other, and that we do this in number of ways, from slapping "Refugees Welcome" stickers on the boots of our cars to advocating tolerance and celebrating difference as part of an all-welcoming multicultural society.

However, imagining the subaltern outside the "struggle of two opposed principles" or the subaltern as a "paradoxical object in which negativity itself acquires positive existence," we arrive at another theoretically interesting idea about the subaltern (Žižek 2012, 797). We do not need to depart from Spivak's singular construction of subalternity as position without identity to remark further that the subaltern is the excluded included of the social, and as such it is the traumatic *extimité* constitutive of but irreducible to the sociosymbolic. The impossible alterity of the subaltern is a threat to hegemony; its eruption in the symbolic defatigates the imaginaries of power, authority, and identity.

L'extimité. Lacan coined this neologism specifically for describing the inside-outsiderly character of the Thing (*das Ding*). I will invoke it here to characterize the subaltern as an exterior that is always already present in the interior, thus assigning to the interior a quality of exteriority (Miller 1994, 76). Put differently, the subaltern makes the interior uncanny, unrecognizable, and violently fissured. The subalterns Spivak has in mind—the indigenous tribal women in South Asia—indeed live out their lives in the absolute obscurity of the subcontinent's withering forests, drought-ravaged interiors, and remote mountainous terrains. It is a rare accomplishment of Indian democracy that these subalterns even feature on the voter's list and the census. But this democratic obligation toward equal franchise apart from supplementing the politics of vote-based democracy (one person, one vote) also pushes us to experience the subaltern as the concrete yet ambiguous within everyday life. Demographic bodies, the subaltern are physically locatable yet metaphysically irreducible. Yet their irreducibility is not simply symbolic difference but irrecuperable impossibility. While symbolic difference can be understood or even overwritten from within the symbolic register, we cannot negotiate the real insofar as it is outside of symbolization. The real is not just a rupture in the symbolic; it is constitutive of the symbolic.

My hypothesis of subaltern nonrelationality is therefore an invitation to think about replacing neoliberal democratic politics with a politics of ontological discordance. Unlike the neoliberal thrust on arranging a "non-totalizable multiplicity of singularities" into a "democratic network," the politics of ontological discordance focuses on identifying nonrelationality as the constitutive condition for the social and the pivot for imagining a new politics of the social (Zupančič 2016, 90).

Let there be no mistake: I know the subaltern exists. I am not seeking to dematerialize the subaltern. My point rather is that by thinking about subalternity as "immanent impossibility" we can revise our understanding of subaltern (re)actions against hegemonic oppression (Žižek 2012, 800). I claim that, far from being non-agental, subaltern acts expose the real caveats of a disarticulated *socius*. What I am calling the subaltern act, though, is nothing more than an exceptional enunciative moment via which the subaltern's negative positivity gains a disruptive social presence. The act re-presents the subaltern as the *inherent non-logic of the social* (Zupančič 2016, 89; Flemming 2015, 155).

II. THE SUBALTERN ACT

Set at the turn of nineteenth-century-colonial Bengal, Rabindranath Tagore's (1861–1941) short story "Jibito O Mrito" ("Alive and Dead" [1892]) revolves around the life and death of a young Bengali widow. In the wake of her husband's untimely passing, Kadombini is condemned to the extreme domestic fringes of her in-laws' home. As the story goes, Kadombini's marginalization within the household is so complete that eventually everyone forgets about her; she becomes a veritable specter in her departed husband's household, and whenever anyone sees her they react as if they had seen a ghost. Kadombini accepts her condition and takes care to keep away from the in-laws, thus pushing herself deeper into the shadows. The situation comes to a head when a child in the family falls sick and "Kadombini's ghost" is blamed for this illness. Desperate to prove that she is not the cause, or that she is not a ghost or even dead, Kadombini jumps into an adjoining pond to prove that she cannot die twice. The story ends with the sound of Kadombini's body hitting the water hard, and as this sound tears through the domestic tranquility of the bourgeois household, Rabindranath is quick to moralize: *Kadombini moriya proman korilo se more nai* (Kadombini died to prove that she was not dead).

Rabindranath's critique of nineteenth-century-Bengali bourgeois is penetrating—vacuous customs, punishing rituals, and habitual neglect from the in-laws reduce the young widow to a nonentity, a shadow of her former self, and though alive a ghost. But this story gives us more than a critique of a particular sociohistorical context. The peculiar character of Kadombini's suicide invites a theoretical possibility, which I am calling "the subaltern act." I will detail the theoretical features of the subaltern act more substantially in my discussion of Mahasweta Devi's "Draupadi" later in this chapter. Here let me introduce two signal points.

It is clear that Kadombini does not commit suicide to end her life of misery but, rather, to convey a message to the big Other, namely, that she is not dead. But in order to prove she is not dead she has to die. Kadombini commits suicide therefore not to die but in order to validate her being alive previously. Apropos my first point: the subject enunciating or initiating this message, namely, Kadombini, is also the object in the message. Or it is by objectifying herself into a dead body that she manages to convey her message. Second, this erasure of the subject *is* the message that Kadombini wishes to convey to the big Other. However, her act both temporarily ruptures the big Other's ability to comprehend and ends up erasing the big Other's authority. Rabindranath tells us that when Kadombini confronts the patriarch of the house to prove she is alive, the latter freezes and fails to react. Then, as Kadombini runs out of the house and jumps into the adjoining pond, the patriarch, still frozen in his place, hears the sound of something heavy crashing into the water but fails to react. I contend that because the subject becomes an object—the speaker and the spoken about, the inflictor of pain and the victim of that pain—she erases the symbolic order by erasing or cutting the big Other out of the scene. The big

Other is rendered impotent to (re)act and can only stand witness to the effacement of its authority from the scene. As further example, let us consider Jose Dolores's death at the end of Gillo Pontecorvo's 1969 film *Queimada (Burn!)*.

Jose's death is similar to Kadombini's suicide. Though Jose is executed and does not commit suicide, it can be argued that by not escaping when given an opportunity Jose actually does commit suicide. A prisoner charged with leading a peasant insurrection against the newly formed decolonial government of Queimada, a fictional Caribbean island in the Lesser Antilles, Jose (Evaristo Marquez) is sentenced to death by hanging. William Walker (Marlon Brando), a retired English navy officer and *agent provocateur*, who knew Jose from before the time of the nationalist government, however, decides to set the prisoner free.[2] It is not clear from the film if Walker's decision to let the prisoner escape is due to his old friendship with Jose or because he is concerned about the political implications of executing Jose. The latter seems more probable, because on the night before the execution Walker cautions the administration against making Jose a martyr: a rebel alive is easier to contain than a martyr because the latter becomes part of local songs, oral histories, and inspires rebellions outside the ken of state surveillance. On the morning of the execution, Walker appearing to be acting on his own conviction and accord, slips unnoticed into the prisoner's tent, cuts his bonds, and tells him to escape. Jose *refuses*. Jose refuses to accept freedom not wrested away from the oppressors, preferring to die instead, especially if his death becomes an inconvenience for the government.

The "ultimate expression of sovereignty," according to Achille Mbembe, "resides, to a large degree, in the power and the capacity to dictate who may live and who must die." Hence, to kill or to allow life constitutes the limits of sovereignty, its fundamental attributes (Mbembe 2003, 11–12). By refusing sovereignty this power, Jose withholds satisfaction from the big Other. Like Kadombini, Jose too recognizes and sends a message to the big Other. But in both cases the message reaches the big Other as a stain, inexplicable and incomprehensible. Struggling to make sense of the subaltern's desire, the big Other finds itself absent from the message. This act of sending a message to the big Other but which the big Other is incapable of hearing or understanding creates a possibility for subaltern freedom. This (speech) act I term therefore as the *subaltern act of freedom*. It is not a freedom into a different or better world but, rather, the freedom to speak. Or, freedom in the (moment of) enunciation. Freedom here is the authentic subjective moment that unravels the big Other's lack—it is not all-knowing and has no power to authorize. Kadombini's and Jose's suicide/execution are expressions of them remaining alive outside the strict jurisdiction of the Law.

Though Kadombini commits suicide, her act appears closer to an execution than suicide. For Kadombini was pushed to suicide as the hegemony silencing her left her with no other recourse. No matter how many times Kadombini screamed "I am alive" no one heard. Similarly, Jose's execution is also a suicide. He had the option to escape but only by not escaping could he articulate his message. Both the subalterns therefore use their bodies to speak; their bodies slithering out from being overwritten by law. By erasing their bodies to correspond with their already erased speech, that is, by unraveling the body as an object of speech, the subaltern shocks the big Other. Their wanton disregard for the body delivers a traumatic truth, namely, there's a difference between having and being a body. As humans, we can have a body but never be the body. The association we make between the self and the body is perpetually flawed. Inaugurated by misrecognition, the image of the corporeal body never stands up against the signifier subjectifying us as lack-in-being. "This lack in being as effect of the signifier divides being and body, reducing the body to the status of having it" (Miller 2001, 21). Therefore, in throwing their bodies away, the subalterns force the big Other to confront its own lack, delivering in process a sharp rebuff to the big Other's promise of a positive relationship between the image and an idea of being.

The subaltern act challenges, foregrounds, and uncongeals the already existing systemic aporias within the dominant symbolic order. As excess of the signifying function or remainder of the signifying process, however we wish to conceptualize the subaltern-in-the-act, the subaltern is the signifier gone missing (Zupančič 2017, 47). It is the name for an unbecoming of signification. Confrontation with the subaltern act is therefore a confrontation with something extremely traumatic, a negative positivized or the coming face-to-face with nonbeing. This results in *momentary lapse of reason* and evisceration of the logic for differential identities, symbolic power struggles, libidinal economies, and commodity cultures.

Before moving forward to a detailed explication of my theory, I wish to clarify that this effort to re-theorize the concept of the subaltern is not exclusively Lacanian in orientation but, in fact, most of my cues for reading the subaltern in this manner comes from Spivak. Lacan aids by giving the framework required for thinking through, especially via the Lacanian theory of acts, to which I will now briefly turn before returning again to discussing the subaltern act in more detail.

III. THE SUBALTERN ACT AND LACAN'S THEORY OF THE ACT

On first reading, the psychoanalytic theory of the act might seem inappropriate or even unusual to analyzing subalternity (for reasons discussed below). But I will underline in this section the braiding I pursue between Lacan's theory of the act and what I term the subaltern act.

The act in psychoanalysis, Ed Pluth explains in *Signifiers and Acts* (2007), must not be conflated with the well-known psychoanalytic concepts of "acting out" and the "passage to the act" (*passage à l'acte*). The act is different from both. The fundamental distinction has to do with their different relations to fantasy. To elaborate: while "acting out" and the "passage to the act" leave fantasy and the big Other unchallenged, *the act* decimates both (i.e., fantasy and the big Other). In "acting out" there's a reenactment of the scene of fantasy, which is why Lacan calls it a (de-)*monstration* (Lacan Sem. X, 2015, 124). By contrast, in "passage to the act," there is the exiting of the scene of fantasy; or, in the words of Lacan, "a rush[ing] and toppl[ing] off the stage, out of the scene" (ibid., 115). Yet, in neither "acting out" nor "passage to the act" is "the plane of identity…crossed and the fantasy traversed," and as such the fiction of the subject as the subject of the big Other's desire remains undisturbed (Pluth 2007, 139). In sum: both "acting out" and "passage to the act" ensure the big Other and the fantasies necessary for ensuring the existence of the big Other as support to the self. Whereas the act in decimating both fantasy and the big Other guaranteeing the function of fantasy leaves the self without mechanisms of (mis)recognition, therefore, strictly speaking, without a self.

"Acting out" is strictly an epiphenomenon of the clinic, mostly involving analysands reacting against their analysts' interpretation or the lack of it. Abrupt and, at times, even violent, acting out is "addressed (unwittingly) to the analyst…as a protest against a faulty interpretation, or a failure on the analysts' part to make an interpretation altogether" (ibid., 100). Its goal is to preserve the scene of fantasy. Or, as Bruce Fink notes, in "acting out" the symptom is renewed as it takes on a "new form" in response to the big Other (Fink 2004, 56). Equally sudden and unruly, "passage to the act" shares a slightly different relation to fantasy. It is "a reaction to (and against)" fantasy, which includes the total exiting of the stage, an evasion of the big Other altogether (Pluth 2007, 100). Note: it is an evasion but not decimation. Apropos "acting out" and the "passage to the act" is different only in degree. While in "passage to the act" the subject evades confrontation with the big Other, "acting out" involves the staging of subjectivity for the big Other. In "acting out," the subject brings "the semblance onto the stage...to make an example of it" (Lacan, Seminar XVIII 20.01.71). In other words, "acting out" sees the reappearance of the subject-as-symptom on the stage of fantasy whereas "passage to the act" involves the subject exiting the stage of fantasy. In either case, they remain tethered to the big Other insofar as the big Other is the guarantor of the object supposed to fulfill desire. Fantasy, as Žižek writes somewhere, is not about the desired object but about how this object comes to represent desire. In other words, when thirsty and longing for a chilled can of Coke, I am not fantasizing about Coke. Rather, fantasy is what makes Coke appear as my true and only object of desire. The modality of encoding an object (of desire) with the *Thing* (object *cause* of desire) that will fulfill me is controlled by the big Other. Traversing of fantasy involves recognizing the *object cause of desire* as trash/shit (*déchet*), and this also implicates the big Other's failure to function as the symbolic support of desire—to authorize, stabilize, and invest meaning (desire) in the rambunctious other. Without this radical traversing there is no negating fantasy for or the prevalence of the big Other. Both "acting out" and "passage to the act" therefore leaves fantasy intact, and consequently the big Other intact.[3] By contrast, *the act* is "purely formal[;]unemotional, with no motives, desires or fears" (Žižek 2008, xli). The act ruptures the big Other.

Pluth identifies four major aspects of the act: (1) it has a signifying function or does things with signifiers;[4] (2) it changes the structure of the subject;[5] (3) it is outside Law or transgressive;[6] and (4) no authority is capable of grounding or making sense of the act.[7] To these, I wish to add a fifth point: the act is "without a clear awareness" over "the outcome of strategic argumentation."

In order to fully render these five points, let me start by citing Žižek on the act. Žižek writes,

> the decision [to act] is purely formal, ultimately a decision to decide, without a clear awareness of WHAT [*sic*] the subject decides about; it is non-psychological act, unemotional, with no motives, desires or fears; it is incalculable, not the outcome of strategic argumentation; it is a totally free act, although one couldn't do it otherwise. It is only AFTERWARDS [*sic*] that this pure act is "subjectivized," translated into a (rather unpleasant) psychological experience. (Žižek 2008, xli)

Notice that Žižek's is not an argument stating the act is free. Rather, Žižek acknowledges the subject could've decided not to act but that, then, the act is the only recourse available to the subject in her specific situation. Therefore, what makes the act truly free is its unhinged existence. It is unglued from the subject acting insofar as, at the moment of acting, the subject is "never fully aware" of what she is doing. "[C]aught in the flow of events" the subject acts "automatically," without planning or strategizing, "under the impression...that there is really no [other] choice" (ibid., 222). This alone makes the subaltern act irreducible, shocking, and "incalculable." It is an act that can be only signified retroactively. Simply put, the subaltern (act) confronts universal fictions of power without conscious intent, thereby underlining that the act is without a subject or the act is "knowledge without a subject" (Lacan "Overview of the Psychoanalytic Act"). In sum: one, the subject initiating the act is not completely aware regarding the ultimate extent of the act; two, the act is spontaneous; and, three, the act is retroactively made meaningful for the subject. At the moment of its eruption, the act is immeasurable, unmoored from and disruptive of the symbolic (big Other).

What I am terming the subaltern act (of freedom) is not provisional to the subaltern's movement from the margin to the center. It is also not proof of subaltern consciousness, agency, and/or desire. Neither, for that matter, should this "freedom" which I lexicalize to the act be understood in the terms of rights-based entry into a constitutionally protected space. Whether directed inward or outward, the act translates the subaltern subject into a speaking object irreducible to History and outside the discursive narratives of global politics. At the same time, keeping to its undecidable character, the subaltern act is extremely local. It brings to surface a shift between the place where it unfolds (the margins) and the place it occupies as a stain in the Other—a material incongruity jamming the structure; the letter dislodged from the signifier (Tomšič 2015, 21–22).

This aspect of the subaltern was not lost on Spivak, which is why she chooses to use the example of Bhubaneswari in "Can the Subaltern Speak" even when her distant relative does not appear to align with Spivak's definition of the subaltern as the Third World woman doubly disadvantaged by class and gender. Bhubaneswari is not a class subaltern. I contend that Spivak uses Bhubaneswari's story because she wishes to underline Bhubaneswari's suicide as an *act*. It is an excessive reaction to the failed mission and is in excess of all possible understanding, a fact that Bhubaneswari seems to anticipate, hence the repeated *écritures* she leaves behind.

At the base, there are two distinct *écritures* or messages. First, Bhubaneswari's suicide note detailing the only reason for her suicide, namely, the failure to complete the revolutionary act and, second, what Spivak terms, a graphic...graphematic note that is brought to bear through her lifeless menstruating body (Spivak 1999, 246). The second note, written through the materiality of her body, is supposed to underline the first handwritten note but functions as well to question writing (*écriture*), that is, the written note, as a valid method of communication. The second note renounces writing for the body. Spivak claims that Bhubaneswari's double *écritures* are aimed toward (doubly) establishing that she did not kill herself because of unwanted pregnancy and only because she failed to assassinate the magistrate. Yet, one cannot help but notice how these *écritures* equally convert Bhubaneswari's act from being cautious about the lack in the big Other (will a double *écriture* help deliver my point to the big Other) to resting on the truth about the complete absence of the big Other (the second *écriture* merely brings into relief the impossibility of communication as there's no big Other guaranteeing meaning). It is finally through her appearance in Spivak's text, her third differential writing delivered via proxy, that Bhubaneswari's real question stands deciphered: "Can the *center* hear?" Might we not ask the same after Kadombini and Jose? Do they interrogate the big Other's desire or establish the big Other as absent? At the same time, we mustn't overlook that all three acts are directed inward—toward themselves—as a mode for sending a message to the big Other.

What kind of liberatory acts might these be if not directly addressed to the (repressive/prohibitive) big Other? And, by reading the subaltern act thus are we not inviting the charge brought against Spivak by Sunder Rajan regarding the only good subaltern being the dead subaltern? We must reject ideas of the organic body as the subject or the end of the organic body as end of the subject if we are to fully understand the affective impact of the subaltern on hegemony. What truly harasses the big Other is not the subaltern acting to end the dominant regime and/or gaining access to the center. It is not even about the subaltern remaining alive, free to enjoy the fruits of her emancipation. Rather, going against all such commonplaces of thinking about freedom and agency, I contend that the subaltern act exposes the subaltern as equally an agent (speaking or doing subject) and the (target) object (acting against self-interest). This collapsing of the subject-object into the rupture opened up by the subaltern's act, that is, of the space of nonbeing sharply divided between identities of the center and the margin, spotlights the subaltern as inhabiting the lack. The "zone of non-being," as Fanon phrases it in *Black Skin, White Masks*, offers a paradoxical freedom: on the one hand, there is freedom to transcend restrictive boundaries of being or identity and in recognizing the constitutive force of the nonbeing, and on the other, this freedom is only possible in death

(Fanon 2008, xii). *They are in the hour they cease to be.* The zone of nonbeing, which appears through the act, substantiates the social as marked by the ab-sens of meaning and stripped of reproductive futures.[8]

We must not mischaracterize the subaltern act as an instance of "spontaneous" outburst against authority or oppression. If anything, the subaltern act is political only insofar as it substantiates the deadlock prevailing at the heart of the social (Zupančič 2016, 90). But this is not intentional. Not only does the subaltern act have no referents, it is also not guided by some universal aspiration shared by subalterns across the planet. Trending on the side of the local and heterogeneous, the subaltern act eludes both its immediate as well as protracted addressees.

Instead of considering the subaltern act qua the symbolic, that is, a matter of representation, identity, or speech, I propose understanding the concept as the Freudian death-drive. Conceptually isomorphic to Badiou's event, Eisenstein and McGowan's radical rupture, and Edelman's sinthomosexual, the subaltern is an "empirical impossibility": a gaping hole in the imaginaries of self-representation and the symbolic stilts orienting such imaginaries. It is the primeval real that disrupts politics, materiality, history, and ethics by suddenly bringing into relief the intransitive, fragmentary, and traumatic that are inherent to the social (Spivak 1995, 204). But it is only when theorized as death-drive, that the subaltern act appears to arrange a site of freedom. Not freedom understood in terms of closed definitions of individual or class freedoms and/or the theories of liberty, equality, and justice that underwrite such dreams of freedom but, rather, paradoxically, a freedom articulating the impossibility of subaltern freedom. The act does not free the subaltern; it simply underscores the impossibility of freedom for the subaltern (and all) within capitalism. The only freedom for the subaltern is in her unbecoming or becoming the nonbeing carefully eradicated from the capitalist imaginary.

The act is an (re)enunciation of the subaltern's lack of freedom. It is symptomatic of the subaltern's inability to "act out" and/or conceive a "passage to the act." Or, the subaltern cannot send a message to the Other. As such, the act must be kept distinct from romantic ideas of emancipation. As I note below, in certain cases, the subaltern does not know or even care about the political implications of the act. The subaltern acts to survive, thinking only about its self, and has, often, little to no consciousness of the international(*e*) resonances of her act. Also, it is equally important to remember that the subaltern act is not prescriptive and/or reproducible. The subaltern capable of such action is already on the path toward politicizing her destiny.

THE SUBALTERN ACT OF FREEDOM

By contrast, the freedom emerging from the subaltern act must be understood as a possibility without universality. Simply put: the subaltern act can momentarily interrupt hegemony but lacks both the imagination and consciousness necessary to reconceptualize and/or to entirely dispense with the oppressive system. However, it is precisely this localized character of the act that underwrites its potential for waylaying the politics of progressive futurisms. The act is unsymbolizable symbolic action unraveling the inconsistency/impossibility of the symbolic order.

IV. THE WEDGE OF UNREASONABLE UNCERTAINTY

During the 1970s, thousands of India's sharecroppers and harvest workers, predominantly made up of the indigenous tribals, untouchables, and other low castes, encouraged by a peasant uprising in the Naxalbari area of the Eastern Indian state of West Bengal and swelled in ranks by young Maoists from cities such as Calcutta, challenged the might of the Indian state and its comprador classes with the dream of ending an unequal society with the power of the gun. Reason for their uprising: "the long-established oppression of the landless peasantry and itinerant farm worker." Their target: the "unofficial-government-landlord collusion" sustaining class oppression (Spivak 1995, 262, 249). History remembers these revolutionaries as the Naxalites and their uprising as the Naxalbari movement. Mahasweta's "Draupadi" is set in this historical moment and tells the story of Dopdi Majhen, a tribal woman and a Naxal foot soldier, who, at twenty-seven, is a most-wanted criminal. Her charge: waging war against the Indian nation.

Senanayak, the story's main antagonist, whose name translates simply as "army chief," is a "pluralist aesthete" and "specialist in combatting extreme-Left politics." His expertise eventually leads to Draupadi's arrest and it is under his command—"Make her. *Do the needful*"—that Dopdi is raped in custody (Mahasweta 1995, 245, 258, 267). Her captors hope that shame and pain will compel Draupadi to divulge the names of her comrades. Yet, in spite of undergoing multiple rapes and grievous physical torture, Dopdi does not sing. The next morning, while being readied for meeting the Senanayak, she does the unexpected: first, she refuses to wear clothes, putting on full display her violated, bloodied body—her "[t]high and pubic hair matted with dry blood. Two breasts, two wounds"—and, then, once presented in front of the Senanayak, she yells with a "terrifying, sky splitting": "There isn't a man here that I should be ashamed. I will not let you put my cloth on me. What more can you do? Come on, *counter* me—come on, *counter* me—?" (ibid., 269).

Because my discussion will largely focus on this final moment in the story, the last few paragraphs are worth citing in full here:

> Draupadi stands up. She pours the water down on the ground. Tears her piece of cloth with her teeth. Seeing such strange behavior, the guard says, She's gone crazy, and runs for orders. He can lead the prisoner out but doesn't know what to do if the prisoner behaves incomprehensibly. So he goes to ask his superior.
>
> The commotion is as if the alarm had sounded in a prison. Senanayak walks out surprised and sees Draupadi, naked, walking toward him in the bright sunlight with her head high. The nervous guards trail behind.
>
> What is this? He is about to cry, but stops.
>
> Draupadi stands before him, naked. Thigh and pubic hair matted with dry blood. Two breasts, two wounds.
>
> What is this? He is about to bark.
>
> Draupadi comes closer. Stands with her hand on her hip, laughs and says, The object of your search, Dopdi Mejhen. You asked them to make me up, don't you want to see how they made me?
>
> Where are her clothes?
>
> Won't put them on, *sir*. Tearing them.
>
> Draupadi's black body comes even closer. Draupadi shakes with an indomitable laughter that Senanayak simply cannot understand. Her ravaged lips bleed as she begins laughing. Draupadi wipes the blood on her palm and says in a voice that is as terrifying, sky splitting, and sharp as her ululation, What's the use of clothes? You can strip me, but how can you clothe me again? Are you a man?
>
> She looks around and chooses the front of Senanayak's white bush shirt to spit a bloody gob at and says, There isn't a man here that I should be ashamed. I will not let you put my cloth on me. What more can you do? Come on, *counter* me—come on, *counter* me—?
>
> Draupadi pushes Senanayak with her two mangled breasts, and for the first time Senanayak is afraid to stand before an unarmed *target*, terribly afraid. (ibid., 268–69)[9]

To most (postcolonial) readers Dopdi is the ultimate figure of subaltern feminist resistance. Dopdi acts against institutionalized patriarchy, racial, and gender oppression. Her final actions, critics claim, disrupt authority in two ways: One, the sight of her horribly mutilated bare body visually shocks the Senanayak. Two, her stinging words challenge patriarchal authority by reversing the subject-object positions. Stephen Morton, for example, writes,

> Draupadi's refusal to be clothed stands as an unequivocal sign of political resistance and agency. [And,] this threat to patriarchal authority is *reiterated* in Draupadi's interrogation of her torturers. (2003, 133; my emphasis)

Rajeswari Sunder Rajan nuances this idea further by underlining that it is not a matter of simple reiteration. Rather Draupadi's resistance is "simultaneously a deliberate refusal of a shared sign-system (the meanings assigned to nakedness, and rape: shame, fear, loss), and an ironic deployment of the same semiotics to create the disconcerting counter-effects of shame, confusion and terror in the enemy," affirms Sunder Rajan (1999, 353–54). From a Lacanian perspective, we can earmark Draupadi's actions as mapping in the scopic and the enunciative registers. The disturbing image of her naked body (image) belongs to the first, and her words (signifiers) in the second. More appropriately, it is by appearing as the real that the image of her naked body and her words put Senanayak's authority to crisis.

In the scopic register, Draupadi's mangled body is the real. Following arrest, Draupadi was interrogated for an hour without anyone laying a hand on her. However, with dinnertime approaching the Senanayak retired for the night giving instructions to his subordinates to "Make her. Do the needful" (Mahasweta 1995, 267). Next morning, after breakfast and informing HQ about Draupadi's apprehension, Senanayak orders Dopdi back in his presence. Dopdi is to be cleaned, clothed, and presented before him as if nothing happened overnight. We have here the attempt to foreclose the events of the night and, more pertinently, the consequences of his orders from the night before on basis of his most recent enunciation. The night before, Senanayak had retired after giving the orders to "make her" but he does not wish to accept the full extent of his order the next morning. And this is exactly what Draupadi returns to him—the full consequence of the order, the desire of Law, via the horrific image of her raped body. Spivak is correct in identifying Draupadi as a "terrifying superobject" (Spivak 1995, 252); her bleeding body appearing in the scopic field (Senanayak's as well as ours, readers who are Senanayak's class compradors) as an intolerable image, pulverizing the anticipated image of a women cowed by patriarchal violence. Instead she surfaces as an image too disproportionate and too overbearing for the frame—an image too traumatic for the symbolic to contain.

Dopdi's nakedness is an intrusion; it disintegrates the imaginary to which the Senanayak is habituated—though his practice takes the form of mercilessly squashing Naxalites, in theory he respects them. This is Mahasweta describing the Senanayak:

> [H]e knows that, as in the old popular song, turn by turn the world will change. And in every world he must have the credentials to survive with honor. If necessary he will show the future to what extent he alone understands the matter in its proper perspective. He knows very well that what he is doing today the future will forget, but he also knows that if he can change color from world to world, he can represent the particular world in question. Today he is getting rid of the young by means of *"apprehension and elimination,"* but he knows people will soon forget the memory and lesson of blood. And at the same time, he, like Shakespeare, believes in delivering the world's *legacy* into youth's hands. He is Prospero as well. (1995, 259)

Wanting to remain relevant in all ages and wishing one day to magnanimously deliver the world to the youth, the Senanayak prefers to stay away from the dirt and the grime of his practice. But Draupadi's naked confrontation upends this plan by exposing the true meaning of his practice. The sight of Draupadi's brutalized body forces Senanayak to confront the unavowed connection between his theory and his practice.[10] As much as he likes to think that his theory and his practice are separate, they are not. Spivak correctly notes in her "foreword": "Such a clean break is not possible, of course. The theoretical production of negative capability is a practice; the practice of mowing down Naxalites brings with it a theory of the historical moment" (ibid., 254). But the unavowed connection between theory and practice—violence—is not just the product of this specific historical moment because it enjoys a more universal presence in the social. This is *necessary* violence, *civilizational* violence, one required for establishing the basic minimum of social contract. It is law-preserving violence or violence that seeks to sequester the human from its own fundamental inhumanness. This is violence necessary for grounding the idea of the human (Žižek 2008, 206; also, 2008b).

It is, therefore, in context of Senanayak's exercise of law-preserving violence, or what this exercise accepts as given, namely, that every individual has a specific place marked for by destiny or class which they may not seek to transgress without expecting strict censure, that we should locate Dopdi as an unmanageable stain dislocating Senanayak's position in society as the big Other or the omniscient subject who "alone understands the matter [Naxalite uprising] in its proper perspective" (Mahasweta 1995, 259). Senanayak had hoped to inscribe his authority on Draupadi by overwriting her body with signifiers of gendered violence. The morning after, he had hoped to see absolute submission imprinted in her eyes. Instead, he struggles to see any recognition for his authority in her gaze. Confronted with the enigma of her desire—What does Draupadi want?—and unable to pierce this enigma, the Senanayak is rendered speechless. He sees (*the*) nothing in those eyes. His expansive field experiences and theoretical insights come to naught as Draupadi's nakedness composes "a space of withholding, marked by a secret that may not be a secret but cannot be unlocked" (Spivak 1999, 190).

Senanayak undergoes an experience similar to the young Lacan on vacation in Brittany. One day, on board a rickety fishing boat with some local fishermen, Lacan saw a can of sardines bubbling up and down in the ocean. The fisherman who first drew his attention to the object also offered him a curious information: "you see the can but the can does not see you." Draupadi is not unlike this can of sardines, exotic and trifling at the same time. We oftentimes pass by the physical bodies of subalterns in society, ignoring them unless their alienated labor is useful. But what happens when, like Senanayak, we find ourselves captured in their dark gaze? What does our sudden reduction to the status of an object in their gaze portend for our imagined sovereignty? Recall here Spivak's reading of the Magistrate in J. M. Coetzee's *Waiting for the Barbarians*: the otherwise "capable and senior official who is able to summarize the characteristics of empire" cannot "perform what would be recognizable as an act of sex with [a] young [captive] barbarian woman" (2003, 22). Unable to decipher the blank stare of the barbarian woman as he uses her body, the Magistrate is left feeling benumbed. Detumescence of authority here is linked directly to evaporation of the woman as fantasmatic support to the imaginary of phallus as signifier of power. The barbarian in this scene is the Woman expounding the uncomfortable truth: *there is no sexual relation*. It is interesting that Spivak who commonly pursues interrogations of gendered violence emerging from the politics of social relations would choose to comment on a scene that most explicitly echoes this infamous Lacanian maxim. Perhaps we would do better to short-circuit Spivak and Lacan, postcolonial politics and psychoanalysis, to see the overlap between what Lacan claims as the founding principle of psychoanalysis—*there is no sexual relation*—and Spivak's contribution regarding the impossibility of communication between the subaltern and the master. I will return to discuss this later,[11] because I wish to address Draupadi's appearance as real in the register of speech before.

Spivak weighs in most effectively on Draupadi's vocal challenge to the Senanayak. She claims Draupadi's final words to the Senanayak—"Come on, *counter* me—come on, *counter* me—?"—overturn the established subject-object/center-margin relationship through "a deconstructive practice of language" (Spivak 1995, 255). Though "Dopdi does not understand English,...she understands this formula and the word," that is, the vernacular code within which the English word *counter* counts for extralegal killing of suspects by police and paramilitary forces. In this context, Draupadi's articulation of "encounter" as "counter," mysteriously resembling "the 'proper' English usage," constitutes the menacing appeal of the objectified subject to its politico-sexual enemy" (ibid.). What silences the master according to this reading is a sudden upsurge of the "intractable," or what Spivak at one point terms the "wedge of unreasonable fear" and at another instance in her text as "wedge of unreasonable uncertainty" (ibid., 246, 254). Confronted by this *unreasonable* other, the Senanayak is left incompetent of asking even the most common "authoritative ontological question[:] What is this?" (ibid., 253). As an instance of the symbolic real, Draupadi's deconstruction of the word exposes the instability of the symbolic order, thereby leaving sovereignties claimed on basis of words or symbols unprotected. The symbolic guarantee for his position, which the Senanayak derived from his army handbook, the Indian constitution, and reading Hochhuth's *The Deputy* (1963) and David Morell's *First Blood* (1972), stands exposed in the wake of Draupadi's "counter." As one critic puts it, Senanayak's "theoretical knowledge of the tribals, even about information storage in their brain cells" proves inadequate in the face of Draupadi's *counter*-move (Dhillon 2013, 76).

My theorization of the act differs from these readings insofar as I contend Dopdi's naked parade and vocal challenge as unraveling more than the dysfunction or shakiness of language. What stands exposed, rather, is the incompleteness of reality. The act substantiates the radical negativity occupying the heart of the sociosymbolic. An unruly "shattering force of negation," the act is blatantly dismissive of imagined sovereignties and casually destructive of symbolic networks (Glyn Daly 2004, n.p.).

The first step in reconceptualizing Draupadi's actions as act, therefore, involves recognizing the rupture caused due to the act as not resulting from an outside intrusion, rather, because of the inherent condition of the sociosymbolic as constitutively fractured. Habitual readings of Draupadi's nakedness and speech are galvanized by an understanding of subalternity in terms of center-margin binary positions. Correspondingly, these represent Draupadi's actions as an intrusion from the outside, the margin crashing into the center. But I have been insisting here for understanding subalternity as already inhabiting the center, that is, as the real inherent to social reality and its negation or depreciation being the minimum necessary idealization required for the subject to sustain its identity against the real (Žižek 1997, 22). The subaltern's marginality is a symbolic appropriation of this negation and the subaltern's invisibility a fantastic cloaking of the negativity. Both secure the sociosymbolic by keeping the radical core of the social at a distance.

Draupadi (re)embodies the real through her act. Her act awakens the terrifying Nothingness, the *Thing*, and returns it square and center in the social. This succeeds in waking up the Senanayak from his dream of self-mastery, and as he apprehends the real in the "experience of rupture" he awakens to the knowledge of being "knocked up" in a world "ontologically incomplete, traversed by an impossibility" (Lacan Sem. XI, 1998, 56; Žižek 2017, 1).[12] Draupadi's act draws its affective strength from exposing a radical truth about the social, namely, that the composition of equal social relations is immanently impossible due to our ontological incompleteness. In the following section, I illustrate this point by comparing Draupadi's act with another example of subaltern action from the story. This will help further distinguish the subaltern act from other kinds of subaltern actions. Though both subaltern act and subaltern action involves the use of signifiers, only one of them qualifies as act because only one, namely, the act, has the potential to implode the big Other. Subaltern action, by contrast, as I show below, is more of an intrusion—a challenge from the outside—and often being quickly symbolized fails to reach the magnitude of the act. In spite of both challenging authority, they function on two different levels.

V. THE HOLE IN THE REAL VERSUS THE REAL THING

Dulna Majhi, Dopdi's husband and another Naxalite foot soldier, dies after being shot by the counterinsurgency force. His death by encounter is Senanayak first success in the mission. Yet far from uplifting his spirit, Dulna's death pushes Senanayak to the edge. Because at the very moment the fatal bullet hit Dulna, flinging his body across ragged rocks and filling his mouth with blood, "he had roared 'Ma-ho' before going limp" (Mahasweta 1995, 260). These two words, "Ma-ho," became a concern to the mission and for Senanayak. The words simply made no sense to the all-knowing Senanayak or to anyone in the Department of Defense or even to the tribal experts brought in from Calcutta. Finally, a local water carrier explained: "The Santals of Maldah did say that when they began fighting at the time of King Gandhi! It's a battle cry. Who said 'M-ho' here? Did someone come from Maldah? The problem is thus solved" (ibid.).

Spivak's translation here is interesting, especially the last sentence "The problem is thus solved." The original Bengali sentence is: *samasya forsha hoy* (Devi 2004, 63). *Samasya* = problem; *hoy* = doing verb; and, *forsha,* which Spivak translates as "solved." In Bengali, *forsha* is commonly used to designate "fairness" or specifically someone with "fair" skin tone. It contrasts with *kalo* or black or dark skin. *Forsha* as "fair" however does not mean "white skin" for which the preferred word is *shada*. *Forsha* is used more in the context of the South Asian imaginary of caste-determining whiteness. But when used in the context of a problem or puzzle, as in Mahasweta's story, the word implies the eventual clearing off of confusion or mystery and/or whatever was clouding judgment. In Mahasweta's text, *forsha* carries the connotation of unveiling or uplifting of a cover hiding the truth. Therefore, my preferred translation of the sentence *samasya forsha hoy* is: "The problem thus cleared" or "The fog of confusion thus lifted."

Interestingly, Mahasweta uses *forsha* twice in this paragraph; the second time in the context of the Senanayak's confident assertion that he is very close to deciphering the meaning of Dopdi's song. (Dopdi, it is reported, danced around the bodies of her dead victims ululating and singing in some obscure language.) On this instance, Spivak opts for "clear" and not solved. She translates Mahasweta's original—*sob forsha hoye jabe. Je sob gaan geyeche Dopdi tar mane ber kore fellam bole*—as "All will come clear, he [Senanayak] says. I have almost deciphered Dopdi's song" (Mahasweta 1995, 260). As a native speaker of Bengali, Spivak is well aware of the different meanings of the word *forsha*. What could be her reasoning for translating *forsha* as "solved" in the first instance and "clear" in the next? It could be that she was trying to avoid using "clear" twice in the same paragraph but, again, in that case, she could have gone with "lifted." But the use of "solved" in this instance, I will claim, reinforces a conceptual misreading of subalternity and Spivak's theorization of subalternity in terms of the hermeneutic model of the hegemonic center and the subaltern margin. Within this model the subaltern exists as a gap in knowledge or unknown that invites interpretation. "Solved" becomes a validating signifier for those misreading Spivak's theory of subaltern-hegemony relation as hermeneutic, where resolution is dependent on one set reinscribing the other in desire. The translation is unfortunate because as I note in the conclusion of the book, Spivak's theory never situates the subaltern strictly on the margins. Instead, as with the example of Bhubaneswari, the subaltern is the uncanny alterity—the extimate—existing already within the weave of the social/text. But on this instance her translation almost unwittingly encourages readers to situate the subaltern within a strict coda of positional opposition.[13]

The first step toward understanding the last words of the revolutionary couple—Dulna's "Ma-ho" and Dopdi's "counter me"—requires us ditching this idea of the subaltern as binary opposition. Subalternity is not an issue of epistemological limit but names the radical indeterminacy at the heart of the social, and every effort to cloak this inherent antagonism by striving after communicative social relations or interpretative understanding (of what the subaltern wants?) only ends up producing more confusion and concomitant excuses for exclusion, othering, and intolerance (Zupančič 2017, 30).

Let us take the examples of the couple's last words. First, Dulna. "Ma-ho" is not a word. It represents the *lack* in the symbolic order. It represents the moment when the symbolic system encounters a bump—"impediment, failure, [or] split"—that challenges the efficiency of the symbolic by proving it as inadequate or lacking (Lacan 1981, 25). "Ma-ho" unravels the *insistence of the unconscious* against the brutal domination of sovereignty imagined on the crutches of a symbolic order. Yes, we can argue that what insists is the subaltern's desire for recognition, but we can also read this as the insistence of the excessive other. Dopdi's word/act similarly reveals the incompetency of the symbolic order but the two are not wholly alike. Entering the symbolic from the outside, Dulna's words tear a hole in the established knowledge of the dominant center. But this tear or the hole in the real it is still edged by the symbolic. Suturing such ruptures are easier than what Draupadi's words realize. Because unlike Dulna's words, which are neatly packaged away in official knowledge, archived for future reference, no such closure is possible against Draupadi's outburst. Her words cause the total devastation of the symbolic compared to Dulna's melodramatic slashing of the symbolic.

Consequently, Draupadi's words evaporate the Senanayak's will to know and *will to power*, fully exposing the constitutive negativity operating at the core of reality. Faced with this implosion, the Senanayak is left aghast, unable to make even a rudimentary onto-phenomenological inquiry—"What is this?" Draupadi's word(s) *unleashes* the Freudian *Thing*—the incomprehensible gushing of the death-drive which irreparably horizontalizes all imaginaries of the self. Her act is an open wound refusing to heal. Even Mahasweta withholds giving us any further information, thereby keeping the story unclosed and Draupadi's act real or without symbolization. I will return to discuss this a little later in the chapter. At this point, it is important to note though that Dulna's words, while eventually sutured, still force the Senanayak to relinquish some of his authority. This is because the "omniscient Senanayak," having exhausted all official channels, only figures out the meaning of Dulna's words by consulting the regiment's tribal water carrier. It is the lowly water carrier, who gives the history and context of the word, and as such it is he and not the Senanayak who functions as the subject-supposed-to-know in this scene. Though Senanayak acts to validate and/or theorize the knowledge offered by the slave, by allowing the slave's experiential know-how into the official report he retracts himself from the position of the subject-supposed-to-know.[14]

Mahasweta writes about Dopdi (and her husband) as if they are the *living dead,* alive but dead, the *undead.* After escaping police action at Bakuli *by playing dead*—they lay stiff among the dead pretending to be dead when the police fired—the couple remain untraceable for a long time, their bodies lost in spectral "*Neanderthal* darkness" (Mahasweta 1995, 257). *Neanderthal darkness.* What does this phrase mean? An extreme space of extinction? A space evoking fear, anxiety, and evolutionary dread? The abysmal point of no return impressioned on the collective consciousness of *homo sapiens*? Or does Mahasweta use the phrase to draw attention to the fact that Dopdi and her kin today occupy the other side to humans, that is, the side once occupied by Neanderthals in evolutionary struggle. Isn't the Naxalite also engaged in an evolutionary struggle? Are they not seeking a new species of the human, one not derived from the *homo economicus*? And, in representing this dream and appearing in place of the evolutionary other, do subalterns such as Dopdi—the indigenous who although of the same species but treated differently in society—challenge our humanity on the inverse scale of evolution? The excluded/included, the undead, the surplus of society raising their clenched fists against the hegemon's visions of a cosmetically undifferentiated social order to be accomplished by virulently eliminating all irritating alterities (of being, thought, and vision). By presenting India's dehumanized and spectral indigenous as not just class enemies but an evolutionary threat to the ruling elite, Mahasweta makes a brilliant point. For with one fell stroke she presents class struggle as the fight for survival. The fight of the indigenous to end oppression is a struggle against rampant state-endorsed decimation of indigenous habitats, languages, cultures, and (bare) life. It *is* a fight for survival; a struggle against extinction.

Neanderthal darkness designates a space best avoided, kept at a distance, its inhabitants not welcome into society. It is therefore unnerving when the denizens of this dark realm appear in our world as speaking subjects. When the dead speaks, its voice from beyond is symbolized by the fantasmatic horizon separating the living from the dead. However, when a putrefying corpse speaks, its speech transgresses the sacrosanct boundary between the alive and the dead. The latter hits us without the defense of fantasy. With the decomposing body channeling the voice, we are caught in the dread of the embodied voice, nay, we are enthralled by it, for we stand arrested, spellbound by the image of the ghoulish dead and the words escaping its moving lips. This is what happens when Dopdi Majhen speaks. Her alien tongue coming out of her badly beaten (barely recognizable as human) body puts the Senanayak in thrall.

VI. DRAUPADI'S ACT

What makes Draupadi's actions an act?

First, Dopdi "does something with signifiers" (Pluth 2007, 101). She *asks* the officer to "counter" her. But I do not think Dopdi uses the word knowing that it will elicit an intense affective reaction from the Senanayak. Critics often misinterpret Spivak's point about Dopdi being illiterate in English but aware of the meaning of "counter" as the "code description for death by police torture" (Spivak 1995, 255). Typically, they misconstrue Dopdi's use of the word as "*intentional* political struggle," or the moment when subaltern voice and agency finally finds expression (Morton 2003, 131). But these readings overlook Spivak's concluding sentence in the paragraph: "What is it to 'use' a language 'correctly' without 'knowing' it?" (Spivak 1995, 255). Let me elaborate.

It is clear from Spivak's own commentary that Draupadi understands the code in the most rudimentary way, that is, in its immediate context of the political situation where "counter" describes the only existing relation between the military and the Naxals. But, otherwise, she possesses no knowledge about the word. Put differently, Draupadi derives a political agency through her historically specific understanding of this word but possesses absolutely no knowledge of the language from which this word comes.[15] As her political displacement allows her to "operat[e] the language of the other side," Draupadi's word composes a "menacing appeal of the objectified subject to its politico-sexual enemy—the provisionally silenced master of the subject-object dialectic—to encounter—'counter'—her," thereby reversing the established positions of the interrogator and the interrogated (Spivak 1995, 255). This reversal, along with her "refusal to confess her meaning," attests both subaltern agency and the subaltern's impossibility (Morton 2003, 132). My problem with this argument is that it does not think beyond symbolic politics. The other gains agency or identity only by symbolically negating the self or moving from its position of the negated other to occupying the center from where she enact her own negation of others, including the previous occupants of the center. But this sort of reversal is exactly what Spivak advises that we avoid.

I propose, therefore, that, first, we rethink Dopdi's *doing with signifiers* by focusing on the gap that emerges between her enunciation of the word based on a historically specific understanding and the excessive reaction that her enunciation elicits from the Senanayak. Secondly, instead of thinking of the speaker as subject we consider how the real subject appears in the aforementioned gap between the enunciation and its effect. Dopdi uses "the Other's language against, despite, and without, the Other, in what could be called a profound indifference to the Other" (Pluth 2007, 104). What she really *does* with the signifier or what the signifier *does* in spite of the speaker is not to reverse positions of power but, rather, to pulverize the very symbolic ordering necessary for imaginations of and material exercises of power.

This brings me to the second point regarding what makes Dopdi's action an act, namely, Draupadi's words have direct effects on the structure of the subject. We read that Draupadi's words affect Senanayak but we are not told what truly affects the Senanayak. Is it the confrontation with the traumatic enigma of the subaltern other? Or, is it the constriction of the gap separating desire from jouissance: Dopdi's vulgarization of the signifier catalyzes a moment of molting when a terrifying sublime super object surfaces through the raped female body? Taking cue from Spivak, I contend that the signifier challenges the assumption of the "individual subject who theorizes and practices is in full control" (Spivak 1995, 254). Or, the act destroys the *subject-supposed-to-know* by transforming Dopdi as subject to Law into "a jewel that glitters by itself and bears all its value in itself" (Zupančič 1992, 91). The end of "Draupadi" substantiates the homologous relation of the real to the Hegelian notion of *appearance qua* appearance: "the Thing or truth is precisely the ontological appearance of this distortion" (Vighi & Feldner 2007, 182). In "Draupadi" the known or symbolic is horizontalized by the sudden appearance of the real as the inherent limit of the symbolic. It is the appearance of the real not from a threat from the outside but as the condition of the inside which destabilizes the fiction of the subject as omnipotent.

The third point about the act's transgressive character is to be found in this extimacy—it is as the uncanny inside that the word threatens. Its *extimité* character means we are not simply dealing with a signifier but what Pluth terms a "new signifier." According to Pluth, the "new signifier" is "a signifier that is not bound up with the production of meaning already recognizable by the Other but one involved in the repetition of a resistance to signification" (2007, 105). This new signifier is the signifier of the real, and, accordingly, does not "directly produce new significations" but "mark[s] the presence, within language, of an essential impasse in and resistance to signification" (ibid., 106). If the signifier is what stands in for another signifier, and the Master-signifier is the signifier that halts this process of continual reference by positing itself or pointing to itself as *the* signifier, then the new signifier announces the impossibility of the signifier and/or signification. Or, put differently, the new signifier discloses the inadequacy of the signifier, including the Master-signifier. As the real, the new signifier exposes the other side of difference or what discourses of symbolic difference and signifiers designating such difference strive to hide.

We can approach this in another way, namely, by claiming Dopdi's use of the word extracts the *letter* from the signifier. Often conflated with the signifier, the *letter* (in Lacan) is different from the former. Whereas the signifier belongs to the symbolic order, the letter is (of) the real. When contrasted, the two lead down separate if eventually knotted routes. Thus, while the drift of the signifier is toward meaning-making, the letter resists or insists beyond signification.

But we must avoid the common mistake of thinking the letter and the signifier as mutually opposed: the word kills the thing, true, but there are times when the thing *returns* to disrupt the word. Though Freud formalizes thinking about the unconscious as that which has been repressed but which nevertheless reappears, Lacan teaches us to move beyond this structural model for understanding the unconscious as the real or "*that which has not yet been symbolized, remains to be symbolized, or even resists symbolization.*" The unconscious per Lacan is not hidden but already on the surface in the actions of the subject who repeats. In other words, the unconscious is inextricably part of the conscious and the constitutive force behind reality. In the words of Žižek, the unconscious is *the* wheelbarrow (2006, 21). This is the reason why Fink also writes that the letter exists alongside, to wit, in spite of the signifier (Fink 1995, 25). The real is not outside of but inherent to the symbolic.

Tom Eyers tries to clear the confusion over the "letter" and the "signifier" by offering another set, namely, the "signifier-in-relation" versus the "signifier-in-isolation":

> [T]he signifier-in-relation designates the signifier as it exists negatively, defined purely by relation to other signifiers and producing meaning as the result of its perpetual displacement along the axes of metaphor and metonymy. The signifier-in-isolation designates the signifier as Real, isolated as a material element apart from the networks of relation that would render it conducive to meaning....[T]he signifier-in-isolation and signifier-in-relation should be considered as potential "states" for *any* signifier, rather than as different signifiers or fundamentally different modalities of signification. (Eyers 2012, 57).

Following Eyers, it is possible to argue that Dopdi's act exposes the big Other's failure to arrest the slippage/divorce of the letter from the signifier. As such, her act renders present the traumatic *unrealizable* in the habitual, the routine, and the programmed.

If there is a rule for language it is this: there is *no* rule for language. Language is characteristically unruly—constantly slipping, sliding, and slithering—therefore making signification impossible. Yet how many times do we hear people speak as if there exist rules for our use of language? As Hook and Vanheule perceptively observe:

> The self-referring quality of a given oft-stressed signifier has to suffice when no overarching explanation can be given ("Well that's *Jeffrey* for you...!," "Boys will be boys..."). This, after all, is what self-referential answers do: they don't as much provide sufficient reasons, as loop back on what has already been said, and elevate one signifier over others ("My *children* mean everything to me," "For me it boils down to *faith*," "Evolution does not adhere to the principles of *Christianity*"). The signifier here overreaches its signified; it exceeds what it literally signifies to perform a different discursive function, that of drawing a line, halting a sequence of inadequate explanations by the imposition of a master-signifier ("We know it is true because *science* tells us so"). In this way such responses enable a temporary point of fixity; they ground a point of belief and/or authority. (2016, n.p.)

We negotiate the absence of rules or the constant sliding of signifiers by inventing Master-signifiers that function as "self-validating points of attachment to a broader ideological or personal worldview" (ibid.). What Pluth terms the "new signifier" counters this fantasy by turning the symbolic order inside out.

It is critical to remember though that Dopdi's words are not directed at the big Other with intention of collapsing authority. While her conscious intent might have been of confronting the big Other seeking moral redress, her action becomes an act insofar as it presents her (via her words) as totally outside the influence of *all* symbolic Laws. In the climactic moment, she is free from the compatriot urban male voices of authority—voices that taught her how to fight as well as how to stay unbroken under police torture—as well as the unembodied voice of patriarchy, which lays down codes of gendered existence and teaches women to assume the full responsibility for their rape on themselves. What did you do to deserve this? Were you wearing appropriate clothes? Were you staying out late, drunk? Women are socially interpellated to be ashamed for what happens to them, to remain silent, to acquiesce to their being the lesser gender. Yet, as Spivak poetically notes,

> Once Draupadi enters, in the final section of the story, the postscript area of lunar flux and sexual difference, she is in a place where she will finally act *for* herself in *not* "acting," in challenging the man to (en)counter her as unrecorded or misrecorded objective historical monument. (Spivak 1995, 253)

I read Spivak as saying Draupadi *exits* the symbolic order. But not in the way the subject exits the scene in "passage-to-the-act." Rather, Draupadi exits the scene not to preserve the big Other but rather to dismantle it. It is only by virtue of her exit, a result of her body and mind being thoroughly chewed up and spit out as trash (*déchet*), and her embracing of being this trash, the abject refuse of society, that is, as never having an existence that was not violated by the forces of hegemony, which results in her becoming the traumatic nothingness that suspends the Senanayak's authority. Outside the symbolic codes determining how she is supposed to act, believe, feel shame, or pray, Draupadi is the stellar *Thing* whose radiance proves too unbearable for the Senanayak.

Draupadi's act is neither her own (i.e., aimed at self-preservation) nor addressed to the big Other (for recognition). Her act is "explicitly placed 'beyond the pleasure principle,' beyond the care of the subject's welfare," and "beyond any exchange, calculation, beyond any model or logic of equivalence" (Žižek 1992, 91). Though as the subject of the act Draupadi is never "fully aware of what [she is] doing" or never fully present in the act (Žižek 2008,

222), and the act once articulated can be only eventually "subjectivized" or "translated" into discourse (Žižek 2005b, n.p.), yet the moment of the act as devoid of both an actant and the big Other capable of symbolizing it, discloses the independent traumatic impact the act exerts on everything around. "Counter" with the "en" dropped yet implied is a "crumpled word" (Lacan XXIV cited in Pluth 2007, 106–107)—it is a word stretched between meaning and non-meaning, between meaning and resistance to meaning, and, as a piece of the real, this "garbling of signifiers" (encounter as extralegal killing; encounter as meeting; counter as encounter; and, counter as resistance, and counter as sharing) goes beyond seeking the recognition of the Other (ibid., 109).[16] It presents nonbeing as subject but not the subject of castration.

The vulgarization of the signifier—the catachresis of the dropped "en"—prompts a space for this subject. The subject emerges in the interstice between the intended meaning of the signifier and its unintended effect by momentarily suspending the onto-phenomenological. This is a freedom from the "what is." That is, from the interrogative and from interrogation; from surveillance, discipline, and control. The subaltern comes into transient being between enunciation and her (dis)-appearance in the enunciated word. It exists as an incorrigible subjectivity irredeemably flickering between the garbling and clearing up of meaning.[17] This is not freedom in the sense of Liberty as a metaphysical attribute. But, rather, freedom here is action illuminating the lack of freedom. What the act confirms, which is also the reason why it is so threatening to the symbolic, is that real freedom is the freedom of the death-drive (Pluth 2007, 3). Dopdi's freedom is in (un)becoming what we truly are in this universe: conceited trash. The subaltern act of freedom is an act of debilitating excess—tribal mimicry announcing the nonsense of (non-)meaning into the language of colonial and postcolonial oppression.

VI. CONCLUSION: THE ACT IS WITHOUT A FUTURE

It is important that we do not overtly romanticize the subaltern by claiming Draupadi's act is universal or transferable. For though Mahasweta ends her story with the Senanayak frozen in inaction, bereft of any ability to verbalize or authorize the situation, we should be cautious reading this moment as Spivak does, that is, that the story ends at "the place where male leadership stops" (Spivak 1995, 252). Unlike Spivak, I remain chary about attributing a universal pan to Dopdi's act because such a gesture is problematic within the field of desire. Let me give three reasons for this claim.

First, while Senanayak might find Dopdi's act paralyzing, another subject in his place might find the same act extremely desirable. What hooks or unhinges desire for one individual is often not similar for another individual. In other words, though Dopdi's act unnerves the Senanayak, this act might not produce the same result with a different army chief. This is why Žižek claims that Gandhi's nonviolent active resistance cannot be universalized. Gandhi's movement worked because the British Empire was liberal-democratic or possessed "certain minimal ethico-political standards" or "conscience." But if it were the Nazis, the same strategy would have failed (2013, 122–23).[18] The requirement of a common minimum moral code is reason number two why Dopdi's act should not be universalized. Lastly, three, even though the act is distinct from reaction, it is still a product of local, material, and risky historical contexts. Even though it has been my claim in this chapter that the subaltern act appears on the side of the real, I stake claim equally in the historical realities via which Kadombini, Jose, and Draupadi independently reach their acts. Each of their acts originate in specific needs for survival, demands for love, and desires for recognition, however, at the time of expression, these acts transcend their symbolic particulars to gesture the real as universal.

The subaltern is another name for the impasse constitutive of yet unaccommodated in the space of the social. Subalternity is the expression of the failure of the social, a brutal commentary on the fragility of the symbolic and our ontological scandal. Indeed, no one wishes for the subaltern to remain in subalternity. But, as debates over Rigoberta Menchu's memoir demonstrate, the "end" of subalternity does not necessarily end the question of the subaltern. There exists thus a curious parallel between the subaltern and Lacan's notion of jouissance as surplus. The latter, in the words of Žižek, "always eludes our grasp…one can never get rid of it, that its stain forever drags along" (2005, 321–22). Similarly, the subaltern's existence is not contingent upon the presence or end of social inequality, for the subaltern is the reminder of our riven ontology; the real cause why we are alive; the death-drive that keeps us repeating, encountering, and working-through our irredeemable nothingness.

We should not forget though that while the subaltern act manifests the radical negativity constitutive of social relations, the subaltern herself remains a material or positive figuration of this impossible lack. In other words, the subaltern's inability to speak is not a particular condition even though we attribute to this exception an identifiable symbolic position for purposes of grounding our logic of difference. If anything, this excluded interiority divulges the universal condition demarking all subjects, namely, we are ontologically determined by lack.

But what implications does this theorization have for politics? Does my theorization not risk the charge of abstraction for ignoring the real sufferings endured by the wretched of the Earth as well as their real struggles against unimaginable oppressions? My response to the charge of abstraction is to fully embrace it. This has been one of the common charges against using psychoanalysis for studying postcolonial culture and politics. As I see it, the problem with this charge is its assumption that only historically and culturally specific commentaries on the native indigenous are valid whereas deconstructive or psychoanalytic expositions are invalid. The emphasis on historicism, as we know, derives from the Foucauldian notion of everything being historically specified discursive formations. This means that questions about subalternity are meaningful only within certain historical formations of power, and our task is interrogation of this power and resistances against it. To ignore historical formation of power by abstracting subalternity into universality is inadmissible to this view. I find it bizarre that adherents of this view, while passionately interested in rescuing silenced subjects, are themselves complicit in intellectual or disciplinary exclusion. To these acolytes of history and power all other analytic paradigms are excrement. Apart from stultifying emergence of new theoretical directions or *thinking* (in the sense Heidegger posits thinking against philosophy), this obsession with historicism conveniently redoubts postcolonial studies within university discourse. In fact, this is the most effective way for participating in the neoliberal culture—excavate "lost" narratives and faded memories of victims and represent them afterward for consumption in the U.S. classrooms. University classrooms today have become sites for sentimentalized liberal self-flagellation over human and nonhuman victims. The real purpose for teaching to empathize with the less fortunate is to reclaim the sovereign subject of the West as *the* subject capable of being human, self-reflexive, and charitable. Returning "abstract" thinking to these classrooms effectively challenges this neoliberal rearrangement of the self-pitying subject via pedagogical thrusts on empathy and community engagement.

Insofar as the question of politics is concerned, I claim the subaltern act renders possible the political in contrast to politics. Politics names "a positively determined sub-system of social relations in interaction with other sub-systems (economy, forms of culture)," whereas political represents the "moment of openness, of undecidability, when the very structuring principle of society, the fundamental form of the social pact, is called into question" (Žižek 2008, 193). Spivak makes an almost parallel expression when she writes, "[G]iven the irreducible curvature of social space—the heteronomic curvature of the relationship with the other—the political must act in view of...a 'perhaps.'" She cautions further: "Any political philosophy that does not take this grounding errancy into account will cover over the impossibility of simple collectivities with various ruses" (Spivak 2003, 29, 30). As Zupančič notes, the political is the real; it is another name for the impossibility of social relations, and it is to ordain or negotiate this impossibility that politics intervenes with its mythic discourses of the social contracts (Zupančič 2016, 87). But the function of the political or real is not only to explode fantasies organizing social relations but through this explosion to carve out a new space for the emergence of new radical political relations (ibid., 89, 96, 99). In my reading, the subaltern as simultaneously inaccessible to and as the barrier preventing access to the hegemonic center, marks the subaltern as the *political* itself (Žižek 2003, 77). Reintroducing the subaltern as real into navel-gazing discussions about subalternity as extreme victimhood is already a political gesture.

TWO

Postcolonial. Animal. Limit.

I. THE POSTCOLONIAL ANIMAL

Graham Huggan and Helen Tiffin are often credited for initiating dialogue between postcolonial studies and animal studies. In their 2010 book *Postcolonial Ecocriticism*, widely recognized as a foundational text of postcolonial zoocriticism, Huggan and Tiffin posit: "If the wrongs of colonialism—its legacies of continuing human inequalities, for instance—are to be addressed, still less to be redressed, then the very category of the *human*, in relation to animals and environment, must also be brought under scrutiny" (18). At the center of their analysis is the figure of the Enlightenment Man whose subject-constitution is predicated on identifying the animal as the Other. The animal is the symbolic armature of Enlightenment Man–making and central to the zoological foundations of modernity. Huggan and Tiffin summarize the last four hundred-odd years of this history thus: During the seventeenth and eighteenth centuries, the animal helped trace the margins of a normatized Enlightenment European identity. Thereafter, during Europe's colonial expansions, animals mediated metropolitan relationship with the far-flung colonies by representing the colonized as dehumanized and/or by nominating entire cultures being under the influence of bestiality (Sotadic or otherwise). Beginning at the end of the nineteenth century, however, the animal was repurposed into self-reflexive discourses about the hidden/repressed animality of (European) Man himself for purposes of imagining European Man as white, able-bodied, and rational. Static and perfunctory, the animal functioned in all these versions to index the privilege of the European Man. As the "master of beasts" the latter exacts unconditional sovereignty over the animal world and the animalistic Other worlds. The animal is the dialectical Other vis-à-vis whom human identity is formed, and communitarian values grounded.

Looking back from the late twentieth century, Huggan and Tiffin put this normalizing discourse under scrutiny.

> While the Enlightenment trajectory of humanist essentialism demanded the repression of the animal and animalistic in all its latent and recrudescent forms, it is not until our own century, in the urgent contexts of eco-catastrophe and the extinction of many non-human species, that a radical re-drawing of this foundational relationship has occurred. (134)

Huggan and Tiffin show that far from being simple epistemic exercises, the abstraction of the animal and the animalistic from the conception of the human gave Europe the license to freely exploit Nature and "destroy or marginalize other human societies" (135, 138, 158). The animal is a "transparent metaphor" for sustaining unequal power relations and therefore must be placed at the *forefront* of postcolonial concerns with difference and Othering (Heise 2013, 640).

Broadly speaking, postcolonial zoocriticism examines representations of animals in colonial discourse, the imperial use of animals for dehumanizing the colonized, and the latter's use of animals to question imperial power and reconvene alternative imaginaries of nationalist or nativist sovereignties (Tiffin and Huggan 2010, 158). In the words of another critic duo, DeLoughrey and Handley, postcolonial zoocriticism underlines the role played by the animal in unraveling the Empire's structural exclusions of gendered, ethnic, sexual, and racial minorities alongside examining the "ethics of resistance" arranged through animal figures against the colonial and postcolonial politics of apartheid and exclusion (2011, 32). As such, along with the third world subaltern, the animal today is central to postcolonial interrogations of representational politics and a clarion cause for "political advocacy" (DeKoven 2009, 367).[1]

For me, though, the question remains: What animal are we talking about? That is, are animals in discourses real, imagined, or symbolic? Inscribed under the sign of the human, the latter either as its name giver and/or as its deliverer, the animal cannot exist other than as symbolic prop facilitating subject-composition or as the imaginary other in whom I first see my image. If there is a real animal, it is neither in the text nor in the reading of critics because the (real) animal cannot exist in language. I am not saying that the signifier/word *murders* the animal-in-itself or the signifier fails to cohesively grasp the signfied, but, rather, that the real animal can only exist as a rupture in the symbolic—its *fearful symmetry* beyond the possibility of human symbolization and its excess unbearable to sight. I concur with Rosi Braidotti: the *real* animal is always an anomaly, unavailable in language and apprehended only as disruption in speech or as a tear in cognition (2009). In other words, the animal's presence in language is a semblance underlining the absence or impossibility of the (real) animal. The real animal eludes, evades, and resists human nomenclature, it exists only as a missed encounter. Insofar as the animal is not in relation to the logic of the signifier, commanded to speech or desire via castration complex, there exists an irreparable chasm between animals and humans. This gap has nothing to do with the privilege of humans as subjects capable of speech; rather, paradoxically, because we are speaking subjects, that is, due to our subjection in language. Human existence in the symbolic order must be recognized as the fundamental reason for our alienation from the animal. The animal exists in nonrelation to the human.

This theoretical perspective is missing in Huggan and Tiffin's analysis, and this absence is peculiar because Huggan and Tiffin broach the topic of the real animal versus the animal as semblance a number of times in their book. For example, they write that subject-making is never complete and never secure; rather, the idea of the human remains persistently "haunted" or "dogged" by "the wild, savage and [the] animalistic" (2010, 134). Soon after, in their soulful reading of J. M. Coetzee's 2003 novel *Elizabeth Costello* and Barbara Gowdy's 1999 novel *The White Bone*, Huggan and Tiffin observe that the idea of the animal handed down to the general public by Cartesian dualism, science, and Christian theology obfuscates "animals as *animals*" (ibid., 160). They emphasize instead the necessity of liberating animals from their "metonymic, metaphorical or fabular enclosure[s]" (ibid., 154). But it is in referencing Steve Baker's *Postmodern Animal* (2010) that they come closest to articulating the impossibility of the real animal in the symbolic, although they never quite manage to hit this point. In fact, they misrecognize Baker's complaint as an issue of verisimilitude. In speaking about the absence of the animal in cultural representations, Baker is not asking that we make our representations more real by loosening our anthropocentric grip on animals, but, rather, that real animals are impossible or *unavailable* to man. In Baker's words, the animal points "to the *unavailability* rather than the inescapability of an anthropocentric perspective" (2010, 83). The "real" animals Baker speaks of exists only *in absentia* or when present in confrontational (non-)relationship to the human. It is good that the real animal does not exist because its presence can only result in our *ex-sistence*. Our anthropocentric cocoon is a defense against such traumatic confrontations. Postcolonial zoocriticism, and to a large extent the broader field of animal studies, has failed to understand this and have remained reticent about *the* real animal. Their animal consciousness serves their desire for rescuing these victims and rewriting a new narrative of our anthropo(s)cene history of (colonial) modernity. My term for their blind spot: "postcolonial animal limit."

My intention is not to dismiss existing criticisms. They are valid in their own right. Instead, without discounting discussions about discursive appropriations of animals for dominating racial, gendered, and deformed others, I wish to inaugurate in this chapter a parallel discussion about the *real* animal as substantive of the *charnel reality* of (postcolonial) planetary ecology. Taking my cue from Timothy Morton's suggestion that we recognize the volatile character of the ecological above our habitual celebrations of Nature as harmonious or restorative (2015, 188; also 2009) and Gayatri Spivak's notion of planetarity (2003), which, as I understand it, calls attention to the irrevocable subject-destabilizing unhomeliness (*unheimlichkeit*) of the planet, I propose below a necessary counterpoint to habitual postcolonial readings of animals. Specifically, I propose moving beyond studying animals as neglected and/or marginalized, an exercise that reinscribes the animal back within human-oriented analytics or displaces them further via romanticization of their irreducible naturality, in preference of animals that are unassimilable by human imagination.

Animals that interest me most are ones that shock the imaginary of the human by appearing suddenly and debilitating the symbolic order. I am not thinking of creatures about which we have no scientific knowledge—a hitherto undiscovered species of spider or some extraterrestrial biological organism. No doubt these prospects are terrifying for humans, as Hollywood has made a point of repeatedly reminding us.[2] Animals I have in mind instead are known or scientifically classified animals, but which either by appearing outside the laws of Nature and/or by rendering our known universe uncanny put human imaginary and the sociosymbolic under duress.

Let me be more specific on this point. Firstly, by speaking of the animal, as it exists outside of human knowledge, I am not hinting that there is a secret or inner life of animals that remains unavailable to us. Secondly, I am also not speaking of the animal in-itself; the noumenon that is the true reality of what only appears as the phenomenon to humans. Both these propositions suggest that the real is hidden from or repressed in reality, when I prefer to think of the real as the manifest irreducible kernel of reality (Žižek 1989, 7). The real is never hidden but exists in plain sight though we prefer to overlook or overwrite through fantasy its traumatic thingness. Therefore, when speaking about the real or uncanny animal, I am speaking about human encounters with animals that escape the grid of symbolization, challenge human knowledge, and expose us to the traumatic truth of living on this planet without the possibility of ever adequately knowing our relation to this planet.

In experiencing the real animal, we experience this world as gashed by unsymbolizable fissures, which, unless mediated through fantasy, risk unraveling the fragility of the symbolic and our incompleteness within. The real animal eviscerates our imaginary of *being human*. Confronted with the uncanny animal, humans feel stripped of the minimum idealization necessary for surviving as a desiring subject. In the animal's radical alterity the subject witnesses its own absence; the animal's appearance manifesting a vanishing point at which reality folds into the real and the subject is left to fend the agape with nothing but its body.

In the next two sections, I focus on explicating this argument further through discussions of Mahasweta Devi's "Pterodactyl, Puran Sahay, and Pirtha" (1995) and Amitav Ghosh's *The Hungry Tide* (2005). Parting from postcolonial discussions of animals that enjoy privileged positions in European and non-European literary traditions (the large mammals, the domestic and farm animals, and the anxiety-provoking reptiles) or animals that function as props enabling the human amid the uncertainties of imperial, postcolonial, global politics (environmental crises, terrorism, shifting gender roles, power struggles, economic collapses, etc.)—I turn in this chapter toward animals whose excessive otherness disrupt the human as the subject-supposed-to-know. Lurking on the limits of postcolonial écriture, these animals open up the fundamental deadlock at the heart of the social and push readers to recognize this antagonism as necessary for the emergence of new political relations. I look specifically at creatures lurking on the limits of Mahasweta's and Ghosh's writings—the demonic chthulucenes (as Haraway might identify these)—the annelids, the cryptids, and the crustaceans—which evade symbolization, vex human agency, and threaten to erase the human. The anomalous Tithonian flying reptile in Devi's novella and the ordinary multitude of crustaceans in Ghosh's novel are the real animals of this study, animals that disclose the impossibility of our establishing a positive relationship with the planet. These animals (dis)appear in the texts as unplumbable holes, *detranscendentalizing* or trans-/dis-forming the world into a planet and, subsequently, the planet into an unsettling, to wit obscene, experience of planetarity. *Experience of planetarity*: the experience of irreducible margins inhabiting the center; of awakening to the rude fact that life on this planet is borrowed, shared, and nonhierarchical (Spivak 2003, ch. 3; Thacker 2010, 6–7).

II. THE POSTCOLONIAL ANIMAL 1: THE EMPIRICAL IMPOSSIBILITY OF THE PTERODACTYL

In "Pterodactyl, Puran Sahay, and Pirtha," a real live pterodactyl flies over a drought-ravaged landscape. Its first inscription is discovered in a tribal village located in the heart of this parched land. Puran Sahay, a city journalist sent to report on the famine at Pirtha, learns about "this unearthly terror" from a photograph in possession of the SDO.[3] Withheld from the press, its negative confiscated, the photograph is of a painting made by a tribal boy, Bhikia. But how could an uneducated tribal boy paint a creature that has been extinct for millions of years? (Mahasweta 1995, 95, hereafter in text as PPP).

> A boy painted this on the stone wall of his room. The picture was taken by Surajpratap, but no, this photo is not for a newspaper, *not for publicity*.
> He did not print a photo.
> No, we took away the negative. He cannot print this, he doesn't have a copy.
> What is it? Bird? Webbed wings like a bat and a body like a giant iguana. And four legs? A toothless gaping horrible mouth.
> But this is...
> Don't say it. I won't hear it.
> How did he paint this?
> I don't know. The boy's shut up.
> Where? Where is the picture he painted?
> In Pirtha.
> Now the SDO begins to speak in bursts. As if a badly wounded person is making a last-ditch effort to make a deposition to hospital or police, to the killers or to friends. (PPP, 101–102; italics in the original)

The SDO's struggle with speech symptomatizes a deep "communication gap," a "mental and linguistic suspension of contact" between him, an educated state official, and the illiterate tribal child (ibid., 102). The failure of speech marks the empirically impossible, for there are no words to describe something that cannot be, yet is. Is it a ghost, a demon, a relic species, or something else altogether? All that there is, however, is a trace—the child's drawing on a wall—but it is a trace apropos of nothing. It is apropos of nothing because the creature cannot possibly exist. Dinosaurs went extinct sixty-five million years ago. Yet if the child drew this picture, he must have seen it. He did not see it in a book as he does not go to school. There is no television or computer at his village. Then how could he have drawn the picture? Problematically, the child has since gone silent. There is thus no knowing why he drew this picture: Did he see it alive, is it a demon from a nightmare, or just his accidental imagination?

Flickering between myth and reality, cognition and misrecognition, nature and the supernatural the mystery of the cryptid is a metacommentary on the impossibility of representing the subaltern caught in the proverbial jaws of the animal (ibid., 99). The tribals who inhabit this neglected, exploited stretch of the subcontinent "have no resource" and "they will never." Hundreds of years of neglect have made these people inured to "perennial starvation." "They don't [even] know how to ask" for redress anymore. They "don't ask" but "take if given." They are themselves an empirical impossibility, ungraspable by our "urban mentality" (ibid., 104). Even the map of the district resembles the extinct creature that now supposedly soars over it as if an omen of extinction that is the future of these tribals.

The creature has haunted postcolonial critics since Spivak's translation of Mahasweta's novella hit the English-speaking world back in 1995. And the mystery over the creature has only deepened with conflicting accounts from the author and the translator. For while Mahasweta has categorically earmarked the pterodactyl as a symbol for the suffering of tribal peoples across the world, Spivak, and postcolonial critics following Spivak, has often understood the animal as a metaphor for the impossibility of expressing subaltern speech.

Jennifer Wenzel, for example, claims that Mahasweta's work enunciates the problem of ethical narration. As we have seen, speech fails the SDO— the government official narrating the plight of the tribals and the incredible absence-presence of the pterodactyl. Puran too struggles deciding which of the many stories he has discovered should make it into his paper—the disastrous famine, the government's complete apathy toward the tribals, corporate exploitation of the tribals, *or* the existence of a living fossil? At the end, he decides *not* to report on what would have made him and Pirtha famous—the creature. He chooses to remain silent about the pterodactyl because news of a surviving pterosaur would further displace Pirtha's tribals. But it is the literary critic whom Wenzel specifically has in mind when she comments on the problem of ethical narration. "[C]aught between [Puran's] urgency of making a story heard" and the "difficulty of distinguishing between mediated layers of Puran's experience of the pterodactyl, Mahasweta's explanation of it, and Spivak's evolving interpretations," the literary critic ponders "who *tells* stories of subaltern life and which of their many stories should be told" (Wenzel 2000, 236, 239–40).

This mode of reading retains the pterodactyl as symbol, a myth or metaphor, representing the suffering of the indigenous. And that is vital, according to Mahasweta. In conversation with Spivak, she states:

> *Pterodactyl* is an abstract of my entire tribal experience.... If read carefully *Pterodactyl* will communicate the agony of the tribals, of marginalized people all over the world.....*Pterodactyl* wants to show what has been done to the entire tribal world of India....Modern man, the journalist, does not know anything about it. There is no point of communication with the pterodactyl. The pterodactyl cannot say what message it has brought. (PPP, xiv–xv)

Spivak, though, refuses to identify the pterodactyl as a symbol. In the "Appendix" to *Imaginary Maps*, she notes:

> For the modern Indian the pterodactyl is an empirical impossibility. For the modern tribal Indian the pterodactyl is the soul of the ancestors. The fiction does not judge between the registers of truth and exactitude, simply stages them in separate spaces. This is not science fiction. And the pterodactyl is not a symbol. (1995, 209)

Following Spivak, if we strip away the author's symbolic thrust and claim the creature is neither a visitation by the ancestral soul of the Nagesia tribals nor a metaphor for the silenced fourth world subaltern, then we can arrive at an obvious question: Is the pterodactyl real? As I see it, Spivak allows for reading the pterodactyl *literally* (Spivak 1995, 143). By categorically dismissing the idea of it being a symbol, Spivak opens up the possibility of accommodating the radical question of the real. Not real in the sense of a surviving relic but as "alterity...underived from" the human (Spivak 2003, 73). Put differently, human encounter with this animal results in an experience that is "subtracted from" or unassimilable to "the 'natural' totality" of experiencing the animal (Žižek 2016, 12). "Real" here qualifies this excess of experience; excess that by remaining insoluble, as alterity underived from the human, manifests the radical antagonism constitutive of human (non)relation to the animal (Zupančič 2016).

This theory is not entirely lost on postcolonial critics. Sangeeta Ray considers, for instance, the dilemma of "impossible inhabiting," that is, of extinct and current species coexisting or the harsh reality of modern India and the abject poverty-ridden tribal India existing together (2009, 44). Similarly, Ben Conisbee Baer refers to the creature as a "blank or dark spot" in the text (2011, 178). It is an impediment or stumble in the text that forces us to think about what we are reading. Though both critics are primarily concerned with problems of reading, I find their identifications of the creature as limit (to soul making and Enlightenment critique) especially relevant for my argument here. In particular, Baer's argument that the pterodactyl as void both interrupts and sustains the enterprise of Enlightenment connects to my point regarding the pterodactyl as real. As real it is both constitutive of as well as disruptive of subjectivity. "[S]ubjectivity emerges when substance cannot achieve full identity with itself, when substance is in itself 'barred,' traversed by an immanent impossibility or antagonism" (Žižek 2016, 10). In the context of the story, this means that Puran's encounter with the pterodactyl strips him bare as well as reconstitutes him as subject. Let me elaborate.

At one level, the pterodactyl is a stain on or traumatic excess in ordinary reality. In this role it ravages the imaginary of the human as subject-supposed-to-know. Puran specifically finds himself stretched between what he knows, and the non-knowledge presented by the creature's (non-)being. He does not know if what he witnesses is matter—its body made of "liquid darkness"—or if the creature has a message for him—he sees "no communication between [its] eyes" (PPP 157). With its mute presence, the pterodactyl reduces all life on this planet as irrevocably "endangered" (ibid., 163).

> There is no communication-point between us and the pterodactyl. We belong to two worlds and there is *no communication point*. There was a *message* in the pterodactyl, whether it was fact or not, and we couldn't grasp it. We *missed* it. We suffered a great loss, yet we couldn't know

it. The pterodactyl was *myth* and *message* from the start. We trembled with the terror of discovering a real pterodactyl. (PPP, 196; italics in the original)

Experienced as a presence and loss, possibly bearing a message yet that which seems to have slipped through our fingers, the pterodactyl unmakes the subject-supposed-to-know. I borrow from Lee Edelman when I claim the animal as death drive. The pterodactyl undoes "the structuring fantasy undergirding and sustaining the subject's desire, and with it the subject's reality" (Edelman 2004, 73).

Consequently, and following such an encounter, Puran can no longer remain satisfied with the human present with which he identifies. He therefore questions science, history, and technology: "[H]ow can a *computer* possibly *process*…time and give birth to a *data-sheet*?" (PPP, 156). Eviscerated in the tired gaze of this out-of-place and out-of-time flying reptile, Puran stands bereft of all symbolic politics of difference distinguishing human from the animal. Even as he contemplates on deep time or the analogous situation of the Nagesia tribals, he is left facing the creature with nothing except one connecting point: an extinct species being witnessed by another (soon-to-be-extinct) species.

Anxiety over the collapse of the human stems from the anxiety over the evaporation of the symbolic big Other guaranteeing meaning. Unless Puran embraces the truth of human abjection qua the absence of the big Other, his only way out of this nightmare is through transforming his anxiety about human nothingness into a subjective trauma over something appropriately symbolizable. As death drive—outside time and depositing both historical and chronological time under stress—the only way Puran can recuperate the imaginary security of linear time, that is, the time of desire against the circuitous time of the drive, is by symbolizing his "being outside time" as trauma (*après-coup*). *Après-coup* designates a nonlinear form of temporality in contrast to linear developmental time. Lacan highlights this time (*après coup*) by drawing attention to Freud's concept of *Nachträglichkeit*, which is commonly translated as "deferred action." Laplanche and Pontalis underline at least three different possible meanings of the word in Freud. My use here derives from what they identify as the third, a more philosophical "conception of temporality": something is perceived in the present, an irreducible kernel of real, but is resignified retroactively and aligned with linear developmental time and the fantasy of the human supported by it (Laplanche and Pontalis 1973,

111–14). It is via the logic of the *après-coup* that the existence of the cryptid interlocks with the political problems of government injustice and the politics of symbolic difference.

While Puran and the animal remain deadlocked—"each aporetic to the other"—limits encountered by Puran in Pirtha (the superstitious tribals, Bhikia's muteness, and the mystery of the pterodactyl) impact the "rest of his life" (PPP, 162). The enigma of this Other space—"Pirtha *Block* is like some extinct animal...fallen on its face"—will remain a mystery, a void, and (almost) a code, thoroughly irreducible to human logic (ibid., 98). Yet, through all this, Puran is able to reclaim his subjectivity by repurposing his desire. The end of the novella replaces the unresolvable mystery of the pterodactyl with a "tremendous, excruciating, explosive love." We read: "Puran's amazed heart discovers what love for Pirtha is" and that "perhaps he cannot remain a distant spectator anywhere in life" (ibid., 197).

It is the use of "perhaps" in this sentence that folds love into desire. It aids readers to slide from a direct expression of love for Pirtha to its displacement or metaphorization in Puran's future. This is not a temporal move from Puran's present to Puran's future. It is not a simple exposition of a change working through inside of Puran as a result of his encounter with the cryptid. This is a move from love to desire and must be understood as such.

Love constitutes a response to the unknowable alterity of the other. By contrast, desire sustains itself by not knowing the Other's desire. Desire, as such, does not engage with the radical alterity of the other, preferring to symbolically reduce the other into object traits. Love, by contrast, is directed straight toward the heart of the other's traumatic nothingness. As Adrian Johnston explains, love is "linked to an indeterminate *je ne sais quoi* in the beloved," that is, "to the void of an un-specifiable 'x' that eludes being captured in a catalogue of determinate empirical attributes, characteristics, qualities, and so on" (2005, 67). The void (x) here is not simply what eludes symbolization but one that is substantive of the asubjective ontology of the human.

The pterodactyl is real only insofar as it substantiates the humanly impossible task of comprehending the planet. Questions about the creature's existence (Is it a relic of an extinct species?), its unplumbable gaze (What do the Pterodactyl's eyes say?), and the difficulty of synchronically situating the creature in the secular scientific history of the planet (Are dinosaurs still alive?) force readers toward that impossibility. In this sense, the pterodactyl is a radical tear in the (human) symbolic universe. Love for its unbearable otherness, therefore, can only effectively lead Puran to recognize human existence as trash, thus bringing out the most ethical response to a monstrous other.

But that does not happen in this novella. Instead, Puran's explosive love is reframed by a desire and by moral alternatives. The conclusion of the novella, accordingly, presents an exasperating parade of two diagonal positions: if Mahasweta enunciates a framework for determining the *unheimlich* other, Puran professes an unbearable love for that other. However, authorial intent sweeps in as Puran's response is ultimately encased into a synchronic human history. Love is first translated into labor (work) and then into a future as responsibility:

> Only love, a tremendous, excruciating, explosive love can dedicate us to this work when the century's sun is in the Western sky, otherwise this aggressive civilization will have to pay a terrible price, look at history, the aggressive civilization has destroyed itself in the name of progress, each time...we are destroying the primordial forest, water, living beings, the human. (PPP, 197)

Couching love in civilizational history and transforming the animal into a "myth" are two expedient ways for returning the human to the safety of desire, and thus away from the other excessive to symbolic logic. To make matters worse, the future is also made conditional to human action taken toward removing social inequities. Primal forests and their cryptid secrets become metonyms for humans ostracized, exploited, rendered sterile, and/or, as in the case of Puran, a catalyst for reawakening modern humans from privileged stupor.

I concur with Susan Abrams: the pterodactyl *is* the radicalization of a detranscendentalized planet (2011, 83). Yet her subsequent argument about the animal's role in helping humans recognize "the complex interdependent living that comes from sharing a home with many and neglected others" fails to impress me as it reduces the creature to a metonym for human suffering (ibid., 94). In the final analysis, Abrams puts the animal in the role of begetting or restoring a (lost) natural totality on this planet, similar to the conclusion of the novella, which imagines another totality, a future without human inequalities, and sublimates Puran's violent love into desire as means to achieve social good. The pterodactyl's catastrophic presence, by contrast, distresses human thought, collective activism, and sexual futures. The pterodactyl intimates to

Man that his "normal" existence "is a condition of persistent [and inescapable] crisis" (Baer 2011, 180).

How, then, are we to read the pterodactyl? I submit three options:

1. The pterodactyl is real. It substantiates the constitutive alienation of the human from the 4.5-billion-year-old planet. As real, it is the impossible, the unreal, and the unsymbolizable.
2. The pterodactyl substantiates the fundamental ontological condition of all humans: speech does not exist. It does not exist for the subalterns, just as it does not for anyone else. Speech must always be mediated by desire, so what we hear is displaced from the other's message. But, insofar as the pterodactyl substantiates the crisis of human ontology, it functions to symbolically situate the human against a Nature that is deemed whole, even in the face of its mysteries.
3. The trauma of inhabiting an uncanny world must be recuperated through the other's alterity. The pterodactyl's radical alterity and uninterpretable message must be employed to anoint the human desire as the way to final unravelment.

III. POSTCOLONIAL ANIMAL 2:
"A STRANGENESS BEYOND RECKONING"

Amitav Ghosh's novel *The Hungry Tide* (2005) presents readers with an ethical conundrum: Should they side with refugees seeking resettlement in the deltaic islands of the Sunderbans or should they oppose human settlement in an area declared a national preserve for the fast-depleting population of Bengal tigers? The novel appears to ask what is of greater value: the last preserve of the Bengal tiger, an animal, or humans displaced by the partitioning of the subcontinent and the Bangladesh Liberation War?[4]

Unfortunately, there exists no simple solution to this problem, and the novel concurs to an extent. In fact, the choice offered between saving a near-extinct animal and rehabilitating human refugees fleeing a genocidal war is a "forced choice." Siding with refugees imply overlooking the Sunderbans' fragile ecosystem—the settlement of the refugees on an island earmarked for Bengal tigers threatens these big cats and portends an eventual, and far greater, destruction of the entire archipelago's ecology. But, then, one also cannot simply forgo the human refugees without being complicit in and responsible for the conditions of their suffering. Supporting one will always mean acting *against* the (survival of the) other; a choice made in this situation can therefore be always partial, brutal, and immoral.

Insofar as the refugees in Ghosh's novel have no refuge, *The Hungry Tide* is a novel for the Anthropocene (Haraway 2016, 100). It is also peculiarly of the present, by virtue of its conscious foregrounding of the dilemma noted above. The human-animal/refugee-tiger conundrum draws its affective import from our environmentally conscious multicultural societies at a time when the politics of globalization has become inseparable from the crises of climate change (Chakrabarty 2009, 199). Today we champion the right of every creature, not just man, to share this planet, and the deadlock presented in the novel gestures this phenomenon while raising important questions otherwise sidelined in our unconditional advocacy for animal rights. Two such questions are: While we believe this planet should be shared with animals, that is, as long as each of us stays within our demarcated habituses, what happens when resources shrink and boundaries are truly crossed? Second, What is the relevance of identity politics—human versus animal—when humans inhabit a planet totally indifferent to their cause, being, and future?

Predictably, postcolonial interests in Ghosh's novel focus on this interesting braiding of postcolonial history with the now pressing issue of environmental crisis, most specifically the novel's implicit demand that readers seriously audit their roles in the depredation of colonial and postcolonial ecologies. I do not have the space for a detailed discussion of existing criticisms, but briefly: these tend to applaud the novel's sensitive portrayal of human-animal "symbiotic codependency" (Kaur 2007, 128); its insistence on understanding refugee crises in its "historically differentiated" contexts (Mukherjee 2006, 156–57); and, relatedly, for underscoring "culture-specific, location-based environmentalism" (Sen 2009, 367). Taken together, these readings champion the novel for recomposing the anthropo(s)cene via local contexts, animal rights, and developmental issues based on local and subaltern politics.[5] And while their arguments hinge on the human-animal/refugee-tiger conflict, they mostly overlook the animals in the text that are irreducible to matters of symbolic politics and knowledge constitution. I find these criticisms therefore as failing to transcend the symbolic sphere of human-nonhuman relations and enter the realm of the planetary through considerations of the animal as catastrophic.

There indeed is a case to be made about postcolonial criticism teaching us the ethics of "being human" in a troubled (unequal) world. But the "art of living on a damaged planet" cannot simply consist of making humans more human(e). Today, we have merely replaced the positive form of Enlightenment anthropocentrism ("I am the master of animals") with a more self-conscious, negative albeit feelgood form of anthropocentrism ("I admit guilt of violently mistreating/misrepresenting animals"). Twenty-first-century neoliberal humanism admits the privilege of the human as the subject who concedes mistreating, misrepresenting, and mystifying animals for her own pleasures. Consequently, this subject willingly vacates the scene in order to give animals center stage but only so far as these animals fulfill her deepest fantasies of *becoming human again*. From *subjects-who-know* their superiority over animals, we have today become *subjects-who-know* their culpability in the systematic exclusions of animals. This does not mean we have relinquished control over representation or surrendered our moral privileges. Rather, the subject enunciated by the non-anthropocentric turn is still the subject of speech, capable of representation and knowledge but fully charged on imagined moral privilege.[6]

Badiou identifies the recent turn toward the nonhuman, ecology, and abiotic matter or what he calls the messianic environmentalism of the present as nothing more than a "new age" response to class antagonism. If anything, the current environmental crisis should help us reflect further about the fiction of human sovereignty in a planet impossible to symbolize (Žižek 2016, 30). This in turn should lead us toward a realization of "the real peril" facing humanity today, namely, "the impasse that globalized capitalism is leading us into" (Badiou n.p.). Only an acknowledgment of subjectless-ness can help us fully grasp the import of living on a dying planet. By inhabiting the condition of nonbeing—unpropped by symbolic supports, uncoupled from an imaginary ego, and unmediated by fantasies of our humanness—can we fully comprehend the inconsequentiality of our existence on a 4.2-billion-year-old planet.

In contrast to existing criticisms of Ghosh's novel, I wish to consider therefore the implications of the question: What if the human-animal/settler-tiger/Man-Nature conflict in the novel is a false ideology? That is, what if this conflict serves to detract attention from something else in the narrative, something that exists under the surface of the text, in the murky depths of the deltaic ecology? Something that is indifferent to the political and moral tensions over refugee resettlement and protection of endangered mammals.

This is not a new point: Huggan and Tiffin charge Ghosh with displacing the man-tiger conflict onto the relatively easy-to-resolve human-dolphin issue (2010, 188). However, neither of these issues comes close to considering the

Sunderban crabs. In ignoring the crustaceans, we overlook that which is not mammalian, not large enough to invoke moral debate in the event of their exclusion or death, and not political enough to deserve place in the animal question. The novel's focus on mammalian conflicts forecloses these ecological minutiae simply because they are too insignificant to matter to our current Anthropocene concerns.

The novel's narrative, by contrast, does not ignore these ubiquitous inhabitants of the Sunderbans' deltaic ecology. Even though Ghosh's focus is on mammals—the dolphins and tigers—the crabs scrawl all over the narrative. They appear in the past—Sir Daniel Hamilton, a Scotsman who first decided to establish settlement in the tidal islands was greeted by "crab-covered shores of the tide country" (Ghosh 2005, 42, hereafter in text as HT)—and they appear in the present—they are the source of Fokir's livelihood. Piya also catches sight of the crabs the moment she sets foot on his boat. In "storage spaces in bilges below" and "in the hold at the fore end of the boat, crabs could be seen crawling about" (HT, 59). Though commonly overshadowed by "gargantuan crocodiles" and the iconic Bengal tigers, these miniscule crabs are, in fact, some of the first creatures to greet human visitors to the Sunderbans (ibid., 105). Seething to the surface from their subterranean lairs, these crabs routinely invade the shores at dawn and at dusk "to salvage the rich haul of leaves and other debris left behind by the retreating tide" (ibid., 96). Alongside being a rich source of nutrients for the poor humans who inhabit the tidal islands, the crabs are also the custodians and architects of the archipelago. Constituting a "fantastically large proportion of the system's biomass," they are "the keystone species of the entire ecosystem." They keep "the mangroves alive by removing their leaves and litter" thus helping the cycle of life to continue unabated in the harsh deltaic ecology (ibid., 119).[7]

Then there is the other side to these critters. Metonymic of a brutal nature—fickle and ambivalent, "always mutating [and] always unpredictable" (ibid., 7)—the crabs aggressively challenge human imaginaries of belonging and dismiss human efforts to mold their natural surroundings. The novel tells us that when the crab-covered tidal beaches caught Daniel's attention and he resolved to build a new community on these lands, he was quickly reminded by well-wishers that no human settlement has managed to survive against the wild tempests, floods, tigers, and wasps of the mangrove forests. Nature here was different—"the realities of the tide country were of a strangeness beyond reckoning" (ibid., 66); it was not the reality of rural India, categorized into simple boxes as either picturesque or impoverished. In fact, nature here "erase[s] history," making writing the history of this land and its peoples and creatures impossible (ibid., 43). The tide country vanishes everything, digesting shipwrecks, leveling villages, and devouring entire islands; everything vanishes without trace (ibid., 186). Crabs are the metonym of this nature. For instance, when Piya first catches sight of these crabs in the hold of Fokir's boat, the critters are described as "crawling about in a jumble of mangrove branches and decaying sea grass." And, we are told, if not for the putrid sea grass offering them nutrients and moisture, the crabs would have been "tearing each other apart" (ibid., 59). We see nature, and the animal in a different light here. It is indifferent, asocial, and brutal. But, at the same time, they are the pulverizing life-force occupying the heart of this nature where the only drive is the drive to remain alive, even if that means tearing off the limbs of another member of the same species. The crabs thus introduce another reality, an-*other* scene. Lurking adjacent to yet unseen by humans, they force us to encounter an irrecuperable otherness as a sense of absolute human alienation from or nonrelation to nature seeps into our reality by way of their musty presences. And similar to Mahasweta's cryptid, these crabs rupture the text, challenge its protagonists, and vex meaning-making. Occupying the lowest rungs of the archipelago's environment, these critters unravel Man's irredeemable experience of the animal as real.

The brutality of these crabs finds the most robust illustration at a particularly reflective moment in the novel. Nirmal, recounting about the 1737 Calcutta tsunami that leveled "Englishmen's palaces" alongside native huts and tenements, insists that these intermittent "big" cataclysms are not the real ends or beginnings of History; rather, it is the small crabs who, with their constant burrowing of the dikes, make History. It is they who really tear down human civilizations (ibid., 170). Nirmal instructs a young Fokir to listen carefully to the sound of the crabs burrowing the dikes, the grating noise coming from deep inside the mud banks is the sound of these crabs, in free coalition with the surging and ebbing tides, untiringly chipping away at the manmade dikes or *badhs* constructed to keep the saline tidewater away from the cultivable fields. Without these dikes, human life is impossible in this environment and this makes their relentless burrowing of the dikes a situation of palpable danger for human life and human History. It is not that they are attempting to bring down the dikes to put an end to human settlement. In fact, there's really no telling what their intentions are. Like the pterodactyl, there is also no knowing them. They could be burrowing for food or for shelter. They might be even burrowing for nothing. But their action means that sooner than later the dikes will collapse. Unless continually inspected and constantly patched up, the dikes cannot withstand the onslaught of this alliance. The crabs and the tidewater capture the human in their time.

I read the crabs as the unstoppable life force (the *lamella*) that exists outside human authority. Their uncontrollable, mindless appetite poses a direct threat to everything we know as human. Like the "white noise" that lingers through the universe bearing proof of the Big Bang, the rough grating of crabs coming from inside the dikes is the sound of an irrepressible, uncontrollable nature. Humans have no space in this nature; they have no agency to govern, control, or secure this planet. And, when human civilizations collapse, neither "angels [nor] animals" come to their aid for they know already that, as humans, "we're not comfortably at home in our translated world" (ibid., 171–72).

Lacan describes the lamella as an immortal amoeba that survives death and regeneration (1981, 197). The lamella is the "incorporeal[,] indestructible life substance that persists beyond the circuit of generation and corruption" (Žižek 1995, 205). Its intrusion in the world only makes us uncomfortable—it is "not very reassuring" (Lacan 1981, 197). The lamella brings with it a damp, unwholesome experience of decay, putrefaction, and death mixed with a disgusting lusting after the sexual (Žižek 1995, 206, 216). In other words, the lamella is the real. Its unceasing flitting in and out of our lives qualifies it as an "extreme [and] visible manifestation of the death-drive" (Evans 2008, n.p.). This is why Žižek writes of the lamella as the undead, the Thing and alien within:

> A lamella is indivisible, indestructible, and immortal—more precisely, undead in the sense this term has in horror fiction: not the sublime spiritual immortality, but the obscene immortality of the "living dead" which, after every annihilation, re-composes themselves and clumsily goes on. As Lacan puts it in his terms, lamella does not exist, it insists: it is unreal, an entity of pure semblance, a multiplicity of appearances which seem to envelop a central void. (2006, 62)

As lamella or real, the crabs are of the "unwarped primal world" (Žižek 2007, 209). They are impossible to contain and impossible to battle. Swarming under the currents, too numerous to count, they appear as dark shadows in the water, and, when on land, as blankets of red, they shroud miles upon miles of tidal beaches. These indestructible, flexible, floating masses transform entire landscapes, leaving nothing to destiny, as nothing appears to be able to keep their invasive population in check. Immortal, they tirelessly engineer the tidal country by simply going about their routine animal business—feeding, procreating, and hiding from predators: their impossible alterity holding up the truth about our ontological scandal.

The animal-lamella is the *nonbeing*. Distinct from the self-consolidating Other, or the Other as correlate of the Self, this nonbeing marks the animal's nothingness; a nothingness that makes the animal irreducible to modalities of Othering and as such a threat to the sociosymbolic. We encounter these critters suddenly and in *suddenly* appearing these animals draw into relief nonhuman, nontemporal sites of existence. But while their (re)appearance in human reality is catastrophic—they inaugurate the *world-in-itself* as Eugene Thacker puts it—their absent-presence also gives consistency to our reality. As I see it, the problem with (real) animals is not that they force us to recognize lingering signatures of our bestiality (Agamben 2004) or that they express multiple points of view rendering grand narratives hollow (Derrida 2004, 125). Instead, the problem with animals has to do with the human incapacity to *witness* the traumatic otherness of the animal. *Real, unsymbolizable, and nonrelational,* the animal is the radical instantiation of Man's subjective rupture.

Humans inhabit a *translated* world. A radical gap separating the world we inhabit from the world we imagine we inhabit. In this context, the exchange between Nirmal and Fokir is extremely critical because it functions to shift focus from the catastrophic to normalizing the catastrophic as habitual. And this habitual condition necessitates that humans tend after the dikes. In other words, the narrative shifts focus to the human as the caretaker of his world. But as I have been arguing so far, a slightly different focus, one that takes the crabs as metonym of a nature beyond human control, offers a radical new reading of human-animal relations. In this reading, the crabs substantiate the radical gap between a world we claim for ourselves and the planet that refuses human occupation. The crabs decouple the planet we inhabit from the world we imagine to dote on.

The human-animal ideological deadlock addressed in the novel by contrast seeks to restore human privilege. It renders possible the politics of accommodating a multitude of singularities within a democratic habitus. Occupying the farthest position from this imaginary center and bereft of any privileged ontology, the crabs transform the novel from being a text about conflictual symbolic boundaries to a text about unceasing becomings. As unremarkable figures of insistent violence, the crabs join the chorus of the "chthonic ones"—the tentacled monsters of Haraway—whose monstrosity stems from their total indifference to our symbolic universe. Haraway understands the dangers of critters, writing: these are "not safe" because they have "no truck with ideologies," that is, with "the sky-gazing Homo" and their worldly imaginaries. Worse still, these critters escape the grid of symbolization—being made and unmade in the muck of the planet while they, themselves, "make and unmake" that muck at will, "they [actually] belong to no one." Rather, they compose "a fierce reply to the dictates of both Anthropos and Capital" (Haraway 2016, 2). Metaphysics is problematized by these crabs as they metonymize the volatile ebb and flow of the rivers, the islands birthed and devoured by tidal waves, and dictate the interconnected lives and movements of all animals, humans and tigers included, across the bedraggled archipelago. Simply put: the crabs are irreducible to and the cause of the onto-phenomenological.

IV. INHABITING A TRANSLATED WORLD: THE ANIMAL AS SURPLUS IN POSTCOLONIAL LITERATURE

Mahasweta's cryptids and Ghosh's crabs force us away from the animal-as-difference in order to consider the animal as nonrelation. Formalized in terms of irreconcilable antagonism, these creatures are the empty core of *socius*, arranging as well as disrupting symbolic rights and imaginary identities. They rehabilitate concerns over knowing and knowledge, meaning-making and meaning-production. Staying with them means, "staying with *the* trouble."

Note: it is not "staying with trouble" but "staying with *the* trouble." What can the inclusion of this definite article possibly mean? To me, staying with the crabs means staying with the death-drive. The death-drive does not connote death, but rather its opposite. It means embracing that exuberant excess of life that is indivisible, irreducible, and insistent. Excluded from or unmediated by symbolic division, it represents a persistent force that gushes around the constitutive lack of the symbolic with unrestrained candor. It does not seek to fill this lack but continuously encircles the lack. The death-drive unravels life as it exists outside of desire.

Instead of shying away from these critters—animals that embody the uncanny excess of life—we ought to include such troublesome animals in our discussions of the postcolony. For only by moving beyond arguments about lingering signatures of bestiality within humans and/or the hollowness of human grand narratives positing animals as less-than-humans, can postcolonial zoocriticism address the real animal.

But what is the Lacanian real? Is it a gap in reality that results from our inability to properly articulate in language the exact character of reality? Or, is it an unsymbolizable obstacle, a radical unknown that is destined to remain in excess of the human? Žižek explains this well by distinguishing between three orders of the real—the imaginary real, the symbolic real, and the real real—and, by claiming the Lacanian real as the scientific real (2007a). If the imaginary real is the picture of the pterodactyl that puzzles Puran and pushes the SDO into a fit, the symbolic real is the message or code that Puran believes remains unknown to him at the end of the story. By contrast, the crabs are scientific real. Their unmistakable radical otherness, and the tidal country they metonomize, make them completely alien to or beyond our ken. The alterity of the crabs frustrates the humanism of the larger narrative.

The need to constantly secure the human against the animal is a symptom of our ontological lack, that is, our need to avoid confrontations with others who might substantiate this lack, return it back to as us the irrevocable condition of our being. The real dilemma of *The Hungry Tide* is not therefore what the author identifies—"the dilemma of how to balance human needs with nature" (quoted in Pulugurtha 82). Rather, it is the impossibility of achieving balance with nature while being human. Being human means recognizing the impossibility of connecting to the animal, to the natural world, and to others except either by symbolizing/Othering them or through fantasy. We must consider this human-animal nonrelationality, explore the fact that "being human" means recognizing the animal's radical alterity as the obscene core of our enjoyment, if we are serious about rethinking the ethics of living in a translated world.

V. *THE SECRET LIFE OF PETS*:
THE NEOLIBERAL FANTASY OF ANIMALS

The 2016 animated film *The Secret Life of Pets* has a very simple premise: what our pets do when we are not home. Or, to frame it in terms of the perennial human question: "What does the animal want?" The answer given in the film is interesting: it shows animals enjoying complex social relations and their real lives starting only after humans exit the scene.[8] Unlike what many of us think when we leave our pets behind home—"My pet will be sad not seeing me for so long"—the film claims it is the opposite. The pets in the film wait eagerly (except for one) for humans to leave so they can start enjoying *their* lives—listen to music on stereo, play video games, and just have a good time.

The standard criticism to be made here is as follows: the film models the "secret life of pets" on human wants and activities and its description of animal social life mimics human social life of a "civilized" upper city versus a dark social underbelly. While correct, we must not hastily write off the film, either. For its lesson is found exactly where we expose its weakness, namely, in its representation of the secret or real life of animals. What the film shows us is actually what we want to see. No matter how disturbing we might find thinking that our pets enjoy a carefree and independent life in our absence, the fact remains that this idea satisfies our vicarious pleasure: "Oh I know the animals have a life of their own away from us." Put differently, the ideology of the film is twofold. First, it makes us feel good about keeping a pet. Even though I keep a dog on collar or a bird in a cage I know they have an inner life about which we will never know but I am happy that they have a separate life, etc. Second, more importantly, the real life of pets shown in the film has nothing to do with the secret life of pets but everything to do with our fantasy about what we think our pets do when alone. It is about being able to think the unthinkable (Thacker 2010, 1). And although this appears to overwrite the first function—being in the unknown—, it actually does not. The first ideology is foremost an attempt to satisfy our conscious self, whereas the second functions to secure us against the unconscious anxiety of not knowing. Furthermore, the first has an important function in today's world. In our neoliberal world where we no longer wish to come across as sovereign "master of animals," and where we are willing to accept our historical self-culpability in violently mistreating animals, a film such as *The Secret Life of Pets* promotes a new imaginary of the human. In the strict context of the film, this human is willing to imagine her absence from the anthropo(s)cene in order for animals to take over. It is this formal willingness to render the human absent in favor of animals that constitutes the signature ideological gesture of anthropocentrism of today. As Zupančič observes,

> [T]he official ideology of the contemporary "secular" form of social order and domination, which has abandoned the idea of a (harmonious) *totality* to the advantage of the idea of a non-totalizable multiplicity of singularities forming a "democratic" network [is] to make our voices heard in a complex, non-totalizable social network. There is no predeter-

mined (social) relation, everything is negotiable, depending on us and on concrete circumstances. (2017, 26)

It seems our task in the neoliberal present is to *tolerate* difference and seek ways to (re)connect with different biotic and abiotic others in a networked universe. The responsibility, mind you, is on us humans to make this planet whole again. *Secret Life* teaches us to think about the unintelligible life of animals by devising a framework: *pets without us*. A fantasy scenario allowing us to navigate the unknowable animal world without risking our identity as subject-supposed-to-know (Thacker 2010, 4–5).

Similarly, postcolonial zoocriticism focuses on animals that help us reimagine the human without appearing to claim the human as master signifier. Symptomatic are the broad directions of the field—excavate untold histories of animals in the Empire; underline the Empire's use of animal symbolism in dehumanizing natives; and, lastly, revitalize through accounts of these encounters the broad ethics of human-animal exchanges. Common to all three is the acknowledgment of the role played by humans in silencing animal histories, exploiting animals for human gains, and, most importantly, in the context of the current climate of messianic environmentalism, putting the planet in crisis through unrestrained predation (Badiou 2018, n.p.). The human imaginary secured through postcolonial zoocriticism is, therefore, of the human as less than perfect but still human for recognizing, auditing, and, hopefully, undoing some of its past mistakes. As university discourse, postcolonial zoocriticism attempts to address the lack arising from the collapse of the traditional subject-of-knowledge and the increase in contingencies of human life on this planet—disasters, cataclysms, and global wars. And though galvanized by a wish to mediate the unthinkable and the unknown, the university discourse is the product of the big Other's desire. Accordingly, it carefully substitutes the real reason for the condition of the planet—capitalism—with the crisis of the animal's marginality in cultural productions. The real ideological work performed here is that of inventing the so-called animal question, which does nothing except obscure the real peril of global capitalism (ibid.).

All this is not to say that postcolonial zoocriticism as a field completely avoids identifying and characterizing capitalism for mercilessly predating the planet.[9] But, as we know well, university discourse is one of those sites through which capitalism mandates or even legitimizes critiques against the system. No less problematically, these academic critiques, being often translated through the cultural spectrum, that is, being represented as problems of human identity and ethical action, emphasize the notion of culture over politics.

VI. WHO'S AFRAID OF THE ANTHROPOCENE?

In Seminar XVII, *The Other Side of Discourse*, Lacan defines discourse in terms of distinct arrangements of "social and sexual behavior" which influence our understanding of "nature" in relation to the "function of science and knowledge" (Clemens and Grigg 2006, 2). He introduces *four* such arrangements or discourses, namely, the Master's discourse, the Hysteric's discourse, the Analyst's discourse, and the University discourse. As *discourse,* each describes the arrangement or social link particular to each situation. (The first chapter focuses on the Master's discourse and the third on the Hysteric's; I focus here on the University discourse).

The University discourse does not mean discourse coming out of the university but it describes a specific sociopolitical climate and the social links therein. But then discourse coming out of the university is also part of the University discourse, and I use it here in both these senses. That is, discourse coming out from the university that seeks to establish a specific kind of critical behavior appropriate for the current sociopolitical climate. In this section, I turn to the "Anthropocene" as a discourse that is symptomatic of the neoliberal global present.

Lacan writes University discourse as:

$$\frac{S^2}{S^1} \longrightarrow \frac{a}{\$}$$

In this matheme, the lefthand side is populated by: $\frac{S^2}{S^1}$, where S2 performs the role of neutral knowledge or knowledge based on "factual state of things" such as empirical data, scientific reports, etc. Appearing under the bar (on the lefthand side), thus, technically detached from S2/Knowledge but hiding just below the surface is S1, the master signifier or Power, which is the real source of or support for S2. Zupančič explains: the "constitutive lie of this discourse is that it disavows its performative dimension" (2006, 168). In other words, S2 is not the neutral, objective knowledge it pretends to be. Rather, S2 is "a master's knowledge;" or, knowledge stolen by the master from the slave (Feltham 2006, 183; Lacan 2007, 148–49). Knowledge (S2), Lacan claims, is neither objective not original, rather it a product of violent approximation. Knowledge first appears in the other, the slave. It represents nothing more than the slave/other's practical knowhow or *savior-faire*. Encountering this "excess" in the other, the Master intervenes, abstracts the slave's technical knowledge, and gives this raw knowledge the shape of an episteme. Episteme, as Lacan puts it, is constituted via "an interrogation [and] purification of" the slave's raw knowledge (Lacan 2007, 149). It is an "act of theft, of plunder," but critical for guaranteeing the Master's sovereignty. It helps the Master overwrite the surplus in the Other and this formalization of the slave's technical knowledge into episteme gestures to the final inscription of the slave in the desire of the Master. By abstracting and then returning to the slave its own knowhow as "knowledge," the Master completes the final dispossession of the slave, his gesture pushing the slave into the realm of the episteme from which the slave is to remain constitutively amiss or alienated (Dolar 2006, 139–40; Feltham 2006, 183).

On the righthand side of the matheme representing University discourse, we have: $\frac{a}{\$}$. The a represents surplus or waste (that counts) and, under the bar, we have what this surplus as waste withholds, namely, the "truth" of the divided subject $\$$ (Clemens and Grigg 2006, 3; Zupančič 2006, 170). I read the upper level of the matheme after Žižek, $S_2 \rightarrow a$ represents "university knowledge endeavoring to integrate, domesticate, and appropriate the excess that restricts and resists it" (Žižek 2006a, 107). More specifically, in the context of this chapter, I read this part of the matheme as: knowledge attempting to symbolize the unthinkable in Nature. We confront in planetary disasters the unspeakable horror of seeing Nature ruptured from itself; a Nature that is not whole but constitutively chaotic, unstable, and demonic. A Nature that is indifferent to manmade symbolic divisions of class, race, gender, etc. and unresponsive to our symbolic interpretations (Eisenstein and McGowan 2012, 224). The "nature" that escapes or remains outside of our habitual imaginary of Nature is the real nature. The indeterminacy at the heart of this real nature, expressed in natural disasters and environmental crises, might very well be the responsibility of humans but science also reminds us that natural causes often predate the human or emerge from outside the domain of human influence. Hitherto undiscovered fault lines under the ocean can lead to the next devastating tsunami just as a comet impact can start continent-wide wildfires, usher in a sudden global ice age, and impose species extinction.[10] To think that humans alone have pushed nature to the precipice is indeed to give too much significance to the human and human efforts to classify.

Ben Baer Conisbee, Donna Haraway, and Eisenstein and McGowan repeat the same point: confrontations with real nature/animals return us to our incomplete ontology, thus making our existence on this planet a matter of living in the eye of the catastrophic. And science as the study of the real (that's where psychoanalysis connects to science) also backs this up. What "the Anthropocene" as University discourse does is nothing more than (attempt to) cover up the disharmony we inhabit (in nature). The larger plan, of course, is to obviate the role of capitalism in the destruction of the planet. In the University discourse, the objective knowledge (S2), that is, episteme reinvented through the Master's (S1) violent intervention into the slave's labor, addresses the radical contingencies of the universe to discipline the unbearable surpluses (*a*) of global capitalism in order to conclusively hide the knowledge of the human as a split subject ($).

This point has been already made by Žižek (2015, 2016) and by Badiou (2018). In a recent Verso Blog, Badiou lambasts the contemporary messianic environmentalism for its hyperbolic, ideological lamentations of Mother Nature. Badiou insists that our growing concerns over the death of the planet (and technology run amok) prescribe an intensely ideological response in form of *return to nature*—taking responsible stewardship of the planet, relying less and less on technologies that harm our natural surroundings, etc. But these are just "ideological noise" intended to drown out the irksome grinding of the Juggernaut wheels of global capitalism as it rolls over the bodies of millions.

As the political and social landscape from United States to Western Europe to South Asia turns toward being democratically totalitarian, we witness concerns over class antagonism being replaced by populist interest in fickle and ever-changing factors. The university in this world functions to hide this shift and validate these ever-changing factors. The aim is to evade addressing capitalism as responsible for social inequality and pin hopes on recycling of plastic straws as the way out from an impeding catastrophe. "The fact that so many species are endangered, that climate change cannot be controlled, that water is becoming like some rare treasure, is all a by-product of" globalized capitalism is not recognized (Badiou 2018). Instead, this crisis is reinvented in human terms—humans are responsible for carbon emission for their consumption of fossil fuel, therefore, humans must rectify these problems by acting as one homogenous species. These action plans almost always pay no attention to specific geopolitical contexts, as such they show no regard for why banning the eating of beef might be disastrous for the Indian indigene for whom beef is a cheap source of protein. At stake is the question, how to organize societies at a global scale for responding to the crisis without however erasing the local histories and cultural contexts.

I have noted elsewhere that the recent nonhuman turn seeks an exclusive rearrangement of the fantasy for being human in eye of the global present. Within this fantasy, the human is held accountable in discussions of the biotic and abiotic world but never completely displaced or erased. While nonhumans and things/objects are allowed space for expression, this rejection of the human or human-centered approach to understanding reality is a rejection of Kant's "Copernican" proposition, namely, the external world must conform to human cognition. Simply put, the idea of an autonomous object—an object with inner life (volcanic core), which remains unavailable to humans, is another way to render the human totally absent from the scene of objects. But, as I argue above, this human fantasy of witnessing the self as missing from the world—"[P]erhaps the ancients had it right after all. Perhaps it was the crab that ruled the tide of her [Piya's] destiny"—is yet, another, surefire way of controlling the anthropo(s)cene and avoiding the trauma of apprehending our absence in the gaze (of the other) (Ghosh 2005, 119).

The nonhuman turn is doubly ideological. On the one hand (as Badiou notes), it seeks to deflect attention from the real reason regarding why the planet is coughing up blood. By focusing exclusively on receding glaciers and treelines, climbing summer temperatures and dropping ozone layers, we can signify the planet suffering from overconsumption. But, at the same instance, we also overlook how human communities across the globe and in our neighborhoods are suffering daily from the tyranny of capitalism and our consumerist economy. Or how, marginalized and displaced from the global economic system, certain communities are left with no options but to act in ways identified as responsible for heralding the end of this planet. On the other hand, by mystifying human (non)relation to the planet, that is, by claiming that animate and inanimate objects are independent of the human, the traumatic incompleteness of human ontology realized apropos our alienation from the external universe gets cleverly disguised.

But the funniest thing about the Anthropocene is that while claiming to put an end to the human, or at least appearing to put the human under censure, as University discourse it actually serves to ensure that the human does not leave the frame of the anthropo(s)cene. Recently, Peter Brannen, a science writer whose work has appeared in *The New York Times* and *The Washington Post*, has drawn attention to the human *hubris* implicit in the discourse of the Anthropocene:

The idea of the Anthropocene is an interesting thought experiment. For those invested in the stratigraphic arcana of this infinitesimal moment in time, it serves as a useful catalog of our junk. But it can also serve to inflate humanity's legacy on an ever-churning planet that will quickly destroy—or conceal forever—even our most awesome creations.

What paltry smudge of artifacts we do leave behind, in those rare corners of the continents where sediment accumulates and is quickly buried—safe from erosion's continuous defacing—will be extremely unlikely to be exposed at the surface, at any given time, at any given place, tens of millions or hundreds of millions of years in the geological future. *Sic transit gloria mundi.*

[But] What humans are doing on the planet, then, unless we endure for millions to tens of millions of years, is extremely transient. In fact, there exists a better word in geology than *epoch* to describe our moment in the sun thus far: *event.*

[And] until we prove ourselves capable of an Anthropocene worthy of the name, perhaps we should more humbly refer to this provisional moment of Earth history that we're living through as we do the many other disruptive spasms in Earth history....

The idea of the Anthropocene inflates our own importance by promising eternal geological life to our creations. It is of a thread with our species' peculiar, self-styled exceptionalism—from the animal kingdom, from nature, from the systems that govern it, and from time itself. This illusion may, in the long run, get us all killed. [But] we haven't earned an Anthropocene epoch yet. If someday in the distant future we *have*, it will be an astounding testament to a species that, after a colicky, globe-threatening infancy, learned that it was not separate from Earth history, but a contiguous part of the systems that have kept this miraculous marble world habitable for billions of years. (2019: n.p.)

Readers have responded cautiously. Some have characterized Brannen as a denier while others have tried to situate his queries in the context of disciplinary debates between geologists and climatologists. Still a handful got Brennen's point: all our categorizations and descriptions including those that speak about our impending extinction are products of anthropocentrism.

Let us take another example. This time Dipesh Chakrabarty's essay "The Climate of History: Four Theses" (2009), which also draws on geology to support its arguments. I only mention this because many who are approaching

Brannen with the geology versus climatology argument are or have been in the recent past admirers of Chakrabarty's essay to the extent of characterizing this essay as a foundational text for the Anthropocene.

In "The Climate of History: Four Theses," Chakrabarty writes that humans today are a geological agent directly impacting the life of the planet and leaving behind their distinct carbon footprint in the geological layer, thereby marking the era of the Anthropocene (209; 217). This thesis proposes the past existence of a vital connection between humans and the planet, a harmony that no longer exists because the connection has been cut due to human's transgressing boundaries. In other words, because humans have upset a set quota of their claim on this planet, today they suffer misery and extinction. What we term "climate change" or "environmental crisis," therefore, is the result of human *hubris*. The actual reasons for our planet's weakening health, Chakrabarty appears to suggest, as such, must be sought in the past, beyond recorded history and beyond the history of capitalism. In his words, real knowledge must be sought in the deep history of this planet because species knowledge is connected to deep history. Here is how he presents this and I have rearranged Chakrabarty's sentences slightly from the original:

1. If the industrial way of life was what got us into this crisis, then the question is, Why think in terms of species, surely a category that belongs to a much longer history? Why could not the narrative of capitalism—and hence its critique—be sufficient as a framework for interrogating the history of climate change and understanding its consequences? It seems true that the crisis of climate change has been necessitated by the high-energy-consuming models of society that capitalist industrialization has created and promoted, but the current crisis has brought into view certain other conditions for the existence of life in the human form that have no intrinsic connection to the logics of capitalist, nationalist, or socialist identities. They are connected rather to the history of life on this planet, the way different life forms connect to one another, and the way the mass extinction of one species could spell danger for another. Without such a history of life, the crisis of climate change has no human "meaning." For, as I have said before, it is not a crisis for the inorganic planet in any meaningful sense. (217)
2. In other words, whatever our socioeconomic and technological choices, whatever the rights we wish to celebrate as our freedom, we cannot afford to destabilize conditions (such as the temperature zone in which the

planet exists) that work like boundary parameters of human existence. These parameters are independent of capitalism or socialism. They have been stable for much longer than the histories of these institutions and have allowed human beings to become the dominant species on earth. Unfortunately, we have now ourselves become a geological agent disturbing these parametric conditions needed for our own existence. (218)

3   [T]he knowledge in question is the knowledge of humans as a species, a species dependent on other species for its own existence, a part of the general history of life. (219)

4   Without such knowledge of the deep history of humanity it would be difficult to arrive at a secular understanding of why climate change constitutes a crisis for humans. Geologists and climate scientists may explain why the current phase of global warming—as distinct from the warming of the planet that has happened before—is anthropogenic in nature, but the ensuing crisis for humans is not understandable unless one works out the consequences of that warming. The consequences make sense only if we think of humans as a form of life and look on human history as part of the history of life on this planet.. . .Species thinking, on the other hand, is connected to the enterprise of deep history. (213)

and,

5   Climate change, refracted through global capital, will no doubt accentuate the logic of inequality that runs through the rule of capital; some people will no doubt gain temporarily at the expense of others. But the whole crisis cannot be reduced to a story of capitalism. Unlike in the crises of capitalism, there are no lifeboats here for the rich and the privileged (witness the drought in Australia or recent fires in the wealthy neighborhoods of California). (221)

In his response to Chakrabarty, Žižek spells out the "standard Marxist counter-argument" (2015, n.p.). Zizek draws out the fundamental difference between Marx's notion of the human as "species being" or the human as the only animal species to actively relate to its being a species. This makes the human distinct from all other species and, as such, alienated from the natural world. The human in the current stage of anthropogeny is an anomaly, an abnormality in nature, our universality appearing first with(in) capitalism (as) uniting humanity via a global market of commodities. The human, which the nonhuman turn seeks to dislocate as naturalized, therefore, is already always denaturalized and posthuman. It is a condition *post-commodification*. In fact, if anything, Chakrabarty's proposal of the human as one of the species returns the human to a position of privilege, and the current environmental crisis is made to appear as resulting from or lexicalized to this human.

> With the idea of humans as species, the universality of the humankind falls back into the particularity of an animal species: phenomena like global warming make us aware that, with all the universality of our theoretical and practical activity, we are at a certain basic level just another living species on the planet Earth. Our survival depends on certain natural parameters which we automatically take for granted. The lesson of the global warming is that the freedom of the humankind was possible only against the background of the stable natural parameters of the life on earth (temperature, the composition of the air, sufficient water and energy supply, etc.): humans can "do what they want" only insofar as they remain marginal enough, so that they don't seriously perturb the parameters of the life on earth. (Žižek 2015, n.p.)

If Chakrabarty's idea of human responsibility for current environmental crisis sounds cannily biblical that's because it is so. As if it were not enough for a Marxist, subalternist historian to claim "the existence of life in the human form [has] no intrinsic connection to the logics of capitalist, nationalist, or socialist identities" (2009, 217), the terrain of the Anthropocene expanding out of Chakrabarty's essay unwittingly reinscribes the Christological framework back onto "secular" postcolonial thinking. For if Chakrabarty is to be believed, then, the ecological crisis facing mankind today is a product of our violation of the sacrosanct command (Thou shalt not overbear).

For both Žižek and Badiou, the more important question is how do we think about the link between social history and Capital (cf. Žižek 2015, n.p.). Or, as Žižek puts it: "the key of the ecological crisis does not reside in ecology as such" but, rather, in questions we ask about ecology (ibid.). Challenging Chakrabarty's understanding of the human universal, through Hegel, Žižek attests the point he makes earlier via Marx, namely, the universal is not an aggregate of particulars, where each particular must perform its specific role and otherwise the "organic" harmony of the planet will collapse. But, instead, the only universal condition recognized by psychoanalysis (and, Zizek) is the essentially negative ontology of all humans. In other words, the natural condition of the human on the planet is one of radical alienation from the planet and the only way to resolve this universal problem, it appears, is through the particular issue of capitalism. If anything, Badiou merely stretches the time line of capitalism to the start of the Neolithic age to repeat the same point:

> For four or five millennia, humanity has been organised by the triad of private property—which concentrates enormous wealth in the hands of very narrow oligarchies; the family, in which fortunes are transmitted via inheritance; and the state, which protects both property and the family by armed force. This triad defined our species' Neolithic age, and we are still at this point—we could even say, now more than ever. Capitalism is the contemporary form of the Neolithic. (2018, n.p.)

Marx, Badiou claims, does not mark the beginning of capitalism but rather the beginning of its end. Because of Marx, and after almost ten thousand years, we learn about the need to replace the old age (neolithic/capitalism) with the new (communism).

The Anthropocene does not begin with the Industrial Revolution, the rounding of the Cape, or the establishment of the thirteen colonies in the New World, and the colonizations of Asia and Africa. But, rather, it begins with the Neolithic—the establishment of temples, the division of labor, the privatization of property and the corresponding allotments of social positions (priests, kings, serfs/the domestic and the public/the woman and the man).[11]

Humans have unforgivingly damaged the planet through their desire to control and consume natural resources. There are no two ways about this. Even Chakrabarty admits as much. Then what purpose is there to diffuse capitalism's inexcusable role in creating today's global ecological crises? Why argue for the deep history of the human species, naturalize the human, when it is the most unnatural thing in nature—the biped ape acting uppity by mistaking its reflected image as proof of its bodily autonomy! Why cloak the responsibility of capitalism if not to make discussions about the crises culturally appropriate for the U.S. academia? (The academia that Eagleton once famously dubbed the "gaudy, all-licensed supermarket of the mind" [1999, n.p.]). Make no mistake: *I am not a denier.*

I am not dismissing the threat humanity faces today because of climate change. Indeed, there is much to fear in this era of the Anthropocene but the ideology at work in how we frame questions for our anthropocene age cannot be overlooked. By representing the nonhuman turn in terms of species consciousness and species rights, for example, and thereby obfuscating direct interrogations of capitalism's role in destroying the planet, the University discourse reflects, sustains, and extends the neoliberal logic of tolerant pluralism.

This ideology understands social inequalities as a matter of rights—give the other their rights, listen to their stories, welcome them to your neighborhood—that is, tolerate the other in spite of their difference because different parts make up the whole. In other words, the assumption here is that once every part of the social, and the biotic and abiotic, are conferred equal rights to exist on this planet, there will no longer remain inequality between humans or between different species. What gets lost effectively, though, is the role of capital in creating social inequality and the depredation of local ecologies. However, when we substitute the notion of social/planetary harmony with the scandal of nonrelationality, that is, the impossibility of securing particulars in a relationship of wholeness, a condition that results directly from our divided human ontology, we escape both the fantasy of capitalism as the ultimate redeemer of the planet and realize the importance of reorienting our politics around fundamental antagonisms—radical impasse compromising social relations between humans and separating humanity from the natural, animal world. To articulate politics around this condition means reimagining politics ethically. Or, reimagining politics to best respond to the human condition of knowing that a fundamental nonrelationship structures our attempts at establishing useful relationships and this enterprise also forms the basis of all forms of oppression (Zupančič 2016, 87, 96). The Anthropocene unveils the real condition of the planet and human ontology, and we must accordingly recognize the real and respond with a politics of the real.

THREE

Hysterization of Postcolonial Studies; *or,* Beyond Cross-Cultural Communication

I. WE DO NOT WANT WHAT WE *DESIRE*.

Human life in contemporary global societies is structured by the dialectic of lack and excess. We believe that constant accumulation of wealth will somehow give us a sense of satisfaction, thus guaranteeing happiness, when in reality our endless pursuits of desired objects only unravel the paradoxical relation of desire to lack. Desire remains unfulfilled because what we want is never what we desire.

We do not want what we desire. Lacan underlines this important point in Seminar II. He writes (I rearrange the order of the sentences):

> Desire, a function central to all human experience, is the desire for nothing nameable. And at the same time this desire lies at the origin of every variety of animation.... Desire is a relation of being to a lack. The lack is the lack of being properly speaking. It isn't the lack of this or that, but lack of being whereby being exists... as an exact function of this lack. Being attains a sense of self in relation to being as a function of this lack, in the experience of desire. In the pursuit of this beyond, which is nothing, it harks back to the feeling of a being with self-consciousness, which is nothing but its own reflection in the world of things. (Sem. II 1991, 223–24)

In gist: the cause of desire is lack and lack is the unconscious of the subject. This is what Lacan means when he says the subject does not desire this or that—object x or person y—but *lack* itself—*manqué-à-étre* or want-to-be or the wanting-in-being (Sem. XI 1981, 29).

Lorenzo Chiesa accordingly suggests that we revise the Freudian understanding of the subject. The subject is not a subject-of-desire or even a subject-of-lack but, rather, *subjectivized lack*: the "subject remains a subject only insofar as…he is a desiring *lack-of-being*" (2007, 6, 155). To remain desiring, desire itself must stay unsatisfied, the lack haunting the subject against (her) desire. Psychoanalysis teaches us to recognize this irreconcilable fulcrum as the *materiel* of subjectivity or that the human subject is irreparably marked by contradiction because we repeatedly act against our desire and what is in our best interest. We seek an intense satisfaction from the objects and the people we desire, however, a wholesome enjoyment that can satisfactorily fill our lack is impossible. The objects we strive to possess or the people we (think) would make us whole ultimately fail to satisfy because *desire has no object* (Fink 1995, 90).[1]

We can understand the Lacanian maxim "we do not wish what we desire" another way. Because desire is unconscious it is barred to the conscious subject. Hence, what we consciously wish is never that which we unconsciously desire. Relatedly, given our inability to transcend the symbolic order, we can only express desire in language. However, it is impossible to render *the thing* we desire in words or through symbols without first murdering the thing-in-itself. Language murders the thing by replacing it with a symbol, thereby making desire unavailable or barred. The exact moment desire is expressed in speech there occurs a translation from unconscious desire to conscious wish, leading to the diffusion of the former into the latter.[2] In the words of Bruce Fink: "We ask for things we do not want, only want what we cannot have, and no longer want what we ask for the minute we get it" (2004, 59). This is desire for desire only, or, the desire to remain in desire without satisfaction. The desire to lack is the fundamental signature of the human. It is what makes us human.

But the paradox of desire is more complicated than being a matter of the imaginary—what we imagine as desire is not desire—or the symbolic—language bars our way to true desire. The conundrum of desire is, rather, the real deadlock or impasse constitutive of the subject. As Lacan puts it: "Desire is neither the appetite for satisfaction nor the demand for love, but the difference that results from the subtraction of the first from the second, the very phenomenon of their splitting" (2006, 580). Desire exposes the subject as split: forever marked by the irresolvable antagonism between desire and lack. The only enjoyment possible, therefore, is what leaks out as loss (Žižek 2007, 2010). In other words, what we desire in the other is the *objet petit a*, which like the paradox of desire and lack is also a paradox: it both exists in but is more than the other.[3]

Being in lack allows us to continue desiring, feel self-composed via our endless quests for lost objects of desire, barring which our being risks evaporation. For the moment we confront or possess (the object of) desire, the subject ceases to exist, that is to say, it dissolves into the nothing (Lacan 1981, 263–76). As such, as subjects we are always wrestling with the lack of intense satisfaction and settling for the painful enjoyment of the lack of satisfaction. This is the only way humans come closest to experiencing the satisfaction of an impossible unavailable enjoyment, that is, by enjoying the impossible as surplus. Fleeting, evanescent, and lacking, the enjoyment of this absolute Enjoyment (*jouissance*) is derived via accumulating objects that promise an intense enjoyment only for experiencing the subsequent loss of enjoyment through these objects. These objects could be literally lost and/or eventually found unsatisfactory. Both result in the experience of loss of enjoyment which in itself is an enjoyment. In other words, enjoyment is derived through the absence of enjoyment—in experiencing the emptiness of the promise of accumulation as the route to satisfaction. In the fantasy of gaining intense enjoyment through objects promising plenitude, desire for accumulation stands in for the irrevocable lack as well as for keeping us interested in the surplus enjoyment of these objects. This surplus leaks into our experience as lack—the coming up short of enjoyment in an object or person, which reorients the existence and possibility of experiencing a more fulfilling enjoyment.[4]

Substituting accumulation of wealth/objects with the accumulation of knowledge, I wish to argue in this chapter that the fantasy of knowing or, in Foucauldian terms, the production and control of knowledge for purposes of dominating the Other, has a similar paradoxical relation to lack. As Edward Said and Alain Grosrichard show, fantasy is critical for *Othering* because in reality no amount of knowledge proves adequate for exhaustively knowing and controlling the other.[5] Homi Bhabha explicates this quandary well when drawing our attention to *colonial non-sense*, his term for the irreducible remainder that escapes symbolization or Othering and which, lingering as the *thing*, ruptures the newly composed self-Other symbolic order. As empty sound—the "Ou-boum" in E. M. Forster's *A Passage to India* (1924) and the muteness of the captive Barbarian woman in J. M. Coetzee's *Waiting for the Barbarians* (1980)—, the *non-sense* eviscerates mechanisms of personal and bureaucratic knowing besides exploding the archives responsible for storing, containing, and disseminating knowledge about the other (Bhabha 2006, 176–78).[6] Reading the archive as a symptom for negotiating subjective lack, I explore in this chapter the dramatic role archives play in postcolonial narratives of cross-cultural communication and cultural documentation.

Specifically, my discussions of Leila Aboulela's short story "The Museum" (2001) and Tony Gatlif's film *Gadjo dilo* (*The Crazy Stranger*) (1997) examine how both texts underline the impossibility of cross-cultural communication and expose the fallacy of imagining the archive as a repository useful for storing knowledge about the other and/or as a resource from which one can learn about the other. Relatedly, I show, both texts share the theme of trying to know the other's desire and striving to escape from being completely sucked into this desire. The failure of cross-cultural communication in both narratives discloses the important role desire plays in intersubjective relations, thereby undercutting the habitual postcolonial exercise of archiving lost voices as a means for guaranteeing (self-)representation of the marginalized. What if the excised do not wish to see themselves represented in the public space of the archive? What if the other does not desire the inscription of the archive? My discussion of Aboulela's story and Gatlif's film asks: What are the dangers of the other lingering outside the archive—outside desire or symbolization—as excess, a disembodied voice, a fervent "No." Before discussing the texts I wish to explain how I view the archive, beginning with a broad understanding and concluding with its relevance in the neoliberal present.

II. THE FANTASY OF THE ARCHIVE[7]

The archive is a repository of material documents (handwritten, printed, digital) including books, maps, personal diaries, quilts, recordings of oral narratives, music and interviews, photographs and videos, etc. The archive is a record and attestation of history. It produces knowledge alongside acting as an objective repository of empirical records (Manoff 2004, 12). This definition of the archive as a self-attesting neutral source for historical knowledge has been questioned in recent years by postcolonial academics. Following

Jacques Derrida's and Michel Foucault's identifications of the vested processes that go into making the archive, postcolonial critics have drawn attention to the politics of *archivization*. Or, the highly political processes through which the archive is constituted, and the ideological role of the archive on historical memorization and the organization of the social on basis of archival knowledge. In other words, archivization refers to the constitution of the archive as a totalizing system, which orders "historical truth," nominates what are and validates what aren't credible sources for knowing the past, thereby using this knowledge to anchor "national identity" and foreground authority. Whosoever controls the archive stakes claim on both history and authority (ibid., 16).

Put differently, the archive is a site of interpretation, production, and alteration where power is maintained through each of these braided processes, with every new interpretation of the archive producing a new archive, contributing to the expansion of the existing one, and every new production allowing further alteration or repurposing of the archive in order to better suit the prevailing hegemony. The archive is a space where information is posed as knowledge and knowledge re-presented as universal, sanguine, and irrevocable.

But the archive is not a simple "objective representation of the past;" rather, its "selection of objects" is curated with the aim for maintaining desire, power, and knowledge (ibid., 14). In other words, there is no direct or unmediated access to the past through the archive but the archive (selectively) represents the past through its selective collection. In this sense, the archive is always a reconstruction and reinterpretation of the past (ibid.). Mediated by those in power for preserving their specific hegemonic interests, the archive is most importantly a system for counting bodies, composing minds, and controlling speech. For example, apart from functioning to consolidate positive identities, such as national identity, the archive classifies, catalogs, and creates knowledge in order to identify and control social misfits—the mad man, the criminal, the destitute, and the wanker. Surveyed within the carceral or disciplined through institutions such as the university and the legal system, these excessive bodies are produced, interpreted, and altered through the archive. The archive wields political power insofar as it controls memory and the narrative of social desire (Derrida 1995, 4n1; cited in Manoff 2004, 9).

The archive is the big Other guaranteeing disciplinary speech, underwriting meaning, and instituting disciplinary limits. According to Michel Foucault, the archive is "the first law of what can be said." It "governs the appearance of statements as unique events" and "defines...*the system of its enunciability* [and] *the system of its functioning.*" In other words, the archive names the system that makes speech (*parole*) possible by laying down the rules of language (*langue*). As such, the archive is:

> Far from being that which unifies everything that has been said in the great confused murmur of a discourse, far from being only that which ensures that we exist in the midst of preserved discourse, it is that which differentiates discourse in their multiple existence and specifies them in their own duration. (1972, 129)

The archive backs up history or what claims to be history. Whatever is absent from the archive, therefore, qualifies as outside of history. Thomas Osborne defines the archive as "a principle of credibility [that] functions as a sort of bottom-line resource in carving out of claims to disciplinarity" (1999, 53; cited in Manoff 2004, 18–19). If we replace "disciplinarity" with "subjectivity and otherness," the definition still stands. For what the archive truly seeks to determine is the position of the self in relation to the other. The latter is under scrutiny within the archive. Firstly, the other must be known in order for the self to declare autonomy and, secondly, as part of recognizing or knowing the other the self must be expunged of all irritating otherness. The archive is the public battleground for staking claim over symbolic difference.[8]

Postcolonial interrogations of imperial archives have unraveled, for instance, that collection and collation of information into archival data is never objective. During the nineteenth and twentieth centuries, imperial archives served the British empire's dual ideological agenda of justifying colonial rule and misrepresenting native cultures. Thomas Richards (1993) has further extended this argument to underline the essentially fantastic character of the imperial archive—it equates gathering information about native cultures with effective control of the colony. In reality, though, the vast landmasses occupied by the colonial forces were often without direct supervision, and at times of colonial crises such as anticolonial insurrections and local riots the colonial administration found their data incomplete and their fantasy of control compromised. Bhabha illustrates this limit of the imperial archive in his discussion of the stereotype. Supposedly a product of objective empirical knowledge, the stereotype "is a form of knowledge and identification that vacillates between what is always 'in place,' already known, and something that must be anxiously repeated" (Bhabha 2006, 94–95). Imperial knowledge however claimed is always flawed, always incomplete, and always self-congratulatory (paranoiac). The archive functions to legitimize this (paranoid) knowledge in order to consolidate the image of the sovereign self. As such, the archive is a site of subject-formation through knowledge-production. Its "assurance of concreteness, objectivity, recovery and wholeness" substantiates the self as subject-of-knowledge (Bradley 1999, 119; cited in Manoff 2004, 17).

Today, the meaning of archive has broadened. Partly from postcolonial questioning of the traditional archive and partly due to emerging modes of representing and recording, the archive today is more than the literal site of the library, museum, the clandestinely hidden warehouses storing all sorts of artefacts from recovered UFOs to the Excalibur, etc. Recent interrogations of the archive from different disciplinary viewpoints have shown that the archive can be held accountable, revised, and absent ontologies written back into it. Omissions in the archive can be questioned and filled out. All these in turn prove the archive to be fluid—a fluidity that both explains the assembled character of the archive and allows for correctives: the archive is "the general system of *formation* and *transformation* of statements" (Foucault 1972, 130). The notion of writing in and writing out of the archive, however, only authenticates the privilege of the archive: it *delimits* us. Simply put, we are suspended in the desire of and for the archive. Though recent interrogations reveal it as lacking—the inconsistencies of the archive materialize its contingency and artificiality—our return to plug these gaps by writing in those who have been excluded merely illustrates our desire for the archive or the guarantee of knowledge it upholds. Furthermore, this response to the incompleteness of the archive underlines our inability to exist outside the desire of the Other. Nothing has changed in the contemporary neoliberal universe because the desire of the archive maps onto our desire for celebrating difference: "We are different, that Reason is the difference of discourse, our history the difference of times and we the difference of masks" (Foucault 1972, 131; I have tweaked some words). To be disconnected from the archive is thus to be disconnected from Reason, history, or desire—a severance implying death or an existence in lack at best. To exist outside the symbolic space of the archive is to exist outside desire; this is the *not-all* disruptive of the logic of castration and dismissive of the supremacy of the phallus. It is the trauma of nonbeing, of being bereft of desire, that we desire to avoid. But what are the politico-ethical implications of refusing to write the excluded back and/or the other refusing to be included into the archive? In what follows I explore these (im)possibilities.

III. THE IMPOSSIBILITY OF FALLING IN LOVE: LEILA ABOULELA'S "THE MUSEUM"

> Wherever we turn in our culture, we're told that sustaining passion over time takes effort—that we should do everything in our power to keep desire alive. But, truthfully, sometimes letting passion run its course is better than putting it on life support. Aren't we already working hard enough? Why do our love lives have to become a site of endless exertion? Particularly when it's unlikely that our efforts will pay off? One of the paradoxes of love is that our attempts to render it stable tend to suppress the spirit of improvisation that makes it so enjoyable to begin with. Our protective measures can cause us to lose the very thing we're trying to protect; they can destroy the very ardor that initially mesmerized us. (Ruti 2011, 234–35)

I cite this long passage from Mari Ruti's deceptively titled Lacanian book *The Case for Falling in Love: Why We Can't Master the Madness of Love—and Why That's the Best Part*, because the entire narrative of Leila Aboulela's award-winning short story "The Museum" can be said to be contained within these nine lines.

"The Museum" is about a budding romantic relationship that hits an impasse. Shadia, a foreign student studying statistics in Aberdeen, Scotland, finds herself out of place in both the city as well as within the classroom. She struggles with the damp wet cold and a city very different from her hometown Khartoum in Sudan. "She could scarcely hear or eat or see. Her eyes bulged with fright, watered from the cold" (Aboulela 2001, 244; hereafter TM). Things were no different with her course of study. It "required a certain background [that] she didn't have," and, as a result, she felt battered and lost. She struggled to understand the formulae, how the copier worked, and even how to retrieve books from the library (TM, 243–44). Shadia, though, is not alone, her experiences are shared by a motley crew of third world students all of whom suffer from and bond over similar issues. In her desperation, Shadia eventually reaches out to Brian—a native of Scotland and the best student in class. But this is not easy for Shadia, as she has always found Brian weird: his silver earring, unkept hair, and careless and disrespectful attitude in the classroom has alienated Shadia from him. To her he was a metonym for "the strangeness of the West" (TM, 243). Yet, forced by circumstances, Shadia asks for his notes, and over time their friendship grows before eventually Brian asks her out to the local museum. Once at the museum, however, Shadia realizes the impossibility of their relationship. They come from different worlds, and though both their worlds have been shaped by the history of colonialism, their respective understandings of colonial history and the (postcolonial) cultural imaginaries generated by that history are not compatible. Looking at the African exhibits on display and realizing how these carry very different "messages" for Brian compared to her, Shadia recognizes the impossibility of ever bridging the chasm between them (TM, 256–57). Therefore, notwithstanding Brian's pleas that he will change his views about Africa, Shadia decides to call off their relationship. She remains unconvinced that Brian could ever *unlearn* what generations of racial privilege have taught him about "Africa." An irreparable communication gap between the West and non-West thus clips the wings of this fledgling love story. The museum that was supposed to provide support to the libidinal coupling by inaugurating cross-cultural communication between Shadia and Brian fails. In fact, it does the opposite. The museum's lopsided African exhibits reopen the wounds of colonialism and reestablish the futility of cross-cultural conversation between these "lovers" even decades after the end of colonialism.

"The Museum" deals with common postcolonial themes, notably, experiences of diasporic existence, raising first-generation immigrant children in the West, and the challenges of these children growing up with/between two cultures. In Aboulela's writing, though, these themes gain a distinct flavor from her unapologetic Islamic worldview: she writes about the importance of retaining Islamic cultural, ethnic, and religious identities in the post-9/11 world, especially among Muslim diasporic communities spread across the globe. Aboulela's stories openly depict struggles between "worldly desires" and "spiritual discipline," often presenting cultural communication as contingent on religious conversion (as in *the Translator*). On top of that, Aboulela carefully isolates spirituality from politics—the spiritual struggles of her characters are never allegories for or symbolized as ideological struggles but presented always as strenuously cultural in provenance and character. Unlike Salih, from whom Aboulela draws direct inspiration, the latter's fiction ultimately champions a distinct Islamic resolution to all human conflict. Or, to put it bluntly, her characters appear disposed toward a very categorical approach to cultural difference—no communication without complete translation. This has led Wail Hassan to dub her work as "Muslim immigrant fiction" (Hassan 2014, 180). Specifically, Hassan explains, Aboulela's work represents "two historical developments since the 1970s: the Islamic resurgence that has attempted to fill the void left by the failure of Arab secular ideologies of modernity (something that Salih's fiction as a whole dramatizes), and the growth of immigrant Muslim minorities in Europe and the United States." But, according to Hassan, her work is nothing more than a fringe phenomenon in modern Arabic literature: a "minor literature within a minor literature" (ibid., 180–81, 186).

Religion plays a critical role in Aboulela's first novel *The Translator* where Sammar (from Sudan) gives Rae (from Scotland) a simple choice: convert to Islam and I will marry you. I will discuss this novel in some detail below. For now, I wish to ask whether Aboulela's Islamic worldview also explains Shadia's decision to call off her fledgling romance with Brian. Or, is it possible to read Shadia's external conflicts over identity, culture, and tradition in terms of her personal or inner conflicts; that is, her inability to bridge the gap between what she thinks she desires and what she truly desires?

The Impossibility of Unlearning

"The Museum" was published a year after *The Translator*, and both share many similarities in plot, setting, and characterization. In both narratives the central protagonists are strong Sudanese women living in Scotland. Sammar in *The Translator* and Shadia in "The Museum" endure bitter social isolation and the brutal Lowland cold, and both characters to certain degrees seek solace in religion. They also get romantically involved with Scottish men—Sammar with Rae Isles, a secular scholar of Islam, and Shadia with Brian who hails from the working class. Again, in both texts, their interracial love stories get complicated in part by the presence of another man—Sammar is a widow who devoutly clings onto that identity, while Shadia is engaged to Fareed, a businessman in Khartoum. Their affairs, though, end differently. At the end of *The Translator*, Sammar and Rae overcome their cultural and religious differences, but "The Museum" ends with Shadia terminating her relationship with Brian. And unlike the novel published the previous year, Aboulela's short story does not seek resolution through Islam.

The Sudanese Ambassador to the UK notably characterized *The Translator* as a "dialogue of civilizations." It stands in contrast to the predominant worldview of the "clash of civilizations," and tells how a secular Western man and a devout Muslim woman come together (Abbas 2011, 449). By contrast, we can say, "The Museum" depicts the failure of any such dialogue. The story candidly posits the impossibility of cross-cultural communication between the East and West by reviewing the West's continuing *inscription* of and/or archiving of the non-West under signs of negation. The story confirms that unbridgeable differences between two cultures result from their binary or unequal positions in colonial and postcolonial history, and this means Shadia is forever marked by images and symbols of the *non-*, and as long as she occupies the locus of the Other there cannot be any communication between her and Brian.

But does this mean that Aboulela moves away from emphasizing culture as identity to characterizing identity as political? Does her short story politicize culture instead of culturalizing political difference (as Hassan claims she always does)? Truth be told: I remain unconvinced about Shadia's sudden political awakening at the end of "The Museum." In fact, I will argue that her political awakening has nothing to do with politics, because it is just symbolic posturing—Shadia uses politics of difference as defense against losing her desire. She enjoys being distressed, her desire unsatisfied, more than she desires the satisfaction of a successful relationship—she prefers the surplus enjoyment of *remaining* in dissatisfaction. By refusing Brian, Shadia only recovers her subjectivity from being dissolved or objectified in the desire of the other. She secures herself from becoming an object.

The Impossibility of Communication

The Translator begins with a dream. Sammar dreams that she cannot meet Rae due to inclement weather. In her dream the unceasing rain spoils the translation she prepared for Rae, making her feel anxious about handing him pages smudged by raindrops. Shadia's story, however, begins not in a dream but in the "strangeness" of her waking reality. It begins with Shadia, the subject of the sentence, feeling afraid to ask "him," the object of the sentence, that is, Brian, about his class notes: "At first Shadia was afraid to ask him for his notes" (TM, 243). Brian is not introduced to us by name till three paragraphs into the story, and during this period he only appears as the object of Shadia's enunciation and as an object in Shadia's gaze. Brian exists in bits and parts, defined by negatives and as metonym for the coldness and cruelty of this foreign land: "The earring made her afraid; the straight long hair that he tied up with rubber band. She has never seen a man with an earring and such long hair. But then she had never known such cold, so much rain. His silver earring was the strangeness of the West, another culture shock" (ibid.).

But encountering Brian Shadia experiences more than *culture shock*. Brian shocks Shadia for the memories he evokes from her childhood. Brian's hair throws Shadia back to the past, to her recollection of a doll she owned as a young child, a doll with hair like Brian's—"a dull color between yellow and brown." Shadia reminiscences spending hours "combing the doll's hair," "stroking it," and "longing for such straight hair." She remembers fantasizing about getting similar hair after death: in Paradise this straight hair would "fly behind her" and "when she bent her head down it would fall over her like silk and sweep the flowers on the grass" (ibid.). Brian traumatically manifests for her a long-forgotten fantasy and the desire lurking in that fantasy, namely, to be someone else. This makes Brian at once culturally alien and extremely known. We learn that he repels Shadiya with his unforgiving differences but equally charms her by making the doll from her childhood fantasy come alive. And even though in a sense this is a grotesque realization of the fantasmatic in lived reality, Brian's strangeness functions as the hook of desire that keeps Shadia attached to her new, albeit difficult reality, and importantly safe from a complete anxiety breakdown.

At another level, Brian brings to life Shadia's desire for (her) desire. The doll, specifically its hair, possibly reminds Shadia of her fantasy about being whole. For the doll's hair promises not just the fulfillment of what Shadia lacks, namely, straight hair, but also the emotional freedom to run and touch the ground with her hair. Yet in materializing in the other, that is, Brian, the doll, along with the fantasy it supports, no longer remains Shadia's own. It is displaced in the other, thus alienating Shadia from her desire. This feeling of uncertainty is clear from Shadia's anxiety over her doll becoming "vivid suddenly" or human. It is the stuff of nightmares: the inanimate object becomes animate—Frankenstein's monster or Chucky, both objects of fantasy and anxiety-provoking objects, both challenge the sovereign self, its knowledge and mastery, and both demand lives of their own. Shadia feels sick encountering her desire; she finds Brian appalling.

Read thus, "The Museum" is a story about Shadia's slipping into and recoiling away from (acknowledging) her desire. In fact, because there's a similar encounter at the conclusion of the story, we can say that the story is bookended by Shadia's traumatic close encounters with her desire and her consequent rejection of desire. In between, though, we get the story of Shadia's attempted negotiations of Brian—the other—who moves from being the uncanny thing to, first, becoming the symbolic object of fantasy (the *objet a*) and, ultimately, the big Other, only to be rejected at that point in the story's conclusion. I should clarify at this point that there's no denying that this love story is indivisible from the historical narrative of European colonialism as well as contemporary Muslim immigrant fiction (which of course results from the long history of colonialism). Yet my claim is that by focusing exclusively on these histories we obfuscate a vital aspect of the story, which is Shadia's struggle with her subjectivity and desire. History alone does not explain Shadia's reluctance to discontinue her relationship with Brian. In fact, her sudden awakening to history is surprising unless we consider this consciousness as nothing more than an expedient excuse for ending the relationship without having to acknowledge the unconscious (a traumatic task in itself). I show below that Aboulela's story is more than a commentary upon the impossibility of cross-cultural relationship in the wake of divisive colonial history; it is *also* a story about Shadia's struggle with desire.

The Othering of Brian

Shadia's struggle with desire is integrally tied to her need for Othering Brian. From being an inapprehensible alterity, namely, the traumatic strangeness of the West, Brian gradually transforms into a more human other. This is reflected in Shadia's descriptions of Brian: for over time she starts attributing him with more human qualities such as "immature" and "silly." In contrast to her earlier descriptions of Brian as object—earrings, ponytail, doll-like hair—this humanization gives Brian a more developed role in her life. This begins with Shadia taking a closer look at Brian's *face,* body, and individual character habits: "He had spots on his chin and forehead, was taller than her, restless, as if he was in a hurry to go somewhere else....His blue eyes behind his glasses." Shadia also notes that "She spoke better English than he did! How pathetic. The whole of him was pathetic. He wore the same shirt every blessed day. Grey and white stripe" (TM, 245). By this stage in the narrative, Brian is transformed from an unapproximated other—one who acted as if Shadia did not exist—to being symbolized as the intersubjective other. From not finding her in the gaze of Brian to finding too much of her self in the gaze, Shadia now locks him down in her vision: she has managed to look through him, found his behavioral ticks and physical flaws—his small town, low-class origins—and reduced him into one word: "pathetic."

The narrative structure of Aboulela's story supports this progression. Resembling Elizabethan tragedies, Aboulela's narrative has five parts, or acts or tempos. The first, third, and final tempos focus on Shadia and Brian; the short second and fourth tempos punctuate these longer three tempos and function like cinematic flashbacks. The inclusion of the second and fourth tempos provides greater relief to Shadia's character and aids in our gaining better understanding of her desire. For example, as the first tempo comes to a conclusion with Shadia's symbolization of Brian as pathetic, readers are introduced to Shadia's past life in Khartoum, especially her fiancé, Fareed. Here we get more details about Shadia's longing for her home but also her growing alienation from Fareed. "Shadia was engaged to Fareed. Fareed was a package that came with the 7-Up franchise, the paper factory, the big house he was building, his sisters and widowed mother. Shadia was going to marry them all. She was going to be happy and make her mother happy" (TM, 247). Fareed features in both of the short tempos as a caricature of patriarchy: an overweight, sweaty, and conceited entrepreneur with no time for his fiancée and obsessed with installing gold-colored toilet seats in his bathroom. This caricature almost justifies Shadia's indiscretion—she is engaged to a man she does not love; Fareed appears to have no emotional attachment to her, has no time to listen to her anxieties about her studies or even the weather, thereby explaining Shadia's growing emotional proximity to Brian. But equally importantly, Shadia's distance from Fareed aids Brian's Othering in the following section, where from the immature, silly adult Brian becomes a child. Reading his class notes, Shadia admires Brian's clear handwriting, "sparse on the pages...rounded like a child's" (TM, 248). This infantalization goes hand in glove with Shadia's earlier characterization of Brian as working-class and poor, further allowing Shadia to fantasmatically contain Brian without realizing that by doing so she is unwittingly enunciating her desire for Brian. Brian fills her lack.

Brian's notes help Shadia regain her confidence. After reading these, she feels sure of doing well in the course:

> Understanding after not understanding is fog lifting, pictures swinging into focus, missing pieces slotting into place. It is fragments gelling, a sound vivid whole, a basis to build on. His notes were the knowledge she needed, *the gap filled*. She struggled through them, not skimming them with the carelessness of incomprehension, but taking them in, *making them a part of her,* until in the depth of concentration, in the late hours of the nights, she lost awareness of time and place, and at last, when

she slept she became the epsilon and gamma, and she became a variable, making her way through discrete space from state "I" to state "j." (TM, 248; my emphasis)

What Shadia does not know or what she does not consciously acknowledge is that it is not the notes but, rather, Brian who fills her gap. The very notations that first eluded Shadia, appeared impenetrable, have now become one with her, and all because of Brian. In this moment he becomes the Other who implicitly orchestrates a new becoming for Shadia. For at the moment she admits becoming a part of his notes, of making the notes into her, she also unconsciously acknowledges him as the big Other. Historically constituted cultural differences that had earlier alienated Shadia from Brian is replaced in this scene by statistical notations—pure and ahistorical notations—which make Shadia part of the script. She *became* "the epsilon and gamma" in Brian's notes. With this, we arrive at the final moment of Brian's Othering. He has moved from being the uncanny other to the ideal ego/other to finally becoming anointed as the big Other. As the big Other, Brian promises plenitude, the Other capable of filling Shadia's lack. He is not only the author but also the guarantor of the notes: "Everything was clear in his mind, his brain was a clear pane of glass where all the concepts were written out boldly and neatly" (TM, 249). And it is as the object of the Other's desire, that Shadia gains her (new) subjectivity. Shadia desires to be Brian's desire.

But does she? If she did, then this love story might have had a happy ending. For even as Shadia idealizes Brian, whose voice and gaze seduces her into agreeing to go out for coffee and later visit the museum, she always appears to remain uncertain about her choices. She regrets making these choices. And though it is never clear why she makes these "mistakes"—Aboulela does not tell her readers, noting, "Perhaps because she had been up late[,] she made that mistake. Perhaps there were other reasons" (TM, 249)—but we see Shadia wavering on every decision she takes, from asking Brian for his notes to having coffee with him at the university cafeteria to agreeing to go visit the museum with him. This tells a lot about her subjectivity. As a reader, I feel compelled to ask: If she desires to be desired by Brian, why then does she seek every opportunity to make him dislike her? For example, she confesses to being deliberately rude with Brian and trying to make him uncomfortable with flippant suggestions like he become a Muslim (TM, 253). Why would anyone agree to a date and then try to sabotage it? And this brings us to an important question: What does Shadia *really* want?

What Does Shadia Want?

Shadia desires to keep Brian's desire for her unsatisfied. Freud has a term for individuals like this: *hysterics*. The hysteric desires to be wanted but never fully enjoyed by the big Other. Put differently, the hysteric derives surplus enjoyment in withholding herself from satisfying the big Other's desire. This is why Shadia resists being Brian's love object, humiliates him on every occasion, and wants him to dislike her. Yet the paradox of hysteric's desire lies in the fact that the hysteric, namely, Shadia, also demands constant reaffirmations from the big Other about remaining the big Other's desire. And though Shadia does not know what she desires, because desire is unconscious, what keeps Shadia awake at night is not some moral "guilt" but, rather, the anxiety over confronting or knowing her desire (TM, 253).

Shadia wants to avoid knowing her desire. She does not want to be reduced to the status of the object of the big Other/Brian's desire even though she desires being the big Other/Brian's object of desire. As Patricia Gherovici puts it, "The hysteric's *jouissance* seems to be constrained to appearing desirable, to becoming the object of desire but not being that object" (2014, 62). Put differently, since Shadia does not want what she desires, she seeks to evade the traumatic truth of her desire by holding the big Other as lacking. This can mean the big Other no longer remains a figure of plenitude and/or that Shadia withdraws from her position as the object of the big Other's desire. Either way, the big Other's desire remains unsatisfied. But, in spite of her trying, Shadia fails to distance herself from Brian. Therefore, in the conclusion of the story, she resorts to the clichéd: explaining the impossibility of their relationship in terms of symbolic difference. Shadia recycles the Kipling dogma: "The twain can never meet!" Separated by the phenomenon of colonialism, an event that cannot be forgiven or forgotten, Brian must remain deadlocked in antagonism to Shadia. He cannot erase the sins of his ancestors. Scottish involvement in Britain's imperial project bars Brian forever from loving a woman from Sudan. This history submits, at least for Shadia, that he can never be anything more than a negated other, and this means, as long as Shadia holds onto her identity or desire to not withstand her desire, Brian must die! It is therefore only appropriate that Aboulela sets up her story against the backdrop of a Statistics course. In Statistics, there are no confirmations but only variations and fluctuations. Nothing is ever one, whole, or complete but always a set of many parts. Shadia too desires to remain a variable, pulsating desire of Bryan. A desire that is impossible to localize in one object.

Does this narrative of desire connect to the political dimension of Aboulela's story? Or do we have to sideline postcolonial interrogations of Shadia's opposition to the West's representational politics from a psychoanalytic reading of Shadia's desire? We have again at our hands the old conflict between psychoanalytic theory and postcolonial analysis. However, I believe there is indeed a connection between Shadia's subjective struggle with her unconscious or desire and the conscious ideological stance she assumes against the West's representational politics. I claim that the narrative of hysteric desire and the questioning of arbitrary objectification of the other can and indeed come together in this story.

IV. THE HYSTERIC'S DESIRE AND THE DISCOURSE OF THE HYSTERIC

In Seminar XVII, Lacan proposes the Hysteric's discourse as one of the four specific types of social link or relationship we establish as speaking beings. The other three are the Master's discourse, the University discourse, and the Analyst's discourse. Interestingly, the hysteric is the only psychic structure to have a discourse named after it. After all, Lacan does not propose the Obsessional's discourse or the Psychotic's discourse. In any case, it is possible, as Gherovici illustrates, to draw a straight line between the hysteric's desire and the discourse of the hysteric (Gheorvici 2014, 57–58). In other words, we can connect the subjective to the social; or, Shadia's personal struggle to her conscious political critique of the West's disparaging representations of Africa.

Let us begin by reviewing the Hysteric's discourse. Lacan represents the discourse as follows:

$$\frac{\$}{a} \longrightarrow \frac{S^2}{S^1}$$

I read this as the speaking subject' or hysteric's ($\$$) questioning of the Master (S1) or the Master's response in terms of production of new totalizing knowledge (S2) being called out for what it lacks or what the attempt to totalize knowledge inevitably produces, a remainder in excess to knowledge, that is, the a as the excess eluding/escaping knowledge. Zupančič characterizes the Hysteric's discourse as "discourse about injustice"—the speaking subject is unable to reconcile its real lived experience with the symbolic role assigned to her by the big Other. The hysteric's discourse is, therefore, an expression of her impossibility—there's always a part of the hysteric that exists outside the sociosymbolic and the logic of the Signifier. The hysteric's discourse demands recognition for the right to exist outside and, in turn, exposes the fragility of the Signifier (Zupančič 2006, 164–65). For to push acknowledgment for being outside of symbolic laws reveals the big Other as lacking and questions the accepted operational logic of the cut/castration as fundamental to being. Put differently, to exist outside the symbolic is to exist in spite of or in indifference to the dialectic of "having" and "being." This is an existence unbound to desire, an existence that ex-sists. Another name for such existence/ex-sistence is the death drive. Ex-sistence distinguishes being human through human subjection in the dialectic of an imaginary lack versus an unfulfilled wholeness (Miller 2003, n.p.). The hysteric only demands to know the truth about this conundrum (Gherovici 2014, 58). Her question to the big Other is "am I in the symbolic or also (am I) by being outside of it?" And this simple query opens up a gap in the guarantee of the symbolic order underlining that "man's identity cannot be constituted entirely by reference to others" because every single individual contains "elements that resist all systems of collective designation" (Ruti 2011, 3).

The resistance organized by the Hysteric against the all-knowing big Other is palpably evident even in the hysteric's desire (for the desire of the big Other). The hysteric masquerades as the love object only up to a point (where the other, the intersubjective other who also acts as the big Other in the hysteric's fantasy, starts to desire). Once there, it starts to pull out. In fact, no sooner does the hysteric occupy the position as the object of the Other's desire than it begins to refuse becoming that object. For the hysteric's questions about the relation of desire to truth pushes the other/Other into confronting the emptiness behind its desired object—this object is not special and hides nothing except the traumatic nothingness of being and nonrelation between ontologically castrated subjects. The hysteric enjoys seeing the other/Other falter in the face of this truth (Brousse 1991, 123). But this is not an instance of masochism or the hysteric enjoying the suffering of the other. Rather, the hysteric destabilizes the system of knowledge-making—difference and value—and habitual mechanisms of interpellation. *Hysteria means failed interpellation* (Žižek 2008, 101).

One finds the notion of the hysteric's discourse in some of Lacan's early observations on the hysteric's desire in Seminar V. Most important of these being that the hysteric cannot constitute the other as big Other, the ultimate guarantor of meaning and the executor of the law (of castration). The other as Other hence must always come up short (cited in Gherovic 2014, 61). If we follow this line of thinking, then, the connection between hysteric desire and the discourse of the hysteric becomes clear. The hysteric's desire and the discourse of the hysteric conjoin on the point of challenging authority. As Gherovic puts it,

> In the larger context, this productive and inspiring pathology also proposes a mode of social link, a discourse. The hysteric demands that the Master produce an answer. Once this happens, the hysteric will render this answer incomplete or inconsistent. The question ultimately is aimed at exposing where the Master's knowledge is lacking. (ibid., 63)

The hysteric *prefers not to* accept the big Other.

Shadia's challenge to the West's *archivization* of Africa qualifies as the hysteric's discourse because she interrogates the museum's posing of "Africa" as objective knowledge by underlining the circulation of colonial modes of representation in the arrangement of the museum's exhibits and via questions about what always remains absent from representations of Africa, namely,

> disconnected objects out of place and time.... Nothing was of her, nothing belonged to her life at home.... She wanted to see minarets, boats fragile on the Nile, people. People like her father.... [T]here was nothing for her here.... Here was Europe's vision, the clichés about Africa, cold and old. (TM, 255–56; I have slightly altered the order of the sentences)

Shadia is speaking about the gap between her lived experience of Africa and the West's (re)presentation of Africa as (universal) knowledge. We must not mistake this simply as knowledge about Africa. Critically, this knowledge is also or even only about the West. The museum performs the same ideological role of cultural representation that Spivak charges nineteenth-century literature with generally doing: they culturally represent England to the English (1985, 243). Looking at the dioramas of Scottish soldiers, adventurers, and reformers Brian *learns* the "truth" about his ancestors. He does not see them as marauders, religious fanatics, and vile opportunists but as simple men wanting to escape their small towns, communities, or economic conditions. But then, and by contrast, Shadia's hysteric resistance deflates these mechanisms of interpellation, and affiliate production of knowledge, thereby distressing the authority of the museum.

Aboulela dismantles the idea of museums as objective spaces. She shows that as archive the museum is no less ideologically organized than a Nazi political manifesto. As Shadia disturbingly discovers, museums sustain power by controlling knowledge; that is, by exercising power through what they choose to display and how they arrange their displays for viewing. The African exhibit in the Scottish museum was meant to be a paean to the "Africa," that is, the land that lured European colonialists to its coasts for gold, for saving natives, and for the thrill of big-game hunting. Today the "image of Africa" continues to support Europe's capitalist markets and its imaginary notions of theological modernity and bullfrog-toxic masculinity. The Africa we wish to save today is conveniently homogenized into a landmass ravaged by poverty, civil wars, and widespread regressive religious practices such as female genital mutilation. What Shadia experiences in the museum is therefore not just a radical dislocation of her being but also the gendered naturalization of Africa into a land awaiting, to wit inviting, deep penetration from the West. In segregating herself from Brian, she complains against and exposes these overarching objectifications. Shadia worries about being similarly reduced in Brian's desire to the metonym for Africa, the exotic other, whom the Scottish have "enjoyed" and "penetrated" though the ages, then displayed in cages, cabinets, and photographs. Africa's heterogeneous cultures and regional uniquenesses have only always existed lexicalized to the desires of the white colonizer—the missionary's zeal, the hunter's thrill, and the adventurer's passion. In the West's cognitive map there are no individuals in Africa but only souls needing to be reformed; animals to be hunted; and magnificent vistas awaiting discovery by the white man. Shadia recoils at the anxiety of confronting the object she has become in Brian's desire.

Hysterization of Postcolonial Studies

The hysteric asks a simple question: "What am *I* to your desire"? In other words, the hysteric inhabits the lack without the adequate forbearance in the big Other's ability to assign or secure for her a position within the symbolic order. For such a position is never satisfying to the hysteric, who finds her lived experience divorced from the social identity given to her by the big Other. This is the reason why Ellie Ragland claims that the *hysteric lives castration*, wears the fact of castration as a badge of honor, even flouts it on the face of the Other (2006, 85).

Apropos of the points made about the hysteric, namely, that the hysteric (1) challenges authority/knowledge; (2) demands the rights/acknowledgment of all that is outside the symbolic; and, (3) inhabits the unsymbolizable volatile space of the lack, I wager an alignment exists between the hysteric's discourse and the discourse of postcolonial studies. The latter, as we know, is equally concerned with (1) questioning the role played by West as sovereign authority; (2) advocating for those who are on the margin or outside the sociosymbolic; and (3) articulating the impossible condition of postcolonial being. That is, at least, what we find in the foundational writings of Fanon, Grosrichard, and that of the Holy Trinity, namely, Said, Bhabha, and Spivak. It would serve postcolonial studies today to realize that this similarity between the hysteric and the discipline is more than a matter of parallel ideological aims. Yes, they both seek to uncover the limit(s) of symbolic truth, but more importantly the relationship between them is isomorphic: postcolonial concerns over lost, buried, hybridized identities are the same as the hysteric's questions, even though the hysteric does not attempt to excavate or reclaim lost identities but rather unravels all identities as fiction. The goal of postcolonial studies cannot be the reversal of the self-Other binary but the rendering uncanny of the symbolic ordering of this binary as insufficient (Spivak 1999).

The postcolonial position must be outside battles over identities. It should understand the colonizer-colonized difference as irreducible to dialogue or symbolic appropriation and, as such, akin to the inevitability of sexual difference which too carries no logical explanation or congruous restitution. This means no *new* identity is possible within colonial and postcolonial societies, as all identities forged and recovered are strictly underwritten by the inequality of the system. It is only through violent destruction of this system can we theoretically begin envisioning the coming of (Fanon's) *New Man*.

The Fanonian subject—the colonized fraught in-between—is the universal subject. This subject inhabits the radical cut instituted by colonialism, and by speaking from within this space or as an embodiment of this space challenges the universality assumed by the West. But it is not the colonial system alone that is threatened by the colonized; it puts postcolonial identities under equal duress. Like the hysteric, the colonized underlines the impossibility of achieving identity.[9] Postcolonial studies needs to embrace its hysteria—its provenance as an excessive rem(*á*)inder of colonialism and its brutal questioning of the Master's discourse for unraveling the fragility of all symbolic identities.

V. *GADJO DILO* AND THE PROBLEM OF READING

Tony Gatlif's 1998 film *Gadjo Dilo* tells the story of Stéphane, a young Frenchman, who travels from Paris to a Roma settlement deep in the interiors of Romania. Stéphane, we learn, is in search of a "gypsy" singer, Nora Luca, whom he has never met but only heard in recordings. However, we learn later, his search for Luca is more than a search for a person or a beautiful voice. He is searching for his deceased father's favorite singer. To put it in Lacanese, Stéphane is searching for the object of the Other's desire. Stéphane did not know his father well because the latter mostly stayed away from home, traveling across the globe, documenting ethnic music. It is possible that Stéphane believes by finding the singer he will come to know his father a little better. It is also possible that by traveling alone through foreign lands searching for a Roma musician, Stéphane is physically and emotionally trying to follow in the footsteps of his recently deceased father. For Stéphane this is a journey with deep psychological implications. It is about knowing what made the nomads and their music, specifically Luca, desirable to his father. It is about knowing the nomads, in order to be like them, and thus get a feel of the desire of the Other.

Most critics, however, read the film differently, choosing to debate instead Gatlif's representation of the Roma. Opinion, though, is divided. While many applaud his authentic recreation/representation of the daily life of the Roma, others, including Roma activists, commonly consider the film's representation of the Roma offensive. The latter claim the lived experience of the Roma is very different from the film's infantilizing, romantic, and pejorative depictions of the community.[10] I will return to discussing these in some detail later. Before that though let us focus on the structure of the film and the central theme of finding Luca.

Finding Luca

The film is structurally similar to Western narratives about white men journeying into dark, mysterious spaces of the Other for purposes of self-discovery and "soul making" (Spivak, 1985). Spivak describes "soul making" as "the imperialist project" of "mak[ing] the heathen into a human so that he can be treated as an end in himself" (1985, 248). Self-discovery is integrally related to soul making, and typically involves the white man encountering alien cultures, learning from and then reforming or saving these native cultures, and ending usually with the native woman as prize. Though often identified as "white savior" narratives these are more notorious than the former for disguising the imaginary of self-composition in self-righteous critiques of Western civilization. In one version of this narrative, the white man's experiences in the colony cleanse his soul of the West's competitive individuality and return him back to his essential nature. The European man then either returns to Europe rejuvenated or stays back as the naturally anointed leader of the natives.

The metonym of this cultural exercise of representing England to the English (Spivak 1985, 243), Joseph Conrad's *Heart of Darkness* (1899) is read as much as a tale about the darkness of the other space as about recognizing the darkness within the self of the West. Marlow's journey leads to self-revelation and self-substantiation.[11] These quests, Spivak reminds us, are about feeling Enlightenment positive and carry little sincerity of purpose. When time comes to be reimagined by the other's culture, the subject of the West retreats frantically to the refuge of European privilege, proving yet again that there can be *no communication* between the West and the non-West. Even the most liberal European accounts end up stereotyping non-European others into a singular negative image against which a universal "European" positive self is (re-)posited and/or (re-)attested (Spivak 1988).

Indeed, a narrow reading of Gatlif's film might lead some to see similarities between Stéphane's "Eastern" journey and Marlow's travels upriver in Africa (Belgian Congo). The spitting, cursing, and fornicating Roma in the film pose a stark contrast to a soft-spoken, technologically inventive, and chronicling Stéphane. Unlike the Roma, whose daily lives are taken up by subsistence living and illegal trades, Stèphane is the subject of history. It is *his* quest that brings the otherwise invisible Roma community into a film narrative—his quest both frames and gives substance to the Roma. This inclusion gives the Roma entry into history, to wit, even makes possible a telling of their particular history, for which Stéphane takes the responsibility of documenting and archiving. But this coming into history would not have been possible without Stéphane's perseverance: though initially treated as an outsider—a crazy white stranger or *"gadjo dilo"*—Stéphane gradually gains the trust and acceptance of the Roma. He forms friendships with Izidor, a Roma elder, played by Izidor Serban, and falls in love with Sabina, played by Rona Hartner. Subsequently with their help, Stéphane reembarks on his quest to find Nora Luca, thereby completing the circuit of his personal history as well.

The search for Luca, however, remains unaccomplished in the film. After running into repeated dead ends, Stéphane seems to shift focus on his developing relationship with Sabina and on documenting other local musicians. However, the latter exercise comes to an abrupt end after the Roma settlement is burned down and Stéphane is forced to leave (possibly back to Paris) with Sabina. The film ends with Stéphane destroying all his recordings and notes. This ending leaves a number of questions unanswered, the most important of which is: Why did Stéphane destroy the tapes, the archive he spent so long preparing?

Sean Homer's essay "Voice as *objet a* in Tony Gatlif's *Gadjo dilo*" (2010) makes a rare departure from habitual critiques of the film. He argues that "far from perpetuating stereotypes, whether negative or positive, Gatlif's film questions the stability of stereotypical representations and the verisimilitude of the image" (Homer 2010, 38). According to Homer, Gatlif uses the disembodied voice of Nora Luca, "a voice for which there is no source or origin within the narrative," that is, an "acousmatic voice," to radically undermine "the possibility of self-expression and self-presence" (ibid., 40). Homer's point is simple: it is difficult to pin down Nora Luca's voice to one source. It is not only disembodied and dislocated in the narrative, it is also not as exclusive as Stéphane makes it out to be. As Izidor tells Stéphane early in the film, "There are songs like [this] everywhere around here." Later, Sabina echoes the same when she asks Stéphane: "What's so special [about Nora Luca], there are other singers as strong as fire" (Gatlif, *Gadjo dilo*). As Homer sees it, Gatlif's film is precisely about the problem implicit in Izidor's and Sabina's comments. Namely, Why is Stéphane fixated on Luca? The film is an extension of this problematic insofar as it underlines the impossibility or stupidity of attributing values and ideals to specific bodies, cultures, and/or communities. Far from privileging one identity over another, that is, anointing Stéphane's bourgeois Parisian bohemianism over the foul-mouthed, *mafioso* Roma, Gatlif uses the "acousmatic voice" to nullify such representational politics. There's nothing special about Luca's voice. It is, firstly, untethered from any individual and/or space, and secondly, the voice is effortlessly transferable. At one point in the film, Sabina starts lip synching Luca's song as a visibly emotional Stéphane looks on before surrendering to her: "As the band begins to play the song *Nora Luca*, Sabina sings along. Slowly the voices of Nora Luca and Sabina segue together in the score, and Stéphane snuggles into the nape of Sabina's neck, murmurs the name of the 'singer' " (Homer 2010, 47). This impossible song and Stéphane's failed search for it, Homer claims, subverts the clichéd surface narrative of the film. *Gadjo Dilo* is not a film about competing cultural identities (West versus the Roma), but, rather, through its gradual unraveling of the emptiness of the song and by showing Stéphane's alienation in desire, the film depreciates the imaginary of authentic cultural identity (Homer 2010, 50).[12]

I want to add two points to Homer's reading. First, the film can be read usefully as a commentary against the neoliberal fantasy of the (im)possibility of (cross-cultural) communication, which, in the film, takes two distinct forms, namely, (1) a lack of communication between Stéphane and the Roma, and (2) a gap in the audience's understanding of the film's ending. My second addition to Homer's reading is also about the film's ending. For some reason, Homer's essay does not adequately address why Stéphane destroys the recordings or the politics of desire behind his action. These two points are crucial if we are to pursue an immanent reading of the film. Not connecting the problematic presented by Luca's dislocated roving voice to issues of cross-cultural communication and the politics of the archive risks overlooking Gatilf's engagement with an old historical problem, often highlighted by postcolonial studies, namely, the problem of communication between a privileged West and its muted margins.

The Problem of Communication

Communication is a problem in the film. Stéphane does not speak Romanian and knows a few words of Romani. The Romanian villagers and the Roma mostly do not speak French. The only member of the Roma community who knows some French by dint of having spent time in Belgium is Sabina, but she refuses to entertain Stéphane for the first half of the film. Thus, for the greater part of the film Stéphane fails to explain his journey, and it is not until late in the film that he finally meets someone fluent enough in French to help him communicate to Isidor his reasons for traveling so far in search of a Roma singer. This sets off the first real search for Luca in the film. Isidor and Stéphane head out to visit Milan, a Roma singer who knows all other singers, but again Stéphane meets a wall as they discover upon reaching Milan's village that he is dead. This dead end, though, marks a turn in the film's narrative because after this Stéphane appears to give up his quest for Luca and turns his focus on recording other local musicians. With Sabina as his guide, Stéphane travels from one Roma settlement to another, recording Roma music, sagas, and history. As Homer puts it,

> It is only when Stéphane understands the import of Isidor's remarks [i.e., "there are songs like that everywhere around here"] that he abandons his attempt to find the singer [Luca], the presence behind the voice, and to capture and definitively fix the object of his desire, the objet a. [Stéphane realizes] these songs are not the property of an individual voice. (Homer 2010, 43, 47)

Stéphane's search for Luca was doomed from the very beginning; its incompleteness being the mainstay of Stéphane's desire. Yet Stéphane does not know that what he wishes—to find Luca—is not what he desires. Luca is an impossible object sustaining Stéphane's desire, and even if Stéphane were to meet Luca, I am sure he would have found her a disappointment. Stéphane desires to be the desire of the Other. For only via this impossible search—traveling from one nomad village to another—can Stéphane emulate what he imagines to have been his father's desire. It is therefore only appropriate that he finds his desire only after he relinquishes his father's desire. In the film this is captured by the fact that his relationship with Sabina starts to gain momentum only after he ends his search for Luca. By sacrificing *his* desire for the desire of the big Other, Stéphane succeeds in finding Sabina and begins to appreciate the rich diversity of Roma music. Sadly, though, this promise of communication across desires and cultures does not last long. The burning down of the Roma settlement by Romanian villagers following a fight at the local bar between the two communities puts an end to Stéphane's stay with the Roma. The final scene of the film shows him driving back on the same road on which the film began. He appears to be returning to Paris with Sabina but we do not ever get to know whether he is indeed returning back to Paris or going somewhere else, just as we never know whether Sabina will accompany him all the way to Paris or whether she gets off at another Roma settlement, thus not affronting bourgeois Parisians with the presence of her unimpeachable otherness.

All these questions get buried, however, under a far more difficult to understand final scene where Stéphane steps out of his car to destroy the recordings of Roma music he had collected during his time at the settlement. How are we to understand this ending? Are we to understand this as saying that popularizing Roma music in the mainstream is not enough to redeem the suffering the Roma experience on a daily basis? In destroying these tapes is Stéphane symbolically protesting against the commonplace idea that we can end inequality by knowing the other? I discuss these questions below. At this point, I wish to turn to the other gap that comes to exist between the audiences and the film as a direct consequence of the film's ending. Gatlif, I claim, frustrates audience desire to know in order to fully deliver the point of his film: one cannot know the whole truth since there exists no single truth. In fact, Gatlif plays with audience desire from the very start, starting with the opening shots of the film, even though his auteurial resolve might not be as immediately apparent in these as with the ending of the film.

The Impossibility of Knowing

The radical gap between our desire to know and the impossibility of ever fully knowing finds expression in the opening scenes of the film. We do not realize this till we complete the film but the opening scenes *play* with our desire as much as the ending of the film. The opening is composed of four shots: two mid-shots punctuated by two back-to-back close-ups. The first mid-shot introduces an unnamed protagonist (Stéphane) walking away with his back to the audience. But before we see the traveler on screen, we hear his footsteps: as the opening credits roll up, audiences hear the sound of someone walking over a gravel road. After the screen illuminates, we see this as-yet-unnamed traveler walking alone on a dirty icy road extending to the horizon. With electric poles on the righthand side of the road cutting through the vast tundra-like landscape, the protagonist with his back still to us fills out what is otherwise an uncomfortably flat scene. Other than the traveler, the only vertical references in this scene are the electric poles that line one side of the road, resembling crucifixes used by Romans to punish thieves. If audiences were expecting an establishing shot, then this opening mid-shot offers nothing. It is with the following two close-ups, however, that audiences come closer to knowing more. Close-ups of the protagonist's tired feet, torn shoes, and worn face establish him as a weary traveler. The opening sequence of shots closes with another mid-shot, this time showing the tired protagonist sitting down by the road propped by what appears to be an old milestone, possibly even a Roman milestone, but now in a state of total disrepair and resembling a headstone more than a milestone.

Before moving ahead, I should note that the opening scene is extremely important in the context of the film's ending as well. For the film ends by returning to the opening *mise-en-scène*—the same road, the same electric posts standing like tired crucifixes, and possibly the same milestone or headstone. It will be under this milestone that Stéphane will bury his tapes, notes, and other documents, thus formally transforming it into an unmarked headstone. I discuss this in the next section. For now, let us continue with the opening scene and examine how Gatlif uses the scene to set up audience desire. In other words, I am saying that the opening scene prepares audiences to view the film in a specific manner or learn how to desire what they are watching.

The opening scene establishes a distance between the audience and Stéphane that is never undone. Simply put, when audiences first see Stéphane walking away they have no idea about who he is or what he wants. At the same time, this very unknowability which frames the mise-en-scène hooks audiences into desire: Are we to stare at Stéphane as he walks away from us and civilization or should we join his journey? There is also no push back against audience desire at this point. In spite of seeing a stranger, audience can still identify with his type. Alone and weary on the road, Stéphane embodies the enigmatic yet classical figure of the traveler, which helps audiences identify with the unknown protagonist. We know that we are seeing the quintessential traveler—the traveler we meet time upon time in the pages of literature and in celluloid; the traveler whose journey makes for satisfactory entertainment, social and political commentary. We are thus willing to follow him. Journey is a common theme in world cinema, and so are auteurial attempts to use the trope of the everyman traveler in order to variously orient and/or disrupt audience desire. There are many different ways in which this is done, but I will give here two examples for better contextualizing Gatlif's auteurship in the opening scenes.

Raj Kapoor's *Shree 420* (1955), which was tremendously popular in Romania in the late 1950s, opens with an extreme long shot of a traveler in the distance resembling nothing more than a dark blot. The shot holds as the traveler comes closer and the blot gradually takes the form of the tramp/everyman figure popularized by Kapoor on Indian screens. The figure walks toward the audience before stopping at a crossroads trying to decide which way to go next. The traveler's Chaplinesque gait (Kapoor developed his tramp/everyman figure after Chaplin's) along with his disheveled clothes and torn shoes evoke audience sympathy; his apparent lack of direction endears him as a lost soul out to seek an anchor. Audiences embrace him as a commoner, pity him for being a tramp, and inscribe his desire after their own desire, namely, the tramp/traveler desires to enter the security of the bourgeois metropolitan space. But will he succeed, or will he lose his way in the city? Kapoor's opening scene establishes this desire for knowing and the film satisfies this desire by following the adventures of the tramp, Raj (Raj Kapoor), as he navigates through love, corruption, and redemption in the big city. As such, in Kapoor's film, the traveler himself is devoid of desire as the opening scenes carve him according to the desire of the audience. In this case, at least, audiences get what they want. The success of the Bollywood blockbuster: first create audience desire, then satisfy said desire.

Let's take a different example, Stanley Kubrick's *The Shining* (1980). *The Shining* opens with the camera following, hovering above, a speeding car on a winding mountain road. Though this scene has no human characters, the shot of a moving car implies it is being driven by someone and also possibly carrying passengers. Like *Gadjo dilo* and *Shree 420*, Kubrick's audience at this point does not know anything about the occupants of the vehicle. They do not know who is driving, who besides the driver might be inside, and where the car is headed. But, in contrast to Kapoor, Kubrick puts his audiences in a tizzy in pursuit of their (object of) desire—a yellow car speeding along a scenic highway. Interestingly, Kubrick uses the God's-eye point of view for shooting this scene. Thus, paradoxically, the camera appears to give audiences an omniscient eye at the very moment it impairs their knowing. The ensuing emptiness of the image is all due to the object: engrossed in following the car, the audience pays scant attention to the natural beauty of the surroundings. The emptiness parallels the emptiness of the desired object. In our pursuit of desired objects we similarly often block out everything else that exists around the object. Put differently, the enigma of the speeding car that hooks our desire is the perfect example of the unknowable Thing (*das Ding*), the excess in our visual frame, which fantastically attaches us to an object of desire and alienates us from the object at the same time. As such, audiences occupy the position of desiring subjects, yet they do not know what they desire or that the emptiness of the object is what makes it desirable.

By putting the camera on a relentless pursuit, Kubrick transforms an otherwise picturesque scene into something ominous. What truly makes the scene ominous is desire or the impossibility of satisfying desire. For it is by hooking audiences into the desire for knowing about the speeding car and paradoxically withholding the satisfaction of knowing that Kubrick fills the scene with obscene desire: desire is for (the) nothing. It would have been easy to cut the opening God's-eye view for a mid-level shot of the car's inside. Take, for example, the opening scene from *I Know What You Did Last Summer* (1997).

Jim Gillespie's film begins with a shot of the inside of the car—showing us the four drunk teens—before giving us a long shot of the car steering dangerously over a mountainous road. The moment we see drunken teens in a speeding car, we know this is not going to end well. But Kubrick does not give his audiences that opportunity. He frames the scene in such a way that audiences are compelled to feverishly follow the camera as it tracks the car but does not quite catch up. And this nothingness is what attaches our desire to the vehicle. The object's enigma is the object cause of desire.

At this point, Kubrick makes a brilliant cut. After pursuing the car for some time, the camera actually appears to catch up, putting audiences within titillating visual range of the inside. Then, exactly at this moment, the camera abruptly pans left moving away from the car for the first time since the beginning of the film. Leaving the car on its journey the camera shifts focus onto the surrounding natural scenery, thereby frustrating audience satisfaction once again. This camera cut captures an important psychoanalytic wisdom about desire: even though we want to know our desire, when in close proximity of knowing, we step away. We desire to not know, to remain unsatisfied. This is because only by remaining alienated from desire we can enjoy being (dissatisfied) in desire. Kubrick, though, does not keep his audience suspended in their alienation too long. As if aware that a confrontation with the real desire or real of desire can only put an end to the subject, he turns the camera back to its former pursuit, thereby reorienting audience attention back toward desire as desire-for-something and away from desire-for-nothing. In contrast to Kapoor, who dunks his audience in auteur-crafted desire from the start of the film to the end without allowing them to understand that they are actually enjoying the auteur's/Other's desire, Kubrick both crafts the desire for his audiences (follow the car) and pushes his audience toward a fleeting recognition of desire being essentially alien. Kubrick sneaks in a subtle piece of the real before returning audiences to their happy place as desiring subjects.

At one level, Gatlif also appears to play safe. His opening scenes capture audiences in the auteur's or Other's desire but they are not made conscious about their alienation in desire. Instead, the film leads them on, first with the figure of the traveler, followed by the mystery of Nora Luca, and, then, with Stéphane and Sabina's romantic relationship. It is only in the final scene that audiences are shocked into an awareness of their alienation in desire.

That said, the opening scenes of *Gadjo dilo* are not entirely unsuggestive about the real of/in desire. The footsteps we hear before actually seeing Stéphane walk into the frame from the righthand bottom corner of the screen reference the outside of the diegetic space. I interpret this as a dual reference to the outside where the audience is sitting and the outside reality from where the audiences and all the characters in the film come. I read these further to mean the everyman figure of Stéphane is not just a character on screen but also someone from this outside. Yes, he now walks within the frames of celluloid but within him already exists a piece of the outside—a piece of the real in the reel: the other space or unconscious, where he communicates with his father, desires to be the desire of the Other.

Compared to Kapoor's opening shot, where the traveler appears as a blank smudge, *the thing,* in the distance and becomes recognizable as human only after coming within visual range of the audience, the unknown *thing* in Gatlif's film appears fully formed and already coming from the space of the audience. It is part of the self yet dissociated from or unknown to the self. In this we have a parallel with Kubrick, but in following the *thing* from their inside Gatlif's audiences are truly chasing their own desire alienated in the other. Yet the satisfaction they receive when they catch up with this desire is hardly fitting. For, at one level, as Homer illustrates, the emptiness of desire is showcased by the emptiness of Luca's voice and Stéphane's search for an "authentic" voice that never existed. At another level, and more directly, the film frustrates audience desire to know about the future of Stéphane and Sabina's relationship and the reasons for Stéphane's burying of the tapes. At the end of the film, audiences are no closer to knowing their desire or Stephane's than they were at the beginning. By keeping desire open like a wound that cannot be healed, Gatlif directs our attention to one of the primary characteristics of desire: we do not desire as an end but as a means (to repeat or continue desiring). The only way to heal this open wound of desire or to put an end to desire is to end life. For as long as we live, we are cursed to *enjoy* this festering wound. It is only by following the footsteps of Chiron and giving up our (im)mortality that we can rid ourselves of desire.

If desire is for recognition, and if in this contemporary era recognition means "understand me for who I am without judging me by my skin color, ethnicity, gender, etc.," then, by destabilizing desire Gatlif is actually checking the desire for exclusive or authentic identities. By repeating rather than representing the narrative of the white man's journey into the other's space, Gatlif is exposing the ideological obscenity of the Master's enunciation. In the words of Bhabha, mimicry "*repeats* rather than *re-presents*" and in so doing mimicry discloses the emptiness (ambivalence) of authority that interdicts the other (Bhabha 2006, 125, 126, 128; italics in the original).

> In mimicry, the representation of identity and meaning is rearticulated along the axis of metonymy. As Lacan reminds us, mimicry is like camouflage, not a harmonization or repression of difference, but a form of resemblance that differs/defends presence by displaying it in part, metonymically. Its threat, I would add, comes from the prodigious and strategic production of conflictual, fantastic, discriminatory "identity effects" in the play of a power that is elusive because it hides no essence, no "itself." (ibid., 128–29)

Homer is spot on: *Gadjo dilo* is not about reconstituting or deconstructing identities. It is, rather, about the absence of essential identities and natural cultures. *Gadjo dilo* reveals that there exists "no truth to personal or cultural identity that can give us the 'true picture' " (Homer 2010, 42). Bipolar criticisms of the film—it is not an authentic representation of the Roma but a repetition of the negative stereotypes popular in the Western imaginary, versus the film is a courageous and unfiltered window into Roma life and culture—fail equally to escape the fantasy of exclusive identities.

Put another way, identities cannot be assumed on basis of lack or excess—the Roma lack civility or the Roma are naturally good musicians. Demands for authentic representation and claims of authentic cultural identities are equally fantastic and proportionately ideological in their respective attempts to homogenize the other. Indeed, in explicitly questioning "authenticity of any cultural identity," *Gadjo dilo* "undermines attempts to impose uniformity on the diversity of Roma culture" (ibid., 50). One must add to this argument. First, as all cultural identities are fictional, even transferable, Gatlif could not have *authentically* represented the Roma even if he had wanted. At least, not without resourcing some Master discourse guaranteeing his representation/recognition as genuine. In fact, Gatlif could well have used his own Romani origin to support his representation, but he doesn't. For who doesn't know the dangers of reviving identity claims based on autochthony? These only lead to further divisions in identity and divisive ideologies of identity formations.

Second, what would an authentic representation serve? Even if we accept for a moment that authentic representation is possible and that Gatlif could have authentically represented the Roma, what purpose would that serve? Would that put an end to conflicts over cultural identity and the oppression the Roma face across the world? The idea that social inequality is a matter of representation and correcting representation would eradicate inequality is a multiculturalist fantasy. It asks that we embrace the other as they are, avoid politically incorrect speech, and acknowledge difference as constituent of the whole. Translated into ideology, these mean two things. First, as Žižek teaches us on countless similar accounts, negotiating difference today has become a matter of tolerance: "I am willing to tolerate the other as long as the other does not intrude into my private space." With social relations being defined in terms of rights, the other today has as much right to exist as I do only insofar the other is not actively involved in or complicit in violating my rights, including my right to privacy. Second, and relatedly, the other has a right to exist and to enjoy his/her privacy only if s/he participates in the "homogenizing sphere of consumer economics becoming, as it were, exchangeable through the very process that professes to promote its 'uniqueness'" (Ruti 2012, 196). "Culture" in multiculture is a "nice name for the exoticism of the outsiders" for the right of particulars to exist depends on their obeying the basic rules of civic society and capital (Spivak 1999, 355). The other's desire for recognition in this society cannot be anything but a demand for integration. The other has an equal right to exist in my society only as long as she embraces or finds quaint accommodation in the desire of the Other.

VI. THE PROBLEM WITH APU

Herein lies *my* problem with Hari Kondabolu's "Problem with Apu." This 2017 documentary charges the long-running American sitcom *The Simpsons* (1989–) for propagating a brash stereotype of Indian immigrants through the character of Apu Nahasapeemapetilon (voiced by Hank Azaria). According to Kondabolu, growing up he really liked Apu because the latter was the only Indian/South Asian character on American screens. But later he realized the insidious racism of this cultural representation:

> Apu was the only Indian we had on TV at all so I was happy for any representation as a kid. And of course he's funny, but that doesn't mean this representation is accurate or right or righteous. It gets to the insidiousness of racism, though, because you don't even notice it when it's right in front of you. It becomes so normal that you don't even think about it. It seeps into our language to the point we don't even question it because it seems like it's just been that way forever. (Blauvelt, *BBC Culture*, 2017)[13]

Not unlike black minstrelsy, a white actor, Hank Azaria, voiced the clownish Indian immigrant shopkeeper and, Kondabolu fumes, Azaria's voice acting mimics white people making fun of the Indian accent. Making "fun of my father" is how Kondabolu actually characterizes Hank Azaria's performance, calling it "insulting" and the overall representation of Apu "inaccurate" and part of "a larger problem where people don't get to speak for themselves" (Keveney, *USA Today*, 2017).

Reactions to the documentary have been mixed. While many Indian Americans sided with Kondabolu, recollecting the bullying and abuses they experienced as children because of Apu, many Indian Americans also defended the show.[14] Amar Shah, for instance, noted in an op-ed for *the Washington Post*:

> I didn't feel anger or defensiveness as I saw the conversation unfold. Instead, I felt a rush of memories of my family's second home, a Phillips 66 Gas 'N' Shop in central Florida. Apu and my father are both Indian immigrants and convenience-store owners with questionable mustaches. Both have an affinity for one-letter abbreviations in their store names and a devotion to Hindu gods. Both are fickle Mets fans with arranged marriages and accents. Both are kind, hard-working and entrepreneurial. While most viewers are debating a fictional character, they're also talking about my father and the life he built for us.....For me, the question of Apu is much more complicated. For me, the child of Indian immigrants, raised in stores much like Apu's, it's personal.... To many Indian Americans, Apu is offensive. To me, he's my dad. (*Washington Post*, April 25, 2018)

As with Gatlif's film, the debate around Apu has crystalized over the issues of authenticity and verisimilitude and of the distinct personal experiences of first-generation Indian Americans growing up divided between their parents' culture and that of their own "U.S." culture.

But what are *my problems* with Kondabolu's "Problem with Apu" and, beyond that, with the debate it has inaugurated. My first problem is that both Kondabolu and Shah think the stereotype is complete fiction. This is never the case. Said teaches us that stereotypes are not complete fantasies—lies or myths—because a part of the stereotype is grounded in real life. It is for this reason that a stereotype cannot be simply wished away or exploded by proving it is untrue. Stereotypes do not evaporate if exposed as fiction.[15]

Second, both Kondabolu and Shah seek to validate their respective arguments through the logic of personal experience. In claiming ground for their respective positions on Apu, both are quick to draw on their personal experiences of growing up Indian American. The assumption here is striking: by being born to Indian immigrants to the United States they have a more profound understanding about all things "Indian" and this knowledge extends unequivocally to all immigrants. *Theirs is the immigrant experience par excellence.* Without belaboring a point already noted repeatedly in this chapter, I have to ask: Is there a single idea of "India" or "Indian Immigrants to the U.S." that tallies between them or effectively approximates *all* immigrant experiences in the United States? My question is: Is there *really* an authentic Indian or South Asian identity and, provided there might be, what specifically anoints either Kondabolu or Shah, both Indian Americans, to claim that identity. A nation of 1.2 billion that in parts are as different as Texas is to Guangdong are being parceled out nicely by these two who at best can only represent minute parts of "Indian culture." And, also, how presumptuous is it to think that all immigrants have the same experience postimmigration? We can claim that the sense of cultural alienation, the rampant marginalization, the belief in the so-called American Dream are indeed shared by most immigrants, but the singularity of their individual experiences can never be subsumed under such broad categories without reducing each and every immigrant into an object, *the Immigrant.*

Furthermore, neither the documentary nor the debate afterward distinguishes expats from immigrants. I should not have to explain why this difference is *not* a matter of semantics. However, the fact that Kondabolu forecloses this difference (he also does the same for South Asians of mixed parentage) only discloses his entrenched "American" mindset: if you are brown or speak with an accent you must be an immigrant lured to this "land of the brave and home of the free" in search of a life your homeland could not guarantee. Juvenile thinking at best.

I have now lost count of my *problems* but will persist nonetheless with a few more details, the first of which is Kondabolu's historically specific treatment of the issue. He claims that post-9/11 *The Simpsons* endorsed image of the goofy "Indian" storeowner gets problematized because in the aftermath of the 9/11 attacks *brown becomes the new black*. In this new symbolic regime, Indians or Indian Americans no longer remain characters with funny accents and idiosyncratic cultural mores but become terrorists. Now, this 9/11-oriented historicist argument is problematic because the denigration of the Indian has a long history going back to such Hollywood films as the Cary Grant–starred *Gunga Din* (1939), Peter Sellers's *the Party* (1968), and, even, *Harold and Kumar Escape from Guantanamo Bay* (2008), a film in which Kumar (Kal Penn) embodies South Asian goofiness only to map it onto white America's fear of brown/black people.

Not in the least facile is Kondabolu's acceptance that Homer Simpson, the main protagonist in the show, is also a stereotype. Homer stereotypes the middle-aged white American man with little education. But because Homer is not the only white character in the show, Kondabolu argues, his character does not establish the kind of stereotype that occurs with Apu. Kondabolu here seems to make a curious point: he admits that no representation can be real; however, if there were more Indian representations to choose from then U.S. viewers would not put all their ideas about the Indian immigrant in one basket. Simply put, Kondabolu's logic is that today South Asians are in all walks of life—doctors, lawyers, congressmen, astronauts—therefore, we should not have "stereotypes" of South Asians only as immigrant shopkeepers. This is a neoliberal fallacy, which claims that if immigrants or racial, ethnic, and gendered others find access in the mainstream, social inequality against these communities would automatically end. If we probe deeper into this, we realize that a feelgood argument such as this pivots on the ideological belief that social inequality is a matter of representation (in both the political and the aesthetic senses), and if we correct our representations then social inequalities will evaporate. As I have noted above, this neoliberal ideology waylay difficult conversations by encouraging ego-satisfying solutions. The purpose: continue with white privilege by other means. Purpose 2: mitigate the foundations of the United States of America in genocide and systemic slavery, which continue into the present in the form of directed incarcerations and debilitating exclusions of minorities while holding out the cheerful promise of multiculturalism.

Social inequality in the United States cannot be remedied by claims of cultural belonging but by tackling economic oppression and white racism against nonwhites. Kandabolu's documentary promotes the insidious logic of multiculturalism and rehearses the Klannish solution of scapegoating by isolating Azaria as the problem. Perhaps Kondabolu forgets that Azaria is Jewish or, more seriously, he is the victim of the same system victimizing South Asians in the United States. But Kondabolu needs straw men to avoid directly offending the system arranged by U.S. capitalism. After all, he too benefits from this system: comedy routines and "radical" late night shows appear to severely criticize the wrongs of the system though in reality they function to give common people the impression that wide sections of society are angry for the same reasons the working class is. Feeling thus secured, the working class lives in hopes of change only to dies miserably in camp-like conditions in our democratic societies. Contemporary demands for recognition such as Kondabolu's documentary betray the need for belonging to the Enlightenment center by demanding that the excluded be allowed into the center as particulars that are part of or constituent of the whole. This is far from a radical assertion of self-confident identity. It asks "good" brown men to abstract themselves from "bad" brown men if they are to gain a seat at the table of History.

VII. EXPLODING THE ARCHIVE

Shadia in "The Museum" and Stéphane in *Gadjo dilo* withdraw themselves from the need to belong in the universal. Their acts announce their rejections of the archive as History. If Shadia destroys the archive by entering it from the outside, then Stéphane, the outsider turned insider, refuses the archive from within. In doing so, he dismantles his identity within the historical narrative of the white savior, that is, the one who brings the native other inside the fold of History. Unlike those soldiers, priests, and hunters whose actions in Africa ensured Africa's inscription in the archival space of the museum, Stéphane erases his documentation of the Roma to curtail them from being written into (Western) History.

To be outside the archive or to withdraw from the archive is not tantamount to resistance. This logic of resistance is only Romantic, as such quintessentially fantastic. Lacan is adamant about the fact that there is no existence outside the symbolic. But, hypothetically speaking, what does it mean to withdraw or refuse the symbolic? What does it *really* mean to be truly universal and truly free? To be outside is to be *the* Nothing or to realize fully the condition of being (non-)human. To be nothing or exist without inscription in the symbolic suggests that the subject is excluded from the demand of shared positives (identity) realized only via negated absolutes (the logic of the Phallus). The narratives discussed in this chapter disclose the truth of analysis—unravel as false those imaginaries that appear to bring together disparate elements into harmony and expose elements as inscrutably singular in existence but impotent together. In other words, dispose of the fantasy that the archive constitutes the quilting point guaranteeing social link (Žižek 2006a, 111, 116).

If Shadia withdraws herself from the archive after experiencing erasure within it, then Stéphane destroys the archive after realizing the fallacy of imagining the archive as fulfilling. In the final scene of the film, Gatlif returns his audiences to the exact same spot where the film began—the milestone on the side of the road, the electric poles lined up like ancient crucifixes, except this time Stephane is not on foot and Sabina is accompanying him. Audiences see

Sabina wake up inside the car and look curiously out of the window. She sees Stéphane dancing, his reflection appearing on the glass window almost superimposed on Sabina's face, and a queer smile spreads across her face. Before audiences can understand the reason behind Sabina's smile—is she amused to see Stéphane dance or does she realize that Stéphane has at last transformed from being a "*gadjo dilo*" to being a Roma?—the film ends, leaving us contemplating the meaning of Sabina's smile, Stéphane's burying of the tapes, and even, possibly, the entire film. I claim that Stéphane's refusal to archive corresponds with the film's unsatisfactory ending insofar as both establish the impossibility of exhaustively knowing the truth or the other. Just as audiences cannot fully know Stéphane, similarly Stéphane too cannot know the Roma.

What of communication? Is cross-cultural communication possible when intersubjective understanding is suspect? The fundamental discovery of psychoanalysis attests the singularity of each being. Singularity is what makes every individual distinct from all other individuals, it is the "nonrelational excess" or nonbeing that persists "beyond all social predicates, taxonomies, generalizations, and economies of comparison [and] the logic of...cultural systems of exchange" that construct identities on the basis of imaginary differences weighed out in a symbolic value system (Ruti 2012, 1–2, Santner 2005, 96; cited in Ruti). This means the archive can never fully inscribe the other. Nor is there any possibility of authentic or real communication. Something always escapes communication between two subjects thereby requiring that intersubjective communication is mediated by fantasies. As such, no communication ever hits the mark. What we wish is not what we desire. And what we desire does not drive our being.

FOUR

Fictions of Katherine Boo's Creative Non-Fiction, *or* The Unbearable Alterity of the Other

I. POSTCOLONIAL STUDIES IN THE GLOBAL ERA

As I argue in the introduction of this book, the dissipation of postcolonial studies in the global present results from its failure to constitutively embrace theory. Regardless of claims to the contrary, I believe returning to theory is essential for (the survival of) the discipline. When Fanonian binaries *appear* to have been totally overwritten by neoliberal rhetoric of fluid, networked, and/or entangled identities, the future of postcolonial studies depends on the discipline's ability to theoretically adapt itself to interrogating the lingering "aftereffects of imperial, colonial, and neocolonial rule" in the meshed present (Mezzadra and Rahola 2006, n.p.; Young 2012, 20).

Chapters in this second section of the book, that is, chapters 4, 5, and the conclusion, are devoted to interrogating neoliberal discourses about and representations of the Other. I choose neoliberal discourses over emergent global fascisms because I consider the former to be more deceptive compared to the latter. Unlike conservative discourses, which haven't evolved much beyond their nineteenth-century origins and, as a result, are sadly obvious, unmistakably patent, and without imagination, liberal discourses reflect close knowledge of global politics and colonial and decolonial histories, and consequently are adept at masking their gestures of Othering and subject-making. Supported by the climate of feelgood multiculturalism, neoliberal subject-making hides in plain sight masquerading as ideologically opposed to all forms of discriminatory practices. A white supremacist standing on Main Street spouting indecencies toward refugees, women, and people of color is as much a problem as the tolerant multiculturalist in a Starbucks who, sipping her overpriced beverage, gushingly advocates the need to *welcome* refugees. Both suffer from a sense of emancipated sovereignty that positions them above the minority other so that they both think they have the right to either demand the latter's expulsion from society or invite them to the dinner table (provided the other is willing to learn table manners). For "to insist that you cannot enter my drawing room at all and to insist that you are welcome to enter if you are civilized, wear a suit, know how to use a knife and fork" rehearse the same assumption of subject sovereignty (Menon 2010, n.p.).

In Robert Young's passionate defense of postcolonial studies I visualize an invitation, nay, a plea for theoretically revising the discipline. Speaking about the continued relevance of postcolonial studies in the global present, Young writes:

> [P]eoples [and] cultures still suffer from the long-lingering aftereffects of imperial, colonial, and neocolonial rule, albeit in contemporary forms such as economic globalization. Analysis of such phenomena *requires shifting conceptualizations,* but it *does not necessarily require the regular production of new theoretical paradigms*: the issue is rather to locate the hidden rhizomes of colonialism's historical reach, of what remains invisible, unseen, silent, or unspoken. In a sense, postcolonialism has always been about the ongoing life of residues, living remains, lingering legacies. (2012, 20–21; emphases added)

If we overlook for the moment Young's opinion that no *new theoretical paradigms* are required to investigate *the hidden rhizomes of colonialism's historical reach,* we read in his statement a demand for reconnecting postcolonial studies to contemporary political truths. Specifically, it asks that we engage with the residues or remainders of society; the other—excluded, expelled, and excised— are no longer existing on the margins, but have been reduced to the status of invisible trails in our neoliberal societies. Today, the other subsists in the shadows, barely noticed and rarely represented as they silently toil for the upkeep of our comfortable lives while dreaming of accomplishing a similar life of fortune in the future. Considered abject or leftovers from the previous decades these populations are commonly charged with cleaning the trash our neoliberal societies accumulate through their daily consumptions. Floating populations of disposable labor, these others lack both sustained spatial attachment and social recognition: they are the *walking dead*—the rural and urban poor; the indigenous pushed out of ancestral lands now occupied by mining corporations; the refugee or immigrant as a *thing* of pity or derision—they all exist in the Fanonian zone of nonbeing. They are often fungible data but only inherit identities, often transferable, that are granted to them. Manual scavenger this week, construction laborer the next, night guard at the mall the week after, these precariats at best have a tenuous position in society and almost always no identity. Postcolonial studies must connect to these wretched souls; it needs to redraw critical attention to the contemporary (non-)existences of these "residues" and question the logic or laws responsible for reducing the previously marginalized to the status of *traces* in the global present. But we need to avoid claiming the high moral and spiritual ground when connecting to these others. This means we should interrogate the ideological functions of neoliberal humanitarianism, charity, and empathy when reading, writing, or speaking about these others. We should strive to understand the fantasmatic approximation of these others in neoliberal discourse as well as the inadequacy of neoliberal discourse in fully knowing or controlling these excluded others. These irreducible others haunt discourse, forcing repeated assertions of authority against what these others disclose as the immanent condition of society: namely, that a radical antagonism or impossibility of social (non-) relations is constitutive of the social. These extimité others are physical manifestations of this radical antagonism.

I agree with Young: Postcolonial studies must reconceptualize the notion of the other (Young 2012, 22). But can this be done without theory as he seems to suggest (ibid., 20–21)? I might be biased, but Young himself contradicts his own claim against theory when he encourages us to think *theoretically* about the other:

> The *time has come for postcolonial scholars to rethink the category of the other* according to Levinas's later positions, or according to the arguments of Jean-Luc Nancy, Giorgio Agamben, and others that alterity is not something produced as a form of exclusion but *fundamental to being itself,* which must always involve "being singular plural" from the very first. (39; emphasis mine)

Young here is admitting what I note in my previous chapters, namely, that postcolonial studies must move beyond understanding the constitution of the self against a symbolically negated other to identifying the self as constituted via "a relationship with what can be only 'named' radical alterity (and thus necessarily effaced)" (Spivak 1999, 424). It should be noted that the reason this other can be *only named as radical alterity* is because there is no other way to identify its otherness from within the symbolic order. For what constitutes the self is so beyond the purview of the symbolic that it leaves us with no choice but to approximate: I have no way for knowing what the other is, but let's assume it is evil. Without associating the other to such random and total depravity, it becomes impossible for us to construct our subjective sovereignty. We need to replace the idea of the other as symbolic difference—the other is all those things I am not or cannot be—with a more theoretically rigorous concept of the other as excessive to the symbolic order yet constitutive of the social (Rothenberg 2010, 28).[1] One of the tasks of the postcolonial critic in the present is to underline the ambivalence in neoliberal discourses when it comes to this other. Like the hysteric, the postcolonialist too should focus on this other which enunciates a dilemma in neoliberal discourses resulting from its exasperation with and failure to approximate the other through encyclopedic knowledge.

The two chapters in this section, followed by the conclusion, address some of these contemporary issues. In this chapter, I focus on Katherine Boo's *Behind the Beautiful Forevers: Life, Death, and Hope in a Mumbai Undercity* (2012). Though Boo's work is widely appraised for its critique of neoliberalism and globalization, I argue that her text performs the exact opposite function. It (1) mystifies the real effects of neocolonialism suffered by the urban poor in the global south; (2) distracts attention from the repurposing of Western subjectivity in the context of anxieties provoked by globalization in the West; and (3) allows audiences to critique neoliberalism without having to directly engage in serious activism. Far from being an empathic investigation into the limits of globalization or an earnest attempt to even hear the precariat speak, the book's primary ideological objective is to sustain the continued enjoyment of Otherness without needing to subscribe to conservative beliefs or risk appearing conservative. I contend that Boo's humanizations of poverty and people in poverty constitute the perfect gestures of culturalizing the politics of globalization by strategically redrawing the phantasmatic screen of third world abjection over the real conditions of global inequality suffered the third world. In what follows, I start by listing some palpable reasons for why Boo's book appears to extend a postcolonial critique of neoliberalism before moving on to ask more fundamental questions regarding how this text is complicit in continuing the production of a sovereign West. Or, more specifically, what is the source of enjoyment (*jouissance*) for global readers in contemporary narratives that on first glance appear as radical, self-critical, and liberal.

II. THE FICTIONS OF KATHERINE BOO'S NONFICTION

Behind the Beautiful Forevers: Life, Death, and Hope in a Mumbai Undercity (2012, hereafter BF), is a highly acclaimed and critically appraised work of creative nonfiction about the lives of Mumbai's Annawadi slum dwellers. Closely following their daily struggles, the American investigative reporter Katherine Boo documents in this book the unheard stories of India's poorest of the poor; or, those left behind in the country's meteoric rise as a global economic power.

On the surface, *Beautiful Forevers* is not a typical show-and-tell: it does not seek to present India as an impoverished sinkhole. In fact, Boo makes a conscious effort to steer clear of, to wit, dismantle, routine Western habits of representing third world poverty. As a conscious liberal subject of the West, Boo takes the responsibility of documenting lives in poverty seriously. As with her prior journalistic work with New York City's poor, here too she methodically avoids speaking on behalf of the urban subaltern. She acts as witness to the lives of these people and presents to her readers only what she sees firsthand, without any fictional embellishments, judgment, or ideological interference.[2] Departing from the West's bipolar representations of poverty—poverty as either sentimentalized or sensationalized, "mythic" or "pathetic" (and always existing outside the borders of North America)—*Beautiful Forevers* focuses on real-life characters as they strive to escape poverty through legal and illegal entrepreneurial labor—sifting garbage for recycling to stealing from the nearby airport to prostitution (BF, 249).[3] Using a third-person omniscient voice, Boo foregrounds the crippling poverty, bureaucratic corruption, and syndicated crime that crisscross the lives of India's urban poor, the denizens of India's "undercity," a term she uses for urban slums. In writing about these remainders of global India, Boo shares with the world stories of globalization not commonly told—human voices not heard and human faces made absent from the spectacular narratives of globalizing India (think Bollywood).

But it is not just its content that makes *Beautiful Forevers* such a successful work. Appreciation should be reserved equally for its form. Boo's choice of the genre, narrative voice, and the strategic rhetorical arrangements adds credibility to her objective reportage. In effect, the book is not a first-world author's prying look into the third-world heart of darkness, the "Black Hole" that is India, but an astute and responsible perspective on what has gone wrong with neoliberalism in India, and this builds into a demand from the author that globalized India bring the excluded back into its fold of recently gained national prosperity.

The Fiction of Form

Beautiful Forevers is a work of creative non-fiction. This genre promises unbiased representation of reality with a reasonable dollop of entertainment spread throughout. Creative non-fiction is "fact-based writing that combines the story elements of fiction with the truth-telling elements of traditional journalism," explains Nicola Goc (2008, 281). Or, to skeptics, the recipe for best-sellers (Sharlet 2013). If the book's marketing as a work of creative non-fiction automatically conditions readers to expect a more than ordinary verisimilitude from the book, its obvious fictionlike qualities—novelistic narrative cadence and Dickensian characters—or the fact that in delivering the "truth" the book *still* reads like fiction, only makes it a bigger success (ibid.).

Boo's choice to write in the third person instead of the first person reinforces the book's claim of objectivity. The first-person narrator, Boo tells us, commonly ends up privileging the narrator over the subject matter being narrated. Her decision to use an omniscient third-person narrator ensures that her characters remain center stage. It is important, however, to note that this is a significant departure from genre protocols. Creative non-fiction habitually uses the first-person narrator. In choosing differently, though, Boo could be borrowing from literary journalism, a close relative of creative non-fiction, which *Beautiful Forevers* also resembles, and this relation also makes sense given Boo's extensive career as a journalist for *The Washington Post*. Her decision to not use the first-person voice also echoes Truman Capote's rejection of the intrusive "I" in his writings. A pioneer of contemporary literary journalism and the author of *In Cold Blood*, Capote too claims that the first-person narrative voice forces attention away from the story in preference for the narrator. Many, including Tom Wolfe, agree.[4] Wolfe would even go on to identify the third-person point of view as one of the four devices critical for giving non-fiction its power of immediacy. These are: (1) writing as if witnessing people's lives;

(2) recording dialogues and exchanges in full; (3) writing from a third-person point of view; and, lastly, (4) recording every scene in detail so as to provide readers with the symbolic details of people's status in life. These, Wolfe writes in *New Journalism*, make a work closer to reality—more real and most realistic (1972, 31–32). There's no doubt that *Beautiful Forevers* stands out as a testament to these aims.

But I find Boo's efforts to abstract herself from the narrative deeply symptomatic of her awareness of being an outsider, a foreigner, alienated from the slum dwellers by class as well as race. Her historical determination as a first-world white woman visiting the "third world" affects both her perspective on the Annawadi residents and their reception of her. We notice this hesitation in her "authors note," which she appends at the end of the work in preference over a "preface" appearing at the beginning, thus, again, clearly disclosing her decision to "speak" after her characters have spoken. In this "author's note," she writes, "I felt I couldn't write, not being Indian, not knowing the languages, lacking a lifetime of immersion in the context. I also doubted my ability to handle monsoon and slum conditions" (BF 248). But impatience over seeing routine "snapshots of Indian squalor" and a freak accident that landed her in the ER finally convinced Boo to commit the next four years of her life to "follow[ing] the inhabitants of a single, unexceptional slum...to see who got ahead and who didn't, and why, as India prospered" (ibid., 247–49). But never once in these four years did she let her outsiderness compromise the objectivity of her undertaking. "I tried to compensate for my limitations the same way I do in unfamiliar American territories: by time spent, attention paid, documentation secured, accounts cross-checked," she writes (ibid., 249). Cognizant of the risks involved in a Westerner's overinterpretation of non-Western cultural conventions, she relied on "more than three thousand public records" and employed local translators to ensure the accuracy of her observations (ibid., 250–51). Doubling up on this, she also cautions her American readers against conflating Annawadi with India. She writes, "Annawadi is not representative of a country as huge and diverse as India [and] it is not a neat encapsulation of the state of poverty and opportunity in the twenty-first century world" (ibid., 253). Aware of the West's past and continuing (mis)representations of India's poverty, Boo makes a sincere effort to ensure that her work remains factual in its descriptions of poverty without becoming a metonym of the West's privileged viewpoint. Indeed, as one critic puts it, Boo lays things out as they really are and hopes that policymakers will notice (Rustin 2012). *Forevers* is a conscientious intervention. At least that's how it impresses Amartya Sen.

What Makes Amartya Sen Happy?

Notwithstanding Amartya Sen's repeated warnings to successive Indian governments about their unquestioning embrace of neoliberal market economy, governments since 1993 have made neoliberalism the cornerstone of national policies. As a direct result, India's public sectors are on life support and its agricultural sector thoroughly decimated: in spite of being one of the fastest growing economies in the world, with the third-largest army and the third-largest GDP (PPA), India today ranks one hundredth on the list of 119 countries with the most unnourished, undernourished, and malnutritioned children.[5] No wonder Amartya Sen has been angry and sad because his warnings went unheeded, and today, like many educated intellectuals in the country, he has found himself sidelined by the current Hindu fascist government.[6]

Boo's book however makes Sen happy. Sen writes, *Beautiful Forevers* is

> a beautiful account, told through real-life stories, of the sorrows and joys, the anxieties and stamina, in the lives of the precarious and powerless in urban India whom a booming country has failed to absorb and integrate. A brilliant book that simultaneously informs, agitates, angers, inspires, and instigates. (Penguin Random House Webpage)

Sen is spot on; Boo's narrative is an honest account of the plight of India's poor: *The precarious and powerless in urban India whom a booming country has failed to absorb and integrate.* And Sen hopes that this best-seller's success will spread its message to readers across the globe.

Pulitzer Prize–winning author and social activist Junot Diaz echoes Sen's admiration for Boo's moral courage. Boo, he states, tells the story about the price India has paid for globalization. "She humanizes with all the force of literature the impossible lives of the people at bottom of our pharaonic global order, and details with a journalist's unsparing exactitude the absolute suffering that undergirds India's economic boom" (2012).

Sen and Diaz are not the only ones. Barring Martha Nussbaum's review of the book in the *Times Literary Supplement* and Jeff Sharlet's commentary "Like a Novel: The Marketing of Literary Nonfiction," published in the Summer 2013 issue of *VQR: A National Journal of Literature and Discussion*, every single review of Boo's book only praises the writer and the book. Featuring in such prestigious venues as the *New York Times*, the *Guardian*, *O: The Oprah Magazine*, *The New Yorker*, *The Wall Street Journal*, and *Newsweek*, Boo's unembellished documentation of reality, her humanist vision, and the Dickensian quality of her work have only found rave praise. Shashi Tharoor, the Indian Parliamentarian and author of *The Great Indian Novel* (1989), captures these sentiments in the opening paragraphs of his review for *The Washington Post*:

> This is an astonishing book. It is astonishing on several levels: as a worm's-eye view of the "undercity" of one of the world's largest metropolises; as an intensely reported, deeply felt account of the lives, hopes and fears of people traditionally excluded from literate narratives; as a story that truly hasn't been told before, at least not about India and not by a foreigner. But most of all, it is astonishing that it exists at all...the poor people who are usually, in other accounts, treated as a collectivity, the object of economists' analyses, politicians' promises and ideologues' outrage. In "Behind the Beautiful Forevers," Boo humanizes them as individuals with their own stories to tell.
>
> Overcoming the obstacles to effective reporting posed by her class, gender, ethnicity and language, Boo follows their lives and experiences in an effort to understand the problems of poverty from the bottom up. The result is a searing account, in effective and racy prose, that reads like a thrilling novel but packs a punch Sinclair Lewis might have envied. (2012, n.p.)

Indeed, Boo's resolve to assess nothing at face value and to be cautious about inscribing subaltern life into mainstream rhetoric is immensely praiseworthy. Yet in spite of all her claims about truthful recording and veritable narration, and her sincere wish to give voice to the voiceless without speaking on their behalf, what does Boo's text actually accomplish?

What if far from being a sincere investigation into the limits of globalization or an earnest attempt to hear the silent precariat speak, the primary ideological objective of Boo's book is the obfuscation of the real conditions responsible for global inequality? What if instead of opening Western eyes to the pitiful condition of life in India's slums, Boo's humanization of poverty constitutes the perfect gesture for culturalizing politics via the redrawing of the phantasmatic screen of third-world abjection? What if this attempt to aesthetically capture the excluded-included of a globalized civil society doubly rehearses the negation of the other? Boo's book attempts to discursively erase the other that lingers after aggregating or singularizing identities into imagined communities. The other gets erased once more in this process of aesthetic representation. To me, though, the humanist moral drama crafted by Boo to contain or represent the other only gestures toward the frustration over and the need for filling in the void represented by the urban precariat as the excessive other. The urban precariat is *the Thing*, hence beyond representation, excluded from structured discourses of being and becoming, and removed from both routine experiences of difference and systematized philosophical thinking about alterity. Nothing attaches to this other, nothing captures it and nothing can ontologize its negativity. Unfortunately, this other is already always a part of the socius—it occupies experiential and documentary space but lacks positive identity. I fail to understand why many people misread Spivak's axiom that the subaltern is a position without identity. How much more does she have to say in order to establish a simple fact or truth about the subaltern. Namely, the subaltern does not exist. In the globalized metropolis, the subaltern is the urban precariat—she too occupies physical, visual, sensual, and other spaces but is always without an identity. We consume her just as we detest her. But mostly we do not wish to encounter her. For encountering her would push us toward her unbearable alterity. The subaltern names the excluded-included of the social. The urban precariat is an identifiable and positive avatar representing this antagonistic de-ontologized gap within our contemporary global societies.

Jeff Sharlet argues in "Like a Novel" that the formal arrangements of *Beautiful Forevers* are ideological, being specifically employed by Boo for her Western readers. Symptomatically, repeated emphasis on how the work reads *like a novel*, Sharlet claims, makes certain two things. First, that the book gains "readership far beyond the market share for true tales of relentless filth and poverty," and second, that it keeps readers at a safe distance from the stench and travesties of the said gruesome poverty. To "say that *Behind the Beautiful Forevers* is like a novel is to reassure the reader that the suffering documented on every page isn't what matters. It's the *experience*. The reader's, that is. This book will make you feel close to that suffering, but not too close" (2013, n.p.).

In other words, *Beautiful Forevers* allows readers to experience real conditions of poverty in the Global South without becoming too overwhelmed, uncomfortable, or shaken. This ensures that these readers are not pushed to question how capitalism is responsible for reducing so many people to poverty in a country often cited as one of globalization's success stories. Robert Pfaller has a term for appearing to take action (against social injustice) without really taking any action; he calls it "interpassivity" (cited in Žižek 2008a, 144n28). Interpassivity characterizes the global present, it allows liberals to feel good about participating in mostly pseudo-activism while allowing the undisrupted continuation of neoliberal economy.

This also happens to be Martha Nussbaum's critique of Boo. She claims that while Boo is passionate about "concrete social change," yet she offers no direction or agenda regarding the pursuit of such change. Nussbaum complains,

> If readers are to be steered in the direction of intelligent action aimed at change, the narrative journalist needs to give them not just sympathetic characters, but also historical and economic analysis. (2012, n.p.)

Two examples can be given to underline Nussbaum's charges. First, the book avoids discussing urban poverty as an epiphenomenon of imperialism, neocolonialism, and economic liberalization of Indian markets. Or, there is no unequivocal indictment of capitalism's role in dividing Indian society into the glossy overcity and a dank undercity. Second, the book remains silent about domestic efforts to end the slow violence of poverty and fight state-supported corporate takeover of indigenous ancestral lands. From NGO programs and student protests to armed Maoist insurrections, globalized India is witnessing a range of movements. While the respective causes for and the ideologies underwriting these endeavors are different, their fight is largely to eradicate poverty and against the corporatization of the country. Yet there exist almost no mention of these movements in the book; and these absences constitute the fictive core of Boo's non-fiction.[7]

I understand where Sen or Diaz might be coming from in their respective praises for Boo's book: India today crafts its own fantasies, and in recent years one such fantasy has been about the country's economic growth under globalization. In this context, it can be argued that Boo punctures the fantasy of "Shining India" by bringing to surface the hidden truths about India's globalization—relegated stories and faces and lives from India's undercities. But it can be also argued that while Boo's stated project is underwritten by the temporality of the global present, this story is part of a larger body of Western writing about India's slums that have historically constructed for readers in the West the fantasy of the third world as abject. It can be argued that Boo's work does not gain purchase from excluding the history of this colonial discourse but functions in the present as material practice responsible for sustaining by different means the fantasy that is the "third world." If we do not wish to shy away from this problematic, then, on the one hand, Boo's text must be read in relation to the long history of othering India, which has served to consolidate the image of the West as charitable and efficient. Correspondingly, on the other, we should also read Boo as engaging with a new set of representational practices which, while acknowledging India's rapid modernization, prefers to present this image in tight correspondence with the colonial lithograph of India's unchangeable poverty. Beyond these, if we wish to unravel how Boo's work masks the process of subject-making by adapting to the climate of the multicultural present, then we must heed Gayatri Spivak's critically astute observation regarding how the most radical criticisms of the West's excesses exist only in order to disguise claims of European sovereignty.[8] Today, we need to adduce another point to Spivak's hypothesis, namely, that representational critique alone is not effective for exposing the mechanisms of othering in the twenty-first century. If we are serious about extending our disciplinary roots into the present, we have to move from interrogating politics of (symbolic) difference to exploring the politics of (surplus) enjoyment.

In order to illustrate how this shift proves useful for analysis, I highlight below the lacks, limits, excisions, and assumptions in Boo's representation of the other. I identify this as standard postcolonial work. But, then, I pursue a reading of her book that extends beyond her politics of Othering by asking, What does her narrative really want? The answers will surprise.

III. READING BOO, POSTCOLONIALLY

Boo's realistic account of urban precariats living in poverty is not without lapses. Viewed closely with the intention of interrogating her representational politics, the following intriguing gaps come to the surface. Let me present them schematically, without any particular order.

1. *Globalization and neoliberalism remain unquestioned in the book.* Boo does not examine the relationship between global capital and class inequality shifting all blame for India's lingering poverty to the Indian government's inability to undertake a more managerial role in advancing globalization's benefits to the masses. Alongside, she blames India's newly minted rich middle class for being less charitable and not looking after their more unfortunate countrymen.

2. *Boo never admits that urban slums are essential to the successful running of globalized metropolises* such as Mumbai insofar as slums around the globe make available a flexible, non-permanent workforce necessary for servicing the upper surface or the visible side of global cities. Slums are not a result of inadequate globalization but essential to globalization.

3. *Boo encourages us to think how morality, electoral democracy, and the free media can help the urban poor escape poverty.* But she does not engage with questions about how morality, electoral democracy, and the media in India often collude with neoliberalism to keep the poor trapped in poverty.

Now let me elaborate these three points.

Beautiful Forevers unequivocally gives ground to globalization as an unimpeachable economic principle, blaming instead the inherent or systemic conditions of the Indian nation-state as responsible for social inequality. Among those responsible for the condition of the urban poor, Boo lists the three branches of local and central governments (the judiciary, the executive, and the legislative); the Indian education system; nongovernmental organizations (including Christian missionary charities); India's public health system; and the affluent middle class. Boo claims further that the failure of neoliberal policies in India is not a result of some lack in neoliberalism but, rather, due to the non-West's characteristic incapacity to change or reform itself. As she sees it, Indians prefer to avoid making systemic changes, settling instead for tweaking things in order to get stuff done. Neoliberalization of the economy required completely overhauling the old socialist system, to wit, the purging of socialism, but that did not happen or did not happen quickly enough. In her words: the "chaotic unpredictability of daily life" has helped "produce a nation of quick-witted, creative problem solvers," which in turn has aided India's short-term meteoric rise in the global scene, but in the absence of large-scale social and political reforms much remains still to be done (BF, 219). But nothing can happen unless the educated middle class steps in. Sadly not only are Indians guilty of taking short cuts for short-term gains, they also appear to lack adequate political conscious and/or are too indifferent or too lazy:

> In mid-May, the election results came in. The reform-minded elites had not turned out to vote, after all. Most of the incumbent parliamentarians were reelected, they returned the prime minister to office, and the radical improvements in governance promised before the voting were quietly shelved. (ibid., 233)

Readers get the impression here that the Indian educated elite's indifference to the democratic process sustained the political status quo and the slow pace of reforms. But is it okay to simplify the convictions of the Indian voter thus without first understanding the various regional and cultural complexities of Indian politics? There is nothing in the book that suggests that Boo has any idea about these complexities, let alone knows how Indian democracy works. She is satisfied as long as the ill effects of economic globalization are rendered specific to the East. To this end, *Beautiful Forevers* redraws the phantasmatic screen of the third world as marred by political chaos, lethargy and indifference. The government, the educated elite, and a general state of corruption and crime are responsible for the plight of India's urban poor. Thus, globalization and neoliberal economy remain free from critiques, and their inconsistencies are explained away in cultural rather than systemic terms.[9]

This lack of interest in examining the relationship between global capitalism and class inequality in India, her tendency to culturalize or pathologize Indian society, and a thorough disregard for subcontinental protest movements against global capitalism constitute the major *fictions* of Boo's narrative. *Beautiful Forevers* gives no indication of the role played by Euro-U.S. corporations and U.S. foreign policy in the creation of unequal wealth distribution—not one voice in the text questions the multinational corporations and the West's trade regulations as potential factors for poverty in India as the trickle-down hypothesis remains the unquestioned mainstay the entire book.

Boo's Wellsian imagination of globalized India as divided between an overcity and an undercity establishes an exclusive relationship between the rich, globalized Mumbai and a putrefying ecology existing invisibly inside. While Boo finds this structural geography useful for narrating the story of the "other" India, her narrative (deliberately) misses an important point. The undercity exists not in opposition to or in spite of the rich globalized overcity but as its bulwark. As a source of cheap labor, slums are essential to the successful existence of globalized metropolises such as Mumbai. Simply put: the undercity and the overcity exist in a symbiotic relationship bounded by the arrangements of the urban space. The flexible, nonpermanent workforce made available by Annawadi and other such "unintended cities" around the globe is a product of the current dispensation of capitalism (Jai Sen 1996). Globalization has, on the one hand, dispossessed the rural populations by destroying traditional farming practices, and, on the other, it has herded these rural dispossessed into the slums of urban India to exploit them as disposable labor. The dispossessed, flocking to the cities in hopes of becoming rich, of getting a fresh start, do not realize that they will always remain on the sidelines of this global economy, as the governing principle of globalization as an economic practice is to ensure the accumulation of wealth in the coffers of a select few.[10] The undercity in a global metropolis is the excluded-included—the one not recognized by yet indispensable for the routine existence of the metropolis. It is at once a disgusting excess within the narrative of India's global success and also that without which India's globalization would have remained incomplete.

Boo, though, is nonchalant about issues such as the forced migration of rural populations. If she thought any differently, she would have naturally probed deeper into the causes of urban poverty and drawn out the inescapable links between the acquisition of India's rich agricultural lands by MNCs and the consequent depredation of the country's villages. And that rare instance when Boo does talk about the grievous situation in Indian villages—farmers' suicides, drought, and crop failures—she stays the course, finding fault with local government. It does not strike her that Monsanto may be playing truant.[11]

Boo's argument that nothing is going to change in India is strengthened by yet another strategic elision—she makes no mention of the individuals and nongovernmental institutions protesting against the role of global corporations in today's India. Ongoing "democratic" movements such as the *Narmada Bachao Andolan,* the protests against Vedanta Corporation and the Kundakulam Nuclear plant, the works of filmmakers such as Anand Patwardhan and writer-activist Arundhati Roy, as well as the opposition from a dwindling constitutional Left and the Maoist-Naxalites operating in the "Red Corridor" of the country receive relatively little attention in her book. In the context of this absence, her complaints about the Indian government makes India appear as an elite bourgeois oligarchy and not a multiparty democracy. We read, for instance, that the "parliamentary opposition to the future of a landmark India–United States nuclear treaty was being softened by trunkful of cash" (BF, 138). In reality, it was the Indian parliamentary Left that threatened to withdraw support from the coalition government if the treaty went ahead. Notwithstanding this threat from the Left, the treaty was eventually signed not because the Indian Left was bought over by the centrist-socialist Indian National Congress that was in government at that time but because the Indian Left did not have sufficient numbers in both Houses of the Parliament to effectively make good on their threat. Notwithstanding, they did withdraw support, and this decision has since proved suicidal, as the Left has performed catastrophically in the subsequent elections (2009, 2014, 2019). Worse still, this ideological battle between the Left and the Indian National Congress actually aided the fascist Hindu Bharatiya Janata Party (BJP) to come to power in the 2014 elections (and again in 2019). We never get this "political" story from Boo. We never know whether in criticizing the slow reform of the left-of-center coalition government she was actually hoping that the Hindu fascists would rather be at the helm. The BJP, who are pro-neoliberal but right-wing conservatives in matters of caste, culture, and religion, have since coming to power in 2014 purposefully eroded the fabric of India's ancient republican cultures by demanding unrequited obeisance for privatization and a religio-cultural exceptionalism akin to Nazi ideals. These complexities and risks are missing from Boo's book. Instead her "India" is starkly divided between the rich and the poor, the Hindu and the Muslim (with the mandatory nod to the Dalits thrown in between), and, of course, the overcity and the undercity. This "India" is the legacy of British colonial histories, of Orientalists and James Mill, who divided and packaged the heterogenous political cultures of South Asia into neat divisions of Hindu, Muslim, and Christian social histories.

It therefore comes as a pleasant surprise when Boo concedes to briefly admit into her narrative two snippets of the Maoist-Naxalite movement in India. The movement finds brief mentions: one paragraph on page 139 and one sentence on page 148. These two instances are supposed to tell us about the Indian Maoists, who have been at war against "capitalism and the Indian state" for the last fifty years. Boo writes, "Deprived of their land and historical livelihoods by large-scale corporations and government modernization projects, they'd helped revive a forty-year-old movement of Maoist revolutionaries" (ibid., 139). *They helped revive!* Boo doesn't tell her readers who "they" are, namely, that the rank and file of the Maoist guerilla army is made up of India's poorest of the poor, and that the Maoists are fighting against the systemic oppression of India's tribals and rural poor by class-conscious, casteist central and state governments and their comprador MNCs. Then there is the usual lack of historical knowledge or consciousness about this "forty-year-old" Maoist movement and/or corresponding attempts to genealogically locate the roots of this movement in South Asia's long-standing agrarian revolts against the British Empire and thereafter the big landowners and, more recently, against state acquisition of farmlands for industrial development. Boo is content presenting Maoists as "rural India's problem" (ibid., 148).[12]

This is symptomatic of Boo's general inability to perceive how the problem of the urban poor is integrally connected to India's colonial past and the activities of U.S.-led MNCs in the global present. In fact, throughout all this her only cause of concern is for the violence unleashed by the Maoist insurgents: "This summer, the Maoists had been especially *productive*...they'd sunk a boat full of military commandos, killing thirty-eight, and bombed a police van, killing twenty-one more" (ibid., 139; my emphasis). This is Boo-style "creative" nonfiction at its best—in one stroke of the pen, the real reasons behind the Maoist movement are creatively rendered devious and the seriousness of the Maoist insurrection against the Indian nation state identified as frivolous. Her use of the word *productive* suggests that while, indeed, scarcity of food may have banded the starving Indian villagers together, this band of self-identified Maoists are now productive only in racking up the body count of India's patriotic defense forces. Not only that. Let us don the rhetorician's hat and expose Boo's use of the past perfect—she uses "had stopped believing" and "they'd helped revive" to describe the passivity of the Indian farmer to years of government neglect, corporate takeovers of their hereditary lands, and the resulting (re)birth of the Maoist movement. By contrast, Maoist action is described with the present continuous—*killing*. The Maoists are a vicious force of death involved in carnage of innocents, relentlessly killing, massacring, and plundering the wealth of the nation: Boo articulates here the same rhetoric that Indian governments of the last fifty years, from centrist-socialists to Hindu fascists, have all urged. Maybe in their unequivocal concerns over this movement we can discern the symptom of the global liberal middle-class. No wonder, then, that Boo's concern with directionless Maoist violence is shared by India's burgeoning middle class. To the latter, Maoists are morally despicable—Maoist attacks on police and paramilitary camps a matter of great consternation, as these directly affect foreign investment in the country. In our liberal anxiety over violence, we forget that for these Maoists, who are actually one and the same as the rural poor, violence remains the only option to make their voices heard. Maoist violence is not simply about seeking redress from government apathy, it is, rather, about constitutively remaking reality for India's poor (Giri 2012).

One has to only pitch Arundhati Roy's "Walking with the Comrades" (2011) against Boo's creative non-fiction to witness the full measure of the latter's hypocrisy and to bare her ideological agenda. As Roy rightly infers, it is convenient for liberals (such as Boo) to believe the Maoists are India's rural problem because their efforts are geared toward sustaining a liberal fantasy about Maoists as violent, antidemocratic, and killers. And if Boo's rhetorical use of verbs establishes this very image of the Maoists, then by ignoring the long history of tribal insurrections against colonial and postcolonial oppressions she further conditions her readers to think of Maoists as an anomaly in an era of peace, tolerance, and, therefore, an impediment to democratic dialogue and the growth of the Indian nation. But Roy reminds us:

> It's easier on the liberal conscience to believe that the war in the forests is a war between the Government of India and the Maoists, who

call elections a sham, Parliament a pigsty and have openly declared their intention to overthrow the Indian State. It's convenient to forget that tribal people in Central India have a history of resistance that predates Mao by centuries. (That's a truism of course. If they didn't, they wouldn't exist.) The Ho, the Oraon, the Kols, the Santhals, the Mundas and the Gonds have all rebelled several times, against the British, against zamindars and moneylenders. The rebellions were cruelly crushed, many thousands killed, but the people were never conquered. Even after Independence, tribal people were at the heart of the first uprising that could be described as Maoist, in Naxalbari village in West Bengal (where the word Naxalite—now used interchangeably with "Maoist"—originates). Since then, Naxalite politics has been inextricably entwined with tribal uprisings, which says as much about the tribals as it does about the Naxalites. (2011, 51)

A violent state cannot be countered with nonviolence. State violence perpetrated in the name of globalization and modernity can be resisted only with (Maoist) ethical revolutionary violence. At stake is the need for making present an alternative sociosymbolic to the masses. This would be a sociosymbolic where experiences of difference will not underwrite the logic of violent exclusions but where all (non-)relations would be equally welcome into the socius. The problem is that no previous endeavor has proven fruitful in accomplishing this goal, and there is a growing disapproval of any form of violence in the neoliberal global present. Though right-wing violence is condemned, it is often with the refrain, "Oh! What can we do?" or, "That's how they are." But leftist violence is, ironically, unequivocally opposed by conservatives and liberals alike. They both argue that there cannot be any violent reaction against (licensed) state or state endorsed right-wing actions. In this cultural milieu, it is indeed difficult to offer direct support to the Maoists anywhere in the world. But the reason for India's middle class not supporting the Maoists is a no-brainer: doing so will also mean acting against their immediate class interest. Yet for the rural multitude expelled from their land and labor, the Maoist movement is the only alternative to "another life." Viewed from their perspective, the violent movement is necessary for (*coercive*) *rearrangement of desires*, that is, to decouple our fixation in neoliberal desires and imagine a different future for contemporary India.[13] Our unimpeachable faith in the messianic powers of neoliberalism—we believe the system will eventually usher in social equality and rescue those in poverty—and our reluctance to admit discussions of other alternatives amplifies Žižek's point about ideology: *ideology in the present is not something that is imposed on us, but it determines our social relations and something we learn to enjoy* (Žižek 2012a, n.p.). The fact that ideology today sustains our social relations through enjoyment makes critiquing or disbanding ideology doubly difficult. Why would we risk our social life and renounce enjoyment by opposing neoliberalism? Recall the 2015 *Saturday Night Live* Thanksgiving skit featuring Adele's song "Hello": this skit illustrates our contemporary relation to ideology very well. Adele's song as ideology successfully unites differently opinionated family members across a Thanksgiving table. We prefer not to alienate friends and family. But we also do not wish to sacrifice the various enjoyments offered by neoliberal societies—from interpassivity in social issues to pursuing feelgood multiculturalism—neoliberal societies allow us to remain secured in our privileged bourgeois cocoons. This is the best deal for the middle class. Hence the need for violence. Only a cut can save us today.

Boo writes that the Annawadi slum dwellers are convinced that the free market and not revolutionary politics will liberate them from their impoverished conditions. These precariats believe the overcity rich getting richer eventually benefits them. Even after experiencing marginalization over generations, they retain unflinching faith in electoral democracy, the power of information (media), and the judiciary. In spite of all their experiences being contrary, they continue to believe that eventually it would be possible to transcend their class position. It is not that they are brainwashed or deceived into believing in the fiction of globalization, but more simply that theirs is a classic case of the subaltern lacking class-consciousness. The urban poor fail to make the required connections between their impoverished condition and the riches of globalization they witness everyday while serving the overcity. They do not recognize that the economic chimera they so desperately chase is in fact their grave enemy. Boo's book normalizes this outlook: herself a staunch believer in democracy, activist journalism, and the benevolence of the judiciary in liberal and free societies, Boo also supports their beliefs, thus reinforcing the ideology of the free press, unbiased judiciary, and democracy as absolute. The book does not tell readers that India's urban poor not only lack class consciousness but also have resigned their fates to the dream. Unlike their rural counterparts, who in recent years have marched by the thousands, put the capital city under siegelike conditions demanding government action in reviving farming and protecting the lives of farmers, or the indigenous who have joined the Maoists to directly challenge the state, the urban precariats appear to have become completely inactive, resigned to their zombielike state of existence while still hoping for emancipation. In living for an impossible dream, they have grown indifferent to how they are dying every day in camplike conditions. Where did Boo go wrong? Well, if she really wished to critically expose the condition of these bare lives, instead of writing about what the Annawadi residents are doing to get out of poverty, she ought to have underlined what they are not doing to get out of poverty. Namely, they are not challenging the neoliberalization of the Indian economy, the empty promises of globalization, and the unchecked privatization of farmland and the wanton gentrification of India's metropolises. These are some of the main reason for their depredation.

The urban subaltern is an anomaly: a precariat. They are necessary for doing most of the dirty work of keeping the city glitzy, but they themselves are not allowed to set foot inside the glare of the globalized upper world. But they are not just disposable labor; these dregs of society exist as the radical negative core of the globalized metropolis. In the words of Žižek,

> [The] "rabble" in the modern civil society is not an accidental result of social mismanagement, inadequate government measures, or simple economic bad luck: the inherent structural dynamic of civil society necessarily gives rise to a class which is excluded from its benefits (work, personal dignity, etc.)—a class deprived of elementary human rights, and therefore also exempt from duties toward society, an element within civil society which negates its universal principle, a kind of "non-Reason inherent in Reason itself"—in short, *its symptom*. (2008a, 161; emphasis in original)

The emancipation of this "mob" cannot be logically accomplished from within the parameters of electoral democracy and never simply via our empathy for them. In fact, both electoral democracy and our kindness are killing them slowly, while the liberal media and the judiciary are burying them in the deep end. Simply put, the precariat will not cease to exist unless capitalism comes to end. Their liberation pivots on the absolute and categorical termination of capitalism. It is only by thoroughly laying to ruin the system responsible for producing the precariat and not seeking to make use or manipulate the system for temporary relief that their oppression can end. The characters described by Boo wish to escape their oppressive conditions but are not conscious that such a journey requires them to wake up from their dream of "Shining India." Emancipation will require they align with the Maoists who, as Saroj Giri perceptively notes, represent a small minority's attempt to accomplish an absolute radical revisioning of the socius. Emancipation therefore hinges on action reducing life as we know it to a life in nature, where the playing field is leveled, and each of us without exception has to begin again the experiments of society against a life in Nature that is "solitary, poor, nasty, brutish and short."

Boo *prettifies the Other* (Žižek 2009, 165). Keeping the real of poverty under wraps, she packages abjection for safe consumption for her readers in the West. In addition, her narrative rewrites the third-world Other for the global present. Boo chooses as her subject the topic of poverty in India, which at the very moment of enunciation finds a readymade framework of references and allusions and memes from the long history of European colonialism, and then in the specific context of Boo's text we witness the rehearsals of longstanding habitual rhetorical excisions and accentuations of the other for resituating the latter within a moral humanist universe of European provenance imagined for the global present. Within this new universe, the Others are to be loved, admired, and helped but never despised. Yet in presenting the Other as incapable of direct agency, Boo re-anchors Enlightenment rhetoric of reform in collusion with contemporary forms of displaced Christian dogma of charity: *Beautiful Forevers* gives Western readers the opportunity to both feel pity for and embark on self-reclaiming charities aimed at rescuing India's (overlooked) slum dwellers from their marginal conditions. In this, *Beautiful Forevers* repurposes the same politically correct gestures of feeling concerned about, for instance, patronizing the Other, which a recent slew of Hollywood films can be also charged of doing: *Born into Brothels* (2004), *Slumdog Millionaire* (2008), *Eat, Pray, Love* (2010), *Best Exotic Marigold Hotel* (2011), *I Origins* (2014), and *Million Dollar Arm* (2014) all juxtapose the titillating possibilities of globalized India askance with images, facts, and representations of India's endemic poverty. Like Boo's narrative, these films too acknowledge the globally emergent status of India as a lucrative consumer country and a new economic superpower, but then brings this "new" image of India into circulation alongside the oft-publicized images of "old" India or the third world as the site of death, decay, and dissipation. Recognition of India's emergence as a global power, which itself is a matter of debate and deliberation, is almost always tempered by images of its lingering inexplicable poverty and only diffused by stories about the fortitude of the nation's poor. The latter are the new noble savages of this global world, surviving with dignity against an array of dispossessing circumstances they are the stock of neoliberal Romanticism. Their images help reposition the Global Positioning of the twenty-first-century subject of the West. For while India has embraced neoliberal economy, a lot still remains unaccomplished and it is *still* the West's duty to bring these lapses to attention. *Beautiful Forevers* is an example of what Priyamvada Gopal dubs the well-meaning but ill-informed maternalism of the West (Gopal 2015). Possessed with the desire to save the third world's poor, the globally sensitive Hollywood liberal Marxists conveniently overlook their own complicity in the discursive productions of poverty in the Global South.

IV. THE SUCCESSIVE CAVEATS

Gopal made the remark about the West's "well-meaning but ill-informed maternalism" reacting to Leslee Udwin's documentary *India's Daughter* (2015). Udwin's documentary was made in the wake of the rape and murder of Jyoti Singh ("Nirbhaya") and the public protests that followed throughout India. Udwin's agenda: to expose "India's rape culture" (Smith 2015). The documentary was banned in India following objections from Indian feminists about Udwin's assumptions regarding Indian law, her stereotyping of Indian culture, and her complete ignorance about gender relations in South Asia. Most importantly, though, they charged Udwin for culturalizing rape as a problem that is unique to India and for psychologizing the Indian male as prone to sexual violence. While emphasizing these trivialities, the documentary left out necessary discussions about how rape "is intimately connected to other systems of privilege, exploitation and inequality, including, in the Indian context, caste oppression, religious chauvinism, resource appropriation (including that of mineral-rich land from indigenous tribal communities by multinational corporations) and the vicious economic inequalities fostered by an unfettered capitalism prosperity that has yet to bring basic shelter and nourishment to millions" (Gopal 2015, n.p.).

Unfortunately, these criticisms of Udwin's project got lost in the clamor surrounding the director's claims that the ban imposed by the Indian government was an attack on her freedom of expression and the right-wing Hindu government's counter-charge that Udwin's film was a foreign conspiracy to shame India. One can only wish that instead of the above there was a mature exchange of views between the filmmaker and her feminist critics. Because such a dialogue would have allowed discussion of a universal issue understood in its particular contexts.

Udwin speaking of her sacrifices in making the documentary—"she describes having…made…enormous personal sacrifice [like] her abdication of home comforts to travel with Conradian determination to explore 'the blackest recesses of the human heart' " (ibid.)—recalls Boo reminiscing in the "Author's Note" about her trials and tribulations in writing *Beautiful Forevers*. More importantly, reading Boo's book alongside Udwin's documentary one cannot avoid noticing their ideological entanglement: both projects are undertaken for the uplifting of the Other, with the self supposedly kept at a distance. In both cases, the "authors" assert interest in objectively documenting a reality kept hidden from the rest of the (civilized) world. In making claims of unveiling hidden truths about the Other's reality without worrying about personal interests, these contemporary auteurs join a long list of European writers, adventurers, missionaries, and soldiers who traveled into the Heart of Darkness with the selfless intent of bringing these dark corners into the light of the world. In her appeal to the Indian prime minister for revocation of the ban, Udwin's repeated stress on civilization and how civilized cultures act is metonymic of that habit of thinking that found expression in Laura Bush's radio address to her nation on the eve of the war on terror:

> I'm Laura Bush, and I'm delivering this week's radio address to kick off a world-wide effort to focus on the brutality against women and children by the al-Qaida terrorist network and the regime it supports in Afghanistan.... Civilized people throughout the world are speaking out in horror—not only because our hearts break for the women and children in Afghanistan, but also because in Afghanistan we see the world the terrorists would like to impose on the rest of us.

Interestingly, the same claims have been made separately across centuries by Homer (*Odysseus*, Book 9), Vespucci ("A New World"), and Darwin (*The Descent of Man* [1871]). In all these, the Other is repeatedly chastised for not respecting women and the most disadvantaged in society. These discourses display a mindset that Spivak captures in the maxim: *white men saving brown women from brown men*. Boo and Udwin are the most recent sets in this unending series of Western representations of the non-West's pathological barbarity. Together, they compose the organized episteme about the non-West that Said terms Orientalism.

What distinguishes these twenty-first-century versions of Orientalism is, however, a concerted effort to be politically correct when speaking about the Other. Unlike attitudes of the nineteenth and twentieth centuries, the (liberal) West today cares deeply about representational politics. People are ever conscious about stereotypes and stereotyping, and quite critical of American orientalism in the Middle East and the Pacific. In contrast to Conradian journeys of the previous centuries, contemporary popular culture—from bestsellers like *Beautiful Forevers* to blockbusters like *Eat Pray Love* (2010)—appears to actively embrace a different rationale for traveling to the non-West. These journeys are opportunities for radical unlearning of Western assumptions about life and relationships through immersion in Eastern ideas. The commonly projected result is the concomitant development of the Western subject as more inclusive, more intransitive, and less opinionated. This journey pivots on "learning to unlearn from below," an exercise of stepping into the Other's space "without apprehensions of or fears for possibility of radical self-dislocation," and consequently being radically reimagined by this alien culture (Basu Thakur 2015, 158). Aimed at embracing the "openness and indeterminacy" experienced in the non-West and for achieving a "non-reductive collectivity" that is in stark contrast to "the streamlined, hegemonic collectivity of globalization" (Ghazoul 2003), these journeys are best remarked, following Spivak, as teleopoietic journeys (Morton 2007, 167). They are about the reclaiming the Western subject without appearing to Other the other.[14]

Consider, for instance, films such as *Outsourced* (2006), *Eat Pray Love*, and the *Best Exotic Marigold Hotel* (2011). In each of these, white protagonists find a new lease on life through passing immersion in the Other's culture. These journeys remain as fraught with difficulties as they did when Marlowe sailed upstream, yet, today, as they put it in *The Darjeeling Limited*, a 2007 Wes Anderson comedy about three brothers struggling to connect to one another, and to rectify which they decide to travel through India, "We want to be completely open and say yes to everything even if it is shocking and painful." Anderson's film echoes, to wit, repeats, the rhetoric of self-sacrifice, personal struggle, and individual persistence that we also find in Boo and Udwin. This rhetoric underlines the rational and moral superiority of the Western subject. As for the shock and pain experienced in the East, these are however not treated as they were in the Conradian past. They are no longer to be dismissed or avoided but, rather, shocking differences are respectfully explored for the unparalleled enjoyment of the non-West they offer.[15]

The insidious character of this idea might get lost if we apply it to the West's love for yoga. Rather, I suggest, we try thinking this through with Jordan Peele's *Get Out* (2017). The logic behind Liz Gilbert's journey through Italy, India, and Cambodia is no different from the need of white men and women for a black body, as in Peele's horror flick. Those very aspects of the non-West—pagan spirituality and excessive sexual virility—once denounced are now being widely absorbed in the West albeit in sublimated commodity forms. It is in the Other's excessive enjoyment that the West finds its ultimate rapture. And it is by making the Other's hidden enjoyment universal that the West consolidates its sovereignty: *Originating in India, the festival of colors or the Hindu festival Holi is now celebrated across the United States as a way to promote cultural diversity and inclusivity, and help "young people who want to have fun, but without the alcohol or drug use associated with other kinds of rock concerts or large festivals"* (Davis 2014).

By the same token, Boo's four-year journey through Annawadi is not an innocent attempt to correct clichéd representations of India's poor but an effort to reset these representations as harmless under the excuse of objective reportage necessary for critically pushing global India to accomplish all rounded economic prosperity. Tucked neatly behind this façade, however, is the ideology of subject recomposition—reinstate for the West a new sovereign identity unimpeded by the West's past litany of crimes—genocidal conquests, slavery, pillage, and racism. Faced with these altered or sanitized conditions of subject-production in contemporary cultural productions, we must awaken to the need for focusing attention on the methods via which liberal discourses today mask their Othering and conserve the subject-sovereignty of the West.[16]

V. SUBJECT-MAKING IN THE GLOBAL PRESENT

Boo is not only intent on drawing attention to the lingering poverty in the non-West but also on awakening her readers to the literal and metaphorical poverty existing within the West. To better understand this, let us indulge the common misinterpretation of the Freudian maxim *"Wo Es war, soll Ich warden"* by reading it as "where it (id) was, there I (ego) shall become." Translated in the context of Boo's text, this then becomes: confronting the abjection of the Other allows me to become a better human being through self-reflection.[17] In the "postpolitical multiculturalist universe of tolerance for difference in which nobody is excluded," the Other in whom I scandalously witness a part of my repressed self must not be entirely rejected but gradually accommodated in close proximity for being another person like me (Žižek 1998, 999). What this Other promises is my own self-development through reflecting on what I have for so long repressed or disavowed from my conscious self. It is by recognizing these repressed and disavowed parts through my traumatic interaction with the Other that I grow more wholesome and more composed. In other words, we have a complete reversal of the colonial ideology in contemporary multiculturalist discourses. If colonial discourses were intolerant of the Other for reflecting the self's most repressed desires, contemporary multiculturalism openly advocates embracing the Other for giving us this opportunity to more closely know our selves (Žižek 2002, 545–46). Boo's plotting of the Other follows the same multiculturalist logic: the "pseudopsychoanalytic drama" helps her to avoid the real political questions about poverty in the global South. In sum: far from being galvanized by a desire to help her readers see the underbelly of globalization, Boo's is a self-consolidating project. It is underwritten by the desire to preserve the subject of the West in the era of globalization. To recall Spivak on Kristeva's *On Chinese Women*: "In spite of their occasional interest in touching the *other* of the West…their repeated question is obsessively self-centered: if we are not what official history and philosophy say we are, who then are we (not), how are we (not)?" (2006, 188–89).

There is another way to understand the West's repeated "interest in touching the other," another explanation for the West's repetition compulsion. Insofar as globalization reduces some particularities in favor of the universal, whereby *le Paris* is no different from Dubai or Dubai from Mumbai, this kind of radical leveling after almost three hundred years of the West's exclusive existence only produces anxiety by suddenly putting their sovereign subjectivity at a level with the non-West. It is an anxiety over the disappearance of difference—of Mumbai resembling New York and New York becoming Lagos—another version of the xenophobe's anxiety over the gradual but inevitable disappearance of white majority in mainland United States.

I feel compelled to ask: What if the dark interior of the slum or the slum as the radical kernel of India is not actually a big reveal, far less some truth awaiting disclosure? What if the slum functions as a necessary otherness allowing enjoyment of the glitzy overcity without threatening our privilege as the subject of the West? In other words, what if the dank interiority does not come after an experience of the outside but is the disavowed a priori that makes the outside bearable.[18] The slum functions in this logic for grounding the radical alterity of the Other against which the West can continue enjoying its imaginary identity.

Consider as example this scenario: we can enjoy a cup of caramel macchiato in a Mumbai Starbucks just as we'd do in downtown Chicago. But in Mumbai we'd soon move to an eagerly awaited trip to see the slums for that authentic experience of India as the unchanged, unchangeable pit of squalor.

Meanwhile in Chicago, post-coffee, it is the Magnificent Mile that awaits us. But the flavor of the caramel macchiato is not lost in India, that is, even after seeing the putrefying slums. Rather, it is the reverse: the experience of the slums allows us to savor globalization; we say to ourselves, "How similar a cup of macchiato tastes in India and at home." What allows equal enjoyment of the coffee, however, is the inherent difference between the two cities. For when we are drinking macchiato in Chicago no beggar child tugs at our cuffs hoping, demanding, or pleading emancipation. (In fact, beggars do not even exist in the United States because the poor are "homeless" due to mistakes they have made in life choices, or so the argument goes.) Enjoyment is *only* properly enjoyed when it comes with a caveat or limit. We enjoy globalization apropos the logic of being similar as long as there's an interruption or deviation in this enjoyment of being the same. The veil of fantasy functions to make the subject alive by bringing the other in radical (non)relation to the self. This means, the other as *objet a* is an empirically impossible object of desire as well as an unbearable loss that functions to sustain the subject as the subject of desire. In Boo's neoliberal imagination of the non-West, the slum is the alterity constituting the excess in the Other, and/or that part of India as yet undraped by globalization.

Allow me my second caveat here: let me wonder aloud whether this reading about Otherness and anxiety is not in itself yet another distraction? The *real* ideology of Boo's work, if we may speak of it that way, is to prevent readers from confronting the traumatic nonrelationality of being. For while fantasy does make reality bearable, it does not originate in the Other's self-consolidating difference. Fantasy fills the hole emerging from the confrontation with the other's traumatic nonrelationality. Put differently, fantasy renders bearable a reality grounded in the irrecuperability of the other. This is the other that does not admit the self in its presence. It is the glimmering sardine can, drifting without purpose in the vast ocean, which we see only because of the sunlight reflecting off its surface, though it does not see us. Instead, it captures the aphanitic subject as lack in between the pulses of light beaming off its "body." Fantasy rescues the subject from the trauma of encountering the gap between the pulses; the gap being substantive of our ontological condition. E. M. Forster teaches us that encounters with such gaps, the indefatigable echo of the Marabar Caves, for instance, announce the excess in the Other, and unless written over by dominant fantasies, the rape script, as in the novel, these can have only one other possible result: the death of the sovereign subject or subject-supposed-to-know. J. M. Coetzee and Mohsin Hamid repeat similar scenarios in *Waiting for the Barbarians* (1980) and *The Reluctant Fundamentalist* (2007), respectively, when writing about sudden upstagings of dominant, male, heteronormative subjects in the gaze of excessive others. Desires are upended and self-esteems shredded when the Magistrate fails to see himself in the eyes of the captured barbarian woman (*Waiting for the Barbarians*) or Changez cannot get intimate with his white girlfriend Erica without posing as her dead white boyfriend Chris (*The Reluctant Fundamentalist*). *Beautiful Forevers* crucially envelops the excessive, unsettling, and obscene other, the urban precariat, by folding them into Europe's narrative of, and as an example for, dogged individuality.

V. CONCLUSION: THE DESOLATE UNIVERSAL OF SLUMS

> The gap between "obscure" knowledge-at-work and capitalist enjoyment does not disappear, but returns in the form of "human waste," namely the ghostly masses of slum-dweller produced by, and simultaneously excluded from, the dynamics of value-formation.
> —Fabio Vighi, *On Zizek's Dialectics: Surplus, Subtraction, Sublimation*

On one level, *Beautiful Forevers* makes a provocative point: it characterizes the urban slum as the tipping point for globalization. Slums are unavoidable fixtures in today's modern metropolises. They are all produced by, yet curiously excluded from, globalization. This leads Boo to wonder why don't today's metropolises "with their cheek-by-jowl slums and luxury hotels, look like the insurrectionist video game Metal Slug 3? *Why don't more of our unequal societies implode?*" (BF, 248; emphasis mine). It is evident that Boo is not talking about a moral collapse of capitalist societies but, rather, about a Wellsian uprising of the poor against the rich. Still, this revolutionary concern is nothing more than a self-conscious gesture by Boo, because the general ideological span of her narrative is profoundly against such action. As such, this moment and similar moments where she critiques capitalism and neoliberalism remain purely figural—generic inserts into an otherwise strictly reformed narrative of Western subjective sovereignty.

It is easy to call out Boo if, say, we compare her interest in slums with Žižek's. Žižek also identifies slums as the excessive core of global capitalism or the point at which the system encounters its own inconsistency consequently becoming virally destabilized and in peril of imploding from inside. But he offers a different understanding of these slums. He calls them the *new Universal,* unlike Boo who sees them as a particular condition that will be corrected once the particular accedes to the Universal. Boo and Žižek, therefore, occupy opposite poles in their critiques of globalization. Boo suggests that it is only through the incorporation of the poor-particular into the affluent fold of universal global economy that we can eradicate poverty. Or the poor can become rich within the global economy, and it is only a matter of enacting policy-level changes for this miracle to happen. Therefore, we must first include the issue of urban poverty in current debates over globalization's future, and second, we must undertake extensive policy changes in order to end entrenched systemic inequalities. Hope, she writes, "is not a fiction," as extreme poverty is indeed "being alleviated gradually, unevenly, nonetheless significantly" (ibid., 253).

Žižek, by contrast, makes an entirely different point. On the topic of accommodating the non-part into the social mainstream, he contends that globalization and its neoliberal policies need to end for the global poor to fully emerge out of poverty. This ending however will remain unaccomplished until the urban poor awaken as the *new proletariat* to eviscerate the dominant hegemony.[19] The urban precariats are the future foot soldiers of twenty-first-century communism because "they are 'free' in the double meaning of the word even more than the classic proletariat." On the one hand, they are free "from all substantial ties, dwelling in a free space, outside the police regulations of the state," and, on the other, "they are a large collective, forcibly thrown together, 'thrown' into a situation where they have to invent some mode of being-together." It is from these sites that "new forms of social awareness" will emerge and shape the new class struggle (Žižek 2005a, n.p.).

Let's face it. There's a perfectly simple answer to why Boo raises the question about how to free the urban proletariat from poverty but offers no answer. One, there is no possibility of freedom from the existing social system without radically capsizing the entire system. But such a revolution is admissible to Boo only at the level of the *virtual*—the Metal Slug 3 video game—but never in reality. In fact, an idea of precariat revolution will not be entertained by either Boo or most of her liberal-minded admirers. A precariat revolution is not in the best interest of the global middle class. In the words of Žižek, this "symbolic class" of "managers, journalists and PR people, academics, artists, etc." exists as buffer between those in power and the poor. Indeed, "a New York academic [shares] more in common with a Slovene academic than with blacks in Harlem half a mile from his campus" (Žižek 2004, n.p). And it is in both their best interests—the New York and Slovene academics—to keep precariats distracted with hope, morality, and reproductive futurism. Hope under neoliberalism has reconstructed a new horizon of futurity for the precariat—it convinces them their moral behavior (read: *do not create trouble*) will be ultimately rewarded and even if they might not emerge out of poverty their children might. Through hard work the poor will be able to eventually move from the undercity to the overcity.[20]

Except for that one momentary lapse, the consistent message of Boo's book is of hope. That the poor should not lose hope, keep working hard, and retain faith in democracy, the media, and the judiciary. By replacing "angst" with "hope" Boo ensures that a class struggle between the urban poor and globalized India never happens (BF, 253). It is not just the poor, though, who are deceived by hope; Boo offers hope to the West as well: the latter can now sympathize with the Other, engage with them through organized charities, and learn from their routine struggles for survival about the privileges we take for granted in the West. The West can suffer with the Other without losing class privileges or being threatened by an uprising of the precariat. They—the precariat—Boo assures us, are too invested in chasing their dreams of grabbing a piece of globalization to pose us any threat. For even when individual dreams fail, the poor do not question the system but "blame one another" (BF, 254). And as long as they remain misdirected, the revolution will not happen. Without which the twin tyranny of the twenty-first century—neoliberal economics and democracy—are secure.

If Boo wanted to be ethical in her representation of the urban precariat, then hope should have been the last thing on her radar. For to be ethical apropos the precariat is to acknowledge them as a revolutionary force ready to burst out at any moment. But to imagine the precariat at war is to imagine our social position at risk. Our true test lies here: Can we imagine the end of our class privileges and/or side with the abject, dirty, impoverished yet insouciant other? Can we transcend class to identify the slum-dwelling precariat as the new universal?

In the writings of the Bengali poet and novelist Nabarun Bhattacharya (1948–2014), I find similar questions about precariat revolutions. Nabarun wrote considerably about the condition of precariats in globalized India, especially in his city, Calcutta. Nabarun's satire of bourgeois morality and culture is scathing but his precariats are almost never represented as humans or striving to escape marginalization through hard work and moral consciousness. Instead, his precariats are unrealistic—some of them possess the power of flight (*fyataarus*), while others are trained in black magic (*choktar*). Overly profane, uncouth, and a shock to bourgeois civility, these crepuscular and scatological creatures embody the darkness and abjection that are constitutive of their lives and are composed of those non-parts or excesses of our globalized societies that we wish to see hidden. Their rebellions, accordingly, are equally profane and phantasmagorical. At times, the rebellion involves peeing on city walls in violation of city rules. At other times, as in *Kangal Malsat* (the War Cry of the Beggars), the precariats armed only with a "dickanon" (*nunu Kaman*) declare total war on the state. The ensuing chaos can only be described as nonsensical, bizarre, and a farce. In our global era we have indeed transcended the tragedy of the subaltern, we are in the domain of the farce and the subaltern might very well be its kingpin.

I cannot enter into a detailed discussion of Nabarun's writings here; his work deserves a separate monograph. But my reason for briefly referencing him is twofold. First, Nabarun shows that a precariat revolution today is difficult to imagine and when imagined often resembles a farce more than an epochal event. And, relatedly—the second point—it is impossible from the vantage of our class position to realistically represent the precariat as anything other than crepuscular, scatological, and outlandish. But this exactly is the ethical duty of a writer, namely, to represent the impossibility of representing the other in its overabundant excessive radiance. As excessive, the other is a Thing, only approachable sideways because it restricts or prevents direct access by appearing maliciously threatening (Žižek 2009, 288). As the radically antagonistic core of the social, the other is the Lacanian real. Its excess gives substance to the (notion or concept of the) Thing. The Thing is the lack or impossibility constitutive of the social.[21]

"The Bone Collector"

Narayan Gangopadhyay's (1918–1970) Bengali short story "Hanr" ("The Bone Collector") (1945) offers yet another useful comparison to Boo.[22] Narayan's story is set during the turbulent times of World War II, when Eastern India was suffering additionally from a man-made famine, "the Bengal Famine of 1943," which killed up to three million (some put the figure at 3.8 million) people. But the body count does not do justice to the magnitude of this man-made famine, the responsibility for which goes largely to then British prime minister Winston Churchill, insofar as the impact of the famine lingers even today in the bodies of those who were growing up at that time. Born in 1942, Spivak was a child in a middle-class home, thus relatively protected from the ravages of the famine. Yet a California surgeon diagnosed her brittle bones as resulting from the famine (Brohi 2014).[23] Caught between the war and the famine, the Bengali colonized was the subject proper. Stretched between proving loyalty to the empire by serving in the army or remaining home to face malnutrition, few communities in twentieth-century history faced such an excruciating predicament of being caught between two deaths.

The central protagonist of Narayan's story stayed back, escaping the draft and evading lures of emigration.[24] Home alive but without a stable job, he lands at the gates of a British-subservient Bengali affluent, "Rai Bahadur" H. L. Chatterjee, hoping to procure a recommendation letter. From the very beginning, the story juxtaposes the nonhuman and the human, affluence against debilitating poverty, and the supernatural (against/or) in the natural. As the narrator and the Rai Bahadur come face to face inside the latter's plush, almost soundproof South Calcutta mansion, a range of sounds compose the background: the RAF "lions" circle the skies, two mastiffs bark continuously at the gate, and along the main thoroughfare and across the mansion, barely-recognizable-as-human bodies raise a hellish din scavenging, fighting, and hustling for food scraps. The Rai Bahadur's bourgeois cocoon proves ineffective to keep these noises at bay. The cries of the starving appear to override both the growls of the mastiffs and the roars of the RAF to pierce the Rai Bahadur's heavily curtained room. This noise disturbs the Rai Bahadur, possibly because it makes him uncomfortable knowing that those he oppressed once in his role as a comprador agent of the British colonial regime are today outside his gate.

The city-educated narrator does not belong to the Rai Bahadur's class, but neither does he belong to the class of the dispossessed. The middle class during the war were plagued by economic deflation, rising prices, shrinking jobs, corruption, and black-marketeering, and the influx of the rural dispossessed into an already crowded city added further to their anxiety. Historically a product of colonialism, the Bengali metropolitan middle class were Macaulayian minute-men; their lot have always been inextricably tied to the colonial regime, with many also enjoying "a bit of rental income through petty intermediate tenure-holding in the Permanent Settlement hierarchy" (Sarkar 1992, 1545). It was, therefore, in their interest to retain their loyalty to the landed gentry and the British imperial government, to distinguish themselves as English-educated colonized elite against the illiterate villagers.

No wonder the narrator's descriptions of the famine-stricken destitutes are completely devoid of sympathy. He calls them a "stinking pile of garbage," a stain on his beautiful city: the hungry masses scream "at each other, pick[ing] head lice, and like animals with blackened tongues lap up dirty water from the gutters." They are revolting, he says, adding that one doesn't "feel sympathy [for them], far less sorrow, but an irrational anxiety ripples through the body." This is an anxiety over the question: "Who will satisfy these hungry masses?" The narrator worries "Who will benumb their wretched hunger pangs? Will a fistful of rice or a glob of Bajra prove enough or will they. . .do they need more, lots more, including the picture perfect mansions along Rashbehari Avenue?" ("Bone Collector," 30–31). The point to be noted is that the narrator expresses his feeling without deception—seeing these spectral figures and hearing their demonic cries, he trembles with uncertainty: What if these *living dead* take over the city, destroying the Rai Bahadur's mansion, decimating the colonized middle-class (ibid., 35–36)?

We find similar descriptions of the other in the writings of "the Hungry Generation"—a collective of poets, novelists, and painters whose works captured the traumatic reality of the war and the famine. Narayan's descriptions of the destitutes in the "Bone Collector," for instance, resemble Premendra Mitra's descriptions of the famine-stricken in "*Phyan*":

> On the city streets
> Roam strange creatures,
> Human-like, yet, not quite human,
> Cruel caricatures of humanity!
> Yet they move and speak,
> Like debris they pile up by the road,
> Sit, foraging food, on piles of garbage
> Weary (cited in Sengupta 2016, n.p.)

Like Narayan, Premendra Mitra, too, appears incapable of representing the hungry masses as human or without symbolically encircling their irremediable excess. He cannot put his finger on their existences—do they exist or not, are they real or shadow? From his position as desiring subject, deeply ensconced in his class privilege, this other is "strange," "not quite human," "caricature," and "debris."

There is a fundamental difference between what the "Hungryrealists" consider realism and what realism is for Boo. For Narayan or Premendra reality is always more than what is seen. As Sourit Bhattacharya perceptively notes, representing the Bengal Famine required more than addressing it as an event. The writers wanted as well to expose the historical and material causes responsible for the event and for organizing public reaction against the imperial administration's responsibility in the event (Bhattacharya 2017, 58). These pressing demands significantly modified the notion of realism for the Hungryrealists, and their attempts to capture the "disaster both as a [sudden] event [and] a crisis of historical-structural continuity" resulted in them adapting different genres, including the gothic horror (ibid., 61). The historical reality of skeletal bodies "parading" down the main thoroughfares and bylanes of Calcutta begging for *phyan* thus came to be referenced in their writings via already existing generic trope of zombies and undead walking the city streets (ibid., 69). We can read this in many ways—generic convention, analogous imagination, or, I would insist, the impossibility of seeing these emaciated bodies in any other way except as threat to the city, its clockwork pulse, and bourgeois existences secured within. No matter how hard the Hungryrealists might have wanted to or did empathize with the famished others, in their writings they opted to present them as exceeding the frames of reality. In siding with their class positions, the Hungryrealists stay true to their desires or act ethically.

By contrast, Boo conforms to the moral mandate of realist representation. Both Boo and Narayan set out to describe overwhelming experiences of the other but they respond very differently. Narayan is ethical, while Boo is moral. Sharlet actually makes a similar point about *Beautiful Forevers*. According to him, Boo's book is so realistic that it is not real enough:

> Offered up by blurbers with the best of intentions, the immediacy implicit in like a novel suggests that the book on hand can be engaged with as art rather than as fact, so realist it's not real; a story rather than the state of things, a condition in which we might be complicit. The blurber may be speaking of craft—the use of scene, dialogue, character—but publishers traffic in genre, the overstated distinction between art and fact that makes one book "current events" and another "a timeless story"—that is, a book with a shelf life. (2013, n.p.)

Narayan or the Hungryrealists might offend our twenty-first-century multiculturalist views, but they are at least honest to their desires.

The difference between Boo and Narayan et al., though, extend beyond the issue of ethical representation. For in the case of the latter, ethical representation discloses an important Lacanian lesson about the ethics of desire, namely, to be truthful to desire. Simply put: the narrator cannot overcome his class anxieties in order to identify with the other as Other. In consequence, the other remains for him abject and inhuman or all that he imagines himself to be not. But it can be argued that Boo too remains truthful to her desire for securing the subject of the West at the expense of the Other. Then why should we judge her any differently?

In order to answer this question accurately we must first expand the commonplace understanding of desire as striving for happiness—we desire objects and persons we think will make us happy, complete, and whole again but what we truly desire is the exact opposite: we desire to remain perpetually in desire. At this point, still it seems that Boo is not being unethical to her desire. As I argue above, Boo constitutes the necessary condition for being the subject of desire by humanizing the other as real. In other words, her Othering of the urban precariat constitutes an Other against whom the privileges of the self can be enjoyed at a time when all identities appear horizontalized. As a revived subject of the West emerges due to Boo's representational politics, Boo makes no effort to caution her readers against the fantasmatic framework necessarily indispensable for ensuring the longevity of this new subject. In Narayan's text, by contrast, the assumptions of the narrator are challenged not once but twice: first at the beginning of the story and thereafter at the end. The first is metatextual, the latter metaphysical.

We should be cautious, however, about reading any of this to mean that the end of desire frees the individual from (mis)identifying with either narcissistic images of self-autonomy (I) and/or with the subject of symbolic castration ($). Lacan is quite categorical about the consequences of desire evaporating completely. He asks that we rather change our desire without giving it up entirely. This is because the symbolic cannot be erased or we cannot exists outside of the symbolic. Therefore,

> [a]ctive subjectivization is possible only in the intersubjective Symbolic after we have temporarily suspended it and "reshaped" it through the imposition of a new Master-Signifier and the emergence of a new (partly subjectivized) *jouissance* connected to it. In other words...this subjectivization can be achieved through...what Lacan defines as the "traversal of the fundamental fantasy." Briefly, this means: (1) detaching *objet petit a* from the barred subject $; (2) achieving the void of separation (subjective destitution); (3) resubjectivizing that same void through sublimation; and (4) recognizing [that] the control of *jouissance* [belongs] to the Other. (Chiesa 2007, 347)

We see an almost step-by-step reproduction of this schematic Lacanian theory in "The Bone Collector." But for this we need to loosen the weave of the text, separate out its tactile threads, and read the story free from the knitting intended by its teller. Once we accomplish that, we are left with two stories: one between the narrator and the Rai Bahadur and the other between the narrator and the hungry migrants. Undoubtedly, both are inextricably meshed but for elucidating how these narratives separately traverse the fundamental fantasy and rearrange a new economy of subjectivity that assumes the impregnable void of the other's nothingness as it-self, I will briefly dissociate them before putting them together again. As I see it, the meaning of Narayan's story appears between these two readings.

The Lion Has Wings

The narrator in "The Bone Collector" does not get the recommendation letter he hoped for from the Rai Bahadur. Instead, he gets to see the Rai Bahadur's rare collection of magical bones and hear about how the intrepid Rai Bahadur procured these curios while adventuring across the Pacific. One bone comes from Tahiti. This is a bone of a virgin girl sacrificed on a full solar eclipse by her own tribesmen, the collector details. The body is then burned and interred for the next seven years, after which her bones are ritualistically dug up and dumped into the ocean. Anyone from the tribe who swims across a shark-infested strait and recovers even as much as one of her pinky bones is said to become possessed with supernatural powers. Powers to raise tempests, turn stone into gold, and make the skies rain blood.

    As readers we might wonder at this point if this bone from Tahiti is the eponymous bone from the title of the story. But, interestingly, this is not the only bone in the story. The second bone is of much humbler origin; devoid of any supernatural powers it appears in the "second/parallel" story involving the narrator and the migrants. Unlike the expensive Tahitian curiosity, the second bone is garbage; foraged out from trash by a little starving child who sits beside the road sucking it fiercely. On seeing this beastly child with stick-like arms and a ballooning belly furiously working the bone the narrator is overcome by a strange feeling: he finds a strange affinity between the child's desperation for food and his pleading the Rai Bahadur for a job. The sight allows him to bridge the class difference between the rural hungry and himself—they are both at the mercy of people like the Rai Bahadur, but neither of them possesses the power of the Rai Bahadur or the ability to strip the Rai Bahadur of his power. Rather, the Rai Bahadur has the bone with which he can change the world. The dry bone at the hands of the child has the power neither to satisfy the hunger nor to help the multitude raise a ravaging storm against their historical oppressors.

Interestingly, a phrase that appears early in the story can be identified as hinting to Narayan's readers about the climax. Though chances are that this phrase made more sense to Narayan's contemporary readers than to his readers in the present. The phrase is: "the Lion has Wings." It appears immediately after the narrator hears the low sputter of RAF engines above his head. These are the RAF planes patrolling Calcutta's skies against Japanese bombers. But to Narayan's contemporary readers, this phrase would have carried an additional reference. It was the title of a British documentary-style propaganda film released in 1939. The story revolved around Wing Commander Richardson (Ralph Richardson), his family, and the daring exploits of the RAF. Most interesting is the conclusion of the film where Mr. and Mrs. Richardson (the latter played by Merle Oberon), the former having recently returned from active duty, go on a picnic. The midshot framing the husband and wife, both in uniform, cuts suddenly to a close-up of Mrs. Richardson who, almost on cue, says: "I was thinking about women." As the camera steadies on her face, Mrs. Richardson continues to speak ponderously about the sacrifices women have made for the war yet the short shift they have received. At this moment, the camera suddenly turns toward the husband, only to find him napping—he appears to have fallen asleep at the very moment the mid-shot cut to the close-up. Seeing her husband asleep, Mrs. Richardson realizes that he had not heard a single word of what she was just saying. But she does not wake him up or chastise him for that. She seems okay even if her complaints went unheard because, after all, issues such as gender equality and decolonization are best left for after the war.

Doesn't the position of the wife mirror the position of Narayan's narrator? Both are pleaders yet both their voices go unheard. The wing commander falls asleep possibly at the very moment when his wife utters the words "I was thinking," while the Rai Bahadur precipitously dismisses the narrator's job search as waste of time, advising him instead to "be a man" and seek adventure in the world (32).[25] In both cases, the big Other remains unresponsive to the particular's desires.

A difference emerges, though, in the context of the third element present in the story, namely, the naked hungry masses as the excluded-included of society. Confrontation with this "waste" awakens the narrator to his own displaced stature or lack in the colonial society, but no such prospect is available to Mrs. Richardson. The amorphous hungry masses, by contrast, push Narayan's narrator to identify his abjection in a capitalist society ravaged by war and man-made famine. The other's precarity brings disparate forces together. They identify their shared socioeconomic condition without its requiring them to forge an identity together.[26]

Can Boo Speak?

Allow me one final caveat. I do *not* wish to dismiss Boo as architect of some kind of twentieth-century multiculturalist Othering. Far less, I do not see her as consciously redrawing the fantasy of third world abjection. I consider Boo more as a victim of multicultural political correctness insofar as she is blind to the fact that her work Others the other. If the purpose of postcolonial studies is to spotlight silent and silenced voices, then alongside interrogating Boo's Othering or silencing of voices, we should also inquire to what extent Boo's own voice gets compromised in process. Simply put, alongside emphasizing Boo's strategic misrepresentations of the non-West, we must ask what Boo has failed to do. Or, we need to ask why she cannot write about third-world poverty like Narayan and Nabarun do?

The answer is obvious: Boo cannot write like Narayan or Nabarun and get away with it. She is a victim of the political correctness she endorses. Boo's Othering is not a big reveal, but her need to mask her race/class position in order to write this book is symptomatic of the compulsion liberals face today to disavow their desires. By and large, this is the tragedy of liberals—they are unable to situate themselves ethically apropos the cut. This, many claim, has been the unfortunate result of academic postcolonialism. Insofar as the discipline has reinforced and encouraged ideologies of multiculturalism, tolerant pluralism, and victim narratives, it has in equal measure committed to the kind of performativity that Boo represents. The contemporary climate of political correctness and victim histories does not allow Boo to speak, and if postcolonial studies as discipline is invested in retrieving reproached voices, then, it should also take up Boo's cause. In this climate of political correctness and identity politics, Boo as a white writer cannot represent the other ethically, and though Narayan or Nabarun does not share her situation it is equally important to keep in mind that these Bengali writers lack the ability to speak without being first translated by someone in the first world.

FIVE

Political Correctness *Is* Phallic
IDAHO POLITICS, *BLACK PANTHER*,
AND *GRAN TORINO*

I. IDAHO POLITICS AND THE LIBERAL FIXATION WITH THE IMAGE

In late 2017, when Idaho legislator Paulette Jordan announced her intention to run for governor, few knew her. In fact, there were a number of serious strikes against Jordan in this conservative state: she was a woman, a Democrat, and a rookie representative who had been in the Idaho legislature for only about four years. For someone like her to even think about occupying the governor's mansion, a position occupied by Republicans for the previous three terms in a state that last voted in favor of a Democratic presidential candidate in 1964, was more than a leap. It would require a miracle. Not surprisingly, twelve of Idaho's sixteen Democrat legislators opposed Jordan, preferring to endorse her opponent, Idaho businessman A. J. Balukoff, for the Democratic ticket. Balukoff had unsuccessfully challenged the two-time incumbent Butch Otter in 2014, but from most standpoints this Brigham Young graduate and successful businessman known for creating thousands of jobs in Idaho and for donating generously to the Democratic Party was the obvious choice. Yet

Jordan defeated Balukoff by eighteen points in the primaries to earn the nomination of the Democratic Party going into the 2018 midterms.

The following morning the *Idaho Statesman* reported:

> Anyone who ran an online news search on [Jordan] last year would have come up with a smattering of results, mainly stemming from her position within the Coeur d'Alene Tribe.
>
> Following her quick and focused path to victory, now not only does Idaho know who she is, but so does the nation. Run that Google news search today and 24,500 results pop up, including articles from The Atlantic, The Nation, HuffPost and BuzzFeed.
>
> CNN traveled to Boise to cover Jordan on Tuesday, and more than a dozen national news outlets followed Idaho's elections to learn if someone vying to become the nation's first Native American governor would win the primary. (Sewell, *Idaho Statesman*)

Jordan played her political game well. She secured the national limelight by tipping the incontrovertible logic and suspense of futurity—*Will the United States have its first native governor after three hundred years of calculated genocide, repression, and ostracization of the nation's indigenous?* This was only the first in a series of similar questions: Will Idaho have its first woman governor? Will Idaho have its first Democrat governor in two decades? Will a staunchly Republican state send a crucial message to Washington? And so forth.

But did her win in the Democratic primary have anything to do with her policy positions? Few actually appeared interested in this question. Among the people I met, no one was asking about her positions on social inequality, systemic racism, gun control, single payer healthcare, and the minimum wage. Or about her position on Israel's efforts to programmatically exterminate Palestinians, U.S. police killings of colored people within the nation's borders, education reform, and U.S. foreign policy in Middle East. They were excited because an indigenous woman Democrat was running. Let's face the fact: Jordan did not win against Balukoff because voters chose her on the basis of her policy positions. In fact, Jordan and Balukoff shared the exact same positions on most issues:

> [B]eneath the glitz, beyond the firsts, Jordan isn't all that different from Balukoff. . . . They [both] want to protect the environment, do a better job of educating young Idahoans, repair roads and bridges and make health care accessible. None of them wants to accomplish those tasks

with a major tax hike. In response to inquiries from the Statesman, Jordan and Balukoff both said they support the Second Amendment. (Ganga, *Idaho Statesman*, May 16 2018)

There's nothing interesting, let alone radical, in any of these positions. Idahoans across party lines love nature, so speaking about protecting the environment is a safe bet. Educating young Idahoans is a definite improvement, but what about increasing the salary of schoolteachers? What about making health care accessible to all? Then there's "no tax hike" and "no gun control." Not only did Jordan and Balukoff share policy positions they shared these positions with the Republicans. This, though, is one of the current trends in the Democratic Party, especially in conservative states: more centrist or Republican-like Democrats are being touted in these states to counter Republicans. If, as some pundits claim, the Republican Party has changed in recent years, the same thing has happened to the Democrats as well. This unspoken nefarious coalition, however, sparks the hope of a radical alternative emerging to eventually take down both these behemoths (something of which we might be already seeing with the post-2018 elections' incoming freshmen class of Democrats in Washington, D.C.).

If voters did not choose between Jordan and Balukoff on basis of their policy, then on what basis did they vote? I claim they went with the image, or the candidate with most "radical" image. On the one hand, there was Balukoff, whose image was a close match to Trump's; on the other hand, Jordan was a woman and a member of the Coeur d'Alene tribe, thus everything that Balukoff was not. By most counts, Jordan proved to be a more palatable figure for Idaho liberals—she offered the feelgood image that Idaho's Democrat voters desperately sought in order to distance themselves from anything resembling "Trump," that is, from the gross political and social conservatism gradually becoming the norm in this country.[1] Like Obama, whose appeal among white voters has been identified with the fact that he did not elicit white "feelings of historical guilt" about slavery (Obama being the offspring of an African father and a white mother), Jordan too offered Idaho Democrats a safe bet: not white but not too colored, opposed to Republican conservatism but herself in many ways a Democratic conservative, or, a face that could help invite more capitalist investments into Idaho without completely sacrificing its conservative values (Rodriguez 2006).

It is this fascination with the image that distinguishes liberals today from their conservative counterparts. Nothing appears to please liberals more than a politically correct image. By contrast, conservatives are also attached to the image but tend to highlight the symbolic aspects of an image over everything else. They thus fight for rights—from the Second Amendment to the Ten Commandments—that they believe will strengthen their narcissistic image of themselves as white Christian men with a God-given mandate to police moral, political, and social values both inside and outside the nation.

The liberal fascination with the image no less symptomatically dovetails into their specific ideology of identity and a universe of particulars. That is, liberals operate under the belief that every single individual can share the same social space through mutual tolerance, understanding, and empathy, ideas that function to ideologically subsume questions of political difference to a cultural symbology. Conflicts between communities (as in the 2005 French riots), according to this logic, are not matters of politics—how to exist with the other in the *polis*—but, rather, a matter of culture: Can different types of people coexist? Can different cultures find a common ground in society?

This split between liberals and conservatives over their respective fixations with the image is evidenced not only in the political culture of the United States but also in the cultural politics. As examples, I offer below discussions of two popular Hollywood films, Marvel Studios' *Black Panther* (2018) and Clint Eastwood's *Gran Torino* (2008). Separated by exactly a decade, these are very different films. The latter earned scathing reviews for being overtly racist, replicating the white-savior narrative and overwriting minority cultures. Ryan Coogler's superhero flick, by contrast, received extensive praise for doing the right thing—it celebrated African or black culture with aplomb at a time when racism against African Americans and other minorities is on the rise in the country. My discussion of these films will draw out the limitations of focusing exclusively on representational politics or the politics of the image, and resulting uncritical evaluations as impediments in fully analyzing or comprehending the "real" ideological functions of these films. One concluding point to sum up the discussion with which I started: in the 2018 Idaho gubernatorial election, Jordan lost to the Republican candidate Brad Little by more than twenty percentage points.

II. *BLACK PANTHER*: THE ILLUSION OF DIVISION

Consider this as a thesis for *Black Panther*: the film seeks to obfuscate systemic racial oppression, propagandize the feelgood politics of tolerant multiculturalism, and deracialize U.S. exceptionalism.

Understandably, this thesis will not sit right with the film's liberal viewers who are ecstatic about its positive representations of African and African American culture(s) and its overall message of world peace and reconciliation. But this thesis will also not impress the conservatives: *Black Panther* has avid supporters amongst the alt-right. *Breitbart* celebrated it as a "pro-Trump extravaganza," while white nationalists claimed feeling vindicated by the film's arguments about ethno-states. If "America is to be great again," then, America too must freely adopt policies of isolationism and bravely come down on immigration, they have argued. The "Wakanda Forever" ideology makes it a prosperous peaceful and technologically advanced nation; America should follow suit (see Timberg 2018; Weekes 2018).

I concur with Žižek: "When all sides recognize themselves in the same product…the product in question is ideology at its purest—a kind of empty vessel containing antagonistic elements" (2018, n.p.). This does not mean that *Black Panther* is ideologically empty or that its ideology is open to interpretation with both liberals and conservatives finding traction in it. Rather, the film's true ideological functions are different from those immediately evident. Simply put: *Black Panther*'s most recognizable ideologies—celebration of African culture and black identity—hide another set of ideological functions, namely, to distract audience attention away from real social problems of minority communities and help consolidate a sense of sovereign subjectivity for U.S viewers at a time when the idea of U.S. exceptionalism is under duress. *Black Panther* makes both minority viewers and white liberal viewers feel good. They believe things are changing; with its (mostly) all-black cast, this is a starting point for more minority representation in mainstream cinema, and that it broke all box-office records attests that black actors too can deliver blockbusters. This cinematic celebration of African culture, language, and bodies prove further that white viewers in the United States are more mature than previously claimed. What get lost in all of this are, however, the routine police killings of black youth in the inner cities; the forced separation of children from their "illegal" immigrant parents at the country's southern borders; the decimation of lives and cultures across the globe by the interventions of U.S. military. *Black Panther* is Hollywood in "blackface"—"It lures its audience in with positive representations of black people and black culture…and then feeds it the same neoliberal, neo-colonial politics, except with a black face" (Qurashi 2018, n.p.).

Critiques such as the above have been few and far between. Qurashi's review, for instance, calls out some of the sneaky ideological maneuvers. According to

Qurashi, the film's most insidious message relates to black liberation. It shows that black liberation in the global present is best conducted in cooperation with and not against the white, European (neo-)colonial world order. Similarly, Žižek's review of the film underlines how universalism of black identity in the film is neither truly free nor properly universal insofar as it is impossible to constitute such an identity due to the historical "cut" of the transatlantic slave trade. My efforts in this chapter will be to add to these points as well as elaborating them further. Specifically, my focus will be on three *mise-en-scènes* of fantasy: (1) The construction of Wakanda; (2) the figure of Killmonger; and (3) the logic of the exceptional One.

FANTASY I: THE VEL OF WAKANDA

Black Panther substitutes the Orientalist image of Africa as Dark Continent— its nations poor and mired in chaos—with another equally fantastic image: Wakanda is a site of pure plenitude. Wakanda's prosperity comes from its unique deposits of Vibranium, an extraterrestrial mineral found only in Wakanda, and it has been through strategic isolationism that this tiny African nation has remained unaffected by colonialism. Using a virtual screen of forest canopy, they hide in plain sight. To the world, Wakanda is just another poor African nation, but beneath the veil of the forest canopy it is a nation richer and more technologically advanced than all the countries in the world combined.

The substitution of fantasy is interesting for a number of reasons. For one thing, the replacement of the image of Africa as poor with the image of Africa as rich does not dismantle Othering or the need for fantasy to mediate our relation to Africa. If the fantasy of Africa as the "heart of darkness" supported the West as the subject responsible for rescuing and reforming the Other, then this new fantasy about Wakandan prosperity helps the same subject to comfortably realign its subjectivity in the contexts of postcoloniality, globalization, and multiculturalism. It might appear that by assuming a subservient position to Wakanda's prodigious technological advancements the West is abdicating its imaginary privilege, when in reality the West is still in charge of conceiving and mediating a fantasy of Africa. Grosrichard, Said, and Mudimbe all speak about the West's inability to conceive Africa without fantasmatic support. Africa is always excess—the "non-sensical, pre-ideological kernel of enjoyment"—an overabundance to all our senses, therefore unbearable without fantastic cloaking (Žižek 1989, 124). Untouched by the Spirit of History and the birthplace of the human species, it is the West's disavowed primal scene requiring constant tempering via fantasy.[2]

It can be argued that by choosing to cloak their real identity with the veil of third world depression, Wakandans craftily use a European representational cliché to remain undetected from European corporate greed, and this tantamount to them controlling their fantasy. In fact, it can be asked: Isn't this an instance of "writing back"? In my view, showing Wakandans controlling discourse about their state of existence is one of the many posturings in the film that satisfy audience desire for feeling good about Africa following years of enjoying negative representations of the continent. Wakandans controlling the fantasmatic screen does not overturn the formal aspects of the West's fantasy about Africa and the role this fantasy plays in supporting the West's imaginary about its ultimate sovereignty.

Wakanda repurposes the old fantasies of Africa as a magical and unknowable space. It is magical because it is the hub for saving damaged superheroes and their human sidekicks. This African nation's advanced medical facilities save U.S. Agent Everett Ross (Martin Freeman) after he suffers an almost unrepairable fatal bullet wound. But once flown in, Shuri (Letitia Wright) revives him within twenty-four hours thanks to Vibranium technology. Avid MCU (Marvel Cinematic Universe) followers will also know that Bucky/Winter Soldier (Sebastian Stan) undergoes treatment and rehabilitation in Wakanda. Though the magic of this space is material, with its technology derived from Vibranium, considered in purely formal aspects this magic is synchronous with the magic of the untamed natural Africa we find in Rider Haggard's and Allan Quatermain's adventures as well as in contemporary tourism advertisements promising Western clients "Romance and Rejuvenation at Victoria Falls" (see Elowitt 2015, n.p.).

Wakanda's unknowability is associatively layered and integrally tied to the critical conflict at the heart of the film: isolationism versus global black liberation. In order to peel back the associated layers, let's begin with the fact that this unknowability is the result of Wakanda's secretive existence—it is the most secretive nation on the planet. This again is the result of the technological cloaking of the entire nation. So, what goes on inside of Wakanda is totally unknown. These characteristics already recall nations touted as secretive and unknowable in U.S. media, political rhetoric, and popular culture—the Soviet Union and its Iron Curtain during the Cold War; Iraq and its hidden cache of WMDs during the 1990s; and North Korea in the global present. In the last century, a number of African nations were also represented likewise and in the centuries before that the Ottoman Empire represented the epitome of a secretive, clandestine, enemy state. Though geographically and temporally dispersed, these spaces derive their unknowability, and Western anxiety over this unknowability, via the fantasmatic figure of the (Oriental) despot/dictator (Grosrichard 1998). This old fantasy and the anxiety associated with it returns in *Black Panther*.

Though unaware of Wakanda's Vibranium-driven affluence, the outside world knows a few things about Wakanda. They know it is a monarchy and know about the elite female bodyguards who always surround the Wakandan king, the *Dora Milaje*. They also know that in spite of being one of the poorest countries in the world, the Wakandan king stubbornly refuses international aid, possibly keeping poor Wakandans impoverished. Wakanda could thus very well be Gaddafi's Libya or Mugabe's Zimbabwe or Admiral General Aladeen's (Sacha Baron Cohen) Wadiya (*The Dictator* 2012). This relatable frame invisibly borders the new fantasy, making the film truly about the condition of the nonenlightened despot in the global present. What misdirects us from our enjoyment of this filmic fantasy about non-European despots is the splitting of the figure of the despot into two bodies—T'Challa (Chadwick Boseman) versus N'Jadaka aka Erik Killmonger (Michael B. Jordan). This splitting proves ideologically expedient for two things. First, the question or future of black liberation is presented through their conflict. Secondly, the old European fantasy of the (Oriental) despot is recycled through them.

In the original fantasy, the despot resembles the Freudian primal father insofar as he has access to unbridled enjoyment. The despot's pursuit of enjoyment—his excessive hunger for enjoyment—makes him a bizarre character. The despot is both weak-minded from his constant pursuit of enjoyment and a cause for political trepidation. He is weak because he is negligent of his duties as king, remaining immersed in pleasure all day. This in turn makes him and his rule dangerous: the despot's irresponsibility leads to all-round collapse of law and order, thus giving birth to free radicals who prove politically dangerous.

In *Black Panther* this fantasy is sublimated and split up. For though as a superhero T'Challa is more than ordinary, his excess is not connected to uncontrolled sexual enjoyment. In fact, he appears rather stoic in matters of enjoyment and firmly rooted in heteronormative domesticity. Killmonger, the other king, by contrast, is the raw figure of the excessive despot. He appears full of lust for life, revenge, and revolution. Killmonger represents the drive toward enjoying life fully by way of overhauling existing restrictions, especially restrictions arbitrarily imposed on black bodies: he dreams of emancipating

African's suffering blatant and systemic oppression across the globe by using Vibranium weapons. In the process, he wants to revenge the history of colonization, slave trade, and social discrimination by establishing Wakanda as the *new Empire*. Killmonger unites the political threat of the despot with the anxiety of the despot's excessive desire.

By contrast, T'Challa is a political moderate. He is riven by the Wakandan policy of isolationism because he too believes in helping other not so prosperous African nations. This internal conflict is highlighted a number of times in the film before becoming the central point of contention between him and Killmonger. For example, we see T'Challa discuss isolationism with Nakia (Lupita Nyong'o), the latter in favor of opening the borders, and then with his friend and trusted comrade W'Kabi (Daniel Kaluuya), who is opposed to foreigners and refugees coming into Wakanda. Most importantly, in the opioid-induced reverie in which he "visits" his dead ancestors, T'Challa admits to wavering about kingship: he seeks advise from his father, the late king T'Chaka (John Kani), about how to govern Wakanda at a time when the world has opened up and knowing fully that Wakanda's resources can help other countries and depressed communities in need.

I will return to discussing the film's plotting of the T'Challa-Killmonger conflict. Let me conclude this discussion by noting yet another aspect of Wakanda as fantasy: there are two fantasies in *Black Panther*. The surface narrative—celebration of African culture, Afro-futurism, etc.—is a fantasy veiling the cliched colonial fantasies of African magic, unknowability, and despotic barbarity. The surface fantasy "provides the coordinates of our desire[,] which constructs the frame enabling us to desire" or enjoy the second fantasy (Žižek 1989, 118). This second fantasy is the original colonial fantasy of Africa as "dark continent," but which we cannot openly claim to enjoy or enunciate in the global present. The use of one fantasy to hide another fantasy allows us to enjoy a disavowed enjoyment. Real enjoyment is located in enjoying what has been repressed. In other words, fantasy teaches us how to desire without risking what we truly desire. Or, put differently, fantasy gives us the framework for enjoying what we are not allowed to enjoy and/or that which is impossible to enjoy. This is where the ideological fulcrum of *Black Panther* is situated—not in the images but in what these images hide. Ideology, Žižek writes,

> is not a dreamlike illusion that we build to escape insupportable reality; in its basic dimension it is a fantasy-construction which serves as a support for our "reality" itself: an "illusion" which structures our effective,

> real social relations and thereby masks some insupportable, real, impossible kernel (conceptualized by Ernesto Laclau and Chantal Mouffe as "antagonism": a traumatic social division which cannot be symbolized). The function of ideology is not to offer us a point of escape from our reality but to offer us the social reality itself as an escape from some traumatic, real kernel. (ibid., 45)

Borrowing from Žižek, I wish to claim that *Black Panther* "is not a 'fantasy image of social reality' but, on the contrary, the *mise-en-scène of the fantasy which is at work in the midst of social reality itself*" (ibid., 36). Two hours inside the film theatre watching this superhero flick does not abstract us from the reality outside but teaches us how to understand or negotiate the outside reality. Put simply: the film allows us to continue enjoying the colonial fantasies of Africa without having to acknowledge this enjoyment. In fact, not only are we sheltered from the embarrassment of acknowledging our sick desire, but we are given the option to appear to enjoy something appropriate for retaining our facades of multiculturalism. While a section of the audience is seduced by the romanticism of the images and celebrate the film's progressive bold representation of minorities, another section enjoys what is hidden by the images without necessarily coming across as opposed to multiculturalism, etc. *Black Panther* is neoliberalism perfectly packaged: those with privilege can have their cake and eat it too.

FANTASY II: WAKANDA AND *BINU-R BARI* (BINU'S HOME); OR, HOW TO READ KILLMONGER

The idea of Wakanda as home, a site of extreme plenitude and fulsome happiness, parallels the dream of Binu, the little orphan boy in Bengali *auteur* Ritwik Ghatak's *Subarnarekha* (1965). Binu dreams of a home in a land of fullness: a bungalow in a verdant valley overflowing with blossoming flowers, teeming with sweet songs of birds and the soft flutter of colorful butterflies. This "dream" home of abundance contrasts with the traumas he suffered as an orphan and with the general idea of the "home" or lack of it in the film. Binu's desire, though, is the desire of his mother, and to an extent of his maternal uncle, both of whom were displaced from their ancestral homes in the wake of India's negotiated independence in 1947.

The partition of India created India and Pakistan, the latter being divided into two parts, West Pakistan and East Pakistan (today's Bangladesh). If close to three million people died during the Bengal Famine of 1943, then Louis Mountbatten's cunning plan of partitioning the subcontinent as the condition of India's independence led to the death of millions in sectarian riots, displacement of millions from their ancestral homes, and a further few millions reported missing in the course of the human exodus and ensuing riots. Ghatak (1925–1976) never reconciled to the Partition; his films are troubled testaments to the psychological and material trauma of the displaced. In *Subarnarekha*, Binu's ideal home plays a significant purpose: it is at once the galvanizing force behind actions of all the characters in the film and an impossible space that can never exist. Binu's ideal home is like Wakanda—a fantasy and nothing more.

At one level, Wakanda and Binu's home inspire the wretched of the Earth by urging them to dream a more complete, wholesome, and self-sustaining future. In this future they might yet accomplish a home that would allow them to fully (re)embrace their lost or deformed cultural heritages and mangled identities without needing to reject everything that bears the denomination of the "West." In the specific cases of Binu and N'Jadaka or "Killmonger," the latter another orphan, though, the need to (re)claim "home" is more than a need to belong somewhere, it is, rather, an expression of their respective existential angsts. These "homes" they seek are not what will satisfy them, that is, make them complete; rather, these homes they seek exist as impossible destinations or open wounds articulating their existential pains.

However, like all fantastic spaces the lost ideal home does not exist. They drive us; they invite our attention and solicit our transgressions in hopes that we will find our true homes someday but they do not exist, because they never existed. Yet it is only because they are impossible that desire for these "homes" unravels what drives those like Binu and Killmonger to dream about and fight for "a home." Binu's or Killmonger's is an unending universal fight. For Binu names all those dreamers and rebels and rioters and saboteurs who wish, claim, dream, and demand a new home. We know that this home can never exist, and even if it ever does, this home will not be in the happy valley Binu dreams of. But this impossibility as radical negativity is what arranges Binu's dream, a dream that becomes the forebearer of political thought and pragmatic revolutionary action as Binu grows into adulthood.

Ritwik's Binu returns as an adult in Nabarun's novel *Herbert* (1994). At the end of *Subarnarekha,* Binu was ready to trek across the horizon in search of his home. But Ritwik never shows whether Binu finds his home and/or whether after finding it he likes it or grows disenchanted. Instead, Ritwik leaves Binu on the journey. And that is where audiences have had to leave him too: a young Binu optimistic about eventually reaching his dream home. We do not hear from him till another three decades later when Binu *suddenly* returns in *Herbert*: he is *still* searching for his home but now he is resolved to take direct action in order to reorganize existing society so that it becomes this "home." Binu in *Herbert* is a Naxal: a spectral shadow, moving furtively through the rapidly globalizing city of Calcutta armed with Maoist leaflets and dynamite sticks. He is no longer seeking a home on the other side of the rainbow; instead, he wishes to change society in order to make it home for everyone. In this new figuration, he is an uncontainable force responsible for sudden disruptions (a blast at the local crematorium) in the Bengali bourgeois society—he is the lamella that reappears again and again across decades to announce the dreams of the desperate, the multitude, and the orphaned.

To think of Binu as a desiring subject, that is, Binu desires a home or Binu desires a new political order, is to reduce him into a romantic fantasy.[3] I prefer to read Binu instead as the subject of drive. He is negativity positivized—the manifestation of the real in the symbolic. His search for a home that will never be is the reminder of the impossibility of the subject becoming whole. That is also why Binu will never be happy simply by moving out of or reforming his immediate social position: Binu inhabits the space of routine oppression, but more than seeking to overturn this order he gives body to this space—the condition of this zone—by appearing as its material remainder/reminder. In embodying the impossibility of transcending the margins and in embodying the zone of nonbeing, Binu realizes the impossibility constitutive of the social. As the rem(a/i)nder of class antagonism structuring the socius, Binu is *the* reason for the social.

I draw a straight line from Binu to Killmonger because, like Binu, Killmonger is an orphan. Growing up in "poverty in the United States" Killmonger's life is "shaped by the privation of the American inner-city and his experiences inside the U.S. war machine" (Gray 2018, n.p.). He too desires "a home, a place [where] he truly belongs, and yearns to correct at the point of a gun the injustices of a world order" (ibid.). But more critically, both Killmonger and Binu are effusive stains streaking across our contemporary social order. They are a passionate throwback to Fanonian time—a reminder that only radical violence can emancipate the wretched of the Earth from oppressive neoliberal hegemony. It is therefore not a surprise that Killmonger refuses the dogma of isolationism in preference for using Wakanda's power in helping the exploited. T'Challa/Black Panther stands in deliberate contrast to him because T'Challa represents the *other* viewpoint: he advocates "a gradual and peaceful globalism," or Wakanda responsibly spreading education and technology to impoverished corners of the globe with the ultimate aim of emancipating the world, but only by working "within the coordinates of the existing world order and its institutions" (Žižek 2018, n.p.). T'Challa thus advocates hegemonic collusion with the CIA (who are presented in the film on the side of good and against a ruthless violent "African" leader);[4] he satisfies the neoliberal desires for tolerance and nonviolence while maintaining the particularities of Wakandan culture. As Duane Rousselle rightly observes:

> [W]hat is celebrated here is a "revolution from below"—a "non-violent" and therefore non-confrontational revolution. I name this a "decaffeinated revolution," or, rather, a capitalist revolution (to be distinguished from a revolution *beyond* capitalism). (Rousselle 2018, n.p.)

Christopher Lebron regrets the film pushing viewers to choose between "two radical imaginings in front of them" when these imaginings could have been shown to reconcile (Lebron 2018, n.p.). We can read this as our inability to think outside desire. Structured by the dialectic of having or being, we must choose one in place of the other just as we must also always think everyone is acting out of desire. But what if Killmonger is not acting out of desire? What if Killmonger is like Thanos, who in *Avengers: Infinity War* (2018) quests after the infinity stones only to kill off half the universe with a snap of his fingers? There is no desire, purpose, or motivation in what Thanos wants. He only wants half of living matter in the universe to die. Period. Maybe he has no reason to want this except for wanting this to happen. Following the same logic, I wish to ask, What if Killmonger is not chasing a desire; rather, his actions are illustrative of the traumatic emptiness of desire? Representing Killmonger in terms of desire (i.e., asking "What does Killmonger want?") can only give answers such as he wants world domination, to replace white supremacy with black sovereignty, the throne of Wakanda, etc. These answers function to revitalize the film's conscious narrative strategy of polarizing viewers, as noted by Lebron. In consequence, not only does the film fail to deliver a radical political message, it remains collusive with Hollywood's ideological agenda of representing neoliberalism as humane. But if Killmonger is nothing more than the materialization or embodiment of radical negativity itself, then, unlike T'Challa/Black Panther, he starts to appear as *the* subject. Like Binu, Killmonger is the desubjectivized subjectivity of the hungry, oppressed, and marginalized in our world. Their desires as such confront our class privileges; they appear to us as anamorphic stains decimating the fantasmatic screens of neoliberal worldviews. Hanging outside deliberations of peace, truth, and reconciliation, Binu and Killmonger substantiate an irreducible surplus irreproachable by neoliberal discourse. Their positions in society are irredeemable, which means they cannot be accommodated within society or they refuse accommodation in our societies. In this, they represent the impossible antagonism at the core of the social. But their existence as radical lack is also that which gives "positive ontological consistency" to our society (Žižek 2008a, 97). In other words, they realize the lack constituent of the social, social relations and intersubjective exchanges in the social. Though commonly this lack remains veiled by social discourses of contract, the lack remains nonetheless as the foundation of the social. The erasure of Killmonger therefore becomes necessary to avoid facing the trauma of knowing what occupies the heart of the social, namely, the real, and to return to the relative comfort of our social "reality."

Killmonger dies from a spear wound inflicted by Black Panther. But he refuses Black Panther's offer to be healed by Vibranium. He prefers to die a free man like his ancestors who jumped off ships during the Middle Passage. The film ends with Killmonger and Black Panther sitting side by side, on a mountain overhang, admiring the rich Wakandan sunset. In his "Straussian" reading of the film, Žižek insists that we witness in this scene the dissolution of conflict, as ideological dichotomy makes way for "a scene of extraordinary warmth":

> [T]he dying Killmonger sits down at the edge of a mountain precipice observing the beautiful Wakanda sunset, and T'Challa, who has just defeated him, silently sits at his side. There is no hatred here, just two basically good men with a different political view sharing their last moments after the battle is over. It's a scene unimaginable in a standard action movie that culminates in the vicious destruction of the enemy. These final moments alone cast doubt on the film's obvious reading and solicit us to deeper reflection. (2018, n.p.)

By contrast, Lebron calls this scene "macabre," arguing that the scene only validates that even in fiction "black life does not matter":

> In a macabre scene meant to be touching, Black Panther carries Killmonger to a plateau so that he might see the sun set on Wakanda before dying. With a spear stuck in his chest, he fulfills his wish to appreciate the splendor his father described, when Wakanda seemed a fairy tale. T'Challa offers Wakanda's technology to save Killmonger's life—it has saved the white CIA agent earlier in the film. But Killmonger recalls his slave heritage and tells Panther he'd rather die than live in bondage. He knows the score. He knows that Panther will incarcerate him (as is disproportionately common for black American men). The silence that follows seems to last an eternity. Here is the chance for the movie to undo its racist sins: T'Challa can be the good person he desires to be. He can understand that Killmonger is in part the product of American racism and T'Chaka's cruelty. T'Challa can realize that Wakanda has been hoarding resources and come to an understanding with Killmonger that justice may require violence, if as a last resort. After all, what else do comic-book heroes do but dispense justice with their armored fists and laser rifles? Black Panther does not flinch. There is no reconciliation. Killmonger yanks the spear out of his chest and dies. The sun sets on his body as it did on Michael Brown's. (2018, n.p.)

The difference between Žižek's and Lebron's perspectives can be accounted for by thinking closely about their différanced lived experiences, that is, by thinking about their respective experiences of experiencing difference. Lebron's point of view is anchored in the history of black America, its past and present continuous. Žižek's reading is a distinct gesture of European privilege, which identifies the death of the antagonist (anticolonial revolutionary) as the moment for soulful reconciliation between enemies. As if the death of the rebel resolves the problem of hegemonic oppression altogether. It is an invitation to forget and move on. If anything, this notion is no less cliched than "standard action movie that culminates in the vicious destruction of the enemy," in that this scene rehearses a fairy-tale ending for the dominant power. (Žižek 2018, n.p.). And, as is often the case with these fairy-tale endings, the dominant power gets the opportunity to reenter the folds of humanity by putting on full display its faux humanity. Unlike Lebron, Žižek can admit reconciliation or see this scene as outside ideological conflict because his Eurocentric perspective cannot conceive otherwise. For though Žižek claims to be with Fanon, in his reading of this scene at least he fails to comprehend Fanon's important lesson that there cannot be any communication or settlement between the dominant and the oppressed, even in death. Black Panther's offer to heal Killmonger is insincere, being nothing less than the hubris of the dominant hegemony. At another level, this gesture is symptomatic of contemporary liberals who believe in nonviolence, charity, and equality of all people. But though these liberals express moral shock at the news of children forcibly separated from (illegal) immigrant parents at the country's southern border, they never so much as flinch at the deaths of innocent children in Pakistan from U.S. military's drone attacks. What matters most to the liberals is that their hands are clean of the blood shed by U.S. imperialism, and for this they keep rinsing their hands like Lady Macbeth—by donating to charities and saving hungry children in Africa—with the hope of buying themselves out of their ethical responsibility of condemning U.S. militarism and/or for claiming redemption without needing to recognize their complicity in the violence perpetrated by the U.S. state both inside and outside its national borders. This scene therefore can only appear heartwarming to those with (white/power/class) privilege and those who need to contain Killmonger's final excessive defiance from spilling out of the scene. Killmonger's "nah" to T'Challa's offer frees Killmonger from living a life that is akin to death, the condition of the black man (the Jew, the colonized, and the subaltern), according to Fanon. Choosing death rather than being saved by the class enemy, Killmonger enunciates his final act of defiance, which simultaneously makes him the subject and the object, the agent and the target, of his speech/act(ion) (Pluth 2018, 131). His "nah" is the ultimate full speech giving him freedom; the same freedom his ancestors sought by jumping off the slave ships into the depths of the (black) Atlantic. Killmonger is Jose Dolores of the global present.

My reading so far sides with critics such as Lebron and Qurashi both of whom disapprove of the film's pro-neoliberalism and black liberationist pretension. Quarshi, for example, is spot on when he writes:

> The film is telling black people how to be successful and accepted on the world stage as black people—to be "moderate," to operate within the confines of the neoliberal, neo-colonial world order. If you want to make changes and help people, do so incrementally. Go to the UN, like T'Challa, and announce the creation of a charity organisation that will "help" those that have been oppressed and abused. Don't ever think about "burning it all down and starting over." If you try something like that,

we'll come together in a coalition and destroy you. And you will die, just like N'Jadaka. (Qurashi 2018, n.p.)⁵

While this reading helps us understand how the film ideologically teaches us to remain moderate in our demands, believe in the democratic institutions of (neo)colonial West, and guard against excessive protests, I wish to discuss what is often left out when comparing T'Challa to Killmonger. Namely, the relation of these protagonists to their excessive powers. I would be remiss not to discuss the issue of superpowers in discussing a superhero film. As I see it, Killmonger is not just "a 'radical' black leader with superpowers who wants to reorder the world and redistribute its resources," but he kills for the sake of killing—he is a cold killing machine, inhuman and uncontainable (Qurashi 2018, n.p.; Lebron 2018, n.p.). Siding with him can only mean all-round chaos and death. T'Challa, by contrast, is not only a moderate who acknowledges the West (i.e., the UN) but, more importantly, in spite of possessing superpowers he is still human. Black Panther's humanity endears him to global audiences, whereas Killmonger's inhumanity threatens.

What differentiate the two imaginings of black leadership—Killmonger versus T'Challa/Black Panther—are their respective relations to jouissance: Killmonger's inexplicable enjoyment about freeing the oppressed versus T'Challa's desire for pragmatic nonviolent activism. The latter is quantifiable—a study center here, a food camp there—and provides a cultural solution to a political issue, and thereby is closer to neoliberal worldviews of tolerant pluralism, charitable humanitarianism, and nonviolent mediation of crises. In other words, activism that, being distinct from Killmonger's vision of radical action, poses no threat to the status quo. The latter vision evokes anxiety by resurrecting the specter of proletarian revolution, the establishment of communes, the trials of class enemies, etc.⁶ In discussing this I first turn to the fantasy of the superhero as the exceptional One, then explain why audience sympathy often gravitates toward the exceptional One with *lack*.

Fantasy III: Superhero as the One

Entry into the symbolic order is contingent on castration. Or, alternatively, we can say, entrance into the symbolic order requires a sacrifice, namely, castration. Or, entrance into the symbolic order realizes the void (of castration) that always exists but only finds realization with signifiers (Miller 1991, 32). Castration does not refer to the physical act but, rather, to the institution of symbolic law barring full enjoyment of the (m)other. The responsibility for instituting the law of castration is on the father who intervenes into the mother-child dyad first with a prohibitive "No" (you cannot enjoy the mother) and, thereafter, by substituting the desire-for-the-mother with Law or "Name-of-the-Father." This is also known as the "Father function," that is, the metaphorization or significant substitution of the object of original desire (the mother) with another (the Phallus). The Father function separates the child from the enjoyment of plenitude by pushing it into the laws governing satisfaction of desire and thus inaugurating the desiring or lacking subject. The subject desires wholesome enjoyment or enjoyment lost. The Phallus comes to replace the lost (object of) enjoyment, but regaining our pre-Oedipal paradise proves impossible partly due to the nature of the Phallus as signifier and partly due to the nonexistence of a pre-Oedipal paradise anywhere except in fantasy. Stretched between desire and the absence of satisfaction, the subject is the gap or lack.

We must be careful here regarding one point. The Freudian subject is not a satisfaction-seeking subject. The subject does not desire to return to a pre-Oedipal paradise of a plenitude of mother-child undifferentiated dyad, if anything the subject avoids encountering the mother's desire. To exist in the mother's desire is to exist in constant dread over being totally consumed by this desire, therefore, far from being fulfilling the pre-Oedipal is a horrifying, excessive, and confusing space (Fink 1995, 56; Vanheule 2011, 69). Abstracted from the mythical enjoyment of the pre-Oedipal, the subject might complain about *paltry jouissance* but this nagging subject—unsatisfied and desiring—is the subjectivity preferable to being the object of the (m)Other's desire.[7] The symbolic allows this freedom for the cost of castration.

This is the premise for Lacan's sexuation formula from Seminar XX. Namely, all subjects are castrated or lacking only because there is One who is not (1999, 78–79). It is important to keep in mind, though, that the uncastrated One does not refer to a real person but indexes the formal possibility of such a subject (Hewitson 2013, n.p.). The superhero is the fantastic actualization of this formal possibility. The comic book superhero occupies the position of the One; the exception to castration.[8] As *the* One, the superhero is outside desire, unmarked by death, and often unmarred by the deadlock of sexuality (Žižek 2011, 60).[9]

What makes this fantasy really interesting, however, is the habitual imagining of the superhero's one exception from being the exception. That is to say, though the superhero is more than human, there is always one human aspect or *flaw* in the superhero. This can be a mortal weakness, as with Superman and Kryptonite or Batman's Christ-like sacrifice at the end of Christopher Nolan's 2008 *The Dark Knight*. These human-like qualities make superheroes relatable. As readers and viewers, we start feeling a connection with those who by accident or provenance are outside the laws governing us.

The exception enjoyed by the superhero is not transferable to common people. Simply put: even when the superhero resembles us in some ways, we cannot start claiming the exception and functioning outside the Law. In a scenario such as this, society as we know it, that is, society grounded in and governed by laws, will cease to exist. This problematic is captured in Nolan's *The Dark Knight*. In the scene where three citizens pretending to be Batman interrupt a drug deal, thereby unnecessarily putting themselves in harm's way, the real Batman has the double task of protecting the civilians while busting the criminals. And when Batman tells the citizen vigilantes that he does not need their help, one of them retorts: "What gives you the right? What's the difference between you and me?" Batman's response—"I am not wearing hockey pads"—gives only part of the answer. For what gives Batman the edge over the rest of us is his sophisticated arsenal of innovative weapons that is unavailable to the common man. (We must not forget that this arsenal is possible only because Bruce Wayne is a billionaire; without that kind of money no one can have access to such weapons). But, in my opinion, what this question really asks is: Why only him? How does he get to be the exceptional One? McGowan discusses the politico-legal implications of this exception in his book on Nolan. I do not wish to repeat his points here but I will underline a fundamental psychoanalytic point, namely, the Law is arbitrary and the question "Why only you?" conveys frustration mixed with helplessness, which we, commoners, routinely experience because of this arbitrariness.

The superhero's human-like quality is a corrective imagined for the global present. Today we no longer live under prohibitive laws, the superego no longer bars enjoyment, because in today's world particular pleasures are actively warranted, to wit, permitted. Hewitson reads this contemporary trend as "a kind of reification of the oscillation between the two lines of Lacan's formula"—all men are subject to the Law and there is One not subject to the Law—or, as reiterating the ontological problem of identity, "How can a character be both a man but more than a man? (Hewitson 2013, n.p.). Today, when "we are free to constantly re-invent our sexual identities, to change not only our job or our professional trajectory but even our innermost subjective features like our sexual orientation," the notion of exception is indeed problematic (Žižek 2018b, n.p.). Let's be real: on the one hand, all we need to do in order to appear as Batman is say in a gruff voice "I am Batman," but, then, on the other hand, this shorthand does not work because we cannot be Batman without his gadgets, training, and the butler. How many of us even know what the responsibilities of a butler are or have lived in a household with a butler? Yet we are told continuously that everybody can be anybody, a pauper can become a prince, a beast can land a beauty, the meek shall inherit the earth, etc.

If Nolan's *The Dark Knight* opens discussion over this, then *The Black Panther* performs a straightforward ideological function: make audiences appreciate why not everybody can be a superhero. For as Uncle Ben reminded us in *Spider-Man* (2002): "With great power comes great responsibility." *Black Panther* teaches us that Killmonger is not responsible, but with T'Challa at the helm of a clandestine superpower nation, the rest of the world can sleep in peace. We thus root for T'Challa in spite of the fact that Killmonger gains the throne, as per the laws of Wakanda, after defeating T'Challa in ritual combat. I am sure many of Coogler's viewers also want to end global inequality like Killmonger—they wish to end systemic racism and human and gender rights violations both inside and outside the United States—but they also prefer working toward these goals without acutely questioning or disrupting the real causes for existing inequalities. In other words, they want to appear aggrieved by global inequality but if that requires radical action, they promptly recuse themselves into activism. It is hardly surprising that these people side with T'Challa, the superhero who also prefers to leave capitalism and U.S. imperialism undisturbed. It does not matter that his policy of cultural and technological outreach is programmed into capitalism as tokenized gestures that serve to keep people believing something is really happening for the poor and dispossessed to reclaim their rightful place alongside us in this global economy. In reality, though, these gestures work to numb us against the inaction keeping exploitation, discrimination, and toxic patriarchy alive. It does not matter even if T'Challa's track record as king is most unimpressive—T'Challa "freezes" in his mission to rescue Nakia; T'Challa hesitates taking the responsibility of the kingdom; T'Challa fails to apprehend Ulysses Klaue (Andy Serkis); and, worse of all, T'Challa covers up the actions of his father, who killed his own brother (N'Jadaka's father) and left his orphan nephew in hostile territory. None of these compromises rattle the viewers, just as news of U.S. military killing innocents in Syria or Afghanistan never make it to the headlines of U.S. liberal media. Insofar as we have been taught to fixate over images of happy futures achieved by nonviolent (read: not anticapitalist and/or antiwhite/US) means, our fixation with the image of the nonviolent Other has to overshadow the other's radical political demands for equality.

III. *GRAN TORINO*: FROM THE IMAGINARY TO THE SYMBOLIC

Criticized for its over-the-top use of racial slurs, recycling of the white savior theme, and reducing Hmong Americans into a placeholder for the misguided and the menacing ethnic Other, Clint Eastwood's *Gran Torino* (2008) is not a film liked by liberals (McBride and Shahamiri 2011, 361, 363; Jalao 2010, 1). As liberal reviewers and critics of the film illustrate, again and again, they find the film's attempts to cloak its racist exclusionary ideology unsettling. They see evident bias in the film's attempt to construct a feelgood narrative out of a story about the redemptive transformation of an inveterate racist, Korean War veteran, and retired Ford assembly-line worker Walt Kowalski.

By contrast, the film's conservative admirers see in Kowalski (Clint Eastwood) a man not afraid to speak his mind or not bogged down by liberal pressures (including those from his children) for political correctness. He is a man who has no problem calling things as he sees them. Conservatives therefore praise Kowalski for standing up for his (working-class) values, his old (albeit exclusively white) neighborhood, and for his country. *Gran Torino* is about redemption: it is the story of a lapsed Catholic sacrificing his life in order to help the meek, the oppressed, and the helpless inherit the earth. In the process, he too "transcends his own ugly prejudices by realizing his neighbors are fellow human beings and allies in the struggle to defend their shared and cherished way of life," opines the Republican congressman from Michigan's Eleventh District, Thaddeus McCotter, in his review of the film in *Breitbart* (2009, n.p.).

So far in this chapter, I have stressed the liberal and conservative fascinations with the image. The liberals are totally riveted to the imaginary image whereas the conservatives are attached to the symbolic image. The simplistic reviews of *Gran Torino* show no different orientation. For instance, the image of Kowalski disapprovingly glaring at "new Americans" immediately characterizes him as racist. What gets overlooked in this judgment is the violence inflicted on the character of Kowalski, who does not even get a patient hearing. Relatedly, and speaking strictly in terms of literary or film analysis, such pigeonholing forecloses the possibility of critical reading and alternative interpretations. I have been insisting through my analyses in this book the need to move beyond images and symbols and start considering the real emerging between these. Pursuing this in the context of *Gran Torino* implies that we recognize the absence of stable relationships between signifiers and signifieds and seriously consider the inconsistencies, contingencies, and sheer immeasurability of thoughts, ideas, and intent pockmarking the text as unbearing consciousness about impossibility of seeing our critical reading or conceited imaginaries through. This in turn makes one-way interpretations, such as that *Gran Torino* is nothing but a racist film, or that it is a critique of liberal political correctness, equally problematic.

In what follows, I challenge liberal critiques of the film. I do not engage with the conservative reviews because I do not wish to dignify them. In fact, a discussion with conservative reviews is impossible insofar as these are nothing short of psychotic rantings uninscribed by logic of the symbolic order. Though much of this ranting is for politics—to galvanize, sustain, and support the divisive mechanisms of U.S. capitalism and in return benefit from this machine— some of them are pure psychotic gems. McCotter's review, for instance, calls for "Gran Torino conservatives" to fight off the tide of amoral globalization, radical environmentalists, Global Republicans, the Hippie-Boomers (who have today become Yuppies), and the suburbanite Left radicals. A list of preposterous enemies. I have little doubt that this type of conservative reviewer inhabits judge Schreber's "starlight" zone. They are not divorced from reality but have a specific connection to reality. Possessed of this special connection, they are like Judge Schreber: "Judge Schreber has sunbeams in his ass. A solar anus. And rest assured that it works: Judge Schreber feels something, produces something, and is capable of explaining the process theoretically" (Deleuze and Guattari 1983, 2).

The Polack, His Italian Barber, and a Chink

Early in the film, audiences are introduced to Kowalski's local barber Martin (John Carroll Lynch) and their flippant racist banterings. Later, Kowalski takes Thao (Bee Vang) to Martin's shop in order to teach his young acolyte how real men speak (or, to "man him up"!). The first part of this "instructional" visit requires Thao to learn from watching Martin and Kowalski exchange their characteristic racist and sexist repartee: Martin fires the first salvo by welcoming the duo as a "Polack and a chink" to which Kowalski responds by calling Martin a "crazy Italian prick." Following which Thao is advised to emulate the "man-speech" he just heard, but no sooner does Thao address Martin as "an old Italian prick" than the barber cranks out a shotgun, aims it at Thao's face, and threatens to blow his "gook head off." Kowalski intervenes with the third and final part of the lesson. He tells a shaken and confused Thao that he "cannot come in and insult a man in his own shop," that Thao should've begun the conversation with a "hello" and asked if Martin had time to give him a haircut. "But that's [not] what you said [to Martin]. That's what you said men say," Thao cries out perplexed.

Critics have called this scene "excruciating," "awkward," and, representing the Hmong teenager and Asian American men in general, "as paradigmatically lacking—socially off-kilter, politically mute and sexually undesirable" (Stables 2009; Jalao 2010; Schein and Vang 2018: 97). Two years after the release of the film, Vang collaborated with Louisa Schein on a five minute YouTube short titled "Thao Does Walt" (2010), a project they describe as "queer art," to expose the film's (and Hollywood's) persistent representations of Asian American subservience. In it they ask: "Why is it so funny when a bumbling Asian boy gets tutored in bantering like 'a man' by two patronizing white guys? How much of the audience mirth derives not from the lines themselves—'old Italian son-of-a-bitch prick barber/goddamn dicksmoking gook'—but from Thao's 'failure'?" (ibid., 96).

I agree that this scene uses over the top racist language and does not contribute to the narrative development—there are other scenes showcasing Kowalski's mentoring of the young man, which are not racially insensitive. But I also consider the barbershop scene crucial to the film, especially for understanding Kowalski. This scene gives an insight into Kowalski's mind, which otherwise remains shaded by his cold grumpy exterior and his vile mouth. Critics are right to an extent—the trauma of the war changed him. In addition, the decay of the white working class, the rapidly changing racial makeup of the country, and an all-round shift away from traditional social values and toward consumerism have shaped Kowalski. But to identify him as a xenophobe forecloses his character as stereotype, a rather unfortunate gesture if we are criticizing the film for stereotyping others. Instead, as I show below, the barbershop scene discloses an interesting aspect about Kowalski's character, which is useful for critically understanding the film.

The Other Is Absent!

Thao "fails" in the barber scene because he believes in the big Other. He believes that because Kowalski has said so—"speak like a man"—and because immediately beforehand Kowalski performed this man-speak by freely trading racist and sexist insults with Martin, then manliness must exist in a certain habit of speaking. Free use of racial slurs in this case. This scene shows, however, that signifiers do not correlate to signifieds, that the meanings of words change depending on intersubjective contexts, that is, saying what might be okay in one context may be unacceptable in another. Simply put, the Kowalski and Martin relation does not automatically transfer to Thao and Martin. With no big Other guaranteeing meaning across different contexts, words shift, slide, and take on new meanings from one moment to another.

Freud illustrates this argument throughout his *Interpretation of Dreams* (1900), *Jokes and their Relation to the Unconscious* (1905), and *Moses and Monotheism* (1939): the signifier has no essential relation to the signified, the unconscious to the conscious, and one of the tasks for the analyst is to uncover this (non-)relationship. As Freud writes in "The Technique of the Joke," the force of the joke does not emerge from "bafflement and light dawning," but from "one of the two things; either the thought expressed in [a] remark is intrinsically witty, or the witticism is bound up with the way in which [this] remark has formulated the thought" (2003, 9). Though there's nothing witty or acceptable in Kowalski and Martin's constant harassment of Thao as pussy, nip, and chink, the assumption that everyone laughing at this scene is enjoying seeing Thao racially bullied fails to consider how the real source of enjoyment might be located elsewhere. Specifically, in the unraveling of the absent Other. For it is possible that we are not laughing at Thao but because we identify with him, that is, with his deception. We too, like Thao, believe in the existence of a big Other and like him we often find ourselves in utter confusion.

I am not proposing we understand Kowalski and Martin's exchange as private speech. I am also not asking that we think of racist slurs as innocuous because the signifier does not correspond with the signified and therefore there is no one meaning to any word. As any person of color would vouch, hearing a slur even when it is not directly addressed to you is soul sapping. Rather, I am pushing here for an understanding of the barbershop scene as illustrative of Kowalski's (unacknowledged) awareness about the tenuous connection between the signifier and the signified—the big Other's absence or incapacity to make speech hold. Again, this not to be understood as a free pass for racist speech, or, to imply that Kowalski and Martin share a special bond that supersedes the rules of the big Other. This is also not an issue of linguistic formalization, that is to say, the signifier can never approximate the signified or that at the moment an idea is expressed in words the idea is lost. Rather, my point here is simple: there is no guarantee of meaning by the big Other because there is *no* big Other! The big Other does not exist.

Kowalski's awareness of the Other's absence finds expression in other scenes as well, but most significantly in his exchanges with the parish priest, Father Janovich (Christopher Carley). One easily infers from their interactions that Kowalski hates the Church, calling it out for peddling lies about life and death and for promising hope when none exists. Isn't this distrust of God similar to his distrust of meaningful communication? Kowalski "knows" there exists no ultimate design or plan for humans and this finds poignant expression in one of his exchanges with Janovich. Rebutting Janovich's observation that most traumatic acts are those done under an Other's command, Kowalski says the most traumatic acts are those done without order and yet for which one is rewarded by the Other, no less. Apropos of this scene, we are forced to consider whether Kowalski's war trauma stems from his guilt for killing a young Korean soldier who wanted to surrender—an act mired in linguistic misunderstanding—or for being awarded a medal for this killing. For if there is a law it ought to apply equally to everyone and remain valid at all times. As such, killing an enemy when the enemy is ready to surrender is tantamount to murder, and should not deserve a medal but serious military punishment. Does Kowalski's distrust of the law originate in the trauma of remaining unreprimanded for his action? Is he concerned that the law is partial. and hence cannot be absolute? I detect a Kafkaesque wariness about the law in Kowalski's PTSD. Accordingly, Kowalski's self-imposed social isolation, I would contend, comes from his distrust of the social's possessing collective meaning. To Kowalski, meaning exists at a personal level—his memories of the war, his deceased wife, his 1972 Gran Torino, his lawn, and his dog—but does not extend beyond these, not even to his two sons and their families. Though I am not sure whether Kowalski knows or is unconscious about all this, the point I am making is: Kowalski is not your run-of-the-mill racist. He is also not a "moral absolutist" (Teays 2012, 142). He is an ethical subject to the extent of being socially immoral, a modern-day misanthrope.

Empty Speech versus Full Speech

Those who characterize the barbershop scene as a racist pantomime—full of clichéd sexist and racist banter but otherwise empty of any substantial content—derive their argument from the notion of speech as communication, therefore, by necessity, conditional upon the delivery of meaning. According to this logic, if no meaning is conveyed between a speaker and a listener then communication is considered failure or empty. Successful communication depends on speech fully understood or meaning fully comprehended by both the speaker as well as the listener. An example of empty speech might occur when you step up to the counter at Starbucks and the barista asks, "How are you doing this morning?" We all know that she is not interested in learning about you and is parroting these words to every customer before moving to business proper—"What would you like to drink?" In other words, no significant conversation takes place in the opening exchange; it is an empty preface for the subsequent exchange that is integrated to exchange value. This empty preface is needed, however, to humanize the following cold transaction—to make the customer feel that she inhabits a human world and not a mechanical network of financial transactions.

Returning to the barbershop scene, it is identified as empty because Thao does not understand what Kowalski wants him to do. This communication failure pushes Thao to blindly mimic Kowalski. It can also be argued that communication fails because Kowalski was never interested in communicating anything to Thao. He wanted to have fun with Martin bullying the Asian kid. There is no space for Thao in this scene except as a prop for entertaining the two old white men. Martin and Kowalski's world is far removed from Thao's, and no matter what he thinks or how hard he tries to enter this world it will always remain closed to him. This is the point most vocally championed by critics of the scene: Thao can only exist in Kowalski-Martin's world as a negated subject—without a job, car, or girlfriend; his attempts to blend in only furthers his (self-) depreciation: "Boy, does my ass hurt from all the guys at my construction job" (Jalao 2010, 3; Schein and Vang 2018, 96).[10] But what if we dispense with the commonplace ideas about empty and full speech and choose instead to read the barbershop scene via Lacan's theory of empty and full speech? With Lacan in the scene, I wager a different reading.

Lacan's definition of empty and full speech is different from our common understanding. For what Lacan terms "empty speech" is far from being "empty": it is "expressively full[:] the very kind of speech in which we are in fact trying to communicate at all, authentically or inauthentically." In contrast, Lacan identifies as "full speech" speech that is "noncommunicative, nonexpressive, [and] nonsense" (Pluth 2018, 127). In simpler terms, empty speech is everyday speech, that is, speech we think to be communicative but which, occupying the axis of the imaginary, expresses an individual's ego. The only reason communication succeeds in spite of speakers speaking from their egos is because the big Other functions as the extrasubjective guarantee. The big Other links words to meanings. Hook is right: if two conversing subjects "try to make sense of one another in the absence of such a symbolic Other," the result will be chaos (2011, 188). Full speech, by contrast, is the symptom of the unconscious. But not a symptom that can be deciphered; rather, a symptom resisting speech, meaning, and even articulation. Full speech marks the moment of the eruption of an irrepressible autistic enjoyment; an enjoyment that is in itself unconstrained by communication sequences—"not intended to say anything to anyone" (Santiago 2018, n.p.)—this "automatic, machinic, nonsensical" full speech shocks the subject-supposed-to-know by unraveling its ontological condition: we are split between the speaking subject and the subject of enunciation (Pluth 2018, 127, 129).

The progressive multiculturalist command to empathize with the other—refugees, victims of sexual violence, the LGBTQ community, etc.—unravels an interesting paradox. Since there is no way to assume the other's point of view, what we really do when we claim to empathize with the other is simply adopt the perspective of our individual egos. The governing logic "is that of *how I think they see it*" (Hook 2011, 190; italics in the original). Every time we say to the other, "I understand what you are going through," we actually mean, "I understand what you are going through in terms of *what I imagine you to be going through*." Isn't this the point of Aijaz Ahmad's critique of Frederic Jameson's ambitious, albeit misfounded, claim that *all* third world literatures are national allegories? Shouldn't we condemn the current logic of empathy for circumscribing the other via desires specific to the West? This is exactly why Spivak rebuts first world academic desires for learning about the subaltern. No desire is innocent. Desire functions by approximating the other for self-attestation. But every act of Othering requires readmitting the other, thus exposing the self once more to the other's irredeemable singularity and risking the implosion of the self-Other fantasy necessary for self-identification. What offers security against this threat, both at the moment of encountering the other and in the aftermath of Othering for the smooth continuation of the dialectic, is the big Other. It is only via the big Other's arbitrary, random, partial, or enforced authority that artificial identities come to exist as fact. If empty speech is secured by the big Other's providing the "framework of convention" necessary for transmission of meaning, then full speech is responsible for disrupting this framework and the guarantee operating it. Kowalski's disdain of an all-powerful meaning-guaranteeing authority is evident from his disapproval of institutions (the Church, the police) as well as socially acceptable protocols of speech. Words, meanings, and symbolism in *Gran Torino* are ambiguous, therefore our analyses too should be willing to accommodate alternative interpretations.

This is why we should not jump to a conclusive reading of the final moment of Kowalski's life as iconizing the death of Christ. Brought down by a hail of bullets, the spread-eagled body of Kowalski reminds viewers and critics alike of Christ. Irrespective of whether they condemn this overt display of religiosity or find in it proof that "director Eastwood [is] irredeemably religious," critics unanimously read the scene as reinforcing the Christian values of sacrifice and redemption (McBride and Shahamiri 2011, 361; Kramp 2011, 922; Jalao 2010, 3). But none of these notice that in the scene we get an upside-down shot of Kowalski's body. As Kowalski falls, reciting "hail Mary," the camera first gives an extreme ground-level shot of the body before slowly withdrawing to offer a God's-eye viewpoint. From this point of view, we see Kowalski spread-eagled and dead but upside down and off-center in the frame. We never get a shot showing his body either at the center of the frame or not inverted. We can interpret this upside-down shot as Kowalski's Peterine gesture. Kowalski is *not* Him but *like* Him. The God's viewpoint even strengthens this argument. However, the routine use of the inverted cross in Hollywood horror films and the general popularity of the symbol for antiauthoritarian expressions should make us question interpretations rounding off Kowalski's death as mimicking Christian sacrifice.

The point, again, is ambiguity. Ambiguity that underwrites the barbershop scene returns in this scene asking that we probe deeper for the meaning of this scene. For example, we can argue further that the scene's ambiguity is increased by:

1 God's viewpoint angle is off-center, suggestive of something not quite right, not quite centrally fixed even in this moment of sacrifice,

and,

2 Instead of a bright light of Deliverance, Kowalski's body fades into the flashing red and blue lights of cop cars. These lights of earthly law appear not at moments of redemption but at sites of crime, difference, and violence.

Compare the shot of Kowalski's dead body with the shot of Leonidas's dead body in Zack Snyder's *300* (2006), the latter a patent example of onscreen divinization. In *300*, the camera gives a God's-eye viewpoint of Leonidas and his dead comrades. It remains fixed on the image with Leonidas's body in the center of the diegetic frame. The camera too is flush on top of the center of this frame. There is no doubt in the minds of the viewers what the scene is showing: the king has died so that Sparta can live free! Alongside showing the magnitude of the sacrifice, this shot ensures that audiences focus on the body of Leonidas whose outstretched body resembles the iconic image of Christ on the Cross. Not so in *Gran Torino*, where the God's-eye viewpoint further underscores Kowalski's loneliness and his irreverence for the form of sacrificial gesture.

It's impossible to contain Kowalski within symbolic frames of interpretation. Even the persistent attempts of the priest to bring Kowalski to Confession ends in a mockery of the symbolic value of Confession. In the Confession scene Kowalski basically plays with Janovich by confessing to things that hardly appear worth confessing. In this scene, Kowalski seems to be saying: "You wish to know what I am carrying inside, and believe that if I confess then the guilt is cleansed thus making me whole again, okay here goes. . ." It is absolutely clear that Kowalski does not believe in Confession because he does not believe in some all-forgiving Other. Michaela Driver is correct: ritual speech is tied to the ego and its narcissistic imaginaries. The belief that ritual speech results in "the experience of a complete, integrated, aligned, balanced, whole and non-compartmentalized self. . .an authentic self. . .connected to others and a higher order, fully integrated, balanced, complete and ultimately fulfilled. . .rest[s] on conceptualizations of the self that capture little more than the imaginary function of the ego" (2005, 1091, 1099). Confessing sins to achieve redemption with "five hail Mary's and ten our Fathers" pivots on the same logic; Kowalski is not interested in retrieving his lost unicity.[11]

At the same time, his confessions are not entirely without relevance. His first confession is about kissing Betty Jablonski at the factory Christmas party while Dorothy, his wife, was in another room. The second confession: profiting from selling a boat and a motor but not paying taxes. While these two can be read as his confessions for violating commandment six (thou shalt not commit adultery) and commandment seven (thou shalt not steal), his third confession is different in that it does not relate to any of the ten commandments. Given the backstory of the Korean War, viewers perhaps expect him to confess killing an innocent man (commandment five). Instead, he confesses to not being a good father! The scene therefore not only mocks the idea of an all-forgiving Father in heaven, but it equally admits the impossibility of being a good father here on earth. I agree: the film is depressingly plot driven but this plot is not about a white savior, but rather about the big Other's inability to authorize as proof of the nonexistence of the big Other.[12]

Some claim that Eastwood's films underwent a shift in the 1990s. Since 1993, Eastwood appears to have distanced himself from the kind of films that established him as an icon. His films through the '60s into the '80s established his image as the nameless cowboy or rogue cop who "placed [his] shattered and lonesome faith in the business end of a Colt 45" (McCormick 2009, 44). But with films such as *Unforgiven*, *Mystic River*, *Flags of our Fathers*, *Letters from Iwo Jima*, and *Million Dollar Baby*, Eastwood made a conscious choice in the '90s to step away from boorish masculinity and populist patriotism. In fact, these films from the '90s actually unmask such identities, showing them as hollow or pretentious. I contend that this bent continues in *Gran Torino* as well, where the emptiness of essential identities reified through words and images stands challenged inside a tale of personal redemption.

The Ideology of *Gran Torino* I: The Hmong Gang

At one level, the ideology of the film is simple: surplus enjoyment, especially bodies embodying surplus enjoyment must be contained for a balanced social order. Critics are correct: Kowalski disciplines Thao. By learning construction work, manning up, and eventually getting a girlfriend and a car (the eponymous Gran Torino), Thao gains legitimacy to enter the U.S. sociosymbolic. But in process Kowalski also understands the other's cultural excesses as particular expression of Man's universal quest for meaning in life. But something in the film falls outside this dialectic. The Hmong gang remains unaccommodated as they are too excessive (Jalao 2010). Freely cruising through the arteries of the social body in total disregard of law and without affiliation to morality, the Hmong gang constitutes the real kernel of otherness. They truly "exhibit the kind of agency that approximates the real possibilities and precariousness of life in a Hmong American community" (ibid., 3). They are the (excess) products of U.S. foreign policy and domestic capitalist culture. The Hmong gang is a product of U.S. capitalist imperialism—its military actions around the world and the systemic economic and racial oppression of minorities within the national borders. The precariats thus created through dislocation and marginalization in recent years have suffered further blows due to the Left's shift away from the poor and toward issues of identity politics. "Just as corporate, business, and financial interests were coming together politically, those on the left were fragmenting into particularities by focusing on particular experiences of different identity groups rather than uniting these groups on basis of their shared class position in U.S. society" (Dean 2009, 34). Endless bickering over who is worse off—the man or the woman of color or the nonbinary populations—has completely consumed the Left and transformed its rhetoric into dreary twaddle. And with the Left in such disarray, arguments for further promotion of neoliberalism—privatize, disenfranchise, militarize—have gained in strength. These identify America's inner cities as impediments to economic growth and hold them responsible for restricting social mobility of the economically disadvantaged. In the last U.S. presidential election, we witnessed firsthand the ability of this argument to divide the working class along racial, gender, and nationalist lines.

Jalao is correct in pronouncing the Hmong gang as a paradox. On the one hand, they refuse to conform to a white middle-class moral center, with its hierarchized gendered and racial roles. On the other hand, the only liberty available to economically depressed and systematically alienated racial/ethnic minorities in America is through life in gangs (ibid.). If minority youth refuse to be integrated into white middle-class Christian America, they are left with no choice but to embrace the other side of law and/or perpetually remain outside social acceptance. What Jalao does not discuss, though, is how this paradox manifests the reality of neoliberalism, which, while appearing to be a system based on choice, in actuality has dissolved all alternatives of existence. This is especially true for minorities without class advantage. The paradox of the Hmong gang, therefore, opens a hole in reality, fully exposing the real condition of the Hmongs—they have the choice to accept the system or stand against it. If the latter, then, they will be eventually taken out either by law enforcement or by a conscientious citizen.

The Ideology of *Gran Torino* II: The One

Oliver Davis remarks that *Gran Torino* ends in an extreme expression of "Beauvorian age rage," one "which exaggerates and illuminates[,] the latent 'Eastwoodian' violence of self-assertion...against the alienating chaos of senescence" (2012, 141, 145). McBride and Shahamiri echo a similar sentiment when they note that Kowalski chooses to die a hero instead of from cancer (2010, 363). The fact that Kowalski did not succumb to old age and to cancer but went all guns blazing (without the gun) is the ultimate enjoyment of what is no longer available to a younger Kowalski/Eastwood. For a man such as he, "stuck in the 1950s," this manner of death is the only acceptable end. Mind you, I am not saying this only about Kowalski, but the image Kowalski brings to life. This image is integrally tied to Eastwood's roles in films as well as his directorial ventures. It is not only Kowalski who relives the action but also Eastwood himself. It is the enjoyment of being "Eastwood" and remaining "Eastwood." That is, the enjoyment of being the figure of the "fixer," a role he plays in some of his most celebrated and successful films—from the *Dollars* trilogy to *Million Dollar Baby*. Eastwood's post-1993 films have made subtle adjustments with the explosion of neoliberal demands for political correctness and nonviolence, but while these adjustments have led him to lose his guns his image as the "fixer" remains unchanged.

Eastwood's "desire" hasn't changed post-1993: he *still* wants to be recognized as the Man beyond law (and as such, beyond castration). He demands love for being the One who sticks up for others, stands up for the weak and vulnerable. In fact, with Kowalski, Eastwood moves closer to becoming the One beyond particularities than he ever was in films celebrating rugged masculinity and patriotic jingoism. The plot of *Gran Torino* leads to the One, the self-anointment coupled to the final act of self-sacrifice. As deconstructive practice, let's rehabilitate the argument that the scene of Kowalski's death figures Christ's sacrifice. But instead of reading this as the moment when a lapsed Catholic returns to the fold, and apropos the negative image of the reversed cross, let me propose a more disturbing, to wit, blasphemous reading: instead of being like Christ, Kowalski desires to become Christ. Eastwood/Kowalski desires to replace an absent big Other with a more wholesome, complete big Other. And herein lies the failure of the film. It fails because of its desire for reinstating the big Other. After consistently exposing the impossibility of the big Other, the film ends up espousing the fiction of the big Other. This is also the single most dangerous ideology of the film: the ideology of the (reconstituted) big Other. Danger lies specifically in Eastwood's desire that capstones the film. Kowalski's existence as subject of drive is enclosed and written over at the end in terms of this desire for being.

Who is the possible addressee of Kowalski/Eastwood's beatification? Who most properly enjoys Eastwood's desire to remain Eastwood? What is the most compelling ideology of this film? The addressee is the viewer. The film teaches us how to enjoy an Eastwood film alongside revealing what we desire from Eastwood's movies. We desire that Eastwood remain the same—the fixer fixing things, with or without guns, with or without a name, walking away into the sunset or dying at the end of the film but only to return again with/in another "Eastwood" film. We desire the One. In fact, what I characterize above as Eastwood's desire is actually our desire represented on screen. Eastwood merely frames our desire, giving it back in a form we do not immediately recognize but which we enjoy nonetheless.

IV. POLITICAL CORRECTNESS IS PHALLIC

In *the Emptiness of the Image*, Parveen Adams claims political correctness is "automatically phallic." It matters not, she continues, if the content of a discourse is radical or transgressive, as long as the content is premised on the logic of identification—Us and Them, West and the non-West, Man and Woman— it is phallic in character. In other words, identity is phallic or constituted by the logic of the Phallus as the missing signifier. Or, as Adams puts it, identity is "phallic in the sense of supporting the same mode of identification that supports all norms, phallic identification" (1996, 55).

In the context of identity politics this means all minority demands for identity are mirror images of the dominant/dominating decrees of identity insofar as both share the same logic of identification—of establishing the self against an Other. This is precisely why Spivak disputes all contests over identity as equally violent and equally exclusionary. Claims for identity today, including the most radical or transgressive ones, appear conscious of this structural issue. Consequently, in demanding identity these discourses exercise additional caution to avoid the trap of marginalizing or erasing other identities, remaining gratified instead to be counted as one identity among a collection of different divergent identities. While this gesture does not depart from the inscription of the symbolic order, it does manage to prettify the demand for identity, making it more appropriate for the global present. Demands for identity remain no less grounded in the logic of difference, hence phallic.

In this context we must remind ourselves of two things. First, the Freudian theory about subjectivity as structured between "being" or "having" the phallus is not a teleological argument. Spivak repeats this misreading when she writes, "in the twentieth century psychoanalysis allows the West to plot the itinerary of the subject from Narcissus [the "imaginary"] to Oedipus [the "symbolic"]. This subject, however, is the normative male subject" (1985, 251). Instead, it is clear from Freud that the endeavor to "be" or "have" is an exercise in futility because the Phallus is an impossible object. Or, *the Phallus does not exist*. This leads to the second point, as Lacan never tired of repeating, the *phallus is a signifier* (Lacan 2006, 579). It is not an organ, not even an object (good, bad, internal, external) but a signifier characteristically referring to another signifier for signification. The subject emerges in between the signifiers. At once the irreducible gap and the frayed symbolic that rims the gap, the subject is lack. It is this traumatic truth about our nonbeing, the catastrophe definitive of our being, which we seek to counter through our fantasies of wholeness and exclusive identities. There is no space in these fantasies, therefore, for the ungainly truth of our radically compromised ontology, no understanding of the nonrelation or antagonism constituting intersubjective relations. The right to speech and self-representation on the basis of exclusive identities has therefore become the mainstay of contemporary politics.

Can the White Man Speak?

On August 21, 2017, the *Idaho Statesman* carried a report on the aggravating tension between the then Boise State University president Bob Kustra and Idaho's First District congressman Rául Labrador. Things had been heating up between the two for some time, especially following Kustra's vocal opposition to conservative legislations over concealed carry law and DACA students. Things took a turn in the aftermath of the Charlottesville shooting incident when Kustra publicly condemned President Trump and Congressman Labrador for their reluctance to address the perils of white nationalism. Labrador fired back saying: "It's interesting when you have a 60-something white male from a liberal state [Kustra's home state is Illinois] trying to tell me, a young Hispanic male, how I should react to racism....Maybe it's time for him to go [from the position of president of Boise State]" (Brown, *Idaho Statesman*, Aug. 21, 2017).[13]

This exchange reminds me of sick joke: a white woman goes to an interview and is thrilled to see that all the other interviewees are white men. "I'll surely get this job," she thinks to herself. She delivers a cracker of an interview (no pun intended), further bolstering her belief in landing the job. But as she is exiting the interview room, she stands aghast. A new candidate has appeared on the scene: a black man on a wheelchair. Like most jokes, this gains its cadence by focusing on the disjunction between what we are habitually taught—"Merit alone makes a difference"—and what we know as true: in the era of multiculturalism, who you are in terms of gender, race, sexuality, etc. makes a difference. But far from being serious about this, the joke appears to play off the fallacy of this belief by asking: How different is different enough to matter? Indeed, we can derive from this joke a critique of affirmative action or ask, Where does this stop? Will a brown gay single mother supplant the black man in the wheelchair? Or will she be rejected for someone from one of the many unrepresented silenced indigenous groups? If for a moment we suspend the extremely valid logic for protecting minority job applicants, the joke enables us to see the principal logic of contemporary identity politics. Namely, in order for identity to matter it must feature advantageously on a scale quantifying a hierarchy of difference—a listing of the historically marginalized ordered according to the magnitude of their victimization. In the name of identity, we have today a competition for tragedy—the more historical victimhood you claim, the better it is for your chances of self-representation.

The Kustra-Labrador exchange captures this tragedy: while we ruminate over who has the right to speak against racism, a white man or a Latino man, what gets shoved under the carpet is the need to speak out against racism no matter *who* is doing the speaking. Labrador's argument that only those who have been historically marginalized or come from historically marginalized communities have the right to speak about racism, and that those who are white are disqualified from speaking about racism, leaves me frustrated over what this logic misses. First, it merely reproduces the logic of identity via silencing the Other. Second, is this logic even valid when some of most historically oppressed peoples, races, and nations have transformed in the global present into xenophobic, ethno-nationalist, and racist states? Can we obviate the lynching of religious minorities and African nationals in contemporary India by claiming that such travesties cannot occur in the land of Gandhi? Can we unsee the brutality of the Israeli state against Palestinians because our eyes are still watered up for the extermination of millions of Jews by Nazi Germany? How are we to disavow the genocide of the Rohingyas happening under the eyes of Myanmar prime minister Aung San Suu Kyi?

Labrador's logic is symptomatic of the multicultural present but woefully insufficient. For if someone claims to have more direct experience of racism by being Latino, can I as a South Asian, and embodying otherness in much starker terms than an American person of color (say, in terms of, accent, culture, food habits, love of cricket over baseball, etc.), not stake claim to experiencing far more stringent forms of racism? Furthermore, if there are differences between a Latino man's and a South Asian man's experiences of racism, what happens when gender, ethnicity, disability, sexuality, and class are thrown into the mix? Is a brown man's (U.S.-born or expat) experience of racism the same as a brown woman's (U.S.-born or expat) experience of racism? Is my experience of racism as a South Asian university professor the same as that of an Indonesian hijab-wearing woman working as janitor in WalMart? We can either analyze these very different situations to arrive at a competitive hierarchy of differences or we can identify what is getting conveniently lost in this puerile competition for identity-as-tragedy: we are unequivocally failing to condemn racism and ethno-nationalism as unacceptable.

Does a white man forfeit all right and responsibility to be conscientious just because he is white? Is not saying that an individual is incapable of being conscientious because of the color of his/her skin racial discrimination? There is no denying that systemic/institutionalized racism in the United States allows most white men (including those tenured at the universities) to enjoy privileges associated to their race. But that does not mean no white man can ever come to recognize or express concern over racism. To think that only those who have been racially abused can understand racism is to subscribe to an essentialism.

We must be careful when dallying with equally false premises such as white nationalism versus black nationalism. In Hegel's term, these are false dichotomies or "forced choices": citizens are given false choices in order to (mis)direct them from scrutinizing the real material conditions of social inequality. Following Hegel, Marx defined these forced choices as ideology. What we need to do every time we are assaulted by such forced choices, therefore, is to openly call their bluff: the dichotomy between white and black nationalisms only functions to divert from the fact that all forms of nationalism are equally bad. I might be willing to concur that a white man or woman cannot lay claim to the same life experiences compared to a person of color in America but that does not or should not in any way restrict the former from conscientiously raising his or her voice against immoral acts such as racism. It is the need of the present day that we affiliate ourselves with the dispossessed and dehumanized minorities in order to protest those who seek to further divide humanity in terms of race, gender, and ethnicity.

CONCLUSION
Particular Universal

The conflict between psychoanalysis and postcolonial studies is the same as the old (though, in many ways, current) debate over the singular Universal and the irredeemable Particular. Postcolonial scholars caution against Freudian universalism by raising questions about the cultural specificity of psychoanalytic theory, its patriarchal provenance, and its undeniable Orientalist tendencies. Psychoanalysis as theory and praxis, these critics remind us, has been repeatedly weaponized to justify the dehumanization and genocide of marginalized populations (Hartnack 2001; Hewitson 2017, n.p.). Additionally, they object to using psychoanalysis, a discipline of European provenance, for "reading" *other* non-European cultures (Spivak 1993 and 1999). Drawing attention to essential cultural differences between the West and the non-West and underlining how psychosocial development or subjectivity emerges differently due to cultural differences, these critics ask that we either totally avoid psychoanalysis for examining non-European cultures or that we tweak psychoanalysis in order to make the discipline relevant to diverse cultural contexts.

As much as I agree with these critiques, I cannot overlook how in attacking psychoanalysis postcolonial critics all too often get paradoxically entangled in the desire of the Other or Europe. Simply put, if "colonialism" is a *simplified* name for military conquest and oppression of a community (Fanon 1967, 81–82), that is, Europe's desire to coopt the colonized under its philosophical and cultural systems with the help of the army and the colonial bureaucrat, then the postcolonial endeavor for rescuing or reclaiming particular identities against this universalizing hegemony is a reaction structured by a desire for recognition. On the one hand, postcolonial strategies of identity construction rely on the mechanism of Othering already established by colonial Europe. The demand for rehabilitating previously negated identities and championing these identities by repeating the historical trauma of colonial oppression today has become the means for excusing the domination by these postcolonial nations of other minorities. India's actions in Kashmir cannot be justified any more than Israel's actions in Palestine or Robert Mugabe's actions against white Zimbabweans. What is worse, though, are claims made by these erstwhile colonial nations that they should not be charged for their current actions (read, crimes) against minorities. But insofar as these post-/anti-/de-colonial demands for rehabilitation or recognition of particular identities structurally mimic or resurrect the mechanisms of Othering, these demands remain ultimately inscribed and driven by the desire of the Master.

On the other hand, the postcolonial response fails to introduce any "new element into the classic dialogue of the dominated and the oppressor" but merely changes the positions—the oppressed take on the role of the dominant by claiming recognition for its identity (Fanon 1967, 103). Far from ending the cycle of Othering and the logic of desire set in place by the colonial regime this postcolonial gesture continues the paradigm.

Consider the recent Dabashi-Zabala affair. After reading Santiago Zabala's "lovely little panegyric" to European philosophy ("Slavoj Žižek and the Role of the Philosopher" [2012]), Dabashi responds with "Can Non-Europeans Think?" (2013), wherein he labels Zabala's view of philosophy as Eurocentric. Responding to Zabala's opening paragraph:

> There are many important and active philosophers today: Judith Butler in the United States, Simon Critchley in England, Victoria Camps in Spain, Jean-Luc Nancy in France, Chantal Mouffe in Belgium, Gianni Vattimo in Italy, Peter Sloterdijk in Germany and in Slovenia, Slavoj Žižek, not to mention others working in Brazil, Australia and China. (ibid.)

Dabashi writes,

> What immediately strikes the reader when seeing this opening paragraph is the unabashedly European character and disposition of the thing the author calls "philosophy today"—thus laying a claim on both the subject and time that is peculiar and in fact an exclusive property of Europe.
>
> Even Judith Butler who is cited as an example from the United States is decidedly a product of European philosophical genealogy, thinking somewhere between Derrida and Foucault, brought to bear on our understanding of gender and sexuality.

To be sure, China and Brazil (and Australia, which is also a European extension) are cited as the location of other philosophers worthy of the designation, but none of them evidently merits a specific name to be sitting next to these eminent European philosophers. (ibid.)

What followed was a series of responses and reactions: Zabala's response to Dabashi; Walter Mignolo's response to Zabala's response ("Yes, We can: Non-European Thinkers and Philosophers"); and, lastly, Michael Marder's defense of Zabala ("A Postcolonial Comedy of Errors"). In between, Žižek made matters worse when, at a public lecture at the London School of Economics, he supposedly first called Mignolo "stupid" and then, in reaction to Mignolo's exhortation that decolonial intellectuals should ignore European philosophers, he let out: "OK fuck you, who are these much more interesting intellectuals?" (cited in Kapoor 2018, n.p.). This was reported as a direct attack on Mignolo (Žižek claims he never addressed Mignolo and it was just a general exclamation), prompting yet another response from Dabashi, this time innovatively titled "Fuck You Žižek!" (2016).[1]

In all that has been written and said over the Zabala-Dabashi debate, I find Aditya Nigam's thoughts most balanced and useful. In "End of Postcolonialism and the Challenge for 'Non-European' Thought" (2013), while agreeing in principle with Dabashi, Nigam draws out what he considers the greatest fault in Dabashi's response: In order to prove Zabala wrong, Dabashi gets caught up in citing the names of non-European philosophers and/or philosophers from the non-West.

> He [Dabashi] marshals a formidable list of names which include Ashis Nandy, Partha Chatterjee, Wang Hui, Sudipta Kaviraj, Henry Odera Oruka, Ngugi wa Thiong'o, Wole Soyinka, Chinua Achebe, Okot p'Bitek, Taban Lo Liyong, Achille Mbembe, Emmanuel Chukwudi Eze, Azmi Bishara, Sadeq Jalal Al-Azm, Fawwaz Traboulsi, Abdallah Laroui, Michel Kilo, Abdolkarim Soroush. They are undoubtedly very important thinkers but are they actually doing philosophy? I think some of them are, but most of them think at the borders of philosophy.

As Nigam sees it, philosophy, as such, no longer exists in the non-West. The "postnational" condition of the Global South, Nigam contends, has made "abstract thinking" moot. In place of philosophy we have political thinking in the Global South, which not only defines explicitly political issues of relevance to populations of the Global South but "comes to provide a route to thought in other domains as well [thereby] reducing all intellectual questions to questions of justice and power" (ibid.).[2]

I agree with Nigam. Dabashi indeed makes a mistake by trying to counter Zabala's list of "philosophers today" with his own list of "non-European philosophers today." This exercise, in fact, trips Dabashi into the trap of Othering, and the kind of binary thinking he has criticized for decades. I wish to remind Dabashi as well about the following passage from Fanon's *Black Skin, White Masks*:

> We are convinced that it would be of enormous interest to discover a black literature or architecture from the third century before Christ. We would be overjoyed to learn of the existence of a correspondence between some black philosopher and Plato. But we can absolutely not see how this fact would change the lives of the eight-year-old kids working in the cane fields of Martinique or Guadeloupe. (2008, 205)

This argument connects well to Nigam's point that philosophy as such has ceased to exist in the postnational Global South and has been replaced instead by political thinking. But I feel chary about uncritically agreeing with Nigam's argument that marked by the history of colonialism non-European thought must be only political thought. This notion does more to validate restrictive viewpoints such as Jameson's argument about third world literature being national literature. Far from being untethered to or unmarked by European epistemology, Nigam's conception is intransitively anchored to the West's imaginary of the (postcolonial) non-West. Also, what does it really mean to say abstract philosophical thought is not political? Is Kant's thinking about the man who is offered a night with the woman of his dreams provided he agrees to being hanged the next morning not political in its attempt to determine the social macrocosm via the individual? Or, is it practical to straitjacket Lalon Fakir's (1772–1890) philosophy as social, to wit, unconcerned with abstractions of causation, being, and becoming? These questions require a separate tryst, so I will leave this discussion for another time.

Overall, though, I agree with Nigam: Dabashi's response fails because it devolves into the same politics of recognition and pivots on similar exclusionary politics. Therefore, it is no different from the general tenor of European Enlightenment thinking, which, following Spivak, can be dubbed as the terrorism of Reason, empiricism, and the "categorical imperative" (1985, 248). Insofar as *this* terrorism holds man as a rational creature and an end in himself, it agrees with the premise of bringing all of humanity under a single order. But this can succeed only by exsanguinating particularities in preference for a mythical universality. In reversing the terms of this exchange, we do nothing more than imagine a sovereign center brought up from within the margins and now anointed against a former adversary. But what is the need for invoking, to wit, conceptualizing, quirky margins as fully fledged subjects capable of or willing to participate in the dialectic of the Master-slave recognition? Why must every (postcolonial) response hinge on the other awakening from the cataclysmic smothering of its existence and reclaiming its due? Doesn't this narrative, where every reaction is a story of loss and eventual retrieval, in short, a fantasmatic narrative of self-recomposition against all odds, constitute a secular repetition of the Christological paradigm of death and rejuvenation? Aren't "postcolonial" enunciations of subjective liberation in reality nothing more than a rephrasing of the Kantian notion of the categorical imperative?

The point here is twofold. First (a further illustration of Nigam's point), the fight for identity and recognition privileges no one and only reproduces the imaginary of the self versus the other. When Ta-Nehisi Coates goes in search of the "African Tolstoy" after reading Saul Bellow, he all too soon realizes his mistake: "Tolstoy is the Tolstoy of the Zulus." Why would there be any other? Coates's exact mistake: he was looking for an "unacknowledged equal of Tolstoy" something that Dabashi is "guilty" of doing. As Ryan Engley puts it, Coates's "great error" was in "accept[ing] Bellow's premise," therefore confining black culture, literature, and identity to the logic of the particular (2017, n.p.). Put another way: we cannot reject European thought *tout court* with such claims as "there are better things to do than read European philosophy" or that "non-European thinking on being is more culturally appropriate for the non-West," etc. To do so is to subscribe in the same modality of European Enlightenment self-representation that post/de-colonial thought cares to forsake. To do so is to remain imprisoned in the desire of the Other/Europe.

The second point comes from Spivak. I use it here to demonstrate what Dabashi's response should have been as well to answer my objection to Nigam's solution. *A Critique of Postcolonial Reason* begins with measured words:

> Postcolonial studies, unwittingly commemorating a lost object, can become an alibi unless it is placed within a general frame. Colonial Discourse studies, when they concentrate only on representation of the colonized or the matter of the colonies, can sometimes serve the production of current neocolonial knowledge by placing colonialism/

imperialism securedly in the past, and/or by suggesting a continuous line from that past to our present. This situation complicates the fact that postcolonial/colonial discourse studies is becoming a substantial subdisciplinary ghetto. In spite of the potential for cooptation, however, there can be no doubt that the apparently crystalline disciplinary mainstream runs muddy if these studies do not provide a persistent dredging operation. Because this dredging is counterproductive when it becomes a constant and self-righteous shaming of fully intending subjects, deconstruction can help here. (1999, 1)

Spivak is not asking that we abandon the critical project of interrogating the colonial past and the role of European philosophy, literature, history, and culture in imperialist subject-composition. Instead, she is urging that we think through the impossibility of this critical project for postcolonial studies in the context of its disciplinary situation within the neoliberal Anglo-American University. If the postcolonial project is only about replacing Europe as the subject-making agent and/or about (re-)claiming (moral) ground over European thought by parroting proof of or justifications for independent "native" thought, then there is no actual substantive resolution to the problem of structural hegemony. In *needing* to respond or react to the European Other, Dabashi and postcolonialists fail to effectively hystericize or discombobulate the Master's discourse. As Spivak sees it, there is no critical future in continuing to "act out the part of Caliban," for that only "legitimizes the very individualism that we must persistently attempt to undermine from within" (Spivak 1999, 37, 118). For those who claim to be marked by the disciplinary labels and/or the history of colonialism are "too thoroughly determined" by European thought to entirely reject it. In fact, she posts bluntly, "turn[ing] one's back on [European thought] when so much of one's critique is clearly if sometimes unwittingly copied from them, is to disavow agency, declare kingdom come by a denial of history" (ibid., 9). Instead Spivak advocates replacing the politics of identity with efforts to "rendering (im)possible of (another) narrative" (ibid., 6). I agree with Spivak: it is better to sabotage than mouth platitudes of liberal pluralism (ibid., 9). *Sabotage, dismantle,* and (de-)*construct* the script that secures the master/master's text (ibid., 37). This is how Spivak describes her (cunning) plan for deconstructing European philosophy: "[U]naccusing, unexcusing, attentive, [yet] situationally productive" dismantling of the master text without disregarding European philosophy or competing with intellectual nativism. That is, to unravel the unacknowledged knowledge grounding the master's discourse (ibid., 81).

Spivak writes that an "unacknowledgeable moment that I will call 'the native informant' is crucially needed by great texts [yet] foreclosed" (ibid., 4). What does she mean? Freudians and Lacanians ought to be interested: Spivak's "mistaken" reading of Freud and Lacan leads us to a methodology of reading not too distant from Lacan's (re)readings of Freud's troubled encounters with impossible alterity. In the "Dream of Irma's Injection" (1900) or *the Uncanny* (1919), Freud encounters, for instance, the indecipherable core of the Unconscious. We commonly re-symbolize or overwrite these uncanny experiences from the master's discourse. Yet, for Lacan, Freud's hopeless struggles with these impossibilities are integral to Freud's narrative of the Unconscious, that is, his building of a system, and therefore for Lacan's teaching. In fact, earmarked by Freud himself as critical to his discovery and, later, theoretically repositioned as the constitutive moments in the Freudian discovery by Lacan, Freudian psychoanalysis does not bypass the impossible real in the symbolic but views the impossible real as constitutive of the symbolic. There is a reason why Spivak reaches out to Freud as early as the fourth paragraph of her four-hundred-odd page book: to establish her argument about the need to review European philosophy through the "impossible eye" of the native informant foreclosed from the "source texts of European ethico-political selfrepresentation" (ibid., 37, 9). On this point, Freud and Lacan offer her a suitable theoretical vantage.[3]

The figure of the native informant features prominently in ethnography. Ethnography gives serious consideration to the native informant's narrative, even though, in the final disciplinary pronouncement, the native informant lacks her own distinct autobiography. That is, she cannot authorize "her" self-representation. Celebrated in ethnography, the native informant is nothing more than a function, namely, to generate "a text of cultural identity" malleable to Western inscription. It is true that Spivak borrows the concept of the native informant from ethnography. But it is equally true that on closer analysis it becomes clear that she employs the figure or concept differently in her work. Unfortunately, habitual postcolonial critics have not quite picked up this difference. They understand the native informant instead in terms of her silence and present a managerial effort to rescue or re-present this repressed voice-consciousness, which as I have already noted above is a dubious reversal of the colonial power structure at best, and a gesture unwittingly serving to mystify, if not fully blanket, the complicity between colonial and postcolonial nation-states in oppressing the subaltern. The native informant Spivak speaks of, by contrast, stands "clear out" of both these clusters. As I understand it, the native informant in European philosophy, literature, and history—the source texts of European cultural (self-)representation—is the figure of the Other needed, used, but in the final expression foreclosed (ibid., 6). Now this appears similar to ethnography, but it is not. But first let me discuss a little more Spivak's conceptualization of the native informant. For that, let me share Spivak's reading of Kant, and allow me to do this via the shortcut of citing two recent readers of Spivak—Ola AbdalKafor and Stephen Morton—*summarizing* Spivak's basic maneuvers.

First, AbdalKafor:

> To prove that Kant forecloses the "native informant," Spivak follows two steps. First, she chooses two instances from his Critique of Judgment and deliberately wrenches them out of their philosophical context. The first instance is the appearance of "der rohe Mensch," which she translates as "man in the raw," in the "Analytic of the Sublime." The second is naming 'man in the raw' as the New Hollander, the Australian aboriginal, and the Fuegian, the indigenous inhabitant of Tierra de Fuego in South America, in the "Analytic of Teleological Judgment." She takes 'man in the raw,' the New Hollander and the Fuegian as variables for the 'native informant.' Second, Spivak introduces the discourse of anthropology to conclude that these two instances demonstrate the foreclosure of the "native informant." (2015, 17).

Second, Stephen Morton:

> [Spivak argues] that Kant's theory of the universal subject, or "Man," does not refer to all humanity, but only refers to the educated, bourgeois, masculine subject of the European enlightenment. Citing a passage from Kant's discussion of the sublime in *The Critique of Judgement*, Spivak notes how Kant excluded the "Australian aborigine or the man from Tierra del Fuego" from the category of human subjectivity in his analytic of the sublime. By so doing, Spivak links Kant's philosophical discussion of the "raw man" in his account of the sublime to the "axiomatics of imperialism": "The axiomatics of imperialism as a natural argument to indicate the limits of the cognition of (cultural) man." (2003, 116)

The "native informant" signifies what has been foreclosed from the symbolic order of European thought, hence existing only as the real. This real is "the mark

CONCLUSION

of that expulsion" (Spivak 1999, 5), and by giving this foreclosed a "name," a registration or purchase in the symbolic, Spivak is not only asking that we simply rehabilitate the excluded but that we consider the consequences of this inclusion to the master's discourse. Invocation of the foreclosed signifier—the native informant as "(ex)orbitant"—can free those marked by postcoloniality from their historically determined desire for "Idea, Logos, and Form" (ibid., 67). The native informant is the *exorbitant* or surplus irredeemable within the symbolic. While its rejection "serves as the energetic and successful defense of the civilizing mission," its *return* depresses the self-contained, self-reflexive authority of the West (ibid., 5). It is therefore with the intention of rendering European thought uncanny that Spivak invokes the native informant. She brings the foreclosed back in order to plunge the symbolic into the chaos of what is outside of desire, and thereby effectively rendering the self-sufficient system *not-All*. Put another way, Spivak reintroduces into the text an excessive desire or an excess to desire by identifying it as the excluded-included of the text. This makes a text muddy, pushing it into the chiasmatic and the catachrestic. As doubt replaces agreement and ideology emerges from beneath the mask of objective empirical knowledge, textual authority is exposed as coercive, forcefully shaping the reader's desire.

Spivak's engagement with Lacan appears mediated, and as a result both inexact and hesitant. Her use of the term *foreclosure* is therefore marked by an almost casual shuffling between foreclosure as disavowal and foreclosure as repression—the term primarily standing in for "the rejection of an affect" (ibid., 4–5). This is why, even after characterizing European self-representation as dependent on foreclosing the "name of the 'native informant' *as the name of Man*—a name that carries the inaugurating affect of being human," she wavers identifying European self-representation or knowledge as paranoiac. "We cannot diagnose a psychosis here, but we can supplement the ethical Freud who wrote *The Un-ease [Unbehagen] of Civilization* with this thought: that this rejection of affect served and serves as the energetic and successful defense of the civilizing mission" (ibid., 5; italics in the original).

Two things must be said here. One, the "rejection of affect" or the foundational Law of civilization involves the murder of the primal father by his jealous sons and the subsequent establishment of the now-deceased primal father's prohibitive laws as (social) Law. Put another way, the sons murder the primal father because he restricts their access to full enjoyment (*jouissance*). However, far from allowing the sons unrestricted enjoyment, the paradox of this murder is that restriction on enjoyment becomes law in the aftermath of the crime. We can read this Freudian "myth" as Spivak does; namely, the foreclosure facilitates the rejection of guilt. Or, we can understand the rejection in terms of expelling jouissance. Notwithstanding the fact that the crisis begins with frustration of jouissance, the final prohibition is more to secure the self against the overwhelming character of jouissance than for ameliorating guilt. As Lacan teaches us, we do not wish what we desire. Though we wish full enjoyment, we never desire it. For, to experience desire as full jouissance is to experience the Thing unveiled; an experience best avoided. Murdering the Father whom we identify as the reason for our inability to access full enjoyment therefore only leads us to the accepting Him as the Protector or Law. What is truly enjoyed by humans is the lack of (full) enjoyment; that is, to be suspended in desire without ever accomplishing the goal of desire.

Second, the rejection involved in the establishment of the *socius* is repression and not foreclosure. The former is associated with the clinical structure of neurosis, whereas the latter is associated with psychosis. In neurosis, this Law of the dead father is negotiated but never completely rejected as in foreclosure. Foreclosure is no mere rejection; it is, rather, the foreclosure or closure before the admittance of the Name-of-the-Father as Law. As such, foreclosure occurs prior to the symbolic murder of the primal father, thereby arresting the emergence of Law. This is the Law governing *all men* as subject to castration excluding the One (Lacan Sem. XX, 1999, 80). In foreclosure, the subject rejects this Law totally; in fact, foreclosure describes the operation of shutting off (rejecting, as Spivak might say) the paternal function. Foreclosure, accordingly, plays no role in the constitution of the *socius* as the domain for the subject of desire. Rather, foreclosure enables the psychotic to inhabit and enjoy *his own private world*. A world that is at once within and, yet, isolated from the social world of castration and desire. Even the pervert, who disavows the Law instead of foreclosing or repressing it, enjoys a habitus within the *socius* by virtue of his ability to acknowledge the fetish as the Thing but not quite. No such traction is available for the psychotic who must navigate the *socius* on basis of his special connection to God.

I am not blaming Spivak for not being thorough with Lacan. There are many Lacanians who have not read Spivak, but that does not stop them from criticizing her or postcolonial theory. When asked about their credibility in criticizing Spivak or the discipline of postcolonial studies more generally, the only satisfactory answer they come up with is a version of the clichéd harangue: it is not Lacanian enough. But the point is not to dissolve arguments in a blame game. That is not my intention at all. Going back to Spivak, the fact that she feels the need to engage Lacan or psychoanalysis in the opening pages of what I consider her best book shows the necessity of gathering both disciplines in fruitful dialogue. Mistakes and misreading will happen along the way, but restoration of ties is crucial today.

Irrespective of whether Spivak misunderstands foreclosure or repression, I see her striving after the subject's encounter with the reject. Spivak puts this repeatedly as an encounter with the "wholly other" that "has an unpredictable relationship to our ethical rules" (1999, 173)—(a matter of) reading that unravels, first, truth as trope and, thereafter, the founding lie expedient for establishment of truth (ibid., 18–19). The "wholly other" and/or the founding lie correspond with the expelled—a piece of unincorporated real—or the "native informant," whose return composes a disturbing anamorphic stain on the *universally* accepted idea of truth: "a space of withholding, marked by a secret that may not be a secret [at all] but cannot be unlocked" (ibid., 190). The stain recovers the subject as the subject of lack, alienated from itself and irrevocably lacking. *Every rupture is a repetition* (ibid., 336). The rupture inaugurated by the stain is the signature of the death-drive, of the master discourse as repetition, and of its object, the sovereign European man, an evanescent chimera whose pursuit unravels the nonexistence of that truth.

Encounters with the anamorphic blot, though, are not about reversing the self-other hierarchy, the imaginary and its symbolic props, that is, it neither about the *death of the subject* (I know I am not) nor about recuperating the subject after (I know I lack therefore I am). Rather, the blot as lack must be assumed as the irrevocable condition of being—I, the subject, *am* lack. Spivak's readers commonly pursue the mistake of identifying the native informant as epistemological limit; namely, the limits of European master discourse.[4] This, in turn, opens up the postcolonial exercise of filling in gaps, posed as writing back or resistance. I contend that the native informant substantiates the impossibility of ontology that Spivak locates not outside but within the master text. Acknowledgment of the unacknowledgeable via restoration of the foreclosed— the native informant as real—that is, variously an intrusion of a piece of the real and/or the hole in the real, allows reading the master's discourse "operated by the native informant's impossible eye" (ibid., 37).

"*Wo Es war, soll Ich werden.*" Where it was, there I shall become. It is necessary to bring this "mistaken" translation of the Freudian maxim back here in order to augment Spivak's point: the task is not to dismiss European philosophy, literature, and history but revise the framework within which they are held; that is, expose the commingling of European cultural texts with imperialism as well as the postcolonial complicity in the *muting* of the subaltern (ibid., 309).[5] *Wo Es war, soll Ich werden*. Not the dispossession of the id by the ego (I); not the overturning of the master discourse by a new postcolonial sovereignty; not even the occupation of the hegemonic center by the wretched of the Earth now risen in revolutionary splendor. Rather, "where it was, there I shall become" means I will approach the truth, embrace it as mine, and live with it. The particularity of experiencing the stain as lack is the universal proper.

The postcolonial debate over the universal versus the particular suffers from a fundamental misrecognition. It associates the universal with an Idea (Logos and Form).[6] Most commonly, the postcolonialist argues against the cavalier attitude with which an Idea of European extraction is imposed over non-European multitudes as the norm and the manner in which the European universal Idea thereafter shapes non-European particulars. Historically, these processes have occurred through immoral violence (colonization) and rhetorical arrangements (European philosophy, literature, history, and culture): European colonization depended on "culture as a form of rhetoric" (Morton 2003, 113) with European ideas *changing the way one knows what one is going to know, namely, the object of knowledge* (Spivak 2014).[7]

Todd McGowan has recently drawn attention to the habitual conflation of universality with the master signifier or Idea. Characterizing the mistake of equating the universal with the master signifier as *commonsensical*, McGowan argues for changing this conception by *divorcing* the universal from the positive notion of the master signifier (2018, 199). But what is the master signifier, and how does it relate to the universal?[8]

The master signifier (S1) is responsible for guaranteeing meaning by establishing links between free-ranging signifiers. In the words of Jacques-Alain Miller, it functions to "make understandable [*lisible*]" speech by "making the signifier and the signified correspond, halting them in their contrary shift of meaning [*glissement*]" (cited in Barker 2014, 752). One can think of the master signifier as the critical component for instituting the prison house of language—it (S1) arrests the endless sliding of signifiers and the continuous deferment of meaning. By being the endpoint, that is, the point at which meaning surfaces from amid the volatile slinging and slipping of signifiers, it occupies the position of the "agent" in the Master's Discourse (Fig. C.1) and represents the moment of formal enunciation via which a "self" is retroactively constituted against an other (S2).

The Master's Discourse

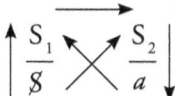

Positions

$$\frac{\text{Agent}}{\text{Truth}} \longrightarrow \frac{\text{Other/Work}}{\text{Production}}$$

Terms
S_1: Master Signifier
S2: Knowledge
$\slashed{S}$: Subject
a: Object (Cause of) Desire

FIGURE C.1

Examples of such enunciation are widespread. Think of Odysseus's assertions about Cyclops as a lawless monster in Book 9 of Homer's epic, the rhetoric then repeated through Vespucci's letters, Darwin's scientific writings, and Laura Bush's radio address to the nation in the aftermath of 9/11 and the Afghanistan war. In each of these, we see an almost verbatim repetition of Homer's/Odysseus's original characterizations of the Cyclops as godless, uncivilized, wife beaters.[9] But how do these "ideas" about the Other become universal? How does the universally accepted idea of "freedom," for example, come to be marked as absent in the non-European Other, thus attesting the latter's particularity as deviation, which in turn justifies the need for civilizing this Other in order to include it into the hallowed grounds of freedom? If we look at the examples in endnote 10, freedom or its lack, especially among women and children, in the non-West is repeated again and again to justify hostile invasions.

Let's try an exercise from the other side: Malcolm X parsing through a dictionary and beginning to understand the politics underlying meanings associated with words. "Black" is "evil," "white" is "pure," and so on. A minimum exclusion formalizes each of these words—black/evil is distinguished from white/pure. White is therefore meaningful only in the context of a negated black. And black is black because it is bereft of white. Apart from the gross dialectic operative here, we must understand the coming-into-existence of meaning as a matter of formal articulation. That is to say, for these meanings to become knowledge (S2) there must be S1 as the master's absolute pronouncement. But, of course, the dictionary is a secular, Enlightenment project and not a matter of authoritarian decree. Also, how did meanings of black versus white ossify in geographically separated societies and cultures? The production of the English dictionary is that moment, spoken by Spivak, when a rhetorical arrangement intersects with the axiomatics of the empire to forever establish "white" as the signature of light and culture versus the impenetrable darkness of the colony. The counter-argument cannot be: Why did the colonized not write their own dictionary? Perhaps they did or maybe they did not. The more important issue here is that institutional, economic, and bureaucratic structures of the empire ensured that the European "word" gained dominance in the form of secular universal education (the dictionary). Like Malcolm X, Fanon too discovered his (negated) identity in the eyes and words of the Master discourse: "I discovered my blackness...I was battered down by tom-toms, cannibalism, intellectual deficiency, fetishism, racial defects, slave-ships" (2008, 92).[10] But credit goes to Malcolm X for understanding that the negated cannot be retrieved—there is no going back and the only possibility of moving forward lies through embracing the negation, claiming it as part of one's identity, hence the "X" in his name (Žižek 2019: n.p.).

The emptiness represented by the "X" is not limited to the negated/negation of the other. On the one hand, as Žižek notes, the "X (the lack of ethnic roots) [is] a unique chance to assert a universality different from the one imposed by the whites" (ibid.). On the other hand, we should understand the "X" as representing the emptiness of the master signifier or the master's name. This is an intriguing fact about the master signifier: while it plays an anchoring role in signification, it is free of a signified. Or, the master signifier is always empty; it does not attach to a signified. Put another way, though the master signifier functions to stitch together (*point de capiton*) free-ranging signifiers into a meaningful whole (a fantasy of wholeness repressing the constitutive antagonism between signifiers), its own incompleteness or disjunction from a signified must remain concealed. This is why Molly Rothenberg terms the master signifier *occulted*: its self-difference "hidden from view," the S1 (master signifier) acts as if "it were the agent of remediation of the incompleteness of the social field" by hiding the "irremediable excess of the subject as signifier" that attests its insufficiency (2010, 210). As Figure C1 shows, the master signifier appoints itself to the position of the "agent" by repressing the "truth" about its lacking/excessive subjectivity ($). The master signifier is incomplete and—like any other signifier—it is empty.[11]

It would be remiss not to mention Homi Bhabha at this point. In such essays as "The Other Question," "Articulating the Archaic," "Sly Civility," "Of Mimicry and Man," and "Signs Taken for Wonders," all of which were later collected in *Location of Culture* (2006), Bhabha makes it a point to remind his readers about the insufficiency, or what he terms *ambivalence,* of colonial authority. Claiming to have been anointed by absolute divine decree and/or Reason to exercise just and moral rule in the colony, the Empire focuses on cultural difference as the logic for colonization. Yet, this "attempt to dominate in the *name* of a cultural supremacy" encounters a frustrating experience, as the idea that culture is a stable model of reference that can be transferred to the colony is almost immediately negated by the experiences of the colony forcing imperial authority to repeatedly revise this model (Bhabha 2006, 51). It is not a stretch to say that one of Bhabha's important contributions to postcolonial analysis of colonial discourse is this underlining of the systemic unraveling of colonial authority as inherent inconsistent. As a symbolic system, the discourse of colonial authority depends on master signifiers such as the "rule of law and reason," "bringing enlightenment to the natives," "rescuing them from paganism for the one true God," etc. These functioned as justifications for colonization in both literature and official documents (*Jane Eyre* [1847] and the British discourse over Sati or the Hindu practice of widow immolation, for example). But, for every stereotype insisted upon as fact, the Empire found itself compelled to guard the boundaries of said fact via repeated assertions of the Other's negation. Every enunciation of a stereotype is a demand for the stereotype which the stereotype disrupts (ibid., 117). This leads Bhabha to remark further: "[D]iscourse of post-Enlightenment English colonialism...speaks in a tongue that is forked." For "every epic intention of civilizing mission...writ large by the finger of the Divine" produces "a text [of colonization] rich in the traditions of *trompe-l'œil*." That is, a text riddled with "irony, mimicry, and repetition" and, as such, unfolding as uncertain, unsure, and hesitant (ibid., 122). The sly native wedges herself into these gaps, giving body to these fissures, thus frustrating strategies to "dominate the 'calculable' individual" and raising questions about symbolic authority (ibid., 137, 141). The native's *persistence* against the behemoth of colonial cultural hegemony is evidenced by her ability to simultaneously inhabit or switch between two worlds (cultures). Skillfully moving between the colonial and the vernacular and from the vernacular back to the colonial, as recorded, for example, in Soshee Chunder Dutt's "Reminiscences of a Keráni's Life" (1877), the native does not simply underline the need for code switching (a habitual topic of discussion in postcolonial circles) or the condition of hybridity (as Bhabha claims) but, instead, their movements reveal the immensely flexible and extraordinarily porous character of the colonial symbolic order. In sum:

> The colonial presence is always ambivalent, split between its appearance as original and authoritative and its articulation as repetition and difference. It is a disjunction produced within the act of enunciation as a specifically colonial articulation of those two disproportionate sites of colonial discourse and power: the colonial scene as the invention of historicity, mastery, mimesis or as the "other scene" of *Entsellung*, displacement, fantasy, psychic defense, and an "open" textuality. (Bhabha 2006, 153)

Bhabha elaborates and explicates this thesis throughout *The Location of Culture*. He challenges the hegemony of colonial culture and questions the (im)possibility of cross-cultural communication by presenting the "unitary sign of human culture" as under duress (ibid., 178). As his restrained reading of E. M. Forster's *Passage to India* (1924) in "Articulating the Archaic" demonstrates, the problem is not with differing cultures or conflicting cultural values as with all declarations of "culture" (from Mathew Arnold to V. D. Savarkar) that gloss the antagonistic nonrelation constitutive of social relations as well as human relations with biotic and abiotic nature. Once outside the cocoon of colonial society, as is the case with the picnickers in Forster's novel, there is no shading this truth: the synapses are cut, run over by repressed discords, the most significant of which in human life is the *actuality* of sexual difference. Actuality is the unbearable law or truth of existence—there is no communication between the "haves" and "have-nots" just as there is no communication between the sexes. The reality is what misinforms or obviates this truth—the endless soap operas and films presenting love as the most crucial harmonizing force in nature, when, truly speaking, "love" discloses the opposite. Love is the signature of disharmony in (all) human relations and in relations between Man and Nature. Bhabha is correct: *How untrue must you be to fail to be happily, if haphazardly human* (Bhaba 2006, 196).

Because the master signifier is empty, McGowan says, we must stop treating the universal as a master signifier. The master signifier cannot guarantee stable identity or assume the inherent sufficiency of an Idea. As Hook and Vanheule claim further, persistent and rigorous interrogations of our most cherished beliefs—love for one's country, say—commonly exposes the impossibility of putting into words why we love our country. "Indeed, the reasons I love someone (or something) can never be wholly rationalized or exhausted by a string of signifiers, partly because such signifiers refer on and on to other signifiers without ever 'hitting the real' " (Hook and Vanheule 2016, n.p.). At times, our best response is often: *I just do*. This "just" however is a filler for an absence or impossibility. It seeks to stop the gap in the symbolic but functions as well to isolate it. As I have noted earlier, the existence of the gap is not an issue of linguistic formalization. Namely, language is inadequate for expressing our core feelings—words are failing me, or I am not finding adequate words to express my real feelings. What is at stake, rather, is this gap (in language) *is* "me!" The stumble I experience in expressing my innermost being through language indexes my real as subjectivized lack. McGowan insists that this subjective condition of lack is the universal:

> The universal is not what subjects have in common but what they don't have in common, the cut that blocks the social structure's completion for the subject. It is an absence that all subjects partake in. This insight cuts against the commonsense conception of universality that associates it with the master signifier. (2018, 201)

To represent the universal in terms of master signifiers is misdirection deflecting attention away from humanity's shared ontological condition. And setting up a master signifier implies excluding those that are not-yet-universal, or, the particular.

Cast in terms of the master signifier, the universal is therefore always political and, as long as the universal predicated on master signifiers is imposed onto particulars for purposes of either excluding them or inviting them to join the hallowed chambers of the universal (as norm), postcolonial objections as acts of political resistance stand to remain valid. Yet postcolonial arguments will fail if, like Dabashi, these end up listing competing ideas and identities as alternatives or supplementary to the master signifier. In proposing new master signifiers in place of old ones does not benefit postcolonial studies. It only sets them up as usurpers who seek the position of old master, that is, instead of white it is black that now becomes the new definition of the pure, the norm, that which must be alloyed to the old in terms of a changing global sociopolitical landscape. Or, worse: The coexistence of the new and the old master signifiers merely reproduce the logic of neoliberal multiculturalism, which sees universalism as an aggregate of particulars. Either way it's a trap postcolonial scholars would do well to avoid.

Postcolonial studies must relieve itself of excavating and archiving competing narratives, hoping that recognition of these narratives as equal to hegemonic narratives would reverse the self-Other binary. Spivak has repeatedly cautioned about this fallacy, noting that this methodology involves *feeling* accomplished at representing yet another lost voice unearthed from the bowels of third world darkness but nothing more. True universalism does not involve being a part of a collective under some signature of the positive. Instead, universalism is found in destroying altogether this regimen of positive framework. Postcolonial politics cannot be about positive representations—being included, recognized, and accepted as a valid text/voice alongside the dominant. Expositions of power and hegemony shouldn't simply be about exposing the obscene structures of power and the institutions upholding structures of dominance. As I see it, the power of postcolonial reading is in antagonizing the space of hegemony, reversing the idea that we have passed the Fanonian time, and restituting the ideology of complete defeat of hegemony for the fashioning of a new politics and a new subject of representation.

NOTES

INTRODUCTION

1. Postcolonial studies evolved somewhat differently in the former colonies, and teaching there one experiences a wide range of variables almost unthought in the United States. Paulomi Chakrabarty, for example, underscores one such difference in terms of South Asian caste politics. She writes:

   To indicate just one site where caste difference explodes the framework of postcolonial theory: what the English language means in India. A few years back, I first heard that the Dalit intellectual Chandra Bhan Prasad celebrates the birthday of Lord Macaulay in Delhi every year with great aplomb. Neither my caste-Hindu upbringing nor my training in postcolonial theory [primarily in North America], which are evidently in great harmony with each other, prepared me to be anything other than just shocked. This is the same Macaulay whose "Minute on Indian Education" (1835) remains indelibly etched in the memory of what I would have thought *all Indians*. I had taught particularly offensive passages from it in multiple courses as an example of colonial violence and the violence done to Indian languages through the English language policy even if English later acquired a complex history in India. However, since then, I have discovered—and included in my postcolonial theory courses—Shefali Chandra's *The Sexual Life of English: Language of Caste and Desire in Colonial India* (2012). Insights from this fine historiography of English in (western) India helps my courses demonstrate how the tremendously powerful binary between English and dominant Indian languages is not oppositional but deployed through a *trope* of opposition by the native elites who marked both English and their mother-tongues as their prerogative in exclusion of the lower castes. In contrast, Dalit intellectual history does not oppose English: Chandra cites a poem by Savitribai Phule (1831–97), the remarkable educationist and Dalit icon, that begins with "English is Our Mother." Teaching Macaulay remains important in my courses. However, putting it alongside Chandra's work interrupts the overwhelming urge to consolidate a nationalist response to the "Minute" that seeks to compel all students to identify themselves as Indians in their common outrage, rather than critically address the differences among them.

2. But this was not always the case. Psychoanalytic theory figures eminently in the writings of Fanon, Alain Grosrichard, Homi Bhabha, and, indirectly, albeit in interesting ways, in Spivak. Psychoanalysts, too, though in a much-limited manner, have addressed the postcolonial question (Bose 1930; Mannoni 1990; Gherovici 2003; Biswas 2003; see also, Hartnack 2001).
3. Spivak not only acknowledges Freud as one of her flawed heroes, but she admits that her well-known maxim "white men saving brown women from brown men" comes from Freud's "A Child is being Beaten" (See, Balibar and Spivak 2016, 863; also, Morton 2007, 113–14). See also Spivak's *Outside the Teaching Machine* (2009), especially the chapters "Women in Difference," "Feminism and Deconstruction, Again: Negotiations," and "Scattered Speculations on the Question of Culture Studies." Fleeting, marginal, or parenthetical her references to psychoanalysis in these chapters speak volumes about her interest in and (dis)engagement with the discipline.
4. In a recent lecture on the "paradox of democracy" (Calcutta, Summer 2017a), Spivak made an interesting observation. She claimed liberty is autonomy and equality is alterity. This is not simply a reduction of the universal into the particular but a cautioning of the fact that the irritating, irreconcilable, intractable particular is *the* universal. Equality is therefore not contingent upon the erasure of alterity but, rather, the product of tense relationship between alterities. Liberty, similarly, is not exclusive of autonomous acts of protest against narrow understandings of the concept of liberty; rather, liberty accommodates all protests including those we do not like. In pushing this argument, Spivak does show her métier, she is *maternal* to the utmost wishing none be left without, but then how can we escape this onerous desire? How do we return to a world not unmediated by difference but different yet symptomatically negotiable?

INTRODUCTION, *POSTSCRIPT*

1. I use the term "master signifier" to designate more than positivity and authority. Europe is the master signifier since it has exclusive command over the symbolic order. For a detailed discussion, see the "conclusion" of this book.
2. I am alluding here to Lacan's observation in "Subversion of the Subject" that as "Being of non-being, that is how *I* comes on the scene as a subject" (2006, 679).

3. "[T]he image of the ideal Father is a neurotic fantasy. Beyond the Mother—demand's real Other, whose desire (that is, her desire) we wish she would tone down—stands out the image of a father who would turn a blind eye to desires. This marks—more than it reveals—the true function of the Father, which is fundamentally to unite (and not to oppose) a desire to the Law" (Lacan 2006, 698).
4. This does not imply that the subject is completely ignorant about the big Other as fiction. Specifically, the subject knows that the big Other lacks but in order to maintain its hard-found subjectivity, even if subjectivity is literally a subjection to desire, the subject voluntarily chooses this servitude. This allows the subject to variously negotiate the Other's lack—the obsessional's negotiation differs from hysteric's and the phobic's—and protect the imaginary of subjective autonomy. To cite Lacan:

> [D]esire institutes the dominance—in the privileged place of jouissance—of *object a* in fantasy [$<>á], which desire substitutes for Ø....the neurotic, whether hysteric, obsessive, or, more radically, phobic, is the one who identifies the Other's lack.... Consequently, the Other's demand takes on the function of the object in the neurotic's fantasy[.] But the prevalence given by the neurotic to demand...hides the anxiety induced in him by the Other's desire, anxiety that cannot be misrecognized when it is covered over by the phobic object alone, but which is more difficult to understand in the case of the other two neuroses when one is not in possession of the thread that makes it possible to posit fantasy as the Other's desire. Once we posit this, we find fantasy's two terms split apart, as it were: the first, in the case of the obsessive, inasmuch as he negates the Other's desire, forming his fantasy in such a way as to accentuate *the impossibility of the subject vanishing,* the second, in the case of the hysteric, inasmuch as *desire is sustained in fantasy only by the lack of satisfaction the hysteric brings desire by slipping away as its object.* These features are confirmed by the obsessive's *fundamental need to be the Other's guarantor,* and by *the Faithlessness of hysterical intrigue.* (Lacan 2006, 698; emphasis added)

CHAPTER ONE. THE SUBALTERN ACT OF FREEDOM

I thank Lee Edelman, Ed Pluth, and Rashna Singh for their comments and suggestions on the conference version(s) of this chapter.

1. See for example, Parry (1995 and 2004), Abdul JanMohammed (1986), Vivek Chibber (2012), Sunder Rajan (2010), Moore-Gilbert (1997), Busia (1989–90). For Spivak's response to her critics, see Spivak (1999). For rejoinders against Chibber, see Spivak (2017) and Brennan (2014). For a case of "subaltern" moving into the center, and the debates that followed, see Beverley (1999; ch. 3).

2. Walker was instrumental in setting up the decolonial government. Employed by the English to push the Portuguese out of the island and set up a de facto English rule through a bourgeois nationalist government, Walker had used Jose, a simple porter, to start the revolution. Following the ouster of the colonial regime by Jose's rebels, Walker played yet another crucial role in restraining Jose from assuming power as the head of the state of the decolonial government. Years later, when Jose leads another peasant/subaltern insurrection, this time against the nationalist government, Walker is brought back as a free agent to help the government capture Jose.
3. We must recognize, though, that fantasy paradoxically grants freedom to the subject from encountering the trauma of the real. In keeping the subject desiring, fantasy keeps her alive. Haunted by a feeling of being offset from the rest of the world, but alive. The unending quest for desire is our only excuse for staying alive. For, if the object of desire is accomplished and/or the object turns out empty, which it always does on realization, the subject loses all conviction to live (unless, as it almost always happens, a new object replaces the old empty one). At the same time, the pathetic existence of always being one step behind the object and, more traumatically, the complete emptiness of the fantastic object of desire can be considered as a condition of unfreedom. Perhaps our subjectification in drive, that is, the striving after the object of desire without any real intention or possibility of ever attaining it, is the most traumatic condition of this entrapment. But, it is also in circling around the object and never touching it where enjoyment is located.
4. The argument that the act involves "doing something with signifiers" does not mean that everything we do with signifiers counts as act. For instance, Pluth explains, we use signifiers in speaking but not every speech constitutes an act. Thus, while appearing similar to J. L. Austin's performative speech act, the act in Lacan is different:

    A performative speech act gets something done with words by virtue of saying the right words in the right context. "I do" or "I hereby declare the meeting adjourned" will achieve marriages and closures by virtue of being said. Lacan shares with Austin the idea that such acts are transformative, and such acts are clearly "signifying," but Lacan's focus is not on acts that change the situation of the world or sets of facts within it. Instead he focuses on acts that change the structure of a subject. (2007, 101)

5. One can imagine a brutal postcolonial riposte to this point: if the act is not about changing the world but something as abstract as the subject, then are we not ignoring the history of the oppressed worldwide? Are we not ignoring the real sufferings endured by the wretched of the Earth and their real struggles against unimaginable oppression? Are we not ignoring the reality of the subaltern? I do not want to belabor the points I've already made in the introduction of this book and which I discuss again in my conclusion, "Particular Universal." Also, later in this chapter, I compare Draupadi's act with another

example of subaltern action in order to illustrate how even though both appear to be speech acts their results are very different. Only one, Draupadi's, shatters the big Other, thus qualifying as the act.
6. It is about "crossing a certain threshold," which puts the subject responsible for the act "outside of law" (Lacan Sem. XV, 11/15/67; cited in Pluth 2007, 101).
7. In Pluth's words, "There is no authority that can ensure the legitimacy" of the act (2007, 101).
8. I owe these thoughts to Lee Edelman, especially his paper "Lacan, Badiou, and the theft of Jouissance," delivered at the 2016 ACLA, "Lacan and Philosophy" Seminar.
9. Unless otherwise noted, the translation is Spivak's. Italicized words (unless noted) are in Spivak's original translation designating English words in the original Bengali story.
10. I use unavowed instead of disavowed deliberately. While the logic underwriting disavowal can be stated as: "I know very well but still...," the critical difference it has from unavowed is this: that which is unavowed is best left unadmitted to the conscious mind. As Zola wrote in *His Masterpiece*: "his *unavowed* dream, the ambition he dared not confess to himself" (1902, 183). I place unavowed in Freud's preconscious.
11. The logic writing class division is isomorphic to the logic of sexual difference; both being different grafting of an impossible ontology. Both assume to imagine the subject in relation to historical reality; both strive to argue that equality between classes and/or genders can be accomplished by erasing difference; and, both as such fail to take into account the impossibility of erasing difference in an ontologically incomplete reality.
12. We ought to be cautious, however, against thinking of the real as a force of social destruction. Instead, as the impossible core of reality, the real is constitutive of the social. It renders possible the political in contrast to politics. See, Žižek 2008, 193–94.
13. I am not suggesting that we all have some part of the subaltern-other within us and once we embrace this interiority a new dawn of equitable social relations will emerge. Far from this new age mumbo-jumbo, I am proposing that we understand the subaltern as the excessive core of humanity. We commonly defray this excess through an array of inventive discourses yet at moments of outburst (such as the ones about which we read in Mahasweta's story), this excessive other substantiates our incomplete ontology.
14. That being said, there is nothing in the story that gives us any satisfactory answers about whether the water carrier was telling the truth, for he could've been lying to appease his bosses by bringing the matter to a close or with the intention of helping the Naxalites. We can never know. But that's not all. He says these words could've come only from someone from Maldah. What are we to make of this? Has the fire of revolution spread so far? He also says that

the war cry was last heard during the Gandhi's nonviolent movements against the British Empire. For what reasons could a war cry popular during India's independence movement and as part of a nonviolent struggle against imperialism come to be employed by a group of violent "anti-state" Maoists? Are signifiers indeed so flexible, random, and arbitrary, or is the use of the same war cry symbolic: it suggests the war of independence still continues?

15. Understanding without knowledge. Common sense tells us that's impossible: How can we understand anything if we do not have knowledge? But we understand a number of things but do not really know. For example, we understand how a car runs—energy drives the axel that in turn rotates the wheels, etc. But do we *know* how gas becomes energy and what exactly this energy does in order for the car to move?

16. Even the catachresis via the vernacular is not singular but contingent upon a variety of factors. In Calcutta, the word *counter* has yet another meaning. When one asks a friend for "a counter," she is asking to share the cigarette her friend is smoking.

17. Lacan does a deconstructive paleonymy with the term *subject*—it is not the classical representational subject nor subject of immanence, rather the notion of the subject is radically (apropos strategically) altered by Lacan to mean the split subject, that is, the subject that comes into being (or, effect) by disappearing from statement. It emerges in "between an extinction that is still glowing" and a presence that is a stumble (See Lacan 2006, 678).

18. Hannah Arendt makes the same argument. See *On Violence*, 53–54.

CHAPTER TWO. POSTCOLONIAL. ANIMAL. LIMIT.

1. For recent scholarship in animal studies, see Cary Wolfe's *Animal Rites* (2003), Philip Armstrong's *What Animals Mean in the Fiction of Modernity* (2008; see also, 2006), and the cluster of essays on "animal studies" in the March 2009 *Publication of the Modern Languages Association*, vol. 124, no. 2 (Yaeger 2009). For the theoretical base of these studies, see Jacques Derrida *The Animal Therefore I Am* (2008) and *The Beast and the Sovereign* (2011). See also Giorgio Agamben's *The Open* (2004). For a sampling of recent postcolonial zoocriticism, see Philip Armstrong, Richard Iveson, Neel Ahuja, Andrew Benjamin, Sara Saliha, and Laura Wright.

2. In *Arachnophobia* (1995) an aggressive species of spider discovered in the South American rainforest accidentally travels to the United States and starts killing people. While in *Prometheus* (2012) we get director Ridley Scott's version of *panspermia* or the theory that cellular biological life was imported to Earth from outer space by comets (most famously supported by the Cambridge astronomer Fred Hoyle and his acolyte, the astrobiologist Chandra Wickramasinghe).

NOTES TO CHAPTER TWO

3. SDO or Sub-Divisional Officer is a junior district magistrate in charge of a subdivision.
4. For history of the incident, see Ross Mallick; Annu Jalais.
5. Kaur (2007) and Mukherjee (2007) both argue that the novel challenges and dismantles (Western) cosmopolitanism, forcing a vision of locally sensitive conservationism to emerge at the end through Piya's transformation. At the end of the novel, Piya returns to Lusibari with renewed funding from the United States to complete her research project on dolphin conservation. But she also comes bearing charitable coffers for Moyna and Tutul, Fokir's widowed wife and son. Taking my cue from Ilan Kapoor's notion of "celebrity humanitarianism," a term describing U.S. celebrities who undertake charity in the global South, I wish to label Piya as diasporic or cosmopolitan humanitarian. As one, she believes in social media and crowd sourcing as exemplary venues for raising concerns over and curing individual cases of poverty without needing to tackle the deep economic reasons responsible for global inequality. I therefore disagree with assessments of Piya's transformation and find the unquestioning acceptance of a locally sensitive ecological consciousness deeply problematic. I have written elsewhere that Western gestures of involving subalterns into politicizing their destinies are mere posturings—a façade that makes the neoliberals feel good about doing something without having to directly confront corporate exploitation of the global South.
6. For the relationship between neoliberal culture and self-culpabilization, see Žižek 2017, especially pages 12–14. This paragraph also draws from Oxana Timofeeva's "The Non-Human as Such: On Men, Animals, and Barbers" (2016) and *The History of Animals* (2018).
7. We should also not forget their role in the narrative development: without them, Piya would not have discovered the dolphins: "because they were Fokir's livelihood and without them he would not have known to lead her to this pool where the Oracella came" (HT, 119).
8. In this, the film shares with Discovery Channel's *Life After People* (2009) the idea that only after the extinction of humans will Nature successfully reclaim what has been lost to humans, the planet for itself, as wildlife will gradually take over our cities, monuments, and homes to fill out a void at the heart of the planet; that is, the void created by humans and represented by humans.
9. Recent postcolonial scholarship is starting to reject "illusions about happy intermingling and egalitarian dialogues" between humans and animals in order to focus on the "intersecting and co-constituted histories" of the two species (Deb 2015, 67). Yet anxiety informs even the slightest suggestion of the human collapsing onto the animal. Ursula Heise's otherwise brilliant essay, for instance, shirks the possibility of the human erased; the human reduced to a metonym and horizontalized with *others* (2013, 638, 642n7).
10. Let us take two examples: (1) the 2010 earthquake that hit Haiti resulted from a previously undetected fault line (cited in Eisenstein and McGowan

2012, 225); (2) the Younger Dryas cold period and the last big extinction, namely, the Holocene Extinction, occurred, according to new research, due to a comet entering the Earth's atmosphere, breaking up into pieces, and resulting in an air burst over terra firma (like the 1908 Tunguska blast) or a direct impact with the Laurentide Ice Sheet. This sudden event arrested the melting of the icecaps and inaugurated a period of global cooling known as the Younger Dryas. Though debate over this hypothesis is ongoing, we should remind ourselves that the Alvarez Hypothesis, which blamed the extinction of dinosaurs on a comet hitting the earth, "Extraterrestrial Cause for the Cretaceous-Tertiary Extinction" (1980), was initially dismissed, mocked, and rebuked. Today however, it is scientific fact, proven further by the 2016 Chicxulub crater-drilling project. For Alvarez Hypothesis, see Kolbert 2014, 72–91. For the Younger Dryas Impact hypothesis, see Rex Dalton's 2007 report in *Nature*, "Blast in the Past?" Also, Carey Hoffman's report in the University of Cincinnati's Website on the fieldwork done by University of Cincinnati Assistant Professor of Anthropology Ken Tankersley, offers proof of the comet/asteroid impact theory. See Hoffman (2008), "Exploding Asteroid Theory Strengthened by New Evidence Located in Ohio, Indiana" (Web).

11. I've often wondered why Chakrabarty chooses geology over archeology. Geology divides time into the Pleistocene (last Ice Age) and, following that, the Holocene. Anthropocene is a geological designator—it identifies the new epoch based on *traces* of carbon in the Earth's crust. But wouldn't a materialist have found in archeology a more suitable reference frame? Archeology divides Earth's history and the history of humans on Earth by locating matter embedded in the Earth's crust (stone tools, pottery, children's toys). Accordingly, it terms Pleistocene as Paleolithic or Old Stone Age and Holocene as Neolitihic or the New Stone Age. The latter is again further subdivided into two parts: PPNA or early Aceramic (that is, without pottery) and PPNB or later Aceramic. Shouldn't buried matter be of more interest than sedimentary traces to a historian? But in speaking about matter, one must relinquish theories of harmony and enter the unnatural domain of the human as a species, a species that needs matter to fill out its ontological void. As archeological records prove, humans were not content with making tools that would serve their needs for survival. Humans also decorated their tools, embellished the aesthetic appeals of these tools, and their gestures of aesthetic tool enhancement coincided with the evolution of the species.

CHAPTER THREE. HYSTERIZATION OF POSTCOLONIAL STUDIES

1. Commonly, humans are caught in an unsatisfied desire (*hysteria*), in an impossible desire (*obsessional*), and/or in a desire sustained by anxiety (*phobia*). In hysteria, the object of desire is never the true object of desire but

a deferment for or strategic replacement of the real, true object of desire. The simplest example of this is Freud's Dora: Dora desires Frau K via Herr K. In obsessional, the object of desire is an impossible object. It is an unrealizable object, in all possibilities nonexistent except in fantasy, and thus the subject's pursuit of this object is doomed from the very start. In phobia, the subject's relation to the object is maintained by anxiety. Common to all three, however, is the paradoxical relationship between desire and lack—the subject does not know what it desires and what the subject desires is either impossible and/or unbearable.

2. It is clear from Freud's *The Interpretation of Dreams* that wish replaces desire for a prohibited/lost object. Consider as an example infant Anna's dream for strawberries. Anna was reacting to what had been withheld from her, strawberries, on account of her vomiting. But strawberries were not the only thing taken off her "menu," yet, as Freud notes, strawberries appear twice in her dream, first as strawberries and second as wild strawberries (German word for each are different). Freud identifies Anna's emphasis on strawberries to her nanny who claims the cause of Anna's vomiting was a result of her eating too many strawberries. "The nurse had attributed her indisposition to a *surfeit* of strawberries. She was thus retaliating in her dream against this unwelcome verdict" (Freud 1900, 129–30). Note: it is the prohibition on excessive eating of strawberries or excessively enjoying strawberries that results in Anna translating strawberries as the prohibited object over all other foods. Second, in demanding not just strawberries but also *wild* strawberries, young Anna is doubling down on wanting to enjoy more wildly, more impetuously, more egregiously.

3. Characterized by Bruce Fink as Lacan's *most* significant contribution to psychoanalysis, the concept of the *objet petit a* evolved over the years through Lacan's seminars, and, as I read it here, this concept has at least three distinct dimensions in relation to the subject (Fink 1995, 83). We can map these three apropos Lacan's well-known triad of the Imaginary, the Symbolic, and the Real. Let me elaborate this point in some detail as it would be crucial for understanding configurations of the other in colonial and postcolonial discourses as well. As imaginary, the *objet a* grounds the subject's fantasy of the other by abstracting an image of the other from the real other—an object, a person, or an idea. Or, the other as Other. The sole purpose of this image is to aid the "subjective organization" of the self, or consolidate the ego (Krishner 2005, 88). By contrast, the symbolic function of the *objet petit a* can be understood as determining the protocols of desire and desiring. This involves recognizing the other as (manageably) different and establishes the rules governing all interactions between the subject and this other. The realness of the *objet petit a* or the object as a piece of the real emerges when an incomprehensible and symbolically irredeemable other surfaces to dismember the symbolic order and eviscerate the imaginary self.

4. These opening paragraphs make use of Todd McGowan's lecture "Citizen Trump," YouTube, February 9, 2017.
5. For instance, Said's *Orientalism* addresses the mechanisms of imagining the other as excessive or lacking, a process he shows was necessary for consolidating European sovereignty: Orientalism is a collection of images about lands and peoples east of Suez; images that aid disciplinary learning about these alien cultures and help establish an unequal "relationship of power, of domination, [and] of varying degrees of complex hegemony" between the West and the non-West (Said 1978, 73, 5). Detached from one's personal experience of the Orient, "Orientalism" is a habit of thought, figure of speech, and methodology of writing (about) the other. All these aim to reduce the other to a "sign of European-Atlantic power over the Orient" (101, 6). "European culture gained in strength and identity by setting itself off against the Orient as a sort of surrogate and even underground self" (3).
6. The British in South Asia, for instance, kept meticulously detailed records of every minute aspect of colonial life, hoping that these would provide them with the required insight necessary for keeping native populations under control. But the inadequacy of this system appeared again and again, especially as the colonial administration struggled to contain a wide range of native quirks and outbursts (*non-sense*), including but not limited to anticolonial insurrections.
7. This section makes use of Marlene Manoff's excellent overview on recent developments in theories of the archive. See, Manoff, "Theories of the Archive from Across the Discipline" (2004).
8. See Agamben 2004, 79–80.
9. "Hysteria would emerge in Freud's writing, that is, as the effect of women's inability to achieve identity through the Oedipal moment of recognition: in effect, he suggested, women are always already psychically scarred by the recognition of their own 'castration' " (Devereux 2014, 24).
10. For a review of this debate, see Homer 2010, 37–39.
11. For a comparative reading of this theme, see Basu Thakur 2015.
12. Stéphane does not know that his admiration for Luca is galvanized by his father's desire: Why did the old man *enjoy* Luca's voice? What did he find in it that made him listen to her on his deathbed? What secrets do the nomads and their music contain that kept his father away from home, family, and Stéphane?
13. http://www.bbc.com/culture/story/20171027-the-simpsons-apu-a-stereotype-hiding-in-plain-sight; accessed April 26, 2018.
14. The most pathetic defense came from the show. At the end of its April 8, 2018, episode, Marge is shown struggling to read a book full of stereotypes to Lisa. Realizing Marge's conflict, Lisa looks directly at the camera and says: "It's hard. . . . Something that started decades ago, and was applauded and

NOTES TO CHAPTER FOUR   207

inoffensive, is now politically incorrect." Right after the camera pulls away to a photo of Apu on Lisa's nightstand. It's signed: "Don't have a cow."

15. In *Orientalism*, Said writes, "One ought never to assume that the structure of Orientalism is nothing more than a structure of lies or of myths which, were the truth about them to be told, would simply blow away." (See *Orientalism* 1978, 6)

CHAPTER FOUR. FICTIONS OF KATHERINE BOO'S CREATIVE NON-FICTION

1. Lack and excess should not be understood in terms of opposition. Rather, they share one boundary; their relation being homeomorphic.
2. Interview with Parvathi Menon, "Being the Subject of a Book Didn't Make Life Lovely in Annawadi." *The Hindu*, December 3, 2014.
3. Not every resident of Annawadi however dreams of transcending his or her class position. The garbage peddler Abdul does not believe he will ever do anything other than buy, sort, and sell garbage to recycling plants. He simply wants to be a *rich* garbage peddler. Mr. Kamble wants money to undergo a heart surgery and live long enough to support his family. While Asha, the local slumlord with connections to petty politicians, aspires to rise in class and grab a piece of the riches globalization offers. And for this she is willing to use unfair means, including entering into salacious liaisons with petty officials in positions of power.
4. There was also a strong countermovement in American literary journalism led by Hunter Thompson and Joan Didion who sought to introduce the "*I*" or first person narrator as a strong character and voice. For this information on Capote and Wolfe, I thank Bruce Ballenger. Personal correspondence with Bruce Ballenger, November 12, 2014.
5. http://www.thehindu.com/news/national/india-100th-on-global-hunger-index-trails-north-korea-bangladesh/article19846437.ece.
6. Cornel West characterizes the "three dominant tendencies in a neoliberal society" as financialize, privatize, and militarize. The Indian tendencies for most parts have been privatize, de-unionize, and militarize. In India, de-unionization proved crucial for privatizing though sometimes public sectors were privatized and then de-unionized through paramilitary force. The current iteration under the Hindu Fascists is again slightly different: financialize, polarize, globalize. The current Indian government encourages private finance, indirectly supports the division of the country's population along sectarian lines, and claims this to be on the shortest route to being on the top of the list of global powers.
7. Martha Nussbaum raises the question of history for making a very different critique than mine. While I am noting the absence of history as strategic to Boo's culturalization of poverty, Nussbaum stakes her claim for defending economic liberalization. According to her, the conditions of poverty described

by Boo existed even before liberalization of the subcontinent and, therefore, Boo's pinpointing the growth of poverty on liberalization is misfounded. Yet, "though increased economic growth certainly does not solve all problems of justice, it is one good thing to which one should have no objection," opines Nussbaum (Nussbaum 2012).

8. "Some of the most radical criticism coming out of the West today is the result of an interested desire to conserve the subject of the West, or the West as Subject. The theory of pluralized 'subject-effects' gives an illusion of undermining subjective sovereignty while often providing a cover for this subject of knowledge. Although the history of Europe as subject [continues to be] narrative by the law, political economy, and ideology of the West, this concealed subject pretends it has 'no geopolitical determinations.' The much-publicized critique of the sovereign subject thus actually inaugurates a Subject" (Spivak 1988, 271–72).

9. There is a brief paragraph toward the end of the book where the condition of poor in Mumbai is presented as being the same in New York City, Nairobi, and Brasilia (BF, 237).

10. For a recent debate on the pros and cons of sustainable economic growth versus trickle-down growth, see exchanges between Amartya Sen, Arvind Panagariya, Jagdish Bhagwati. The following can be a good starting point. Khushwant S. Gill, "Way to Grow: A Look at Trickle-down Effect," November 24, 2013; http://www.tribuneindia.com/2013/20131124/spectrum/book1.htm.

11. See Vandana Shiva, "The Seeds Of Suicide: How Monsanto Destroys Farming," March 13, 2014; http://www.globalresearch.ca/the-seeds-of-suicide-how-monsanto-destroys-farming/5329947.

12. For the "real" story of India's Maoists, see Arundhati Roy, *Walking With the Comrades* (2010).

13. I admit to violently twisting Spivak's maxim of education for uncoercive rearrangement of desires. See Spivak 2004.

14. *Teleopoiesis* is a Greek word. Transliterated and translated over the ages, it has accrued a wide range of meanings. I use it here after Gayatri Spivak who borrows the term from Derrida but in her distinctly catachrestic mode of postcolonial reading transforms it by underlining its signature of endeavor over its programmatic teleology. In *Death of a Discipline* (2003), Spivak not only gives the word a new spelling, *teleopoiesis*, but this change in spelling also organizes a turn in meaning: teleopoiesis in Spivak means the exercise of stepping into the Other's space, the latter's distance or alterity being connoted by the prefix "tele-," and of being radically reimagined by this other, alien culture. It, however, does not imply a teleological end to this exercise. This means that the journey into Otherness is not guided by or aimed to accomplish certain preset results but is aimed at embracing the "openness and indeterminacy" indexed by the prefix *tele* (Morton 2007, 167). Spivak con-

ceives *teleopoiesis* as critical for achieving a "non-reductive collectivity" that is in stark contrast to "the streamlined, hegemonic collectivity of globalization" (Ghazoul 2003). Spivak puts it as: "letting yourself be imagined (experience the impossibility) without guarantees, by and in another culture" (52).

There is another aspect to Spivak's teleopoiesis, one that also comes from Derrida's abstraction of the term from Nietzsche, and this has to do with the second part, that is "*poiesis*" as "imaginative making" as well as an act of "reading, as a creative, productive art" (Scheiner 2005, 243). Remarking on this, Scheiner, for instance, contends that both Derrida and Spivak take ample liberty with their adoption of the original Greek—mediating, translating, and transfiguring the term through transliteration—for suiting their respective thinking. With orthographic changes changing meaning, Spivak's term is, however, *most* ambiguous, according to Scheiner. For, in departing from Derrida's use, she further distances herself from the original Greek, thus settling for something new, something revised by way of writing back to the center of French Greek heterotopic symbiote, *teleopoiesis* in-citing thought rather than guiding thinking and reading along the parallel rails of Euro-endorsed meaning-making. Spivak's derivation of the word and her remaking of it in the Other's image are therefore more than translation; it is a mode of ethical engagement with the Other that involves dismantling privileges of the subject of the West and the disorientation of the West as subject.

15. Gone are the days when Richard Attenborough played Godbole, the Hindu priest, in David Lean's adaptation of E. M. Forster's *A Passage to India*. Today we actually have the opportunity to experience the Indian method actor Naseeruddin Shah in the role of Captain Nemo in *The League of Extraordinary Gentlemen* (2003). As most of us know, Jules Verne's Nemo was also an Indian prince. Therefore, Hollywood today does not shirk from presenting protagonists as who they really are. Yet, contemporary Hollywood remains notorious for whitewashing history and culture by casting white actors in colored roles—Russell Crowe as Noah in *Noah* (2014), Christian Bale as Moses in *Exodus: Gods and Kings* (2014), Emma Stone as a native Pacific Hawaiian in *Aloha* (2015), and, most recently, Joseph Fiennes as Michael Jackson in the British TV movie "Elizabeth, Michael and Marlon" (2016). The point I am seeking to make is that the general understanding that times have changed and a few missteps here and there are all that remain is incorrect. True, every time a misstep occurs it is identified by scholars, criticized by the press, and chastised in social media. This indeed pushes Hollywood today to become avidly self-conscious about its actions in marginalizing the other. It is also true that Hollywood elites regularly stand up for racial and ethnic minorities, gender and sexual minorities, differently abled and those outside our species: recall Patricia Arquette's "equal pay" Oscar speech in 2015 or Meryl Streep's passionate advocacy for the protection of persons of disability, the freedom of press, and immigrant rights in her 2016

Golden Globe speech. In other words, Hollywood no longer seeks to just entertain with their billion-dollar productions but also to make these movies *matter*. Bearing the responsibility of being followed by millions across the globe and in order to be the role model for all, Hollywood seeks to be at the forefront of today's multicultural, tolerant, and species-conscious milieu. As some argue, in this age when the Fanonian binaries have been made redundant by the logic of global or universal time, Hollywood, too, appears to increasingly advocate for inclusion. Today, popular culture is not only regularly audited for its representational politics, it also stringently advocates for relegating self-Other binaries to the past in recognition of fluid identities and transnational relations.

16. Also, we cannot ignore gestures such Gopal's characterization of the West's maternal feminism as tantamount to an (other's) act of Othering.
17. For a more Lacanian reading of the Freudian maxim, see my conclusion. Also, Žižek 2006, 3.
18. I am repeating, of course, Slavoj Žižek's point about enjoyment of kinder eggs. See, Žižek 2012a.
19. "Our main hope for a truly 'free world' lies in the desolate universe of the slums," submits Žižek (2004, n.p.).
20. Symptomatic expressions of this find illustration in reviews of Boo's book. From Amit Chaudhuri to William Dalrymple to Janet Maslin, every single review commends the slum dwellers for their patience and for remaining hopeful against all odds. Dalrymple, for example, gushes about how an "infrastructure of opportunity" allows even the most "economically marginalized" to dream about making it big one day. In spite of all "the deprivation and injustice" experienced by India's poor, Boo believes that "hope is not a fiction" and that "her scavengers can succeed in flourishing against all the odds," writes Dalrymple (2012, n.p.).
21. I thank my good friend Sayandeb Chowdhury for helping me think with Nabarun.
22. "Hanr" is "bone," but I think "The Bone Collector" is a more appropriate translation of the title. All translations are mine.
23. Spivak writes: "My earliest memories are of the Great Bengal Famine. It was specifically meaningful for me as a child. Even the rationed food we were given was of terrible quality. I remember skeletal figures crawling up to our backdoor and begging for the starch water of rice that people throw away. There were people dying everywhere.

    In California, half a century later, I got a stress fracture while running. The doctor looked at the X-ray and asked when and where I was born. When I told him, he searched his World Health Organization handbook, and said, simply, "bad bones." That's how long the effects linger. The famine was so bad that even middle-class children suffered malnutrition." See Brohi 2014.
24. He gets repeated advice about leaving the country—join the navy; embark on an adventure; nine-to-five jobs are for clerks, etc. Interesting point to

note, this advice repeats itself, almost customarily, across the cultural history of colonial and postcolonial South Asian literature as one protagonist after another is told to go abroad and live dangerously. From Bibhutibushan Bandhyophaya's *Chander Pahar* (1939) to Jhumpa Lahiri's *Namesake* (2003), first-generation Indians are advised to eke it out in (British) Africa, United Kingdom, and the United States.

25. The idea of the time-bound clerical job as emasculating has its roots in late-nineteenth-century-Bengali bourgeois reaction to the opportunities available within the colonial regime. As Sumit Sarkar shows, this reaction was further galvanized by the influence of Ramakrishna, a turn of the century spiritual leader, who openly condemned the clerical profession under the British as slavery. (See, Sarkar 1992).

26. "Precarity is the rubric that brings together women, queers, transgender people, the poor, the differently abled, and the stateless, but also religious and racial minorities: it is a social and economic condition, but not an identity (indeed, it cuts across these categories and produces potential alliances among those who do not recognize that they belong to one another)" (Butler 2015, 58).

CHAPTER FIVE. POLITICAL CORRECTNESS *IS* PHALLIC

1. Symptomatic of this tendency: Jordan received celebrity endorsements from Cher and Khizr Khan ("the Gold Star father, Pakistani-American lawyer, Hillary Clinton supporter and Donald Trump target") and funding support from "Planned Parenthood Votes NW" and Jonathan Soros, chief executive of a private investment firm and son of billionaire philanthropist George Soros. See, Ganga 2018.
2. Both the trans-Saharan gold trade and the translations of Greek philosophy by African Arab Islamic scholars proved invaluable for the development of "Europe" through the Middle Ages and into Enlightenment.
3. This argument applies as well to Nabarun. Often regarded as the last Romantic, one who continued to dream of a Bolshevik socialist revolution till the end of his life, I consider Nabarun differently: I think of him as a poet of lack. Nabarun inhabits and writes about the impossible antagonism at the center of the social; a deadlock that cannot be broken without radical violence of the bizarre.
4. "[T]he sole white leading character in the movie, the CIA operative Everett Ross (Martin Freeman), gets to be a hero who helps save Wakanda. A white man who trades in secrets and deception is given a better turn than a black [American] man whose father was murdered by his own family and who is left by family and nation to languish in poverty. That's racist." Writes Christopher Lebron (2018, n.p.).

5. "Killmonger's main dream to free black people everywhere decisively earns him the fate of death" (Lebron 2018, n.p.).
6. Worse still, Killmonger plans to attack New York, London, and Hong Kong—three of the world's largest and oldest stock exchanges. Bringing these cities down would lead to the inevitable collapse of the system. Most fans read this as a subtle reference ("Easter egg") to the three sanctums protected/overseen by Dr. Strange: "Since there's no such thing as a coincidence in a Marvel movie, there is most definitely a reason behind Erik [Killmonger] naming these three locations, which are also the three locations directly connected to *Doctor Strange*" (Paige 2018, n.p.). They contend that these attacks aid Thanos? But I suggest we look beyond the Marvel Cinematic Universe (MCU).
7. As noted already, there are three versions of the impossible object of desire. In obsessional neurosis, the object is unreachable, ungraspable, and impossible. To the hysteric, the object is unsatisfactory. Lastly, for the phobic, the object is unbearable. It is, however, the hysteric who most plainly illustrates the "disharmonious character of desire," that is, the tenuous relation of the subject to the big Other/Law. The (hysteric) subject both desires to defy the Law as much as it demands the Law's riveting attention or authority. See, for instance, Gerovici 2014, 65–68.
8. My reading relies on Lacan's seminar XX; McGowan (2012, ch. 6, 123–46); Žižek (2011); and Owen Hewitson (2013).
9. It does not matter if the superhero is female—Wonder Woman or Black Widow. As Lacan teaches, distinct from biological sex, positions we adopt relative to the Signifier—the Phallus (simultaneously the signifier of plenitude and lack)—determine the male and female positions. Female superheroes by appearing outside the logic of the cut of castration are neither man nor woman. They are the One. Perhaps intuitively the use of "super heroine" for female superheroes is rare. Irrespective of gender, superheroes are superhero.
10. It is also worth noting that what Kowalski teaches as "man-speak" appears as nothing more than small talk that is supposed to work as filler while the business of hair cutting gets done, and it is, therefore, to be kept intentionally empty of direct speech.
11. A quick note about Driver's essay: it makes the common mistake of identifying Lacanian empty speech as empty. As I explain above, empty speech in Lacan is the opposite of empty; it is, rather, full speech that is empty of any other content except for the imaginaries of the self.
12. Bosch complains, for instance, "Eastwood paints this movie in large, easy-to-read strokes without much subtlety. The story by Dave Johannsen and the screenplay of Nick Schenk are part of the problem. The plot and the dialogue both border on simplistic, the plot driven by the obvious, and the dialogue often at the mercy of the need to move the plot along. We end up with characters at the service of the plot, meaning they ripen in the hot house

of the movie plot rather than develop more genuinely as real human beings" (2009, 459).
13. Kustra retired in 2018 after serving as the president of the university for fifteen years, and Labrador, seeking the Republican nomination for governor, resigned from his post as First District Congressman but was defeated by Brad Little by almost four points.

CONCLUSION

1. Mignolo's and Dabashi's pieces are now part of *Can the Non-European Think?* (2018). For a review of the debate see Kapoor 2018.
2. Nigam gives the example of India. "[T]here were pretty robust traditions of abstract philosophical thought—preoccupied with questions of logic, epistemology, causation and being, disquisitions on language and meaning and similar questions—in the pre-colonial period. Why is it that from the 19th century on, 'politics' takes centre stage? It is not just that 'politics' becomes the key object of inquiry; rather it is that all inquiry and thought comes to be colonized by it" (Nigam 2013).
3. My objective is not to unravel Spivak as a closet Freudian. Spivak's engagement with psychoanalytic theory is at best cautious. Her "mistaken" readings of Freud and Lacan are often literally mistaken readings; her criticisms of psychoanalysis being refined spiels of the charge that psychoanalysis is culturally specific, and indifferent to cultural difference. Nonetheless, Spivak's thinking, without being avowedly Freudian, does come very close to certain psychoanalytic arguments, and my "misreadings" of her "mistaken" readings of Freud constitute an attempt to unearth these moments in Spivak. Putting things back on their feet, as it were.
4. "What Spivak implies but does not state is that the nonsystematic experiences and knowledges of such radically disempowered groups present a crisis in imagination when it comes to the cognitive abilities of Western critical theory," writes Morton in his review of *Critique* (2001, 189).
5. The commonplace mistaken translation is: Where the Id was, the Ego shall be. This has led to the idea that Freud is speaking about the need for the ego to keep the Id under check so that the subject does not fall prey to her instincts, etc. But this is not what Freud is saying. He is speaking, rather, about embracing the particularity of human existence as split between the ego and the Id.
6. The multicultural universal, however, is slightly different: it considers the universal as an aggregate of particulars, thus making universality an issue of rights, representation, and empathy.
7. The illustrative example is, of course, Macaulay's "Minute on Indian Education" (1835). Speaking in favor of funding the study of English language and literature in India, this British colonial bureaucrat dismisses the entire

production of Sanskrit and Arabic literature as useless and proposes English education for creating a breed of men English in taste and culture but Indian by blood and color. Spivak's proposal for a deconstructive reading attempts to sabotage both the method of learning and the object of this learning. See, for example, her reading of Coetzee's *Foe* in *Critique*.

8. McGowan reminds us that not all master signifiers are universals (Germany under the Nazis) but all universals are master signifiers ("freedom," "democracy," "nonviolence").

9. For ease of my readers, I boldface the words/phrases/images repeated across centuries to describe and understand the Other in what Spivak terms the "Northwestern European tradition (codename "West")" (Spivak 1999, 6). Homer's "Mediterranean" prejudice coopted into the tradition as the original enunciation of the other's alterity. The similarities between these passages are too striking to be missed. In each of these, the Other is dehumanized in preparation for the labor and enterprise of the European subject. In fact, the logic is simple: represent natives as incapable of tending their own lands and present native women and children as oppressed, thereby mandating the duty of the West to interfere into and intervene for the preservation of a universally valid moral law. In process, as if almost an afterthought, the West also assumes the responsibility for the land. This is code for exploiting the land's resources by using the natives as slaves. But neither Darwin nor Laura Bush is consciously citing Homer. Instead, the verbatim reproduction of the Other in each of these passages is a product of that organized body of Western thinking about the non-West which Edward Said termed *Orientalism*.

   1. "In the next land we found the Kyklopes, giants, louts, **without a law to bless them**. In ignorance leaving the fruitage of the earth in mystery to the immortal gods, **they neither plow nor sow by hand, nor till the ground**, though grain—wild wheat and barley—grows untended, and wine-grapes, in clusters, ripen in heaven's rain. Kyklopes **have no muster** and no meeting, no consultation or old tribal ways, but each one dwells in his own mountain cave **dealing out rough justice to wife and child**, indifferent to what the others do." (Homer, Book IX *Odysseus*)

   2. "They live together **without king, without government**, and **each is his own master**. They **marry as many wives as they please**...observe **no sort of law**...have **no church, no religion**." (Amerigo Vespucci, "A New World" [?])

   3. "The astonishment which I felt on first seeing a party of Fuegians on a wild and broken shore will never be forgotten by me....These men were absolutely naked and bedaubed with paint, their long hair was tangled, their **mouths frothed with excitement**, and their **expressions were wild**, startled, and distrustful. They **possessed hardly any arts**,

and like wild animals **lived on what they could catch**; they **had no government**, and were **merciless to everyone not of their own small tribe**...a savage who delights to torture his enemies, offers up bloody sacrifices, **practices infanticide without remorse, treats his wives like slaves**, knows no decency, and is haunted by the grossest superstitions." (Darwin, *The Descent of Man* [1871])

4. "I'm Laura Bush, and I'm delivering this week's radio address to kick off **a worldwide effort to focus on the brutality against women and children by the al-Qaida terrorist network and the regime it supports in Afghanistan**....Civilized people throughout the world are speaking out in horror—not only because **our hearts break for the women and children in Afghanistan**, but also because in Afghanistan we see the world the terrorists would like to impose on the rest of us."(The Weekly Address Delivered by the First Lady, November 17, 2001 [http://www.presidency.ucsb.edu])

10. I use here Charles Lam Markmann's translation from the 1967 edition of *Black Skin White Masks* (New York: Grove) instead of Richard Philcox's 2008 translation, because I find the former, at least in this instance, more appropriate insofar it captures the experiential angst in this passage more succinctly. Philcox's translation goes like this: "I cast an objective gaze over my self, discovered my blackness, my ethnic features; deafened by cannibalism, backwardness, fetishism, racial stigmas, slave traders, and above all, yes above all, the grinning *Y a bon Banania*." Markmann's translation appears on page 112 and is as follows: "I subjected myself to an objective examination, I discovered my blackness, my ethnic characteristics; and I was battered down by tom-toms, cannibalism, intellectual deficiency, fetishism [*sic*], racial defects, slave-ships, and above all else, above all: 'Sho' good eatin'."

11. For master signifier, in addition to McGowan (2018), see Hook and Vanheule (2015).

WORKS CITED

300. Dir. Zack Snyder, Warner Bros, 2006.
Abbas, Sadia. 2011. "Leila Aboulela, Religion, and the Challenge of the Novel." *Contemporary Literature* vol. 52, no. 3, 2011, pp. 430–61.
AbdalKafor, Ola. *Gayatri Spivak: Deconstruction and the Ethics of Postcolonial Literary Interpretation*, Cambridge Scholars, 2015.
Aboulela, Leila. "The Museum." *The Anchor Book of Modern African Stories*, edited by Nadežda Obradović, Anchor Books, 2001.
Abrams, Susan. "The Pterodactyl in the Margins: Detranscendentalizing Postcolonial Theology." *Planetary Loves: Spivak, Postcoloniality, and Theology*, edited by Stephen Moore and Mayra Rivera, Fordham UP, 2011.
Adams, Parveen. *The Emptiness of the Image: Psychoanalysis and Sexual Difference*, Routledge, 1996.
Agamben, Giorgio. *The Open: Man and Animal*, translated by Kevin Attell, Stanford UP, 2003.
Ahuja, Neel. "Postcolonial Critique in a Multispecies World." *Publications of the Modern Language Association*, vol. 124, no. 2, March 2009, pp. 556–63.
Arachnophobia. Dir. Frank Marshall, Buena Vista Pictures, 1990.
Arendt, Hannah. *On Violence*, Harcourt, 1970.
Armstrong, Philip. "Sympathy." *Satya*, 2006, Web.
———. *What Animals Mean in the Fiction of Modernity*, Routledge, 2008.
Ashcroft, Bill, Gareth Griffiths, and Helen Tiffin. *Post-Colonial Studies: The Key Concepts,* Routledge, 2007.
Avengers: Infinity War. Dir. Anthony and Joe Russo, Marvel Studios, 2018.
Badiou, Alain. "The Neolithic, Capitalism, and Communism." Verso Blog, July 30, 2018, Web.
Baer, Ben Conisbee. "Terodacktyl Apocalypse: Writing Catastrophe in Mahasweta Devi's *Pterodactyl, Puran Sahay, and Pirtha*." *Culture, Environment, and Ecopolitics*, edited by Nick Heffernan and David A. Wragg, Cambridge Scholars, 2011, pp. 177–99.

Baker, Steve. *The Postmodern Animal*, Reaktion Books, 2000.
Balibar, and Gayatri Chakravorty Spivak. "An Interview on Subalternity" (published in partnership with Éditions Amsterdam), *Cultural Studies*, vol. 30, no. 5, 2016, pp. 856–71.
Barker, Jason. "Master Signifier: A Brief Genealogy of Lacano-Maoism." *FILOZOFIA*, vol. 69, no. 9, 2014, pp. 752–64.
Basu Thakur, Gautam. *Postcolonial Theory and Avatar*, Bloomsbury, 2015.
Benjamin, Andrew. *Of Jews and Animals*, Edinburgh UP, 2011.
Beshara, Robert K. *Decolonial Psychoanalysis: Towards Critical Islamophobia Studies*. Routledge, 2019.
Beverley, John. *Subalternity and Representation: Arguments in Cultural Theory*, Duke UP, 1999.
Bhabha, Homi. *The Location of Culture*, Routledge, 2006.
Bhattacharya, Nabarun. *Kangal Malshat*, Saptarshi Prakashan, 2003.
Bhattacharya, Sourit. "The Question of Literary Form: Realism in Poetry and Theatre of the 1943 Bengal Famine." *The Aesthetics and Politics of Global Hunger*, edited by M. Basu and A. Ulanowicz, Palgrave, 2017, pp. 59–90.
Biswas, Santanu. "Rabindranath Tagore and Freudian Thought," *The International Journal of Psychoanalysis*, vol. 84, no. 3, pp. 717–32.
Black Panther. Dir. Ryan Coogler, Marvel Studios, 2018.
Blauvelt, Christian. "The Simpsons' Apu: A Stereotype Hiding in Plain Sight," *BBC Culture*, November 6, 2017, Web.
Boo, Katherine. *Behind the Beautiful Forevers: Life, Death, and Hope in a Mumbai Undercity*, Random House, 2012.
Bosch, James Vanden. "Media Review: *Gran Torino* and *Doubt*." *Journal of Intergenerational Relationships*, vol. 7, 2009, pp. 459–60.
Bose, Girindrasekhar. "The Psychological Outlook of Hindu Philosophy," *Indian Journal of Psychology*, vol. 5, 1930, pp. 119–46.
Bradley, Harriet. "The Seductions of the Archive: Voices Lost and Found," *History of the Human Sciences*, vol. 12, no. 2, 1999, pp. 107–22.
Braidotti, Rosi. "Animals, Anomalies, and Inorganic Others," *PMLA*, vol. 124, no. 2, March 2009, pp. 526–32.
Brannen, Peter. "The Anthropocene is a Joke," *The Atlantic*, August 13, 2019, Web.
Brennan, Timothy. "Subaltern Stakes," *New Left Review*, vol. 89, Sept.-Oct. 2014, pp. 67–87.
Brohi, Nazish. "In Conversation with Gayatri Spivak," *Dawn*, December 23, 2014, Web.
Brousse, Marie-Hélène. "Feminism with Lacan," *Newsletter of the Freudian Field*, vol. 5, nos. 1 and 2, Spring/Fall 1991, pp. 113–28.
Brown, Ruth. " 'Maybe It's Time for Him to Go,' says Rep. Labrador about BSU president," *The Idaho Statesman*, August 21, 2017, Web.
Burn! Dir. Gillo Pontecorvo, Produzioni Europee Associate (PEA), Les Productions Artistes Associés, 1969.

Bush, Laura. The Weekly Address Delivered by the First Lady, November 17, 2001, Web.
Busia, Abena. "Silencing Sycorx: On African Colonial Discourse and the Unvoiced Female," *Cultural Critique*, no. 14, Winter 1989–90, pp. 81–104.
Butler, Judith. *Notes Toward a Performative Theory of Assembly*, Harvard UP, 2015.
CBS. "Behind the Beautiful Forevers Highlights Hope," CBS NEWS, March 14, 2012, Web.
Chakrabarty, Dipesh. "The Climate of History: Four Theses," *Critical Inquiry*, no. 35, Winter 2009, pp. 197–222.
Chakrabarty, Paulomi. "Teaching Postcolonial Theory in Contemporary India: The Question of Caste," n.d. (draft essay).
Chaudhuri, Amit. "Behind the Beautiful Forevers: Life, Death and Hope in a Mumbai Slum by Katherine Boo—review," *The Guardian*, June 29, 2012, Web.
Chibber, Vivek. *Postcolonial Theory and the Specter of Capital*, Verso, 2012.
Chiesa, Lorenzo. *Subjectivity and Otherness*, MIT Press, 2007.
Clemens, Justin, and Russel Grigg, eds. *Reflections on Seminar XVII: Jacques Lacan and the Other Side of Psychoanalysis*, SIC 6, Duke UP, 2006.
——. "Introduction." *Reflections on Seminar XVII: Jacques Lacan and the Other Side of Psychoanalysis*, edited by Justin Clemens and Russel Grigg, SIC 6, Duke UP, 2006.
Dabashi, H. "Can Non-Europeans Think?" *Al Jazeera*, January 15, 2013, Web.
——. *Can Non-Europeans Think?* Zed Books, 2015.
Dabashi, Hamid. "Fuck You Žižek!" Zed Books Blog, July 26, 2016, Web.
Dalrymple, William. "Behind the Beautiful Forevers: Life, Death and Hope in a Mumbai Slum by Katherine Boo—review," *The Guardian*, June 22, 2012, Web.
Dalton, Rex. "Blast in the Past?" *Nature*, May 16, 2007, Web.
Daly, Glyn. "Slavoj Žižek: A Primer," 2004, Web.
Darjeeling Limited, The. Dir. Wes Anderson, Fox Searchlight, 2007.
Dark Knight, The. Dir. Christopher Nolan, Warner Bros, 2008.
Davis, Katherine. "Holi Festival a Hit Not Only Among Hindus." *The Washington Post*, March 17, 2014, Web.
Davis, Oliver. "Eastwood Reading Beauvoir Reading Eastwood: Ageing and Combative Self-assertion in *Gran Torino* and *Old Age*." *Existentialism and Contemporary Cinema: A Beauvoirian Perspective*, edited by Jean-Pierre Boulé and Ursula Tidd, Breghahn Books, 2012.
Dean, Jodi. "The Object Next Door." *Political Theory*, vol. 35, no. 3, June 2007, pp. 371–78.
——. *Democracy and Other Neoliberal Fantasies: Communicative Capitalism and Left Politics*, Duke University Press, 2009.
Deb, Rohan, ed. "Nonhuman Empires." *Comparative Studies of South Asia, Africa and the Middle East*, vol. 35, no. 1, 2015.

DeKoven, Marianne. "Guest Column: Why Animals Now?" *Publications of the Modern Language Association*, vol. 124, no. 2, March 2009, pp. 361–69.

Deleuze, Gilles, and Felix Guattari. *Anti-Oedipus: Capitalism and Schizophrenia*, translated by Robert Harley, Mark Seem, and Helen R. Lane, University of Minnesota Press, 1983.

DeLoughrey, Elizabeth, and George B. Handley. *Postcolonial Ecologies: Literatures of the Environment*, Oxford UP, 2011.

Derrida, Jacques. *The Animal That Therefore I Am*, translated by David Wills, Fordham UP 2008.

———. *The Beast and the Sovereign*. Volume I (The Seminars of Jacques Derrida), translated by Geoffrey Bennington, U of Chicago P, 2011.

Devereux, Cecily. "Hysteria, Feminism, and Gender Revisited: The Case of the Second Wave." *ESC* vol. 40, no.1, March 2014, pp. 19–45.

Devi, Mahasweta. "Pterodactyl, Puran Sahay, and Pirtha." *Imaginary Maps. Three Stories*, edited by Gayatri Spivak, Routledge, 1995.

———. *Srestha Galpa* [Collection of Short Stories], Dey's, 2004.

Dhillon, Monika. "Postcolonialism and Feminist Assertion in Mahashweta Devi's 'Draupadi.'" *Asian Journal of Multidisciplinary Studies*, vol.1, no. 4, November 2013, pp. 72–77.

Diaz, Junot. "By the Book." *The New York Times*, August 30, 2012, Web.

Dictator, The. Dir. Larry Charles, Paramount Pictures, 2012.

Dolar, Mladen. "Hegel as the Other Side of Psychoanalysis." *Reflections on Seminar XVII: Jacques Lacan and the Other Side of Psychoanalysis*, SIC 6, edited by Justin Clemens and Russel Grigg, Duke University Press, 2006.

Driver, Michaela. "From Empty Speech to Full Speech? Reconceptualizing Spirituality in Organizations Based on a Psychoanalytically-Grounded Understanding of the Self." *Human Relations*, vol. 58, no. 9, 2005, pp. 1091–1110.

Dutt, Soshee Chunder. "Reminiscences of a Keráni's Life" (1877). *Selections from Bengaliana*, edited by Alex Tickell, Trent, 2005.

Eagleton, Terry. "Postcolonialism and 'Postcolonialism.'" *Interventions: International Journal of Postcolonial Studies*, vol. 1, no. 1, 1998, pp. 24–26.

———. "In the Gaudy Supermarket: Review of *A Critique of Post-Colonial Reason: Toward a History of the Vanishing Present* by Gayatri Chakravorty Spivak." *London Review of Books*, vol. 21, no. 10, May 13, 1999, pp. 3–6.

Edelman, Lee. *No Future*, Duke UP, 2004.

———. "Lacan, Badiou, and the Theft of Jouissance." Conference Paper, American Comparative Literature Association Annual Conference, 2016.

Eisenstein, Paul, and Todd McGowan. *Rupture: On the Emergence of the Political*, Northwestern UP, 2012.

Elowitt, Karen. "Romance and Rejuvenation at Victoria Falls." *AFKTravel*, June 19, 2015, Web.

Engley, Ryan. "Mobilizing the Universal: Black Lives Matter against the Postmodern 'All.'" Conference Presentation, *LACK II*, October 19, 2017, Colorado College.

Evans, Christine. "M. Hommelette's *Wild Ride*: Lamella as a Category of Shame." *International Journal of Žižek Studies*, vol. 2, no. 2, 2008, Web.

Eyers, Tom. *Lacan and the Concept of the 'Real,'* Palgrave Macmillan, 2012.

Fanon, Franz. *Black Skin, White Masks*, translated by Richard Philcox, Grove Press, 2008.

———. *Alienation and Freedom*, edited by J. Jhalifa and R. Young, translated by S. Corcoran, Bloomsbury, 2018.

———. *Toward the African Revolution*, translated by Haakon Chevalier, Grove Press, 1967.

Felski, Rita. *Limits of Critique*, U of Chicago P, 2015.

Feltham, Oliver. "Enjoy Your Stay: Structural Change in Seminar XVII." *Reflections on Seminar XVII: Jacques Lacan and the Other Side of Psychoanalysis*, SIC 6, edited by Justin Clemens and Russell Grigg, Duke UP, 2006.

Fink, Bruce. *The Lacanian Subject: Between Language and Jouissance*, Princeton UP, 1995.

———. *Lacan To The Letter: Reading Écrits Closely*, U of Minnesota P, 2004.

———. *Lacan on Love: An Exploration of Lacan's Seminar VIII, Transference*, Polity, 2016.

Flemming, G. C. "'By Mutual Opposition to Nothing.'" *Angelaki*, vol. 20, no. 4, 2015, pp. 157–77.

Foucault, M. *The Archeology of Knowledge and the Discourse on Language,* translated by A. M. Sheridan Smith, Vintage, 1972.

Freud, S. *The Interpretation of Dreams* (1900). *The Standard Edition of the Complete Psychological Works of Sigmund Freud*, volume IV, translated by J. Strachey, Hogarth Press, 1953.

———. "Moses and Monotheism" (1939). *Penguin Freud Library*, vol. 13, Penguin, 1990.

———. "Group Psychology and the Analysis of the Ego" (1921). *Penguin Freud Library*, vol. 12, Penguin, 1991.

———. *Jokes and their Relation to the Unconscious* (1905). *The New Penguin Freud*, Penguin, 2003.

Gadjo dilo/The Crazy Stranger. Dir. Tony Gatlif. Princes Films, Canal+, Centre National de la Cinématographie (CNC), 1997.

Ganga, Maria L. LA. "Paulette Jordan Claims Democratic Victory: 'We Won This Race by Everyone.'" *The Idaho Statesman*. May 16, 2018, Web.

Ganguly, Debjani, and Florina Jenkins. "Limits of the Human." *Angelaki*, vol. 16, no. 4, December 2011, pp. 1–3.

Gangyopadhyay, Narayan. "Hanr [The Bone Collector]" (1945). *Narayan Gangyopadyay-er Shreto Golop [Select Short Stories by Narayan Gangyopadhyay]*, Prakash Bhaban, 2016.

George, Sheldon. *Trauma and Race: A Lacanian Study of African American Racial Identity*, Baylor University Press, 2016.

———, and Derek Hook, eds. *Lacanian Psychoanalysis: Interventions into Culture and Politics*, Special Issue of *Psychoanalysis, Culture, and Society*, 2018 [forthcoming].

Get Out. Dir. Jordan Peele. Universal Pictures, 2017.

Ghazoul, Ferial J. Review of *Death of a Discipline,* H-net, 2003, Web.

Gherovici, Patricia. *The Puerto Rican Syndrome*, Other Press, 2003.

———. "Where Have the Hysterics Gone? Lacan's Reinvention of Hysteria." *ESC*, vol. 40, no. 1, March 2014, pp. 47–70.

Ghosh, Amitav. *The Hungry Tide: A Novel*, Harper Collins, 2005.

Gibson, Nigel. "Losing Sight of the Real. Recasting Merleau-Ponty in Fanon's Critique of Mannoni." *Race and Racism in Continental Philosophy*, edited by R. Bernasconi, Indiana University Press, 2003.

Gill, Khushwant S. "Way to Grow: A Look at Trickle-down Effect." *The Tribune*, November 24, 2013, Web.

Giri, Saroj. "Against 'Reality': The Maoists In South Asia." *SACS*, vol.1, no.1, 2012, Web.

Goc, Nicola. "What's in a Name? New Journalism, Literary Journalism and Creative Nonfiction." *Media and Journalism: New Approaches to Theory and Practice*, edited by Jason Bainbridge, Nicola Goc, and Liz Tynan, Oxford UP, 2008.

Gopal, Priyamvada. "Reducing Rape to a Generic Indian Male Mindset Fails Its Victims." *The Guardian*, March 4, 2015, Web.

Gran Torino. Dir. Clint Eastwood. Matten Productions, Double Nickel Entertainment, Gerber Pictures, 2008.

Gray, Jonathan W. "The Liberating Visions of *Black Panther*," *The New Republic*, February 13, 2018. Web.

Greedharry, Mrinalini. *Postcolonial Theory and Psychoanalysis: From Uneasy Engagements to Effective Critique*, Palgrave, 2008.

Grosrichard, Alain. *The Sultan's Court: European Fantasies of the East* (1979), translated by Liz Heron, Verso, 1998.

Grusin, Richard, ed. *The Nonhuman Turn*, U of Minnesota P, 2015.

Haraway, Donna. *Staying With Trouble: Making Kin in the Chthulucene*, Duke UP, 2016.

Hartnack, Christiane. *Psychoanalysis in Colonial India*, Oxford UP, 2001.

Hassan, Wail. *Immigrant Narratives: Orientalism and Cultural Translation in Arab American and Arab British Literature*, Oxford UP, 2014.

Heise, Ursula. "Globality, Difference, and the International Turn in Ecocriticism." *PMLA*, vol. 128, no. 3, May 2013, pp. 636–43.

Hewitson, Owen. "5 Lacanian Cinematic Clichés that Hollywood Loves." *LacanOnline*, 2013, Web.

———. "*Amuse-Bouches* I—The Yerodia Case," *LacanOnline*, 2017, Web.

Hoffman, Carey. "Exploding Asteroid Theory Strengthened by New Evidence Located in Ohio, Indiana," 2008, Web.
Homer, Sean. "Voice as objet a in Tony Gatlif's Gadjo dilo." *Psychoanalysis, Culture & Society*, vol. 15, 2010, pp. 37–52.
Hook, Derek. "Postcolonial Psychoanalysis." *Theory and Psychology*, vol. 18, no. 2, 2008, pp. 269–83.
———. "Empty and Full Speech." *The Social Psychology of Communication*, Palgrave Macmillan, 2011.
———. *A Critical Psychology of the Postcolonial: The Mind of Apartheid*, Routledge, 2012.
Hook, Derek, and Ross Truscott. "Fanonian Ambivalence: On Psychoanalysis and Postcolonial Critique." *Journal of Theoretical and Philosophical Psychology*, vol. 33, no. 3, 2013, pp. 155–69.
Hook, Derek, and Stijn Vanheule. "Revisiting the Master-Signifier, or, Mandela and Repression." *Frontiers in Psychology*, January 19, 2016, Web.
Hudson, Peter. "The State and the Colonial Unconscious." *Social Dynamics*, vol. 39, no. 2, 2013, pp. 263–77.
Huggan, Graham, and Helen Tiffin. *Postcolonial Ecocriticism: Literature, Animals, Environment*, Routledge, 2010.
I Know What You Did Last Summer. Dir. Jim Gillespie, Mandalay Entertainment, Summer Knowledge LLC, 1997.
Iveson, Richard. *Zoogenesis: Thinking Encounter with Animal*, Pavement Books, 2014.
Jalais, Annu. "Dwelling on Morichjhanpi: When Tigers Became 'Citizens,' Refugees 'Tiger-Food.'" *Economic and Political Weekly*, vol. 40, no. 17, April 2005, pp. 1757–62.
Jalao, Ly Chong. "Looking Gran Torino in the Eye: A Review." *Journal of Southeast Asian American Education and Advancement*, vol. 5, article 15, 2010, Web.
JanMohammed, Abdul. "The Economy of Manichean Allegory: The Function of Racial Difference in Colonialist Literature." *"Race," Writing, and Difference*, edited by Henry Louis Gates Jr., U of Chicago P, 1986.
Johnston, Adrian. "Nothing Is Not Always No-One: (a)Voiding Love." *Filozosfski Vestnik*, vol. xxvi, no. 2, 2005, pp. 67–81.
Jong, Sara de, and Jamila M. H. Mascat. "Relocating Subalternity: Scattered Speculations on the Conundrum of a Concept." *Cultural Studies*, vol. 30, no. 5, 2016, 717–29.
Jurassic Park. Dir. Steven Spielberg, Universal Pictures, 1993.
Kangal Malsat. Dir. Suman Mukhopadhyay, AV Films, 2013.
Kapoor, Ilan. *Celebrity Humanitarianism: The Ideology of Global Charity*, Routledge, 2012.
———. "Žižek, Antagonism and Politics Now: Three Recent Controversies." *International Journal of Žižek Studies*, vol. 12, no. 1, Web, 2018.
———, ed. *Psychoanalysis and the GlObal*, U of Nebraska P, 2018.
Kaur, Rajender. "'Home Is Where the Oracella Are': Toward a New Paradigm of Transcultural Ecocritical Engagement in Amitav Ghosh's *The Hungry*

Tide." *Interdisciplinary Studies in Literature and Environment*, vol. 14, no. 1, Summer 2007, pp. 125–41.

Keveney, Bill. "Apu Taints Love of 'The Simpsons' for Comedian Hari Kondabolu, in His New Documentary." *USA Today*, November 15, 2017, Web.

Khader, Jamil. "Žižek's Infidelity: Lenin, the National Question, and the Postcolonial Legacy of Revolutionary Internationalism." *Žižek Now: Current Perspectives in Žižek Studies*, edited by Khader and Rothenberg, Polity, 2013.

———. *Cartographies of Transnationalism in Postcolonial Feminisms: Geography, Culture, Identity, Politics*, Lexington Books, 2014.

Khan, Azeen. "Lacan and Race." *After Lacan: Literature, Theory, and Psychoanalysis in the Twenty-First Century*, edited by A. Mukherjee, Cambridge UP, 2018.

Kirshner, Lewis A. "Rethinking Desire: The Objet Petit A in Lacanian Theory." *Journal of the American Psychoanalytic Association*, vol. 53, no. 1, 2005, pp. 83–102.

Kolbert, Elizabeth. *The Sixth Extinction: An Unnatural History*, Picador, 2014.

Kramp, Joseph M. "Film Review: Gran Torino (2008)." *Pastoral Psychology*, vol. 60, 2011, pp. 921–22.

Kurtz, Stanley. "Statement of Stanley Kurtz Research Fellow, Hoover Institution Contributing Editor, National Review Online Testimony before the Subcommittee on Select Education, Committee on Education and the Workforce U.S. House of Representatives." "International Programs In Higher Education and Questions of Bias." Hearing before the Subcommittee on Select Education of the Committee on Education and the Workforce, One Hundred Eighth Congress, First Session, June 19, 2003, Web.

Lacan, Jacques. "Overview of the Psychoanalytic Act," translated by Cormac Gallagher, 1967–68, Web.

———. *The Four Fundamental Concepts of Psychoanalysis*, Seminar Book XI (1973), translated by A. Sheridan, Routledge, 1981.

———. *The Seminar of Jacques Lacan. Book II. The Ego in Freud's Theory and in the technique of Psychoanalysis 1954–1955*, translated by S. Tomaselli, Norton, 1991.

———. *On Feminine Sexuality, The Limits of Love and Knowledge, 1972–1973: Encore the Seminar of Jacques Lacan Book XX*, translayed by B. Fink, Norton, 1999.

———. *Ècrits*: The First Complete Edition, translated by B. Fink, Routledge, 2006.

———. *The Other Side of Psychoanalysis: The Seminar of Jacques Lacan Book XVII*, translated by Russell Grigg, Norton, 2007.

———. *Anxiety: The Seminar of Jacques Lacan Book X*, translated by A. R. Price, Polity, 2014.

———. 2015. *Transference: The Seminar of Jacques Lacan Book VIII*, translated by B. Fink, Polity, 2014.

———. Seminar XV, *L'acte psychoanlytique*, 1967–68, unpublished.

———. Seminar XVIII, *D'un discours qui ne serait pas du semblant*, 1970–71, unpublished.
Laplanche, Jean, and J.-B Pontalis. *The Language of Psycho-Analysis*, translated by Donal Nicholson-Smith, Norton, 1973.
Lazarus, Neil. *Postcolonial Unconscious*, Cambridge UP, 2011.
LeBron, Christopher. "'Black Panther' Is Not the Movie We Deserve." *Boston Review*, February 17, 2018, Web.
Life After People. Created by David de Vries, Discovery Channel, 2009.
Lion Has Wings, The. Dir. Adrian Brunel et al., London Film Productions, 1939.
Macaulay, Thomas Babington. "Indian Education, The Minute of the 2nd of February, 1835" (1835). *Macaulay: Prose and Poetry*, selected by G. M. Young, Rupert Hart Davis, 1952.
Mallick, Ross. "Refugee Resettlement in Forest Reserves: West Bengal Policy Reversal and the Marichjhapi Massacre." *The Journal of Asian Studies*, vol. 58, no. 1, February 1999, pp. 104–25.
Mannoni, Octave. *Prospero and Caliban: The Psychology of Colonization*, U of Michigan P, 1990.
Manoff, Marlene. "Theories of the Archive from Across the Discipline." *portal: Libraries and the Academy*, vol. 4, no. 1, 2004, pp. 9–25.
Marder, Michael. "A Postcolonial Comedy of Errors." *Al Jazeera*, April 13, 2013, Web.
Maslin, Janet. "All They Hope for Is Survival: Katherine Boo's First Book, 'Behind the Beautiful Forevers.'" *The New York Times*, January 30, 2012, Web.
Mbembe, A. "Necropolitics." *Public Culture*, translated by Libby Meintjes, vol. 15, no. 1, 2003, pp. 11–40.
McBride Debbie, and Lourdes Shahamiri. "Review of *Gran Torino*." *Contemporary Justice Review: Issues in Criminal, Social, and Restorative Justice*, vol. 14, no. 3, 2011, pp. 359–64.
McCormick, Patrick. "Review of Gran Torino." *U.S. Catholic Faith in Real Life*, 2009, Web.
McCotter, Thaddeus. "'Gran Torino' Conservatives." *Breitbart*, February 26, 2009, Web.
McGowan, Todd. *The Fictional Christopher Nolan*, U of Texas P, 2012.
———. "Citizen Trump." Lecture, YouTube, February 9, 2017, U of Vermont, Web.
———. "The Absent Universal: From the Master Signifier to the Missing Signifier," *Problemi International*, vol. 2, no. 2, 2018, pp. 195–214.
Menchu, Rigoberta. *I, Rigoberta Menchu: An Indian Woman in Guatemala*, edited by Elisabeth Burgos-Debray, translated by Ann Wright, Verso, 2010.
Menon, Nivedita. "The Two Žižeks." *Kafila*, January 7, 2010, Web.
Menon, Parvathi. "Being the Subject of a Book Didn't Make Life Lovely in Annawadi." *The Hindu*, December 3, 2014. Web.

Mezzadra, Sandro, and Federico Rahola. "The Postcolonial Condition: A Few Notes on the Quality of Historical Time in the Global Present." *Postcolonial Text*, vol. 2, no. 1, 2006, Web.

Mignolo, W. D. "Yes, We Can: Non-European Thinkers and Philosophers." *Al Jazeera*, February 19, 2013, Web.

Miller, Jacques-Alain. "Language: Much Ado About What?" *Lacan and the Subject of Language*, edited by Ellie Ragland, Routledge, 1991.

———. "Extimité." *Lacanian Theory of Discourse*, edited by Mark Bracher, Marshall W. Alcorn Jr., Ronald Corthell, and Francoise Massardier-Kenney, New York UP, 1994, pp. 74–87.

———. "The Body Event." *Lacanian Ink* 19, 2001, pp. 4–47.

———. "Lacan's Later Teaching." *Lacanian Ink* 23, Spring 2003, Web.More, Max, and Natasha Vita-More. *The Transhumanist Reader: Classical and Contemporary Essays on the Science, Technology, and Philosophy of the Human Future*, Wiley, 2013.

Morton, Stephen. "Review of Gayatri Spivak. *A Critique of Postcolonial Reason: Towards a History of the Vanishing Present*." ARIEL: A Review of International English Literature, vol. 32, no. 3, 2001, pp. 186–91.

———. *Gayatri Chakravorty Spivak*, Routledge, 2003.

———. *Gayatri Spivak: Ethics, Subalternity, and the Critique of Postcolonial Reason*, Polity, 2007.

Morton, Timothy. *Ecology Without Nature: Rethinking Environmental Aesthetics*, Harvard UP, 2007.

———. *Ecology without Nature*, Harvard UP, 2009.

———. *The Ecological Thought*, Harvard UP, 2012.

———. "They Are Here." *The Nonhuman Turn*, edited by Richard Grusin, U of Minnesota P, 2015.

———. *Dark Ecology: For a Logic of Future Coexistence* (The Wellek Library Lectures), Columbia UP, 2016.

Mukherjee, Upamanyu Pablo. "Surfing the Second Waves: Amitav Ghosh's Tide Country." *New Formations*, no. 59, 2006, pp. 144–57.

Nandy, Ashis. *The Intimate Enemy*, Oxford UP, 1983.

#NotInMyName. N.A. Web.

Nigam, A. "End of Postcolonialism and the Challenge for 'Non-European' Thought." *Critical Encounters*, May 19, 2013, Web.

Nussbaum, Martha. "How to Write About Poverty." *Times Literary Supplement*, October 12, 2012, Web.

Osborne, Thomas. "The Ordinariness of the Archive." *History of the Human Sciences*, vol. 12, no. 2, May 1999, pp. 51–64.

Paige, Rachel. "There's a Black Panther Easter Egg that Connects It to Doctor Strange." *HelloGiglies*, February 20, 2018, Web.

Parry, Benita. "Problems in Current Theories of Colonial Discourse." *The Postcolonial Studies Reader*, edited by Bill Ashcroft, Gareth Griffiths, and Helen Tiffin, Routledge, 1995.

———. *Postcolonial Studies: A Materialist Critique*, Routledge, 2004.
Pluth, Ed. *Signifiers and Acts: Freedom in Lacan's Theory of the Subject*, State U of New York P, 2007.
———. "Lacanian Anti-Humanism and Freedom." *Lacan and the Nonhuman*, edited by Gautam Basu Thakur and Jonathan Dickstein, Palgrave, 2018.
Problem with Apu, The. Dir. Michael Melamedoff, TruTv, 2017.
Prometheus. Dir. Ridley Scott, Twentieth Century Fox, 2012.
Pulugurtha, Nishi. "Refugees, Settlers, and Amitav Ghosh's *The Hungry Tide*." *Local Natures, Global Responsibilities: Ecocritical Perspectives on the New English Literatures*, edited by Laurenz Volkmann et al., Rodopi, 2010, pp. 81–89.
Qurashi, Fahid. "*Black Panther*: The Same Old Western Politics with a Black Face." *5Pillars*, February 23, 2018, Web.
Ragland, Ellie. "The Hysteric's Truth." *Reflections on Seminar XVII: Jacques Lacan and the Other Side of Psychoanalysis*, SIC 6, edited by Justin Clemens and Russel Grigg, Duke UP, 2006.
Ray, Sangeeta. *Gayatri Chakravorty Spivak: In Other Words*, Wiley-Blackwell, 2009.
Richards, Thomas. *The Imperial Archive*, Verso, 1993.
Robin Hood: The Prince of Thieves. Dir. Kevin Reynolds, Warner Brothers, 1991.
Rodriguez, George. "Is Obama the New 'Black'?" *Los Angeles Times*, December 16, 2006, Web.
Rothenberg, Molly. *The Excessive Subject: A New Theory of Social Change*, Polity, 2010.
Rousselle, Duane. "Black Panther as Empty Container," *dingpolitik*, February 17, 2018. Web.
Roy, Arundhati. *Walking With the Comrades*, Penguin, 2011.
Rustin, Susanna. "Katherine Boo: Slum Dweller." *The Guardian*, June 8, 2012, Web.
Ruti, Mari. *The Case for Falling in Love: Why We Can't Master the Madness of Love and Why That's the Best Part*, Sourcebooks Casablanca, 2011.
———. *The Singularity of Being: Lacan and the Immortal Within*, Fordham UP, 2012.
Said, Edward. *Orientalism*, Vintage, 1978.
Saliha, Sara. "The Animal You See: Why Look at Animals in Gaza?" *Interventions: International Journal of Postcolonial Studies*, vol. 16, no. 3, 2014, pp. 299–324.
Santiago, Jorge. "Beyond Full and Empty Speech." September 12, 2018, Simon Fraser University, Web.
Sarkar, Sumit. " 'Kaliyuga,' 'Chakri,' and 'Bhakti': Ramakrishna and His Times." *Economic and Political Weekly*, vol. 27, no. 29, July 1992, pp. 1543–59, 1561–66.
Schein, Louisa, and Bee Vang. "Micro-Exclusions, Raunch Aesthetics, and In-Jokes: A Rogue Hmong Raciosexual Parody." *Visual Anthropology*, vol. 31, no. 1–2, 2018, pp. 93–115.
Secret Life of Pets. Dir. Chris Renaud, Universal Pictures, 2016.

Sen, Amartya. Praise in Penguin Random House Webpage for Katherine Boo, *Behind the Beautiful Forevers*. n.d., Web.
Sen, Jai. "The Left Front and the 'Unintended City': Is a Civilised Transition Possible?" *Economic and Political Weekly*, vol. 31, no. 45/46, November 9–16, 1996, pp. 2977–79, 2981–82.
Sen, Malcolm. "Spatial justice: The Ecological Imperative and Postcolonial Development." *Journal of Postcolonial Writing*, vol. 45, no. 4, December 2009, pp. 365–77.
Sengupta, Debjani. "A Metropolis of Hunger: Calcutta's Poetry of the Famine (1943)." *Coldnoon: International Journal of Travel Writing and Traveling Cultures*, "Coldnoon Cities (Mapping the Metropolis) Vol I," 2016, Web.
Seshadri-Crooks, Kalpana. *Desiring Whiteness: A Lacanian Analysis of Race*, Routledge, 2000.
Sewell, Cynthia. "Paulette Jordan Is Idaho's New Political Force; Brad Little Is Its Steady, Guiding One." *The Idaho Statesman*, May 16, 2018, Web.
Shah, Amar. "To Many Indian Americans, Apu Is Offensive. To Me, He's My Dad." *Washington Post*, April 25, 2018, Web.
Shandilya, Krupa. "Writing/Reading the Subaltern Woman: Narrative Voice and Subaltern Agency in Upamanyu Chatterjee's *English, August*." *Postcolonial Text*, vol. 9, no. 3, 2014, Web.
Sharlet, Jeff. "Like a Novel: The Marketing of Literary Nonfiction." *VQR*, vol. 89, no. 3, 2013, Web.
Shepherdson, Charles. "Foreword." Roberto Harari, *Lacan's Seminar on Anxiety: An Introduction*, translated by Jane C. Lamb-Ruiz, Other Press, 2001.
Shining, The. Dir. Stanley Kubrick, Warner Bros, 1980.
Shiva, Vandana. "The Seeds Of Suicide: How Monsanto Destroys Farming." March 13, 2014, Web.
Shree 420. Dir. Raj Kapoor, R.K. Films Ltd., 1955.
Siddiq, Muhammad. *Man Is a Cause*, U of Washington P, 1984.
Smith, Joan. "India Is in Denial about Its Rape Culture." *Independent*, March 8, 2015, Web.
Soler, Colette. "What Does the Unconscious Know about Women?" *Reading Seminar XX: Lacan's Major Work on Love, Knowledge, and Feminine Sexuality*, edited by Suzanne Barnard and Bruce Fink, State U of New York P, 2002.
———. *Lacan: The Unconscious Reinvented*, Karnac, 2014.
Spider-Man. Dir. Sam Raimi, Columbia Pictures Corporation, Marvel Enterprises, Laura Ziskin Productions, 2002.
Spillers, Hortense J. "All the Things You Could Be by Now, If Sigmund Freud's Wife Was Your Mother." *boundary 2*, vol. 23, no. 3, Autumn 1996, pp. 75–141.
Spivak, Gayatri Chakravorty. "Three Women's Text." *Critical Inquiry*, vol. 12, no. 1, "Race," Writing, and Difference," Autumn 1985, pp. 243–61.

---. "Can the Subaltern Speak?" *Marxism and the Interpretation of Culture*, edited by Cary Nelson and Lawrence Grossberg, U of Illinois P, 1988.
---. "Echo." *New Literary History*, vol. 24, no. 1, "Culture and Everyday Life," Winter 1993, pp. 17–43.
---. *Imaginary Maps. Three Stories*, Routledge, 1995.
---. *Critique of Postcolonial Reason*, Harvard UP, 1999.
---. *Death of a Discipline*, Columbia UP, 2003.
---. "Righting Wrongs." *The South Atlantic Quarterly*, vol. 103, no. 2/3, Spring/Summer, 2004, pp. 523–81.
---. *In Other Worlds*, Routledge, 2006.
---. *Outside in the Teaching Machine*, Routledge, 2009.
---. *An Aesthetic Education in the Era of Globalization*, Harvard UP, 2012.
---. "Interview with Gayatri Chakravorty Spivak." YouTube, August 8, 2014, Proyecto Grado Cero AEJ, Web.
---. "Postcolonial Theory and the Specter of Capital." *The Debate on Postcolonial Theory and the Specter of Capital*, edited by Rosie Warren, Verso, 2017.
---. "Paradox of Democracy." Lecture, Calcutta, 2017a.
Stables, Kate. "Gran Torino." *Sight & Sound*, vol. 19, no. 3, March 2009, pp. 61–62.
Subarnarekha. Dir. Ritwik Ghatak, J.J. Films, 1965.
Sunder Rajan, Rajeswari. "The Story of Draupadi's Disrobing." *Signposts Gender Issues in Post-Independence India*, edited by Rajeswari Sunder Rajan, Kali for Women, 1999.
---. "Death and the Subaltern." *Can the Subaltern Speak?: Reflections on the History of an Idea*, edited by Rosalind C. Morris and Gayatri C. Spivak, Columbia UP, 2010.
Tagore, Rabindranath. "Jibito O Mrito" (1892). *Galpa Guccha*, Web.
Teays, Wanda. *Seeing the Light: Exploring Ethics through Movies*, John Wiley and Sons, 2012.
Thacker, Eugene. *In the Dust of This Planet: Horror of Philosophy*, Volume 1, Zero Books, 2011.
Tharoor, Shashi. "Book review: 'Behind the Beautiful Forevers,' by Katherine Boo." *The Washington Post*, February 10, 2012, Web.
Timberg, C, D. Harwell, and S. Zeitchik. "How White Nationalists Are Trying to Co-opt 'Black Panther.'" *The Washington Post*, March 14, 2018, Web.
Timofeeva, Oxana. "The Non-Human as Such: On Men, Animals, and Barbers." *On Culture: The Open Journal for the Study of Culture*, 2016, Web.
---. *The History of Animals: A Philosophy*, Bloomsbury, 2018.
Tomšič, Samo. *The Capitalist Unconscious: Marx and Lacan*, Verso, 2015.
Tsing, Anna, Bubandt, Gan, Swanson, eds. *Arts of Living on a Damaged Planet: Ghosts and Monsters of the Anthropocene*, U of Minnesota P, 2017.

Udwin, Leslee. *India's Daughter*, Women Make Movies, 2015.
Vanheule, Stijn. *The Subject of Psychosis: A Lacanian Perspective*, Palgrave, 2011.
Vighi, Fabio. *On Zizek's Dialectics: Surplus, Subtraction, Sublimation*, Continuum, 2010.
———, and Heiko Feldner. *Žižek: Beyond Foucault*, Palgrave, 2007.
Weekes, P. "Things We Saw Today: The Alt-Right Loves *Black Panther* So Much They Want to Make It About Trump." *The Mary Sue*, February 18, 2018, Web.
Weinert, Friedel. *Copernicus, Darwin, and Freud: Revolutions in the History and Philosophy of Science*, Wiley-Blackwell, 2008.
Wenzel, Jennifer. "Grim Fairy Tales: Taking a Risk, Reading *Imaginary Maps*." *Going Global: The Transnational Reception of Third World Women Writers*, edited by Amal Amireh and Lisa Suhair Majaj, Garland, 2000.
West, Cornel. "Cornel West on Donald Trump: This Is What Neo-Fascism Looks Like." Interview *Democracy Now!* December 1, 2016, Web.
Wolfe, Cary. *Animal Rites: American Culture, the Discourse of Species, and Posthumanist Theory*, U of Chicago P, 2003.
Wolfe, Tom. *The New Journalism*, Harper and Row, 1972.
Wright, Laura. *The Vegan Studies Project: Food, Animals, and Gender in the Age of Terror*, U of Georgia P, 2015.
Yaeger, Patricia, ed. *Publication of the Modern Language Association of America*, vol. 124, no. 2, March 2009.
Young, Robert. "Postcolonial Remains." *New Literary History*, vol. 43, no. 1, Winter 2012, pp. 19–42.
Zabala, S. "Slavoj Žižek and the Role of the Philosopher." *Al Jazeera*, December 25, 2012, Web.
Žižek, Slavoj. *The Sublime Object of Ideology*, Verso, 1989.
———. *Everything You Always Wanted to Know About Lacan (But Were Afraid to Ask Hitchcock)*, edited by Slavoj Žižek, Verso, 1992.
———. "The Lamella of David Lynch." *Reading Seminar XI: Lacan's Four Fundamental Concepts of Psychoanalysis*, edited by Richard Feldstein, Bruce Fink, and Maire Jaanus, State U of New York P, 1995.
———. *The Abyss of Freedom*. S. Žižek and F. W. J. Von Schelling, *The Abyss of Freedom / Ages of the World*, U of Michigan P, 1997.
———. "A Leftist Plea for 'Eurocentrism.'" *Critical Inquiry* vol. 24, no. 4, Summer 1998, pp. 988–1009.
———. "Melancholy and the Act." *Critical Inquiry*, vol. 26, no. 4, 2000, pp. 657–81.
———. "A Plea for Leninist Intolerance." *Critical Inquiry*, vol. 28, no. 2, 2002, pp. 542–66.
———. *The Puppet and the Dwarf: The Perverse Core of Christianity*, MIT Press, 2003.
———. "The Free World...of Slums." *Inthesetimes*, September 23, 2004, Web.

———. *Interrogating the Real*, edited by Rex Butler and Scott Stephens, Continuum, 2005.
———. "Where to Look for a Revolutionary Potential?" 2005a, Web.
———. "The Act and Its Vicissitudes." *The Symptom*, 2005b., Web.
———. *How to Read Lacan*, Norton, 2006.
———. "Objet a in Social Links." *Reflections on Seminar XVII: Jacques Lacan and the Other Side of Psychoanalysis*, SIC 6, edited by Justin Clemens and Russell Grigg, Duke UP, 2006a.
———. "Psychoanalysis and the Lacanian Real: Strange Shapes of the Unwarped Primal World." *Adventures in Realism*, edited by Matthew Beaumont, John Wiley and Sons, 2007.
———. *Slavoj Žižek, the Reality of the Virtual*, Olive Films, Dvd, 2007a.
———. *For They Know Not What They Do: Enjoyment as a Political Factor*, Verso, 2008.
———. *The Plague of Fantasies*, Verso, 2008a.
———. *Violence*, Picador, 2008b.
———. *In Defense of Lost Causes*, Verso, 2009.
———. *Less than Nothing: Hegel and the Shadow of Dialectical Materialism*, Verso, 2012.
———. *Perverts Guide to Ideology*. Dir. S. Fiennes, P Guide Productions Zeitgeist Films, 2012a.
———. *Demanding the Impossible*, edited by Young-june Park, Polity, 2013.
———. "The Future as Sci-Fi: The New Cold War." 2015, Web.
———. *Disparities*, Bloomsbury, 2016.
———. *Incontinence of the Void: Economico-Philosophical Spandrels*, MIT Press, 2017.
———. "Quasi Duo Fantasias: A Straussian Reading of "Black Panther." *Los Angeles Review of Books*, March 3, 2018, Web.
———. "Getting a Grip on Slavoj Žižek (with Slavoj Žižek)." 2018a, Web.
———. *Like a Thief in Broad Daylight: Power in the Era of Post-Human Capitalism*, Ebook, 2018b.
———. "They Are Both Worse." *The Philosophical Salon*. A Los Angeles Review of Books Channel, February 25, 2019, Web.
Zola, Emile. *His Masterpiece*, Chatto and Windus, 1902.
Zupančič, Alenka. "A Perfect Place to Die: Theatre in Hitchcock's Films." *Everything You Always Wanted to Know About Lacan (But Were Afraid to Ask Hitchcock)*, edited by Slavoj Žižek, Verso, 1992.
———. "When Surplus Enjoyment Meets Surplus Value." *Reflections on Seminar XVII: Jacques Lacan and the Other Side of Psychoanalysis*, SIC 6, edited by Justin Clemens and Russell Grigg, Duke UP, 2006.
———. "Sexual Is Political." *Jacques Lacan Between Psychoanalysis and Politics*, edited by Samo Tomsic and Andreja Zernik, Routledge, 2016.
———. *What Is Sex?* MIT Press, 2017

INDEX

AbdalKafor, Ola, 186
Aboulela, Leila—"The Museum":
   and the failure of cross-cultural communication, xxix, 70, 74–79
   and the idea of museums as objective spaces, 86
   and the narrative of hysteric desire, 80–83
—*The Translator*:
   critical role of religion in, 75–76
   "The Museum" compared with, 76–77
Abrams, Susan, 44
Adams, Parveen, 176
Agamben, Giorgio, 107
Ahmad, Aijaz, xix, 169
Alvarez Hypothesis, 204n10
anomaly:
   and the human in the current stage of anthropogeny, 62–63
   and Lacan's *object a*, xxxv
   and the Maoist as an, 121
   and *real* animals, 35–38
   and subalternity, 124
anthropocentricism:
   and *The Secret Life of Pets*, 53–55
   See also human-animal relations
archives:
   and Aboulela's "The Museum," 77, 85–86, 103–104
   and Gatlif's *Gadjo dilo*, 89–91, 103–104
   and the human endeavor to memorialize the other, 38, 70–73

Arendt, Hannah, 202n18
Austin, J. L., 200n4
Avengers: Infinity War, directed by Anthony and Joe Russo, 155
Azaria, Hank, 99–100, 102

Badiou, Alain:
   and the link between social history and Capital, 63–64
   subalterns and the "event," 12
   on twenty-first-century messianic environmentalism, xv, 47, 55, 58, 59
Baer, Ben Conisbee, 41, 58
Baker, Steve, 35–36
Best Exotic Marigold Hotel, 125, 128
Bhabha, Homi, xvi, xix, 87, 198n2
   on the ambivalence of colonial authority, 192–194
   on colonial non-sense, 69–70
   on mimicry, 97
   on the stereotype, 72, 193
Bhattacharya, Nabarun:
   Boo's writing about third-world poverty contrasted with, 142
   Fyataarus and *choktars*, 135
   Herbert, 154
   Kangal Malsat, 135
   as a poet of lack, 211n3
   and precariat revolutions presented as unrealistic by, 134–135
   on precariats as Things, 135

big Other:
   and the act in psychoanalysis, 9–11
   exposure of the fiction of, xxvi–xxviii, 5, 9, 11, 17–18, 87
   the hysteric's resistance to, 5–6, 84–87
   lack of, 199n4
   meaning-guaranteeing authority of, 85, 167, 169–170
   other and *Other* distinguished, xxxiv–xxxvi
   the subaltern's challenge to, 5–7, 11
   unresponsiveness to the particular's desires of, 141
Black Panther, directed by Ryan Coogler:
   and identity politics, xxx, 146
   illusion of division as the thesis of, 146–148, 151–152, 162
   Killmonger compared with Binu (character in Ghatak's *Subarnarekha*), 153–154, 156
   Killmonger's plan to attack three cities, 212n6
   and racism, 146, 155, 157, 211n4
   and the role of the superhero and political demands for equality, 162–163
   T'Challa-Killmonger conflict, 150–151, 155–159, 162
   Wakanda constructed in, 147, 148–153, 155–157, 162, 211n4
Blauvelt, Christian, 99
Boo, Katherine—*Behind the Beautiful Forevers*:
   and creative non-fiction as a genre, 110–111, 115, 121
   and the fantasy of "Shinging Indiz," 115, 124–125
   narratives of globalizing India conveyed in, 109–110, 129
   —representation of urban precariats, 105–142passim
   and Boo's status as an outsider, 111, 113
   and the collusion of morality, electoral democracy, and the media in India with neoliberalism regarding the poor, 116
   globalization and neoliberalism unquestioned by, 116, 117–119, 134
   and slums as essential to globalization, 116
Bosch, James Vanden, 212–213n12
Braidotti, Rosi, 35
Brannen, Peter, 59–61
Burn! (Queimada), directed by Gillo Pontecorvo, xxix, 6–7, 200n2
   impossible figure of the subaltern, xxix
   Jose's subaltern acts, 6–7, 11, 29, 200n2
Bush, Laura, 127, 191, 214–215n9
Butler, Judith, 180, 215n26

Capote, Truman, 110, 207n4
caste:
   and the framework of postcolonial theory, 197–198n1
   and the Naxalbari movement, 13, 119–120
   and systems of privilege in India, 126
   and the term *forsha*, 20
   and the term *shada*, 20
catastrophe of our being:
   and confrontations with real nature/animals, 34–35, 44–51, 57–58
   and the extinction of humans, 203n8
   and fantasies of wholeness and exclusive identities, 176
   and the need to recognize local histories and cultural contexts, 58–59
Chakrabarty, Dipesh, on human responsibility for the current environmental crisis, 60–63, 64, 204n11
Chakraborty, Paulomi, 197–198n1
Chibber, Vivek, xix–xx
Chiesa, Lorenzo, on subjectivized lack, xxvii, 68
climate change:
   and the framing of questions for our anthropocene age, 64–65
   and human responsibility, 61–64
Coates, Ta-Nehisi, 183
Coetzee, J. M.:
   Elizabeth Costello, 35

INDEX 235

Foe, 214n7
  Waiting for the Barbarians, 17, 70,
    131–132
Conrad, Joseph, *Heart of Darkness*, 89
  Boo's *Beautiful Forevers* contrasted with,
    110, 127
  contemporary travel to the non-West
    contrasted with, 128
  and Leslee Udwin's Conradian determination, 127
  and the Orientalist image of Africa as
    Dark Continent, 148–149
Coogler, Ryan. *See Black Panther*, directed
  by Ryan Coogler
creative non-fiction as a genre:
  and Boo's *Behind the Beautiful Forevers*,
    110–111, 115, 121
  and the first-person narrator, 110,
    207n4
cryptid. *See under* Devi, Mahasweta—"Pterodactyl, Puran Sahay, and Pirtha"

Dabashi, Hamid, 180–184, 195
Dalrymple, William, 210n10
Darjeeling Limited, The, directed by Wes
  Anderson, 128
Darwin, Charles, *The Descent of Man*, the
  Other as godless, uncivilized, wife
  beaters, 127, 191, 214–215n9
Davis, Katherine, 129
Davis, Oliver, 173–174
Dean, Jodi, xxi, 173
death-drive:
  and *aprés-coup*, 42
  and rupture as stain, 189
  subaltern act as, 2–3, 12–13, 21–22,
    28–29
  and the uncanny excess of life revealed
    by Ghosh's crabs, 50, 52
Derrida, Jacques, xix, 2, 71, 208–209n14
Devereux, Cecily, 206n9
Devi, Mahasweta—"Draupadi":
  and the Naxalbari movement, 13–17,
    19–20, 22–23, 201–202n14
  and the phrase *Neanderthal darkness*,
    22–23

  and the term *forsha*, 20–21
  —and the theoretical features of the
    subaltern act, 5, 29
  Draupadi/Dopdi's enunciation of
    "counter," 15, 22–28, 200–201n5
  Draupadi/Dopdi's refusal to be clothed,
    13–19
  and the uncanny alterity of the subaltern, 31, 201n13
  —"Pterodactyl, Puran Sahay, and Pirtha":
  and Lacan's "being outside time" (*aprés-coup*), 79
  and the "postcolonial animal limit," 36,
    37–38, 41–43, 45, 52–53
  pterodactyl/cryptid as a metaphor for
    the impossibility of expressing
    subaltern speech, 39–40, 42, 45
  pterodactyl/cryptid drawing by an
    uneducated tribal boy, 38–39,
    53
  unheimlich other enunciated in, 41,
    44–45
Diaz, Junot, 112, 115
Dictator, The, directed by Larry Charles,
  150
"Draupadi." *See* Devi, Mahasweta—"Draupadi"
Driver, Michael, 171, 212n11
Dutt, Soshee Chunder, 193

Eagleton, Terry, xviii, xxiii–xxiv, 64
Eastwood, Clint:
  Gran Torino. *See Gran Torino*, directed
    by Clint Eastwood
  shift in the direction of his film in the
    1990s, 172, 174
Eat, Pray, Love (2010), 125, 128
eco-catastrophe. *See* catastrophe of our
  being; climate change
Edelman, Lee, 12, 42, 201n8
Eisenstein, Paul and Todd McGowan, 12,
  57, 58, 203–204n10
Engley, Ryan, 183
equality is alterity, xxxi, 198n4
  and fantasies of wholeness and exclusive
    identities, 176

equality is alterity, *(cont'd)*
   and the fundamental antagonism structuring all social relations, xxii–xxiii, xxix, xxxiv–xxxv, 3, 12, 21, 37, 41, 52, 65, 69, 87, 107–108, 114, 135, 156, 211n3
   love as a response to, 43
   and neoliberal discourses, 105–106
   and our ontological condition as lacking subjects, xxxv, 131, 169, 195
   and politics of the real, 65
   and postcolonial studies in the global era, xxi–xxii, xxviii, 105–108, 195–196
   and Spivak's critique of othering, 116
   and subalternity as the inherent non-logic of the social, 4, 21–23, 29–30
   and the subaltern's lack of freedom, 12–13
Eyers, Tom, 26

Fanon, Franz, 154, 196, 198n2
   on (negated) identity and the Master's discourse, 192
   Black Skin, White Masks, 11–12, 182, 215n10
   on ontology in relation to colonialism, xvi–xviii, 179, 210n15
   on the zone of *nonbeing,* xxxiv–xxxiv, 11–12, 87, 107
fantasy:
   and the act that ruptures the big Other, xxvi–xxviii, 5, 8–9, 9, 11, 17–18
   of archives. *See* archives
   and desire for the master signifier, xxvi–xxvii, 26–27
   of the ideal Father, 199n3
   neoliberal fantasy of animals, 53–56, 59
   and *object a,* 78–80, 131, 139, 199n4, 205n3
   and othering, xxxiv, 69–70, 169
   and our mediation of the real, 37, 42–43, 53, 176
   of third world abjection, 115, 142

   and Wakanda's constructed in *Black Panther,* 147, 148–153, 155–157, 162, 211n4
   Žižek on, 9
   See also superheroes
Fink, Bruce:
   on "acting out," 8
   desire has no object, 68
   on Lacan's concept of *objet petit a,* xxxv, 205n3
   on *letters* and signifiers, 25
Foucault, Michel, xix, 71–72, 73
   notion of everything being historically specified discursive formations, 30
Freud, Sigmund:
   Chiesa's revision of Freudian understanding of the subject, 68
   concept of *Nachträglichkeit* ("deferred action"), 42
   and feminist psychoanalysis, xxiv–xxv
   on hysteria, 204–205n1, 206n9
   The Interpretation of Dreams, 205n2
   on the joke, 166
   and the Phallus as signifier, 160, 175–176
   on repression and the unconscious, 25
   Spivak on, xxiv–xxv, 185, 188–190, 213n3
   on the split between the ego and the Id, 129, 189–190, 213n5
   the unavowed associated with his conception of the preconscious, 201n10
   See also death-drive; Thing (das Ding)

Gadjo dilo/The Crazy Stranger, directed by Tony Gatlif:
   and the failure of cross-cultural communication, xxix, 70, 91–93
   and negotiating difference as a matter of tolerance, 99
Gandhi's nonviolent movements, 29, 202n14
Gangyopadhyay, Narayan:
   Boo's writing about third-world poverty contrasted with, 137–139, 142

INDEX 237

writings by the "Hungryrealists" compared with, 137–138
–"Hanr" ("The Bone Collector"), 135–142
and the Bengal Famine of 1943, 135–136, 138
bone foraged from trash by a starving child, 140–141
bone of the sacrificed virgin girl, 140
colonial Bengali metropolitan middle class contrasted with illiterate villagers, 136–137
and Lacanian theory of desire, 138–140
Gatlif, Tony. See Gadjo dilo/ The Crazy Stranger, directed by Tony Gatlif
gender:
and feminist psychoanalysis, xxiv–xxv
and Freud on hysteria, 204–205n1, 206n9
and Leslee Udwin's India's Daughter, 126–127
and superheroes, 212n9
unresponsiveness of the big Other to issues of gender equality, 141
George, Sheldon and Derek Hook, xxvi
Get Out, directed by Jordan Peele, 128–129
Ghatak, Ritwik:
Subarnarekha directed by, 152–154
and the trauma of Partition, 153
Ghazoul, Ferial J., 128, 209n14
Gherovici, Patricia, 82, 83–85
Ghosh, Amitav—The Hungry Tide:
crabs in, xxix, 48–51, 203n7
and human refugees vs. near-extinct Bengal tigers, 45–46
and the "postcolonial animal limit," 37–38
Goc, Nicola, 110
Gopal, Priyamvada, 126, 210n16
Gran Torino, directed by Clint Eastwood:
and identity politics, xxx, 146, 169–170
and the ideology of the One, 173–174
image of Kowalski in, 163, 170, 212n10
racism of, 146, 163–168, 172
Greedharry, Mrinalini, xxv, xxvi

Grosrichard, Alain, xxxiv, 69, 87, 148, 198n2, 198n2

Haraway, Donna, 37, 51–52, 53, 58
Hassan, Wail, 75–76, 77
Heise, Ursula, 203n9
hierarchy:
and Fanon's zone of nonbeing, xxxiv–xxxiv, 11–12, 87
and the futility of reversing symbolic positions, xv, xvii, 180, 182, 195
See also hysteric's discourse; master's discourse; subaltern act
Hollywood:
denigration of the Indian, 101
and the multicultural present, 128, 209–210n15
and neoliberal patronizing of the other, 125–126, 128, 155–156
See also Avengers: Infinity War, directed by Anthony and Joe Russo; Best Exotic Marigold Hotel; Black Panther, directed by Ryan Coogler; Get Out, directed by Jordan Peele; Gran Torino, directed by Clint Eastwood
Homer, Odysseus, the Other as godless, uncivilized, wife beaters, 127, 191, 214n9
Homer, Sean, "Voice as objet a in Tony Gatlif's Gadjo dilo," 90–92, 97–98
Hook, Derek, xxvi, 169
Hook, Derek, and Stijn Vanheule, 26, 194
Hudson, Peter, xvi–xvii
Huggan, Graham, and Helen Tiffin:
on the man-tiger conflict in Ghosh's The Hungry Tide, 47
postcolonial zoocriticism of, 33–36
human-animal relations:
the animal as nonrelation, 51–53
and confrontations with real nature/ animals, 34–35, 44–47, 51, 58
and the extinction of humans, 203n8
and the man-tiger conflict in Ghosh's The Hungry Tide, 46–48, 53
neoliberal fantasy of animals, 53–56, 59

human-animal relations (*cont'd*)
  and postcolonial zoocriticism, 33–36, 52, 55–56, 202n1
  See also Devi, Mahasweta,—"Pterodactyl, Puran Sahay, and Pirtha"; lamella (life force)

Hysteric's discourse:
  and castration as a badge of honor, 86–87
  and Lacan's definition of four discourses, 56, 83–84
  and postcolonial studies, 86–88, 108
  and resistance to the big Other, 5–6, 84–87
  See also Devi, Mahasweta—"Draupadi,"—and the theoretical features of the subaltern act

identity politics:
  and animal rights, 46
  and Malcolm X's discovery of his (negated) identity in the eyes and words of the Master discourse, 191–192
  and the ordering of the marginalized in terms of victimization, 142, 173, 177
  and postcolonial studies' advocacy for the marginalized, xiii–xv, xx, 179–180
  real issues obviated by, xxix–xxx

I Know What You Did Last Summer, directed by Jim Gillespie, 95–96

images and image making:
  and Boo's imaging of Maoists as an anomaly, 121
  and identity politics, xxx
  liberal fixation with, xxx, 143–146
  and the relation between postcolonial studies and psychoanalysis, xxvii–xxviii
  scopic register of Draupadi's naked body, 15
  and the symbolic big Other, xxvi–xxviii

  See also Boo, Katherine—representation of urban precariats

Jameson, Frederic, 169, 182
Johnston, Adrian, 43
Jordan, Paulette:
  celebrity endorsements of, 211n1
  and the Idaho gubernatorial election (2018), 140–145, 146

jouissance (enjoyment):
  and *Beautiful Forevers*, 109
  black leadership imagined by Killmonger and T'Challa/Black Panther differentiated by, 159
  and desire, 139
  of the hysteric, 82, 83–84
  nonbeing as surplus of, xiv, xxxv, 29
  and the production of a sovereign West, 129, 148
  and repression, 148, 151–152
  —lack of, 69
  and castration, xxxvi
  and the gap separating desire from jouissance, 24
  and murder of the primal father, 187–188
  and the Other's desire, 199n4
  and the paltry jouissance of the pre-Oedipal, 160

Kant, Immanuel:
  "Copernican" proposition, 59
  Spivak on, xv, 186
  subjective liberation as a rephrasing of the Kantian notion of the categorical imperative, 182–183
Kapoor, Ilan, xxvi, 203n5
Kaur, Rajender, 203n5
Khader, Jamil, xxvi
Khan, Azeen, xxvi
Kondabolu, Hari, 99–103
Kurtz, Stanley, xviii–xix
Kustra-Labrador exchange, 176–178

Lacan, Jacques:

on the Act and the subaltern act, 8–13
on *après-coup*, 42
deconstructive paleonomy with the term subject, 28, 202n17
on desire, 67–69, 138–139, 199n4
empty and full speech defined by, 168–169
four discourses defined by, 56, 83
on the image of the ideal Father, xxxvi, 188, 199n3
lamella described by, 50
on other as radical alterity, xxxiv
sexuation formula of, 160, 212n9
Spivak on, 185, 187–188
on the unconscious, 25
University discourse of, xxvi, 56–57
See also anomaly; Hysteric's discourse; Master's discourse; *objet a*; University discourse
lamella (life force):
Binu in Nabarun's novel *Herbert* as, 154
crabs in Ghosh's *The Hungry Tide* as, 50–51
and Lacan's description of the immortal amoeba, 50
and the nonbeing/nothingness of animals, 51
Žižek on, 50
Laplanche, Jean, and J.-B Pontalis, 42–43
Lebron, Christopher, 155, 157, 158, 211n4, 212n5

Macaulay, Thomas Babington, "Minute on Indian Education," 197–198n1, 213–214n7
Maculayan minutemen, 136
and culture as a form of rhetoric, 190
McBride Debbie, and Lourdes Shahamiri, 174
McGowan, Todd:
on excess and lack, 206n4
on master signifiers, 190, 194–195, 214n8
on *The Dark Knight*, 161
McGowan, Todd and Paul Eisenstein, 12, 57, 58, 203–204n10

Mahasweta. *See* Devi, Mahasweta—"Draupadi"
Malcolm X, 191–192
Manoff, Marlene, 70–71, 206n7
Marder, Michael, 181
Master's discourse:
and colonialist views of non-European thought, 180–185
master signifiers and universals distinguished by Todd McGowan, 190, 194–195
upending of, xv–xvi, 87–88
Mbembe, Achille, 6
Menchu, Rigoberta, 2, 29
Metal Slug 3 video game, 132, 133
Mignolo, W. D., 181
Miller, Jacques-Alain:
on the master signifier, 190
on self and body associations, 7
Mitra, Premendra, 137
Morton, Stephen, 15, 186, 213n4
Morton, Timothy, 36
Mukherjee, Upamanyu Pablo, 203n5
multicultural present:
and exoticism of outsiders, 99
and Hollywood, 125–126, 128, 209–210n15
and neoliberal discourses of the Other, 105–106
and political correctness, 125–126, 146
and reconnecting postcolonial studies with psychoanalytic theory, xiii
See also Boo, Katherine—representation of urban precariats

Nabarun. *See* Bhattacharya, Nabarun
Name-of-the-Father:
Lacan's image of the idea Father, xxxvi, 188, 199n3
and the Phallus as signifier, 160
Nandy, Ashis, xxv
Narayan. *See* Gangyopadhyay, Narayan
Naxalbari movement:
and Binu in Nabarun's *Herbert*, 154
and caste, 13, 119–120

Naxalbari movement (*cont'd*)
    and Devi, Mahasweta—"Draupadi," 13–17, 19–20, 22–23, 201–202n14
neoliberal discourses:
    and anthropocentrism, 46–51
    and *Black Panther,* 152, 156, 158–159
    and India's neoliberal market economy, 112, 115, 207–208n7
    Maoist opposition to, 121–123
    neoliberal fantasy of animals, 53–56, 59
    the Other represented by, 105–106
    and radical alterity, 107–108
    and subalterns politicizing their destinies, 76–77, 134, 148–152, 155–156, 162–163, 203n5
    and the subject-sovereignty of the West, 129, 210n16
    See also Boo, Katherine—representation of urban precariats
Nigam, Aditya, on the Zabala-Dabashi debate, 181–183, 213n2
Nolan, Christopher, *The Dark Knight,* 161–162
non-West's pathological barbarity:
    and *Black Panther,* 151
    and Spivak's reading of Coetzee's *Waiting for the Barbarians,* 17
    white men saving brown women from brown men, 127
Nussbaum, Martha, 112, 115, 207–208n7

objet a:
    and the character of Brian in Aboulela's "The Museum," 78–82
    and Nora Luca's voice in Tony Gatlif's *Gadjo dilo,*" 88, 90–92, 96–97
    and unsymbolizable alterity, xxvii, xxxv, 131, 139, 205n3
One, the:
    and the ideology of *Gran Torino,* 173–175
    See also superheroes
Osborne, Thomas, 72
Othering:
    and the global relevance of postcolonial studies, xiii–xvi, xx–xxi, xxxiv
    the nonviolent Other and the other's radical political demands for equality, xxii–xxiii, 162–163
    other and *Other* distinguished, xxxiv–xxxvi
    See also big Other; equality is alterity
otherness, *See also* human-animal relations

Peele, Jordan. *See Get Out*, directed by Jordan Peele
Phallus:
    and political correctness, 175–176
    as the signifier of plenitude and lack, 103, 160, 212n9
    See also Name-of-the-Father
Pluth, Ed:
    on the act in psychoanalysis, 8, 9, 201n7
    and "doing with signifiers," 200n4
    on Dopi's *doing with signifiers,* 23, 25
    and new significations, 25, 27
political correctness:
    and academic postcolonialism, 142
    and identity politics, xxx
    and liberals fixation with the image, 143–146
    and the logic of the Phallus, 175–176
    and the other in Hollywood films, 125–126, 128, 146, 157–159
    and popular culture's representational politics, 209–210n15
    and twenty-first-century Orientalism, 127–128
    See also Boo, Katherine—representation of urban precariats
Pontecorvo, Gillo. *See Burn! (Queimada)* directed by Gillo Pontecorvo
postcolonial Other, psychoanalytic Other distinguished from, xxxvi
postcolonial studies:
    advocacy for the marginalized, xiii–xv, xx, 179–180, 196
    the future of, 195–196
    global subjectivity as a focus of, xiv–xv, xxii, 105–109
    hysterization of, 86–88, 108

and the intersecting and co-constituted histories of humans and animals, 203n9
and Macaulay, Thomas Babington, "Minute on Indian Education," 197–198n1, 213–214n7
and political correctness, 142
psychoanalytic theory reconciled with. *See* psychoanalytic theory—reconciliation with postcolonial studies
Stanley Kurtz's views about, xviii–xix
Young's reimagining of, xxi–xxii, 106–108
and the Zabala-Dabashi debate, 180–182
—debate over the universal versus the particular:
the habitual conflation of universality with the master signifier or Idea, 190–191
and the multicultural universal, 213n6
and the postcolonial riposte, 200n5
postcolonial zoocriticism, 33–36, 52, 55–56, 202n1
the creature as limit (to soul making and Enlightenment critique), 41, 52–53
and the postcolonial animal limit, 36, 37–38, 41–43, 45, 52–53
precarity:
Boo's writing about urban precariats contrasted with Narayan's, 137–139, 142
as the social and economic condition linking disparate forces, 140–142, 215n26
and the subaltern act, 113–114
the urban precariat as Thing (*das Ding*), 114, 134–135
See also slums
Problem with Apu, The, directed by Michael Melamedoff, 99–103
psychoanalytic Other:
definition of, xxxv–xxxvi
and Lacan's concept of *objet petit a*, xxxv, 69, 205n3

psychoanalytic theory, concepts of. *See* jouissance; subjectivity qua desire or/as lack ($)
psychoanalytic theory—reconciliation with postcolonial studies:
and engaging with otherness as radical alterity, xxii–xxiv, xxix–xxxi, xxxiv, 37, 43, 45, 53, 106–108, 130–131
and the fiction of big Other, xxvi–xxviii
and global relevance, xiii–xiv
and reservations each discipline has about the other, xxi–xxiv, 179–180

Qurashi, Fahid, 147–148, 158–159

racism:
and *Black Panther*, 146, 155, 157, 211n4
and caste-determining whiteness, 20
and colonial constructions of "white" and "black" identities, xvi–xviii
and colonialist views of non-European thought, 180–185
and the false dichotomies of white nationalism versus black nationalism, 178
of *Gran Torino*, 146, 163–168, 172
and the Kustra-Labrador exchange, 176–178
and Malcolm X's discovery of his (negated) identity in the eyes and words of the Master discourse, 191–192
and reestablishing the conversation between psychoanalysis and postcolonial studies, xxvi
and stereotyping of Indian immigrants on *The Simpsons*, 99–103
Ragland, Ellie, 87
Ray, Sangeeta, 41
Richards, Thomas, 72
Rothenberg, Molly, 192
Rousselle, Duane, 155
Roy, Arundhati, *Walking With the Comrades*, 121–122
Ruti, Mari, 74, 84, 99, 104

Said, Edward, xix, 87, 148, 198n2
  on fantasy as critical for *Othering*, 69, 100
  Orientalism termed by, xxxiv, 127, 148, 206n5, 207n15, 214n9
  on Self versus the Other, xv, 69
  Stanley Kurtz's views about, xviii–xix
  on stereotype, 100
Sarkar, Sumit, 136, 211n25
The Secret Life of Pets, directed by Chris Renaud, and anthropocentrism, 53–55
Sen, Amartya, 111, 112, 115
Sen, Malcolm, 46
Sewell, Cynthia, 144
Shah, Amar, 100–101
Sharlet, Jeff, 112, 114, 138
Shining, The, directed by Stanley Kubrick, 95–96, 97
Shree 420, directed by Raj Kapoor, 94–95, 97
Simpsons, The, 101–102
slums:
  and the antagonistic alterity of urban precariats, 113–114, 130–131
  and the excessive core of global capitalism, 132–134
  and the lack of class consciousness of subalterns, 123–124
  Žižek on, 210n19
  See also Boo, Katherine—representation of urban precariats
Soler, Colette, xxxv
soul making:
  identified with self-discovery by Spivak, 88–89
  and Mahasweta's pterodactyl, 41
Spillers, Hortense, xiii
Spivak, Gayatri Chakravorty, 198n2
  and the Bengal Famine of 1943, 136, 210n23
  on distinguishing the "other" from the "Other," xxxiv
  on Draupadi's act as universal, 27–29
  forsha translated by, 20–21
  on Freud, xxiv–xxv, 185, 188–190, 213n3
  on identity politics, 175
  on the inadequacy of postcolongial critique of othering, 116
  on Kristeva's *On Chinese Women*, 130
  on Lacan, 185, 187–188
  on Mahasweta's pterodactyl as a metaphor for subaltern speech, 39–41
  on postcolonial politics, 195
  on postcolonial unease with psychoanalysis, xxiv–xxv
  and rendering the political in contrast to politics, 31
  on "soul making," 88–89
  on subalternity as a position without identity, 2–3
  on teleopoiesis, 208–209n14
  on the terrorism of European Enlightenment thinking, 182–183
  theory of subaltern-hegemony relation as hermeneutic, 20–21
  translation of Mahasweta Devi, "Pterodactyl, Puran Sahay, and Pirtha," 39
  on upending the master's discourse, xv–xvi
stereotypes:
  and Apu Nahasapemapetilon in *The Simpsons*, 99–103
  and identification of Kowalski (in *Gran Torino*) as a xenophobe, 165
subaltern act:
  as the Freudian death-drive, 12–13, 21–22, 28–29
  and Jose's death in *Burn! (Queimada)* directed by Gillo Pontecorvo, 6–7, 11, 29, 200n2
  and Kadombini's death in "Jibito O Mrito" ("Alive and Dead") by Rabindranath Tagore, 4–7, 11, 29, 200n2
  Lacan's theory of the act braided with, 8–13
  localized character of, 9–13, 46, 203n5
  nonrelationality of, 3–4, 21, 29–31
  and the political rendered in contrast to politics, 30–31
  and the urban precariat, 113–114

See also Devi, Mahasweta—"Draupadi"—and the theoretical features of the subaltern act; hysteric's discourse; master's discourse
subalternity:
  and anomaly, 124
  Spivak's theorization of, 2
Subarnarekha, directed by Ritwik Ghatak, 152–154
subjectivity qua desire or/as lack ($), xiv
  and the Hysteric's discourse, 83
  and the Master's discourse, *191*fc.1, 192
  and the University discourse, 56–57
Sunder Rajan, Rajeswari, 11, 15
superheroes:
  female superheroes, 212n9
  and radical political demands for equality, 162–163
  and the T'Challa-Killmonger conflict in *Black Panther*, 150–151, 155–159, 162
—as the exceptional One:
  and castration, 159–160
  human aspect or *flaw* in, 161–162

Tagore, Rabindranath, "Jibito O Mrito" ("Alive and Dead"), 4–7, 11, 29, 200n2
Tankersley, Ken, 204n10
Thacker, Eugene, 51
Tharoor, Shashi, 113
Thing (*das Ding*), xxxv
  and the blank smudge of a traveler in Kapoor's *Shree, 420*, 94–95, 96, 97
  and Draupadi's embodiment of the real through her act, 19, 21–22, 24, 27
  and the experience of desire as full jouissance, 188
  and *extimité* others, 3–4, 25, 107
  and the lack or impossibility constitutive of the social, 135
  the lamella as, 50
  and the object cause of desire as trash/shit (*déchet*), 9, 27
  and signification, 25

the speeding car in Kubrick's *The Shining* as, 95
the urban precariat as, 114, 134–135
300, directed by Zack Snyder, 171

Udwin, Leslee, *India's Daughter*, 126–127, 128
University discourse:
  the Anthropocene as, 58–60, 64–65
  and Lacan's definition of four discourses, 56–57, 83
  and neoliberalism in universities, xxi, xxvi–xxvii, 30
  and postcolonial zoocriticism, 55–56

Vespucci, Amerigo, "A New World," the Other as godless, uncivilized, wife beaters, 127, 191, 214n9
Vighi, Fabio, 132
violence:
  law-preserving violence of the big Other, 16–17
  of Maoists, 120–123, 202n14
  and opposition to neoliberal hegemony, 121–123, 155

Wenzel, Jennifer, on ethical narration in Mahasweta Devi, "Pterodactyl, Puran Sahay, and Pirtha," 39–40
Wolfe, Tom, 110–111, 207n4

Younger Dryas, 204n10
Young, Robert, xxi–xxii, 106–108

Zabala, S., 180–182
Žižek, Slavoj:
  on ecocriticism, 62–63
  on fantasy, 9, 103
  on ideology, 123, 147
  on lamella, 50
  and the link between social history and Capital, 62–64
  on negativity positivized, 3–4, 30–31, 124, 156, 192
  postcolonial studies criticized by, xix–xx, 180–181

Žižek, Slavoj (cont'd)
  real enjoyment located in repression by, 37, 148, 151–152
  and rendering the political in contrast to politics, 30–31
  review of *Black Panther,* 147–148, 156, 157–158
  on slums as the excessive core of global capitalism, 132–134, 201n19
  on the act, 9, 27–28
  on the Real, 37, 41, 53, 201n12
  on tolerance and neoliberal culture. 129–135, 203n6
  three orders of the real distinguished by, 53
  on University discourse, 57–58
  on violence, 16, 29
  and the Zabala-Dabashi debate, 181

Zupančič, Alenka:
  Hysteric's discourse viewed as "discourse about injustice" by, 56, 83–84
  on the impossibility of social relations, xxii, 31, 41, 54–55, 65
  on politics of the Impossible xxii, 4, 12, 31
  on University discourse, 56-57

www.ingramcontent.com/pod-product-compliance
Lightning Source LLC
Chambersburg PA
CBHW020642230426
43665CB00008B/285